Prospects for Monetary Cooperation and Integration in East Asia

Prospects for Monetary Cooperation and Integration in East Asia

Ulrich Volz

The MIT Press
Cambridge, Massachusetts
London, England

For information about special quantity discounts, please email special_sales@mitpress.mit.edu

This book was set in Times New Roman by Toppan Best-set Premedia Limited. Printed and bound in the United States of America.

Library of Congress Cataloging-in-Publication Data
Volz, Ulrich, 1977–
Prospects for monetary cooperation and integration in East Asia / Ulrich Volz.
    p. cm.
Includes bibliographical references and index.
ISBN 978-0-262-01399-4 (hardcover : alk. paper) 1. Monetary integration—East Asia. 2. East Asia—Economic integration. I. Title.
HG1270.5.V65   2010
332.4′566095—dc22

10 9 8 7 6 5 4 3 2 1

Contents

List of Abbreviations

ABF   Asian Bond Fund

ABMI   ASEAN+3 Asian Bond Market Initiative

ACU   Asian currency unit

ADB   Asian Development Bank

AEC   ASEAN Economic Community

AFTA   ASEAN Free Trade Area

AMF   Asian Monetary Fund

ANCOM   Andean Common Market

APEC   Asia–Pacific Economic Cooperation Forum

ASA   ASEAN Swap Arrangement

ASEAN   Association of Southeast Asian Nations

ASEAN+3   ASEAN with China, Japan, and Korea

ASEAN+4   ASEAN+3 with Hong Kong

BIS   Bank for International Settlements

BSAs   Bilateral Swap Arrangements

c.i.f.   Cost, insurance, and freight

CACM   Central American Common Market

CeMCoA   Center for Monetary Cooperation in Asia of the Bank of Japan

CIA   Central Intelligence Agency

CIS   Commonwealth of Independent States

CMI   Chiang Mai Initiative

CNY   Chinese yuan

CPI   Consumer price inflation

DEY   Currency basket consisting of the US dollar, the euro, and the Japanese yen

DTS   Direction of Trade Statistics (IMF)

EAFTA   East Asian Free Trade Area

EC   European Community

ECB   European Central Bank

ECOWAS   Economic Community of West African States

ECU   European currency unit

EEC   European Economic Community

EMEAP   Executives' Meeting of East-Asia and Pacific Central Banks

EMS   European Monetary System

EMU   European Economic and Monetary Union

ERM   Exchange rate mechanism

EU   European Union

EUR   Euro

ERPD   ASEAN+3 Economic Review and Policy Dialogue

FDI   Foreign direct investment

FTA   Free trade agreement

G-3   Group of three (United States, Japan, and euro area)

G-5   Group of five (France, [West] Germany, Japan, United States, United Kingdom)

G-7   Group of seven (G-5 plus Canada and Italy)

G-10   Group of ten (G-7 plus Belgium, Netherlands, and Sweden)

G-20   Group of twenty (Argentina, Australia, Brazil, Canada, China, European Union, France, Germany, India, Indonesia, Italy, Japan, Mexico, Russia, Saudi Arabia, South Africa, Korea, Turkey, United Kingdom, United States)

GATT   General Agreement on Tariffs and Trade

GDP   Gross domestic product

GNI   Gross national income

HK Hong Kong

HKD Hong Kong dollar

ICB Individual country basket

IDR Indonesian rupiah

IFS International Financial Statistics (published by the IMF)

ILO International Labor Organization

IMF International Monetary Fund

IOU "I owe you"

IP Industrial production

JPY Japanese yen

KRW Korean won

Mercosur Mercado Común del Sur

MYR Malaysian ringgit

NAFTA North American Free Trade Agreement

NCB National central bank

NEER Nominal effective exchange rate

OECD Organisation for Economic Cooperation and Development

OCA Optimum currency area

OLS Ordinary least squares

PBC People's Bank of China

PHP Philippine peso

PPP Purchasing power parity

REER Real effective exchange rate

SADC Southern African Development Community

SD Standard deviation

SEACEN South East Asian Central Banks

SGD Singapore dollar

SGP Stability and Growth Pact

SITC Standard international trade classification

THB   Thai baht

UNCTAD   United Nations Conference on Trade and Development

UK   United Kingdom

UN   United Nations

USD   United States dollar

US   United States of America

USG   US growth

VAR   Vector autoregression

WAMU   West African Monetary Union

WAMZ   West African Monetary Zone

WDI   World Development Indicators (published by the World Bank)

WEO   World Economic Outlook database (published by the IMF)

WTO   World Trade Organization

Acknowledgments

The foundation for this book came from my doctoral thesis at the Economics Department of the Free University of Berlin. During the work on this manuscript, I was affiliated with the Hamburg Institute of International Economics, where I was a DekaBank Fellow, and Yale University, where I was a Fox International Fellow and Max Kade Scholar. Since I joined the German Development Institute in August 2007, I held visiting positions at Aoyama Gakuin University, Tokyo; the University of Oxford; and the European Central Bank. The research I conducted at these institutions helped me to produce the book that you now hold in your hands.

I am indebted to the generous support and help of a number of people and organizations that supported the research for this book. First, I would like to thank my supervisor Professor Manfred Nitsch from the Free University of Berlin, who granted me a lot of freedom in conducting my research but was always there to guide me and help me order my thoughts. I also thank Professor Ulrich Basseler, my second examiner at the Free University. Professor Koichi Hamada of Yale University almost became a second supervisor, and I owe him a great deal for supporting my research and continually challenging my work and thus helping me to sharpen and refine my thoughts. Special thanks go to Koichi Hamada also for kindly agreeing to write the preface for this book. Moreover I thank my former colleagues at the Hamburg Institute, especially Carsten Hefeker, Katja Michaelowa, Beate Reszat, and Thomas Straubhaar, for their support and advice.

My research benefited a lot from discussions and exchange with friends and colleagues who challenged my methods and ideas or who commented on earlier versions of various parts of this work. In addition to those listed earlier I would like to mention in person Joshua Aizenman, Mumtaz Anwar, Chris Bowdler, Cai Penghong, Giovanni Capannelli, Yin-Wong Cheung, Menzie Chinn, Ethan Chua, Reid Click, Benjamin Cohen, Joshua Felman, Michael Fidora, Marcel Fratzscher, Manabu Fujimura, Yukiko Fukagawa, Dong He, He Fan, Randy Henning, Heiko Hesse, Jean Imbs, Hiro Ito, Masahiro Kawai, Heungchong Kim, Juljan Krause, Alexander Kriwoluzky, Inpyo Lee, Guonan Ma, Julie McKay, Robert McCauley, Ronald McKinnon, Arnaud Mehl, Naoko Munataka, Shigeto Nagai, Françoise Nicolas, Volker Nitsch, Eiji Ogawa, Maria Oliva Armengol, Michael

Plummer, Michael Pomerleano, Federico Ravenna, Jimmy Reade, Alvaro Santos Rivera, Waltraud Schelkle, Gunther Schnabl, Lotte Schou-Zibell, Eva Söbbeke, Hyun Song Shin, Christian Thimann, Yunjong Wang, Xu Mingqi, Matthew Yiu, Naoyuki Yoshino, Yu Yongding, Zhang Bin, Zhang Haibing, Zhang Liqing, Zhang Yongsheng, and the late Zhang Jikang. I also received helpful comments and suggestions from numerous other colleagues on presentations that I gave at conferences, workshops, and seminars at the Free University, Yale, Harvard, Oxford, the University of California Santa Cruz, the University of British Columbia, Fudan University Shanghai, the Central University of Finance and Economics, Aoyama Gakuin University, Waseda University, Keio University, University of Barcelona, Trinity College Dublin, Maastricht University, centre ifri Paris, the Asian Development Bank Institute, the Hamburg Institute, the German Development Institute, the European Central Bank, DekaBank Frankfurt, as well as at conferences organized by the Japan Economic Policy Association, the International Economic Association, the American Committee for Asian Economic Studies, the Western Economic Association International, and the Royal Economic Society. I also thank the anonymous referees for MIT Press on detailed suggestions on how to improve the manuscript. For reasons of completeness I should mention that all errors and shortcomings of this study are solely my own fault and that the views expressed in this book do not necessarily reflect those of any institution I was or am affiliated with.

Besides my economic research I tried to learn about East Asian societies and their histories in order to avoid producing a narrow-minded economist's work that fails to live up to the real world. In this context I thank especially Ben Kiernan from whom I learned a lot about the rich history of Southeast Asia. I would in particular like to thank my friend Yuichiro Hirano for tutoring me on the Sinocentric tribute trade system. The many informal discussions and conversations with friends from East Asia—academics, government officials, journalists, students, and "normal" people—about the political and cultural relations between various East Asian countries (especially those between Japan, China, and Korea) and their views on East Asian regionalism helped me to get a feel for and understand (or at least think to understand) what is happening in East Asia these days. Some of these thoughts made their way into the last chapter of this book and my thanks go to all who shared their time and thoughts on this topic with me.

My research was made possible through the generous financial support of scholarships of the German Merit Foundation (Studienstiftung des Deutschen Volkes); the German Academic Exchange Service (DAAD); DekaBank, Frankfurt; the Fox International Fellowship at Yale University; the Max Kade Foundation, New York; and the Japan Society for the Promotion of Science. I received conference grants from Yale University, HWWA, DekaBank, and the Royal Economic Society. I hope these organizations will feel that their money was not completely wasted. Whether or not, I thank them for their support, without which I could not have sustained my research. Moreover I thank Shahnaz Khalil-Khan, Jenny Plaul, Andrei Popovici, Maja Rode, and Wendy Soh, each of whom has proofread bits and pieces of the manuscript. Johanna Danielson, Björn Dransfeld, Denise Hassenklöver, Jenny Heithaus, Florian Mölders, Maja Rode, Oliver Schweinzger, and Lars Vogel at times also facilitated my work by providing valuable research assistance. Larisa Satara, the Director of the Fox Fellowship Program, helped me to make the most of my time at Yale. Thanks to all of them. I would also like to thank Jane MacDonald, my editor at MIT Press, for her encouragement and dedication to this project.

It goes without saying that the work on such a project cannot be sustained without the love and moral support of friends and family. Sebastian, Juljan, Eva, Tristan, Richard, Flo, Alex, Justine, Kalyan, and many others (who will please forgive me for not listing them) gave me encouragement, love, and strength. My brother Peter and his girls Shahnaz, Isfahan, and Hanan comforted me whenever I needed it, and my deep-felt gratitude goes to them. But more than anyone else, I would like to express my deepest gratitude to my parents for their never-ending love and support. I dedicate this book to them.

Berlin, May 2009

Foreword

Koichi Hamada

East Asia is one of the most dynamic regions of the world. The economies of East Asian countries, which extend from China to Japan and to the ASEAN countries, are sizzling and well integrated in terms of trade, foreign direct investments, and migration. Indeed, the degree of real economic integration reached in East Asia is beginning to match Europe. While at the end of the last century, Europeans finally achieved the goal of a single currency, the euro, in East Asia, by contrast, monetary unification is still a distant prospect.

The countries in this area show a greater degree of diversity in terms of historical tradition, political systems, ethnicity, religion, and culture than European countries do. Despite the efforts to increase cooperation, this region is far from consensus on what monetary and exchange rate arrangements might be best for individual countries and the region as a whole.

This book by a young European economist addresses the questions about why the pace of monetary integration is so slow in East Asia and if there is any prospect of monetary unification in the future.

Using a clear and nontechnical style, Ulrich Volz explains the benefits and costs of monetary integration, its political economy, and the prospect of currency unification in East Asia. Transaction benefits from a single currency are enormous as has already been shown with the experiment of the euro. There are reasons, however, that the East Asian monetary integration process is slow. First, political competition, for example, between China and Japan, may create an impasse in terms of monetary hegemony as well as in the choice of a common currency unit. Second, economic shocks that affect those countries are so diverse that East Asia cannot be an optimum currency area as defined by Robert Mundell. In other words, countries may be able to navigate macroeconomic crises by maintaining flexible exchange rates.

This book replies to those critics as follows. First, as in Europe, monetary integration itself may work as a political unifier. Second, the benefits from flexible exchange rates apply well only when countries can engage in a truly flexible exchange rate without constraints. The Asian financial crisis and the subprime crisis showed that this premise was not necessarily true. In the latter example, it would be the best for China from a macroeconomic perspective to revalue the yuan substantially and to "kill with one stone two birds," the inflationary pressure and the balance of payments disequilibrium. The existence of a large dollar reserves in China, however, will make this solution hurt her national welfare, making the virtue of flexible exchange rate a "conflicted virtue."

Thus the book contends that under an imperfect, practical environment, East Asian countries will benefit by promoting informal ways of monetary cooperation, then by moving to more mutually calculated policy coordination, and eventually by achieving monetary unification. The Chiang Mai Initiative for monetary cooperation is a substantial and encouraging step in this direction.

In 1964, I attended the lectures of Robert Triffin, a Belgian economist, who was earnestly proposing a unification of innumerable European currencies, which had been, according to him, captured in the "money maze." Discouraged by the ongoing failures of the adjustable-peg system, I was a little skeptical of the need and the possibility of monetary unification. Now his portrait, hanging in the dining hall of Berkeley College at Yale, where he served as a Master, seems to address to me, "Do you now understand what I meant, Monsieur Hamada?" His thinking then, so far ahead of time, has now matured and produced significant fruits of the currency unification in Europe.

A long voyage awaits the East Asian countries before they will achieve a reasonable level of for monetary integration, and an even longer one is ahead before they are to reach a state of unified currency. How long will the journey be? Only history will give us the answer. In the meantime this book will certainly serve as a beacon for those on the voyage.

. . . I'm living in the material world
Not much giving in the material world
Got a lot of work to do
Try to get a message through
And get back out of this material world . . .

—George Harrison, *Living in the Material World*, 1973

1 Introduction

The 1990s have seen dramatic changes in the international monetary landscape. The demise of the Soviet Union and the breakup of Yugoslavia caused the dissolution of existing currency areas and gave birth to new currencies. At the same time European countries decided to abandon their national currencies and replace them with a single common currency, the euro. In 2000, Ecuador relinquished its own currency and officially adopted the US dollar; in 2001, El Salvador did the same; and a year later, Guatemala introduced the US dollar as parallel legal currency. The traditional notion of "one nation—one money" cannot be taken for granted any more. The days in which "virtually all of the world's nations assert and express their sovereign authority by maintaining a distinct national money and protecting its use within their respective jurisdictions," and in which "[m]oney is like a flag; each country has to have its own" (Mussa 1995: 98) seem to be gone. Steil (2007) has announced the "end of national currency." A "new geography of money" is emerging, in which political frontiers do not necessarily coincide with the boundaries of money (Cohen 1998). Especially the introduction of the euro has led to a "redrawing of the map of currency areas" (Mundell 2000: 223) and has propelled thoughts about monetary integration elsewhere. Today, regional monetary cooperation and integration is being discussed in virtually all parts of the world, including East Asia.

East Asian countries were notably unconcerned about regional monetary integration until the late 1990s. The Asian financial crisis of 1997 to 1998 fundamentally changed their perspective on economic regionalism and sparked great political interest in monetary and financial cooperation and integration in the region. The crisis revealed the fragility of the region's prevailing exchange rate arrangements and highlighted the need for a strengthening of the regional financial architecture. Since the crisis, East Asian countries have been engaged in various forums and initiatives to promote cooperation. Cooperation already takes place in the form of regular consultations between finance ministers and central bank governors, the surveillance of regional financial markets, the pooling of foreign exchange reserves, and various schemes to foster the development of regional security markets. There is also a serious debate about establishing a regional exchange rate arrangement or even a common East Asian currency in the longer term. For instance, the Asian Development Bank (ADB) proposed in 2005 the creation of an East Asian currency unit akin to the European currency unit (ECU), which evolved into the euro.

The current developments in East Asia are intriguing and bear great importance for the future shape of the international monetary system. East Asia, which in this study is defined as China, Hong Kong, Japan, the Republic of Korea (which will be referred to as Korea throughout), and the ten member states of the Association of Southeast Asian Nations (ASEAN),[1] has become the most dynamic region in the world economy. With a combined population of about two billion people, almost a third of the world's population, and nearly a fifth of world output, changes in the monetary and exchange rate policies of East Asian countries will have repercussions far beyond Beijing, Seoul, Tokyo, or Jakarta.

This book investigates the prospects for monetary cooperation and integration in East Asia. The central question of this research is to what extent different forms of regional monetary cooperation and integration are promising options for the East Asian countries. Drawing on the traditional and more recent theoretical and empirical approaches to monetary integration, as well as on the European experiences, this work examines the economic conditions for monetary integration in East Asia and assesses the benefits and problems associated with it. It gives a comprehensive overview of all issues of monetary integration in East Asia that are under discussion among academics and policy makers, and provides the theoretical and empirical analysis to assess the policy options available.

While this study is first and foremost an economic analysis, it is key to acknowledge that monetary cooperation and integration is an eminently political process. The political dimension cannot be blanked out. The analysis will hence include politicoeconomic considerations, especially when discussing the choice of exchange rate regime and possible strategies for monetary integration for East Asia.

It is important to clarify what is meant in this book by monetary cooperation and integration. International monetary cooperation can be defined quite broadly to include, for instance, consultations among policy makers regarding the choice of monetary and exchange rate regimes and the exchange of information among monetary authorities. Cooperation is sometimes used interchangeably with the term coordination, which in the definition of Frankel (1988: 1) describes "the agreement by two or more countries to a cooperative set of policy changes, where neither would wish to undertake the policy change on its own but where each expects the package to leave it better off relative to the Nash noncooperative equilibrium in which each sets its policies taking the other's as given." In this characterization, monetary coordination is more specific than the definition for monetary cooperation given above, as coordination already involves the adoption of a mutually agreed policy stance. Maintaining a distinction between cooperation and coordination and adopting a broad definition of monetary cooperation helps to explicate that the latter—like monetary integration—is a gradual process in which lower levels of monetary cooperation may provide the basis for an active coordination of monetary and exchange rate policies.

As with monetary cooperation, there is no generally accepted definition of monetary integration in the literature. This study follows the definition of Schelkle (2001a), according to which monetary integration comprises all forms of coordinated currency stabilization. Besides monetary union, which is defined as an area where there circulates a common currency issued by a single central bank, monetary integration comprises also less far-reaching forms such as coordinated pegging to the same anchor currency or currency basket, and the establishment of a common exchange rate system.

From this definition it follows that an analysis of the prospects for monetary cooperation and integration should not focus solely on the feasibility of and perspectives for an East Asian monetary union. Indeed, as will be argued later, talk of East Asian monetary unification is premature at this point in time—not because the economic conditions prohibit it but because the political determination to see through such a demanding project has not developed yet. Monetary policy coordination is a highly sensitive field that requires mutual trust and understanding; countries pursuing a course of monetary integration need to share common objectives and develop a common ground from which to tackle conflicting issues in a constructive and solution-oriented way. History has shown time and again that ill-conceived or badly managed monetary arrangements are prone to crisis. To avoid crises, it is therefore essential that any kind of coordination failure among the countries engaged in a process of monetary integration is ruled out. National authorities must be willing to subordinate national policy goals, at least at times, for the common goal of stability of the common monetary arrangement. These are requirements that are not yet met by East Asian countries. This study hence recommends a gradual approach toward monetary integration, with less demanding forms of monetary cooperation being pursued first, before highly challenging projects such as the creation of a regional monetary system, let alone monetary union, can be tackled. A step-by-step approach starting with informal forms of policy coordination would give East Asian countries time to develop an integrationist spirit and gain experience with cooperation before moving on to more advanced forms of monetary integration.

There are many sources of skepticism as regards East Asian monetary cooperation. The major concern that is frequently raised, and that was touched upon already, is that the political conditions for monetary integration are not in place, and that the region is lacking historical and cultural commonalities. In particular, it is often argued that the deep-rooted distrust and the historical antagonism that bedevil the relations between China and Japan, the two dominant countries in the region, obstruct cooperation. Relations between the other countries in the region are also strained at times, which is why calls for deeper economic integration are often dismissed as pure rhetoric. For sure, East Asia has not developed an "integrationist spirit" as in Europe as the region continues to struggle with political frictions and historical disputes. But dismissing the prospects for regional monetary cooperation because of an alleged lack of commonality is shortsighted and fails to realize that East Asia is a region undergoing transition, where some modest progress in the areas of monetary and financial cooperation has already been made. One example is the decision taken by the ASEAN+3 countries in February 2009 to institutionalize regionalism for the first time by establishing a common agency to conduct surveillance of regional financial markets. This is a modest step, but it shows their commitment to regional cooperation and illustrates that ASEAN+3 countries have found a practical way to work together despite the existing differences. In this context it is worth pointing out that European economic integration was initiated to overcome exactly the same sort of rivalry between European nations that can be observed in today's East Asia. In any case, the strong economic trade and investment linkages that have developed in the East Asian region over the past decades have resulted in a high degree of economic interdependency which has brought about an ever-growing need for closer macroeconomic cooperation between governments to safeguard growth and stability of the regional economy. What has been an essentially market-driven process of economic integration—which has manifested itself, among others, in the form of extensive regional production networks—has propelled the region's leaders to engage in economic cooperation. As will be discussed later, it appears that the political and business elites of East Asian countries are conscious of the need for government-led cooperation and that they have formed a broad consensus about the principle, if not the detail, of the desirability of monetary cooperation.

A second source of reservation over the prospects of East Asian monetary integration stems from the fact that East Asian countries are diverse not only in terms of population size and political system, but also heterogeneous in respect of economic systems and stage of economic development. While this is obviously true, this is a static perspective which fails to recognize that monetary integration is a dynamic process in which economic structures change as a consequence of this very process. Moreover it disregards the potential developmental effects of monetary integration. It is important to ask what can and what will be achieved through a policy of monetary integration, and how monetary integration can contribute to the development of the least developed countries in the region. Monetary integration is no aim in itself; rather, this study highlights monetary integration as a strategy to overcoming structures that present obstacles to economic development and to create a stable macroeconomic environment that is conducive to investment and growth.

Although the interest of East Asian countries in regional monetary and financial cooperation has developed only recently, a process has been set in motion that might well result in a reshaping of the global monetary system. To be sure, East Asian monetary integration is an open process without predetermined outcome. Despite recurring comparisons with the European monetary integration process, from which many lessons—positive as well as negative—can be drawn, East Asia will have to chart its own course, and it is everything but clear that this course will take it to the creation of a common monetary union like in Europe. But whatever the policy choices of East Asian leaders will be, they will have far-reaching consequences for the international monetary system that will greatly affect us all.

This study is divided into three parts and structured as follows. Part I of the book investigates the main reasons that have prompted East Asian countries to consider a policy of regional monetary integration. Chapter 2 highlights the instability of the international monetary system and the recurrence of financial crises as factors that have nurtured a general, worldwide interest in regional monetary integration. Chapters 3 and 4 discuss two specific factors that have fueled East Asia's interest in regional monetary cooperation and integration: the Asian financial crisis and the rise of China.

Part II turns to an examination of the potential costs and benefits of monetary integration in East Asia. Chapter 5 first reviews the traditional framework for analyzing monetary integration, the theory of optimum currency areas, and the criteria that were developed in this theory to assess whether East Asia constitutes such an optimal currency area. Subsequently chapter 6 explains the flaws and limitations of the standard analysis and extends the traditional framework to take account of the endogenous effects of a policy of monetary integration. In particular, it highlights monetary integration as a dynamic process in which economic structures and conditions change due to a policy of integration. The analysis in chapter 6 includes an estimation of the trade-creating effects of monetary integration, an examination of the likely effects of real and financial integration on output correlations in East Asia, and a discussion of the potential role of regional monetary integration in overcoming the problems of asset and liability dollarization in East Asia. It also extends the discussion of the alleged costs of monetary integration by analyzing the region's current degree of monetary independence.

Part III then considers different strategies for monetary integration in East Asia. Chapter 7 briefly reviews the current monetary regimes in East Asia, which is followed in chapter 8 by a discussion of the principle exchange rate options for the East Asian economies, namely freely floating exchange rates, a continuation of the current system of dollar pegging in most countries, and a coordinated stabilization of intraregional exchange rates. Chapter 9 appraises the arguments for freely floating exchange rates in East Asia and analyzes the feasibility of floating rates with inflation targeting in the region. Chapters 10 and 11 then consider in detail two specific forms of regional coordinated exchange rate stabilization, namely the creation of a regional monetary system and the regionwide adoption of currency baskets, respectively. To assess the feasibility of and delineate lessons for a regional exchange rate system for East Asia, chapter 10 examines the credibility of the European Monetary System and the causes for its 1992 and 1993 crisis. Chapter 11 scrutinizes the regionwide adoption of currency baskets by constructing three different hypothetical currency baskets in order to compare the nominal effective exchange rates that would prevail under the basket regimes with the actual exchange rate policies conducted. Based on these results, it develops a strategy for regional monetary integration in which countries first opt for a managed float regime guided by the use of a common basket as numéraire and in which an Asian currency unit (ACU) is introduced as a virtual parallel currency to circulate alongside national currencies.

Chapter 12 concludes this study with reflections on the future of East Asian monetary relations, giving room also to historical and geopolitical considerations and an analysis of the political economy of East Asian monetary integration. Although the political realization of monetary integration might seem unrealistic because of differences in political systems, historical disputes, and economic rivalry among East Asian countries, a look into East Asian history and an appraisal of economic trends and geopolitical factors make the inconceivable appear less unlikely.

I   The Forces behind Monetary Cooperation and Integration

2 The Instability of the International Monetary System and the Regionalization of Money

. . . for most countries, all but the largest, with the most developed capital markets, the choice of exchange rate policy is probably their single most important macroeconomic policy decision, strongly influencing their freedom of action and the effectiveness of other macroeconomic policies, the evolution of their financial systems, and even the evolution of their economies.
—Cooper (1999: 99)

The interest of both the academic and the policy spheres in regional monetary cooperation and integration is due to several factors. At a general level this interest has been fueled by the instability of the international monetary system. The forces of financial globalization, the recurrence of financial crises, instability between the major international currencies, and a resulting widespread "fear of floating" have made regional monetary integration seem an interesting alternative to existing regimes, which for many developing or emerging economies—including those in East Asia—are one-sided pegs to the US dollar.

In Europe, the breakdown of the Bretton Woods system of fixed but adjustable exchange rates led countries to create regional arrangements that secured relative exchange rate stability and guarded close intraregional trade and investment relations. European monetary integration—which culminated in the creation of the European Economic and Monetary Union (EMU)—is a process that has been closely followed (and sometimes guided) by academic research. Indeed the literature on monetary integration consists for the most part of work related to European monetary integration. The European experience with monetary integration, however, has also stimulated interest in other regions of the world and today, after successful completion of EMU, regional monetary integration has come to be regarded as a viable option elsewhere.

In East Asia, the current interest in regional monetary cooperation and integration can be attributed to at least two additional factors. The first, and most direct one, is the Asian financial crisis, which hit several East Asian economies in 1997 and 1998. The crisis revealed the dangers of financial contagion that stem from close trade and investment relations within the region and highlighted the need for closer financial and monetary cooperation. Moreover the international community's response to the crisis (or the lack of it) caused resentment among East Asian nations and thus fundamentally changed the regional attitude to economic cooperation and integration.

The other factor is the rise of China. The opening of China did not only create a truly integrated regional economy with extensive trade, investment, and production linkages, it has also confronted the neighboring economies, particularly the smaller Southeast Asian countries, with increased competition in international trade and for foreign investment. In the ASEAN countries, but also in Korea, this has nurtured the notion that they need to restructure and integrate their economies in order to stay competitive. For Japan, which for long had been the undisputed economic powerhouse in East Asia, the economic rise of China and its growing influence in the region constitute a challenge for regional leader-ship. Japan, which is not willing to passively cede its influence to China, is trying to respond to this challenge by engaging in trade, financial, and monetary cooperation with the other countries in the region, but also with China. Before turning to the Asian financial crisis and the rise of China in the two following chapters, this chapter will discuss why the instability of the international monetary and financial system has nurtured an interest in regional monetary integration.

2.1 Regionalization of the World Economy

Over the past decades the European Union (EU), and its forerunner, the European Com-munity (EC), has been at the forefront of what seems to have become a general trend toward the regionalization of the world economy. The world is increasingly turning into a "world of regions" (Katzenstein 2005), which has its manifestations not only in regional free trade agreements (FTAs) and customs unions but also in the emergence of currency blocs.[1] The trend for a regionalization of money has its roots in the instability of the international monetary system and the inability (or disinterest) of the international com-munity to respond with adequate reform measures.

The current trend for economic regionalism is in fact nothing new. Already in the 1950s the idea gained prominence that a restructuring of the world economy into regional blocs would mark a step forward in international economic relations and might also help resolve international political problems (Gordon 1961). What is different this time, however, is that emphasis is increasingly on the financial and monetary side of integration. Regional cooperation and integration efforts traditionally went along Balassa's (1961) five-step approach for regional integration in which countries start integration with a free trade area and incrementally move on to a customs union, a common market, economic and monetary union, and finally to political union. Europe has more or less followed this route up to monetary union, but there is no obvious reason why other regions should follow the same path. Dieter and Higgot (2003) have pointed out that this typology was developed in a different historical context and that in today's world of high capital mobility some kind of "monetary regionalism" that concentrates more on the monetary and financial side of integration might be more appropriate. To understand the current interest in regional monetary integration, it is important to be aware of the historical evolution of the international monetary system.

2.2 Brief History of Thought on Exchange Rates and International Monetary Relations, 1870 to 1973

From about 1870 there was a general consensus among policy makers in favor of fixed exchange rate regimes.[2] Most leading economies adhered to the gold standard, a commitment by governments to convert domestic currency into fixed quantities of gold, implying fixed exchange rates among their currencies. The outbreak of the First World War forced the collapse of the gold standard, with laws prohibiting the export of gold (which was needed by governments to finance the expenses of war) and governments suspending statutes requiring them to back currency with gold or foreign exchange. The issuance of fiat money—unbacked paper money—at different rates in different countries caused exchange rates to vary widely.

The period 1914 to 1946 saw a great variation of exchange regimes. Periods of floating rates were interrupted by (unsuccessful and aborted) efforts to restore a variant of the gold standard in the late 1920s and attempts to stabilize the exchange rates among major currencies by coordinating monetary policy and market intervention in the late 1930s. As Cooper (1999: 101) points out, the adoption of flexible exchange rates in the aftermath of the war "did not reflect the preferences of policy makers, but rather their inability, in the immediate postwar circumstances, to re-establish convertibility of the national currency into gold." The experiences with floating exchange rates in the interwar period left contemporaries with no good feelings about them. In an influential report for the League of Nations, Nurkse (1944) concluded from the interwar experience that floating rates were characterized by destabilizing speculation and that they had discouraged international trade and led to misallocation of resources.[3]

Nurkse's antipathy to flexible exchange rates was widely shared both among politicians and within academe (Cooper 1999).[4] It is therefore not surprising that the Bretton Woods agreement of 1944 marked the return to a system of fixed but adjustable exchange rates with a narrow band of flexibility. The International Monetary Fund (IMF) was created to guard the system and to oversee and promote international monetary cooperation and the growth of world trade. The system of fixed parities commenced operation in March 1947 and was initially embraced by 44 countries, with many countries joining later.[5] It delivered a degree of exchange rate stability that stood in stark contrast with the volatility of preceding periods and permitted the expansion of international trade and investment that fueled the postwar boom.

The major exception to the general sentiment in favor of fixed rates in the postwar era was Milton Friedman, who in his classic article "The Case for Flexible Exchange Rates" argued that the

. . . advocacy of flexible exchange rates is *not* equivalent to advocacy of unstable exchange rates. The ultimate objective is a world in which exchange rates, while *free* to vary, are in fact highly stable. Instability of exchange rates is a symptom of instability in the underlying economic structure. Elimination of this symptom by administrative freezing of exchange rates cures none of the underlying difficulties and only makes adjustment to them more painful. (Friedman 1953: 158)

Friedman maintained that a system of flexible exchange rates would eliminate the necessity for far-reaching international coordination. He stressed the importance of the exchange rate as a relative price that should not be artificially determined but should be freely set by the markets through supply and demand. He also highlighted the stabilizing effect of speculation, which he argued would always lead to an equilibrium rate concordant with purchasing power parity (PPP). Initially Friedman was almost alone in his views, but just as the interwar experiences nurtured antipathy to exchange rate flexibility, experience during the 1950s and especially the late 1960s and early 1970s cultivated increasing distaste, particularly among academic economists, for the Bretton Woods version of fixed exchange rates.[6] It soon became apparent that governments held on for too long to fixed rates and that the possibility of an adjustment in case of "fundamental disequilibria" was only used when it became unavoidable.

The Bretton Woods system came under increasing strain in the late 1960s, when the US trade balance deteriorated and when it became apparent that US dollar liabilities exceeded US gold reserves, which shed doubt on the Federal Reserve's promise to guarantee gold convertibility of the US dollar.[7] In April 1971, the US trade balance went into deficit for the first time in the twentieth century, which caused massive capital outflows from the United States in anticipation of a dollar devaluation. In August 1971, US President Richard Nixon officially announced the end of the dollar convertibility into gold. The G-10 nations met at the Smithsonian Institute in Washington in December 1971 in an attempt to restore the system, by revaluing currencies and widening fluctuation margins from roughly 1 to 2.25 percent. These measures, however, came too late and did not suffice to restore credibility in the system. In June 1972 the UK authorities were the first to let their currency float, followed by the Swiss in January 1973 and the Japanese in February 1973. In March 1973, the other European economies suspended the dollar peg and announced a joint float against the dollar, putting a definite end to the Bretton Woods system.[8]

2.3 Experience with Floating Rates since 1973

As a result of the dissolution of the Bretton Woods system, the international monetary system has developed into a *nonsystem* that includes all variants of exchange rate regimes and follows no particular order. Under the IMF's current Articles of Agreement, which were amended in 1978 to reflect the new realities, member countries are basically free to choose any exchange rate arrangement that suits them, provided that it is consistent with the IMF's general objective of fostering "orderly economic growth with reasonable price stability," and provided that countries "avoid manipulating exchange rates . . . to prevent effective balance of payments adjustment or to gain an unfair competitive advantage over other members" (Art. IV 1, iii).[9] While the world's major currencies have been freely floating ever since the breakdown of the Bretton Woods system—except for short periods of intervention, as will be discussed below—many smaller economies have elected to link their currencies to lead currencies in the form of rigid or soft pegs or other forms of exchange rate regimes such as crawling or basket pegs.

The collapse of the Bretton Woods system first seemed to prove Friedman right in his skepticism of fixed exchange rates; his optimistic expectations of exchange rate developments under flexible exchange rates, however, were hardly met: "[i]n reality exchange rates have shown excessively volatile, quite unrelated to macroeconomic fundamentals, thereby increasing risk and uncertainty" (Collignon 1999: 285–86).[10]

The following example gives an illustration. Figures 2.1 and 2.2 depict the nominal and real bilateral exchange rates of the Japanese yen (JPY) and the euro (EUR) vis-à-vis the US dollar (USD) since 1960 and since 1999, respectively. The graphs show that nominal and real exchange rate movements have been quite excessive at times. In figure 2.1, between 1960 and mid-1971, when the Bretton Woods regime was still intact, the nominal dollar–yen rate is stable. Over this period the yen appreciates in real terms,

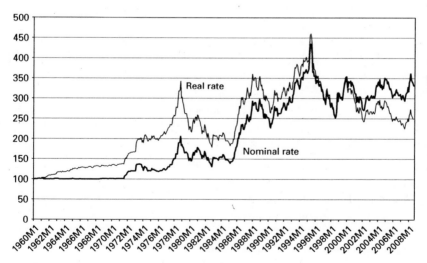

Figure 2.1
USD/JPY (January 1960 = 100)

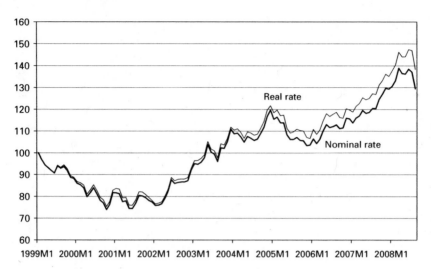

Figure 2.2
USD/EUR (January 1999 = 100)

reflecting higher inflation in Japan than in the United States. This real appreciation is consistent with PPP theory, since the nominal exchange rate was artificially fixed. After the definite suspension of the dollar peg in 1973 and the free float of the yen, however, PPP theory would predict that the real exchange rate should not change, at least not permanently. Instead, nominal and real exchange rates move together, indicating that PPP does not hold in the short or medium run. The same close co-movement can be observed between the nominal and real dollar–euro rates in figure 2.2.

Besides co-movement of real and nominal rates, the graphs also illustrate the enormous swings of the USD/JPY and USD/EUR rates, respectively. The dollar–yen exchange rate, for example, was at 81 JPY/USD in April 1995. Over the course of three years it moved to 147 JPY/USD in August 1998—a depreciation of 80 percent!—and back to 102 JPY/USD by June 2000 (because figures 2.1 and 2.2 depict the exchange rate as USD per local currency, a depreciation of the yen or euro is expressed by a downward movement).[11] It is hard to find a convincing explanation for swings of this magnitude that is related to economic fundamentals. The depreciation of the euro in the first two years after its creation and its strong appreciation in the years thereafter is an equally illustrative example of the unpredictability of exchange rate movements, as both currency areas were successfully pursuing low-inflation policies throughout.

Even this cursory look at the yen–dollar and euro–dollar rates makes clear the problems of exchange rate economists to rationalize exchange rate movements. Going back to the work of Meese and Rogoff (1983), there has developed an extensive empirical literature that concludes that the standard models of exchange rate determination are hardly able to explain exchange rate movements. While most economists today still "instinctively believe in some variant of purchasing power parity as an anchor for long-run real exchange rates" (Rogoff 1996: 647), very few would hold that PPP can be used to explain exchange rate movements in the short or even medium run.[12] Flood and Rose (1999: F671) even believe that macroeconomic fundamentals are "irrelevant" to understanding exchange rate volatility, except in high-inflation countries or in the long run. Krugman (1989: 36) speaks of a "delinking of exchange rates from reality."[13]

The reason for the difficulty of understanding exchange rate movements is that they are increasingly determined by financial transactions that are unrelated to the trade and current account but rather to expectations of exchange rate developments. In April 2007 average daily turnover on the world's foreign exchange markets was USD 3.2 trillion, far in excess of the volume of world merchandise exports, which amounted to USD 13.6 trillion for the whole year of 2007 (which corresponds to a daily value of USD 37.3 billion; see BIS 2007 and WTO 2008). Today over 80 percent of short-term capital transactions are estimated to relate to round-tripping operations of a week or less, being motivated by arbitrage, hedging, or speculation (UNCTAD 2004: 92).

The unpredictable and sometimes excessive movement of flexible exchange rates has led many policy makers and scholars to think of floating rates as a "substantial source of uncertainty for trade and capital formation" (Cooper 1999: 114–15). Calvo and Reinhart (2002) have detected a widespread "fear of floating" among monetary authorities. Exchange rate volatility is commonly regarded as having a negative effect on international trade and investment and on the stability of financial markets, whereas fixed exchange rates are commonly regarded as contributing to growth and macroeconomic stability.[14] Particularly in developing and emerging countries with underdeveloped financial markets, volatile exchange rates can have detrimental consequences. Missing hedging opportunities make them susceptible to exchange rate swings, which not only cause uncertainty for trade and investment decisions but in underdeveloped capital markets often give rise to liability dollarization, which endangers financial stability in the event of a depreciation of the domestic currency because of balance sheet effects.[15]

The last wave of financial globalization and the increasing importance of short-term capital flows have aggravated these problems. In what Stewart (1984) has called the *age of interdependence*, the decisions made by major industrial countries and key emerging economies can have repercussions around the world. Even for large economies it has become increasingly difficult to insulate themselves from developments in the world financial markets. The crises experienced in the 1990s as well as the global financial crisis of the late 2000s have highlighted the problems of international financial contagion that are the result of close international trade and investment ties.[16] Moreover the frequency of recent crises is far greater than the historical average of one per decade chronicled by Kindleberger and Aliber (2005).[17] As Sneddon Little and Olivei (1999: 43) note, "financial crises are viewed as becoming more frequent, more severe, and less predictable." Indeed, the cost of crisis can be dramatic, as is shown through the output losses of the recent crises in East Asia, Russia, Argentina, and not least the global financial turmoil following the US subprime crisis.[18] While financial and currency crises almost always have some homegrown problems at their roots, it is hard to denounce the role played by international investors and speculators who take their opportunities in unregulated international financial markets and an international monetary system that barely deserves such a name.

2.4   Reform of the International Monetary System?

In view of the above-mentioned crises there have been frequent calls for a new international financial architecture that includes a new order for international monetary relations. In the words of several members of the Commission on the Future International Financial Architecture (1999: 129), "reforming the international financial architecture without reforming the currency regime is like watching Hamlet without the Prince."[19] There is no shortage of proposals for international monetary reform.[20] They range from suggestions to create a world currency (Cooper 1984; Mundell 1968, 2003a; Wolf 2004; Bonpasse 2007) over a common monetary standard with "world money supply" targeting (McKinnon 1984, 1988), or cooperation along the lines of the European Monetary System (Bofinger and Gerberding 1988), to target zones between the major currencies (Bergsten and Williamson 1983, 1994; Williamson 1985; Williamson and Miller 1987; Bretton Woods Commission 1994; Commission on the Future International Financial Architecture 1999; UNCTAD 2004). Calls for a reform of the international monetary system have become louder again in the context of the discussion about an overhaul of the international financial system in the aftermath of the 2008 global financial crisis. French President Nicolas Sarkozy, for instance, demanded a return to a global fixed exchange rate system in a speech before the European parliament in October 2008 (LaRouche 2008); Chinese Vice Premier Wang Qishan (2009) urged for exchange rate cooperation to "keep exchange rates of major currencies stable" to ensure financial stability.

Regardless of the appeal and merits of these proposals, the general problem with such grand designs is that they are unlikely to become reality.[21] A "grand fix" is not in sight. The "impossible trinity" (or "trilemma") of international macroeconomics—the incompatibility of fixed exchange rates, a free capital account, and independent monetary policy focused on domestic goals—implies a subordination of domestic policies to the goal of exchange rate stabilization in the face of free capital flows. As capital controls between the major economies are out of the realm of what is politically desired or feasible, the prospects of coordinated exchange rate stabilization between their currencies are very dim. Both the Federal Reserve and the European Central Bank (ECB) are bound to domestic objectives, with mandates to guard domestic price stability (and growth in case of the

Fed). An exchange rate target would inevitably compromise the central banks' domestic policy goals. Hence far-reaching monetary cooperation involving the G-3 economies is not to be expected—and any attempt at global monetary reform without the G-3 is superfluous.

This leaves room only for ad hoc cooperation to correct what are regarded as stark misalignments of major exchange rates. Examples of successful ad hoc cooperation between the major economies are the coordinated (verbal) interventions of G-5 finance ministers and central bank governors through the Plaza accord in September 1985 (to correct the overvaluation of the US dollar) and the Louvre accord of February 1987, where the G-5 finance ministers and central bank governors declared that their currencies were "within ranges broadly consistent with the underlying economic fundamentals" (Funabashi 1988: 177) and that they were ready to intervene to oppose a further decline of the dollar.[22] More recent examples of ad hoc cooperation are the joint interventions of the Fed, the ECB, and the Bank of Japan in September 2000 in support of the euro; after September 11, 2001, in support of the US dollar; or the joint interest rate cuts and provision of liquidity swaps in the course of the 2008 financial crisis.[23] Otherwise, international cooperation between the main economic powers is likely to be limited to the setting of standards and codes as well as to the exchange of information and the surveillance of financial markets.[24]

2.5 Regionalization of Money

If exchange rate stabilization between the core currencies is deemed unfeasible or unwanted, and smaller economies are uncomfortable to pursue a free float, countries and policy makers have to contemplate alternatives. One such alternative—but also a complementary measure—to global exchange rate cooperation is monetary cooperation and integration on a regional scale. Even though regional measures cannot be a full substitute to global governance, the advantage of regional monetary cooperation is that it might be easier to realize than large-scale global cooperation (Dieter 2000a).[25]

The most prominent (and, arguably, most successful) example for regional monetary cooperation and integration is Western Europe. In Western Europe, the end of the Bretton Woods era—which ensured also intraregional exchange rate stability through the common external peg to the US dollar—caused countries to engage in regional cooperation because exchange rate swings within the EC were regarded as intolerable.[26] After a flawed attempt in regional cooperation with the "Snake," which was set up in 1971, the European Monetary System (EMS) was created in 1979 as a kind of "mini–Bretton Woods system" (Cooper 1999: 100). Despite periods of turbulence, especially in the first years of operation and in 1992 to 1993 when the system was hit by a crisis, the EMS was successful in creating a "zone of monetary stability" that, at large, insulated EMS member countries from the upheavals of world financial markets.[27] In 1999 the EMS evolved into the EMU with a single currency.

European monetary integration and the eventual creation of EMU have set a historical precedent. Europe's strategy of regional monetary cooperation to keep exchange rates stable within the region while maintaining flexibility with respect to the outside world has been an attempt at having the best of both worlds. As Padoa-Schioppa (1994: 71) points out,

. . . the EMS has shown that there is a way out of the dilemma often presented to policy-makers: whether to move back to some sort of Bretton Woods system of exchange rate relationships, which is inevitably too rigid and probably not feasible today, or to live in a world of totally unregulated exchange rate relationships, with all the problems, dangers, and difficulties that were a feature of the 1970s.

Ever since the EMS crisis of 1992 to 1993, Europe has experienced a remarkable degree of monetary and financial stability, and even the turbulences in the international financial markets of the late 1990s had only minor impact on Europe. It is safe to assume that several European currencies would have suffered greatly during the 2008 to 2009 crisis, had they still existed.[28] The replacement of national currencies with the euro in 1999/2002 has eliminated the possibility of currency speculation within the euro area once and for all.[29] This success has not occurred unnoticed elsewhere. European monetary integration has developed into a role model of regional integration and there are today many regions that consider emulating the European example.[30]

Proposals for regional monetary cooperation are being discussed in all corners of the world.[31] In 2000 five Western African countries established the West African Monetary Zone (WAMZ), which is supposed to develop into a monetary union by 2010.[32] Plans for regional monetary integration also exist in Southern Africa, where in 2005 the 13 members of the Southern African Development Community (SADC) declared their goal of creating a monetary and economic union by 2016.[33] Even a monetary union for all of Africa is being discussed: in 2003, the Association of African Central Bank Governors announced that it would work for a single currency and common central bank by 2021 (Masson and Pattillo 2004a, b; Masson 2008). In the Middle East, the six member states of the Gulf Cooperation Council (Bahrain, Kuwait, Oman, Qatar, Saudi Arabia, and United Arab Emirates) have laid out a path to a common market by 2007 and monetary union by 2010 (Sturm and Siegfried 2005; Al-Mansouri and Dziobek 2006; IMF 2008a; Buiter 2008).[34] Proposals for monetary union also exist for the Caribbean (Worrell 2003) and in Oceania where six Pacific Islands—Fiji, Papua New Guinea, Samoa, Solomon Islands, Tonga, and Vanuatu—are considering forming a monetary union (Browne and Orsmond 2006). Last but not least, plans for regional monetary integration are frequently raised (and dismissed) also for the Mercado Común del Sur (Mercosur) (Eichengreen 1998; Fratianni and Hauskrecht 2002; De Carvalho 2006; Nitsch 2006) and the North

American Free Trade Agreement (NAFTA) (Buiter 1999a; Helleiner 2006). While serious doubt about the viability of several of these proposals or projects is warranted—either because of lack of political commitment or because of economic problems or both—this enumeration, which is by no means exhaustive, illustrates the prominence that the idea of regional monetary integration has attained among policy makers. Against this backdrop, the next two chapters will turn to the specific causes that have pushed East Asian countries to consider a policy of regional economic and monetary integration: the Asian crisis and the rise of China.

3   The Asian Financial Crisis

Arguably, the Asian financial crisis has been "the key catalytic event to propel regional cooperation" (Padoa-Schioppa 2005: 30) in East Asia. Bergsten (2000) even suggested that East Asia might be on the brink of a historical evolution, as Europe was half a century ago. The Asian crisis has played such a pivotal role in pushing regional integration tendencies for two reasons. First, it has made East Asian countries realize that they are closely tied together economically and that a financial and currency crisis in one country can quickly spread across the region. Second, the crisis has caused resentment at the international community's response to the crisis and has created a feeling of "being alone together."

East Asian countries have long been noted for their lack of interest in regional economic cooperation in general, and monetary and financial cooperation in particular. While embracing an export-led strategy of development, they were more oriented toward the world markets than their regional neighbors.[1] The only forum for regional cooperation in the region for a long time was ASEAN, which was established in 1967 in Bangkok by Indonesia, Malaysia, the Philippines, Singapore, and Thailand as a "zone of peace, freedom, and neutrality." Originally ASEAN's focus was more on regional peace and stability than on economic cooperation. The end of the cold war and the concomitant ideological conflicts between capitalism and communism and ASEAN's inclusion of the other Southeast Asian nations gradually broadened its agenda toward economic issues.[2] The first notable—albeit somewhat half-hearted—attempt at regional economic integration was the creation of the ASEAN Free Trade Area (AFTA) in 1992.[3] Efforts at cooperation, however, were limited to the real sector. The recognition that cooperation in the real and financial sectors need to be extended in tandem had not reached ASEAN yet.

Another platform for regional cooperation has been the Asia–Pacific Economic Cooperation Forum (APEC), which was established in 1989 at the behest of the US government.[4] Despite an economic cooperation agenda and plentiful declarations for fostering trade and investment, APEC's progress has been rather disappointing. And, just like ASEAN, APEC all but ignored financial and monetary cooperation prior to the Asian crisis

(Plummer and Click 2009). This ignorance proved fatal. When the crisis hit Thailand in July 1997, the region was completely unprepared for what was yet to come.

3.1   Chronology, Causes, and Consequences of the Crisis

The East Asian countries were long hailed as "miracle economies," with annual growth rates of partly close to or even over 10 percent in the 1980s and early 1990s.[5] Japan, Korea, China, and the newly industrialized "tiger" economies of Southeast Asia had become the epitome of successful export-oriented growth. This success story experienced a serious setback in 1997.

Even though the export performance of several East Asian countries in 1996 was rather disappointing and there were signs for an abatement of overheating in early 1997, a continuation of the previous growth path was widely expected.[6] The crisis was largely unanticipated and even credit rating agencies such as Standard & Poor's and Moody's did not recognize increased risk in East Asian markets until after the onset of the crisis itself (see Radelet and Sachs 1998).[7]

The crisis took its course when troubles arose in Thailand in March 1997. (A detailed chronology of the crisis is provided in annex 1.) Nonperforming loan problems of financial institutions were interpreted as a sign of vulnerability of the Thai financial sector and attracted selling attacks against the Thai baht (THB) in May and June 1997. The resulting significant capital outflows put the baht, which was closely tied to the US dollar, under heavy devaluation pressure. With ever mounting pressure on the baht, on July 2 the Thai central bank was forced to abandon the dollar peg and let the baht float, which depreciated by 15 percent within one day.

This marked the beginning of what became known as the Asian crisis: not only did the baht lose half its value against the US dollar by the end of the year (at its lowest point on January 12, 1998, it was worth only 44 percent of its value on June 30, 1997)—pressure mounted also on the Malaysian ringgit (MYR), the Philippine peso (PHP), the Lao kip, and the Indonesian rupiah (IDR), all of which were also tied to the dollar (figure 3.1, table 3.1). Unlike the Thai central bank, which exhausted almost its entire foreign exchange holdings to defend the baht, the Philippine, Indonesian, and Malay central banks quickly gave in and floated their currencies within two weeks after the baht's fall. By January 1998, the Malaysian ringgit and the Philippine peso were down 40 percent of their June 1997 value against the US dollar. The worst affected were the Indonesian rupiah, which at times was worth only a sixth of its June 1997 value against the US dollar, and the Lao kip, which had lost three quarters of its dollar value even one and a half years after the outbreak of the crisis.

The Korean authorities initially managed to keep the won (KRW) stable against the dollar, but by the end of October 1997 they also had to give up: the won depreciated sharply and lost more than half its dollar value within two months. The Cambodian riel,

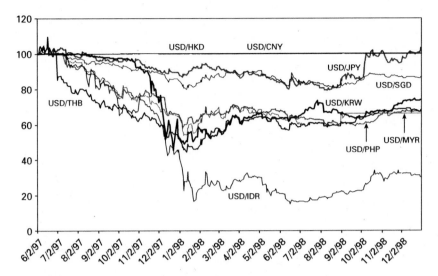

Figure 3.1
Exchange rates of East Asian currencies against the US dollar, June 1997 to December 1998

the Japanese yen, and the Singapore dollar (SGD) were less affected, with declines against the dollar of 12 to 20 percent between June and December 1997. Despite the currency turbulences, China (CNY), Hong Kong (HKD), and Myanmar managed to maintain their tight dollar pegs. Keeping the dollar pegs, however, came at the cost of losing export competitiveness. In Hong Kong, which (unlike China and Myanmar) employed no capital controls, the defense of the currency board regime was only possible because of the Hong Kong Monetary Authority's rigorous high-interest rate policy, which caused a painful contraction in domestic credit, investment, and GDP (table 3.3).

The sharp currency depreciations in Indonesia, Korea, Malaysia, the Philippines, and Thailand severely damaged domestic bank's balance sheets, causing what is commonly referred to as "twin crises"—that is, currency crises and financial sector crises occurring at the same time (see Kaminsky and Reinhart 1999).[8] Basically all East Asian countries except Japan had stabilized their currencies against the US dollar before the crisis (figure 3.2). The stable dollar exchange rates and the apparent absence of exchange risk had led domestic financial institutions to engage in unhedged foreign currency borrowing.[9] A common practice among resident banks and financial firms was to borrow short-term in US dollar and extended medium- or long-term credit in domestic currency.[10] Domestic institutions (particularly in Thailand and Korea) were thus heavily exposed to currency and maturity risks. With the devaluation of the home currencies against the dollar, foreign liabilities in terms of home currency increased markedly, causing a collapse of domestic bank capital and a wave of bankruptcies in the financial sectors of East Asia.[11]

Table 3.1
Exchange rates of East Asian currencies against the US dollar, June 1997 to December 1998

	6/30/97	12/31/97	6/30/98	12/31/98	% Change 6/30/97–12/31/97	% Change 12/31/97–6/30/98	% Change 6/30/98–12/31/98	% Change 6/30/97–6/30/98	% Change 6/30/97–12/31/98
Brunei dollar	0.699301	0.596837	0.585892	0.602228	−14.65	−1.83	2.79	−16.22	−13.88
Cambodian riel	0.000362	0.000290	0.000250	0.000265	−20.02	−13.59	5.97	−30.89	−26.76
Chinese yuan	0.120636	0.120770	0.120763	0.120809	0.11	−0.01	0.04	0.11	0.14
Hong Kong dollar	0.129089	0.129032	0.129114	0.129107	−0.04	0.06	−0.01	0.02	0.01
Indonesian rupiah	0.000411	0.000189	0.000069	0.000125	−54.03	−63.71	82.59	−83.32	−69.54
Japanese yen	0.008725	0.007662	0.007230	0.008853	−12.18	−5.64	22.45	−17.13	1.47
Korean won	0.001129	0.000588	0.000730	0.000831	−47.91	24.11	13.88	−35.35	−26.38
Lao kip	0.000362	0.000290	0.000250	0.000265	−58.99	−41.94	6.17	−76.19	−74.72
Malaysian ringgit	0.396306	0.257447	0.242689	0.263179	−35.04	−5.73	8.44	−38.76	−33.59
Myanmar kyat	0.163148	0.158577	0.156496	0.165485	−2.80	−1.31	5.74	−4.08	1.43
Philippine peso	0.037949	0.024999	0.024097	0.025710	−34.12	−3.61	6.69	−36.50	−32.25
Singapore dollar	0.699594	0.594001	0.594530	0.606061	−15.09	0.09	1.94	−15.02	−13.37
Thai baht	0.040450	0.021731	0.023719	0.027520	−46.28	9.15	16.03	−41.36	−31.96
Vietnam dong	0.000086	0.000081	0.000077	0.000072	−5.09	−5.34	−6.52	−10.16	−16.01

Sources: Pacific Exchange Rate Service Database. Rates for Brunei, Cambodia, Lao, Myanmar, and Vietnam are from IFS.
Note: Exchange rates are presented as USD per local currency.

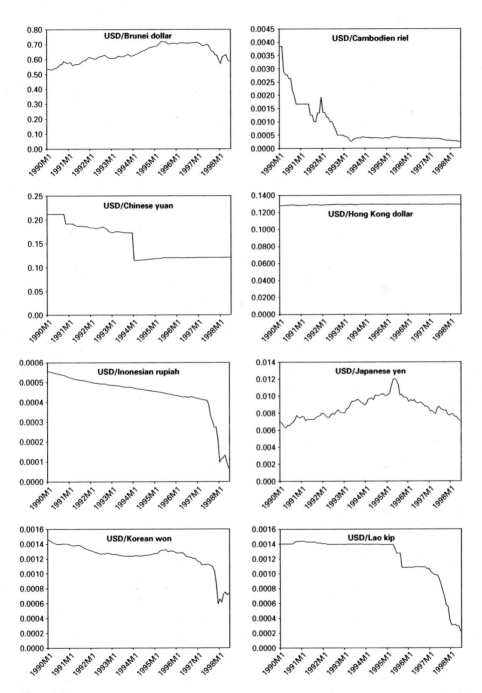

Figure 3.2
Exchange rates of East Asian currencies against the US dollar, January 1990 to June 1998

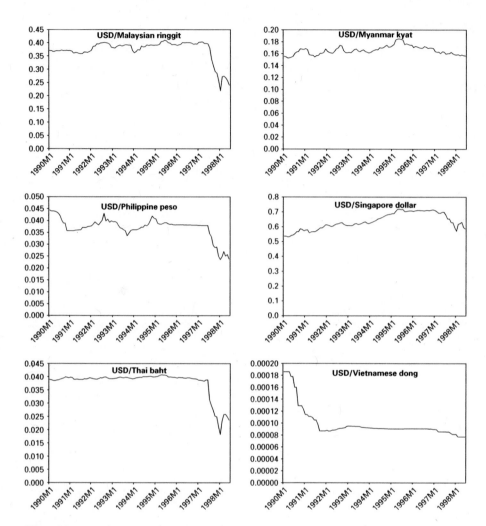

Figure 3.2
(continued)

One of the main characteristics of the Asian crisis was the rapid reversal of private capital flows. According to estimates of the Institute of International Finance (1998), net private capital inflows to the five countries most affected (Indonesia, Korea, Malaysia, the Philippines, and Thailand) dropped from USD 93 billion in 1996 to USD −12.1 in 1997—a swing of USD 105 billion or about 11 percent of pre-crisis GDP within one year![12] The withdrawal of foreign credit caused a liquidity squeeze, a sharp rise in interest rates, and a tightening of domestic credit conditions. Reacting to depreciation pressure on their currencies with fiscal and monetary tightening—policies demanded by the IMF as preconditions for its "rescue" packages (see below)—made things worse. Rising interest rates aggravated nonperforming loan problems, increased the number of corporate bankruptcies, and further weakened the position of financial institutions. Investment fell by more than 50 percent in Indonesia, Malaysia, and Thailand and 25 percent in the Philippines (Branson and Healy 2009: 234).

The outflow of capital, rising interest, and problems in the corporate sector also caused stock prices to decline; equity markets in East Asia recorded falls on the order of 30 to 50 percent (table 3.2). Most severely affected was the Korean stock market, which plunged by 50 percent between June and December 1997. The Indonesian and Malaysian markets also plummeted sharply, with losses accruing to 45 percent by December 1997. Hong Kong, Japan, the Philippines, Singapore, and Thailand all experienced losses in the range of 20 to 30 percent until December 1997. Even one and a half years after the start of the crisis, markets were way below their values of June 1997.

As a result of the crisis, Hong Kong, Indonesia, Korea, Malaysia, and Thailand experienced sharp contractions of real GDP on the order of 5 to 13 percent in 1998 (table 3.3). All other countries in the region, except Myanmar, experienced severe declines or at least a slowdown of economic activity. With pre-crisis growth rates of about 5 to 10 percent a year (except Brunei, Japan, and the Philippines), the cost of the crisis in terms of deviation from trend growth was much higher than the year-to-year decline. Moreover several of the crisis countries (Indonesia, Korea, Malaysia, Singapore, and Thailand) have not recovered back to their original growth paths. The crisis and the following recessions also generated sharp increases in poverty across the region (e.g., World Bank 2000).

There has developed an extensive literature on the causes of the Asian crisis. Several factors have been highlighted as contributing to the crisis, including macroeconomic imbalances, deteriorating external balances, government failure, weak financial institutions and supervision, weak corporate governance ("crony capitalism"), liberalization of capital accounts without adequately developed domestic financial markets, excessive borrowing in foreign currency, reliance on short-term capital flows, and moral hazard.[13] A particular role in the emergence of the crisis is commonly attributed to the de facto dollar pegs before the crisis, which gave rise to three problems (e.g., see Ito 2001). First of all, and as discussed above, the de facto dollar pegs reduced the perceived exchange rate risk and encouraged excessive, unhedged borrowing of short-term capital internationally. It

Table 3.2
East Asian stock markets, June 1997 to December 1998

	6/30/97	12/31/97	6/30/98	12/30/98	% Change 6/30/97–12/31/97	% Change 12/31/97–6/30/98	% Change 6/30/98–12/30/98	% Change 6/30/97–6/30/98	% Change 6/30/97–12/30/98
Hong Kong: Hang Seng Composite Index (HSID)	15,196.80	10,722.80	8,543.10	10,048.60	−29.44	−20.33	68.14	−43.78	−33.88
Indonesia: Jakarta SE Composite Index (JKSED)	724.56	396.53	445.92	398.04	−45.27	12.46	120.43	−38.46	−45.06
Japan: Nikkei Stock Average N225D	20,605.00	15,258.70	15,830.27	13,842.17	−25.95	3.75	21.24	−23.17	−32.82
Korea: SE Stock Price Index (KOSPI)	745.40	376.31	297.88	562.46	−49.52	−20.84	−10.71	−60.04	−24.54
Malaysia: KLSE Composite (KLSED)	1,077.30	594.44	455.64	586.13	−44.82	−23.35	−15.04	−57.71	−45.59
Philippines: Manila SE Composite Index (PSID)	2,809.21	1,869.23	1,760.13	1,968.78	−33.46	−5.84	28.76	−37.34	−29.92
Singapore: Straits-Times Index (STID)	1,921.48	1,507.65	1,009.20	1,392.73	−21.54	−33.06	11.60	−47.48	−27.52
Thailand: SET General Index (SETID)	527.28	372.69	267.33	355.81	−29.32	−28.27	48.71	−49.30	−32.52

Source: Global Financial Database.

Table 3.3
Real GDP growth (in percent), 1994 to 2005

	1990–96	1999–2005	1990	1991	1992	1993	1994	1995	1996	1997	1998	1999	2000	2001	2002	2003	2004	2005
Brunei	1.84	2.83	2.70	4.00	-0.20	0.50	1.80	2.10	2.00	2.60	-4.00	2.60	2.80	3.10	2.80	3.80	1.70	3.00
Cambodia	5.84	7.64	1.10	7.60	7.10	4.00	9.20	6.53	5.35	5.65	4.96	12.55	8.43	5.49	5.25	7.05	7.68	7.03
China	10.74	9.06	3.80	9.20	14.20	14.00	13.10	10.90	10.00	9.30	7.80	7.60	8.40	8.30	9.10	10.00	10.10	9.90
Hong Kong	4.87	5.02	1.87	5.60	6.60	6.30	5.50	3.90	4.30	5.10	-5.00	3.40	10.20	0.64	1.84	3.20	8.60	7.27
Indonesia	8.00	4.18	9.00	8.93	7.22	7.25	7.54	8.40	7.64	4.70	-13.13	0.79	4.92	3.83	4.38	4.72	5.05	5.60
Japan	2.33	1.27	5.20	3.35	0.97	0.25	1.10	2.01	3.43	1.77	-1.05	-0.14	2.39	0.20	-0.30	1.31	2.70	2.70
Korea	7.89	5.80	9.16	9.39	5.88	6.13	8.54	9.17	7.00	4.65	-6.85	9.49	8.49	3.84	6.97	3.10	4.73	3.96
Lao	6.52	6.32	6.67	4.13	6.85	5.91	8.16	7.03	6.89	6.91	3.97	7.31	5.78	5.79	5.85	6.10	6.44	6.97
Malaysia	9.48	5.35	9.01	9.55	8.89	9.89	9.21	9.83	10.00	7.32	-7.36	6.14	8.86	0.32	4.35	5.42	7.14	5.25
Myanmar	5.53	9.41	2.82	-0.65	9.66	6.04	7.48	6.95	6.44	5.65	5.87	10.95	9.85	11.30	12.00	13.80	3.00	5.00
Philippines	2.83	4.46	3.04	-0.58	0.34	2.12	4.39	4.68	5.85	5.19	-0.58	3.40	5.97	1.76	4.45	4.50	6.03	5.13
Singapore	8.76	5.29	9.20	6.55	6.34	11.73	11.57	8.15	7.78	8.33	-1.41	7.18	10.03	-2.28	4.04	2.93	8.72	6.38
Thailand	8.60	4.91	11.17	8.56	8.08	8.25	8.99	9.24	5.90	-1.37	-10.51	4.45	4.75	2.17	5.32	7.03	6.17	4.46
Vietnam	7.93	7.00	5.10	5.96	8.65	8.07	8.84	9.54	9.34	8.15	5.76	4.77	6.79	6.89	7.08	7.34	7.69	8.42

Sources: WDI and WEO.

was the build-up of external debt, denominated in foreign currency, which made the later crisis-hit countries vulnerable and caused devastation in their financial sectors after their currencies started to devalue. Second, if inflation in a country pegging its currency to the US dollar is higher than in the US, this leads to a real appreciation of the currency. Unless the inflation differential is compensated by faster productivity growth, real currency over-valuation will erode export competitiveness and lead to a worsening of the current account.[14] Third, dollar-pegging countries were exposed to fluctuations in the dollar–yen rate (Kwan 1998). The sharp depreciation of the Japanese yen against the US dollar from mid-1995 translated into appreciation of the other East Asian currencies against the yen, eroding their competitiveness vis-à-vis Japan (see chapter 2). As a result exports to Japan, which are an important source of growth for most countries in the region, declined and economic performance was dampened, particularly in Thailand and Korea.[15]

Several East Asian countries did indeed have large current account deficits prior to the crisis (table 3.4).[16] However, as Radelet and Sachs (1998) point out, despite important underlying problems at the macro- and microeconomic level (especially in the financial sector) and weak fundamentals in several East Asian economies, the imbalances were not severe enough to cause a regionwide crisis of this magnitude. Instead, Radelet and Sachs stress the role of financial panic among the international investment community which turned the Thai banking crisis into a full-fledged twin crisis that spread around the whole region. The panic was fueled by policy mistakes of East Asian governments and poorly designed international rescue programs.

It was particularly the role of regional financial contagion and the disappointment with the international community's inadequate policy response to the crisis that prompted East Asia's interest in regional monetary and financial cooperation and integration.

3.2   The Asian Financial Crisis and Regional Financial Contagion

Arguably, the strength of financial contagion was the most remarkable aspect of the Asian crisis (Ito 2001). After Thailand was hit, the crisis spilled over to the other countries in the region, even affecting those that were regarded as pursuing relatively sound and sus-tainable economic policies. Contagion, meaning the cross-country transmission of shocks, makes it increasingly difficult if not impossible for open economies to isolate themselves from shocks to their trading partners or competitors. Research by Eichengreen, Rose, and Wyplosz (1996) and Glick and Rose (1999) has shown that currency crises tend to spread along regional lines, and that trade linkages are an important transmission channel for crises. Glick and Rose's findings suggest that countries may be attacked because of the actions—or inaction—of their neighbors, who tend to be trading partners merely because of geographical proximity. They conclude that "[c]ountries who trade and compete with the targets of speculative attacks are themselves likely to be attacked" (Glick and Rose 1999: 604).[17]

Table 3.4
Current account balance (percent of GDP), 1990 to 1998

	Brunei	Cambodia	China	Hong Kong	Indonesia	Japan	Korea	Lao	Malaysia	Myanmar	Philippines	Singapore	Thailand	Vietnam
1990	68.40	-3.90	3.38	6.20	-2.61	1.45	-0.76	-8.90	-1.98	-25.30	-6.10	8.46	-8.53	-4.00
1991	68.60	-1.20	3.52	4.30	-3.32	1.96	-2.73	-2.40	-8.51	-16.40	-2.10	11.30	-7.71	-1.70
1992	61.70	-1.00	1.53	3.00	-2.00	2.97	-1.24	-3.50	-3.66	-13.40	-1.90	11.86	-5.66	-0.10
1993	48.10	-1.60	-2.64	4.80	-1.33	3.02	0.23	-3.20	-4.47	-10.90	-5.50	7.22	-5.09	-10.60
1994	40.00	-3.40	1.24	-0.80	-1.58	2.72	-0.95	-6.90	-6.07	-7.80	-4.40	16.14	-5.59	-11.50
1995	35.90	-4.90	0.22	-6.30	-3.18	2.10	-1.68	-6.90	-9.73	-3.70	-2.60	17.52	-8.09	-12.80
1996	37.20	-6.20	0.85	-2.50	-3.37	1.40	-4.16	-12.60	-4.42	-10.30	-4.60	15.02	-8.09	-8.19
1997	35.70	-7.90	3.88	-4.10	-2.27	2.25	-1.62	-10.50	-5.93	-10.60	-5.20	15.63	-2.00	-5.69
1998	44.70	-5.90	3.09	1.50	4.29	3.02	11.69	-4.60	13.20	-11.70	2.30	22.30	12.73	-3.95

Sources: WDI and WEO.

In East Asia intraregional trade accounts for more than 50 percent of overall trade.[18] Furthermore, because of East Asian countries' competition against one another in third markets—North America and Europe in particular—exchange rate changes in one country have important spillover effects on its neighbors. The trade channel was indeed an important transmitter of contagion during the Asian crisis (e.g., Ito 2001; Grilli 2002). East Asian countries, which were already caught in a "competitive squeeze" (Grilli 2002: 184) before the crisis, came under increased pressure after the forced devaluation of the baht in July 1997. Their consequent loss of trade competitiveness brought downward pressure on their currencies and led to cascading speculation on their devaluation. Once the Philippine peso and the Malaysian ringgit were floated, the pressure mounted even more on the remaining dollar-pegging currencies. As Branson and Healy (2009) point out, the contagion of this pressure is a strong argument for cooperative exchange rate management in the region.

Contagious effects also resulted from financial linkages. Goldfajn and Valdés (1996) have shown that financial and currency crises can spread contagiously to other countries when institutional investors that encounter liquidity difficulties as a result of losses in one country respond by liquidating their positions in other markets. The selling of risky assets by any trader increases incentives for others to sell as well. As a result sales become mutually enforcing, creating "liquidity black holes" (Morris and Shin 2004). The fact that much of East Asian investment was financed through international borrowing (and in many cases by the same financial institutions) made these countries vulnerable to panic trading among international investors. Moreover the region was confronted with a general shift in investor sentiment that strengthened contagious effects. Many international creditors and investors appeared to consider the region as a whole; a lack of country-specific knowledge might have led them to assume that if Thailand was in trouble, the other East Asian countries probably had similar difficulties. That is, the sudden loss of government credibility in Thailand was projected on governments throughout the region. Another form of financial contagion during the Asian crisis occurred when the Hong Kong dollar came under attack in November 1997 as a result of currency depreciations in the rest of the region. To defend the dollar parity, the Hong Kong Monetary Authority sharply raised interest rates, which caused liquidity problems for Hong Kong banks, which then reacted by calling in loans from the rest of the region, reinforcing financial problems elsewhere (Radelet and Sachs 1998).

The most severe case of contagion during the Asian crisis was that of Indonesia. Radelet and Sachs (1998) note that it is not without irony that Indonesia, which many observers thought would be the least affected country, turned out to be the worst afflicted in the end. The transmission of crisis to Indonesia was a forceful demonstration how a country that is on a relatively stable and high growth path without major macro- or microeconomic imbalances can be thrown into economic and political turmoil.[19] The crisis not only made clear the dangers of contagion, it also showed that the region was completely unprepared to take joint action to contain speculative pressure. The Asian crisis thus acted as a wake-up call for policy makers and showed that in the presence of policy externalities across the regional economy it is simply not sufficient to take national measures to prevent future crises. Probably the most important lesson that East Asian policy makers have drawn from the crisis experience is that effective national and regional crisis prevention schemes are needed and that cooperation in the real and financial sectors must be pursued concomitantly.

3.3   Emancipation from Washington and the US dollar

The Asian crisis not only revealed the dangers of financial contagion and the importance of policy coordination for preventing future crises, it also provoked strong feelings of discontent with the handling of the crisis by the international community, and the IMF and the US government in particular. The IMF has been widely accused of responding too late and giving flawed advice to the crisis economies.[20] The IMF administered crisis resolution measures in Indonesia, Korea, and Thailand (for details of the IMF plans, see annex 1) and gave advice to the other crisis countries. The IMF programs generally called for six actions: a tough stance on bank closures; strict enforcement of capital adequacy standards; tight domestic credit; high interest rates on central bank discount facilities; fiscal contraction; and structural changes in the nonfinancial sector.[21] Of these measures (which were the conditions to receive multilateral assistance and lending), especially the bank closures, capital adequacy enforcement, and tight monetary policies added considerably to the panic and contractionary force of the financial crisis (Radelet and Sachs 1998; Furman and Stiglitz 1998; Stiglitz 2000).[22] Radelet and Sachs (1998: 12) recount that domestic bank lending stopped abruptly in Thailand, Indonesia, and Korea after announcement of the IMF programs and report of "widespread anecdotes of firms unable to obtain working capital, even in support of confirmed export orders from abroad."

Moreover reduced government expenditures shrank the economy further. Even the largest international rescue packages in history, totaling more than USD 100 billion, did not help to prevent the consequences of such policies. In the view of Stiglitz (2000), "[a]ll the IMF did was make East Asia's recessions deeper, longer, and harder."[23] The slow provision of liquidity by the IMF and the detailed conditionality resulted in lasting resentment among East Asian policy makers. Lincoln (2004: 254) asserts that the crisis has caused a "common sense of irritation, frustration, and disagreement with the US government and the IMF" throughout the region, and partly even anti-Western and particularly anti-American attitudes. In the words of Greenville (2004), in Jakarta now, "the IMF label on any policy is virtually a kiss of death."[24] It is hence not surprising that Indonesia took the locally popular decision to exit the IMF program as soon as the economy improved, which was in July 2003 (Leahy 2004). Korea also advanced the repayment of its IMF obligations in August 2001 (IMF 2001). Similarly Thailand repaid its IMF borrowings early in July 2003, not without asking the IMF's Bangkok representative to leave the country (Greenville 2004).

The dissatisfaction with the IMF was also due to the region's under-representation in the Fund, especially that of the Southeast Asian countries. While ASEAN members constitute 8.15 percent of the world's population, they hold a meager 3.4 percent of IMF voting rights (see table 3.5). This contrasts sharply with the influence of the big shareholder countries (United States with 16.77 percent, Japan with 6.02 percent, Germany with 5.88 percent, and France and the United Kingdom with 4.86 percent each). Japan as the second largest shareholder could theoretically raise its voice on behalf of its neighbors, but in practice Japan has so far avoided any friction with the US government.

As a response to criticism on the Fund's ownership structure—not only from East Asian countries—the IMF executive board recently proposed a reform of quotas "to better align the current governance regime with members' relative positions in the world economy and to make it more responsive to changes in global economic realities while, and equally important, enhancing the participation and voice of low-income countries in the IMF"

Table 3.5
East Asian countries' IMF quota and voting rights versus share in world GDP and world population

	IMF Quota		IMF Votes		Share in world GDP in 2007 (% of total)	Share in world population in 2007 (% of total)
	Millions of SDRs	Percent of total	Absolute votes	Percent of total		
Brunei	215.2	0.10	2,402	0.11	0.02	0.01
Cambodia	87.5	0.04	1,125	0.05	0.02	0.21
Indonesia	2,079.3	0.96	21,043	0.95	0.79	3.30
Lao	52.9	0.02	779	0.04	0.01	0.08
Malaysia	1,486.6	0.68	15,116	0.68	0.34	0.38
Myanmar	258.4	0.12	2,834	0.13	0.02	0.70
Philippines	879.9	0.40	9,049	0.41	0.26	1.25
Singapore	862.5	0.40	8,875	0.40	0.30	0.06
Thailand	1,081.9	0.50	11,069	0.50	0.45	0.91
Vietnam	329.1	0.15	3,541	0.16	0.13	1.25
ASEAN	7,333.3	3.37	75,833	3.43	2.34	8.15
China	8,090.1	3.72	81,151	3.66	6.00	18.62
Japan	13,312.8	6.13	133,378	6.02	8.01	1.83
Korea	2,927.3	1.35	29,523	1.33	1.77	0.69
ASEAN+3	31,663.5	14.57	319,885	14.44	18.13	29.28

Sources: http://www.imf.org/external/np/sec/memdir/members.htm#1 for IMF for quota and votes (as of November 26, 2008), WEO for GDP and UN Statistics Division for population data.
Note: Hong Kong does not hold IMF shares of its own. Hong Kong and China's GDP combined equaled 6.38 percent of world output in 2007. China and Hong Kong's population together represents 18.72 percent of the world's population.

(IMF 2006). The proposal included initial ad hoc increases of voting rights for China (from 2.94 to 3.67 percent) and Korea (from 0.76 to 1.34 percent), which were agreed upon by the IMF Board of Governors at the Annual Meeting in Singapore in September 2006.[25] Additional adjustments to member's quotas and voting rights reform were made in April 2008, when a new quota formula was adopted (IMF 2008b), but these hardly affected East Asian countries' voting rights. With now 14.44 percent the share of all ASEAN countries together with China, Japan, and Korea (known as ASEAN+3)[26] is still much smaller than its share in world GDP, and smaller than that of the United States, which is still able to veto any IMF policies or reforms it deems undesirable.

The prospect of further—and more substantial—changes to the IMF's governance structure is still unclear for the time being, although the 2008 global financial crisis has increased chances of a greater overhaul of the international financial institutions which could result in bigger stakes of emerging countries in the IMF. At the London Summit in April 2009, the G-20 leaders declared the aim to reform the international financial institutions' mandates, scope and governance "to reflect changes in the world economy and the new challenges of globalisation, and [ensure] that emerging and developing economies, including the poorest, must have greater voice and representation" (G-20 2009). Whether this aim will be met and credibility of the IMF can be restored remains to be seen.

It is doubtful that any nonsignificant changes in governance structure, or an IMF reform without a scrapping of the US veto right, which seems unlikely, will change East Asian countries' perception of the IMF, which is mistrusted as overly dominated by US interests and unresponsive to Asian concerns (Fukuyama 2005a). The behavior of the US government (which actually declined to participate in a Thai rescue package that was negotiated at a Tokyo meeting in August 1997) and the IMF during the crisis are commonly interpreted in East Asia as narrowly self-interested and aimed at opening up East Asian financial markets to US investment banks (see Fukuyama 2005a, b). Henning (2005: 13) notes that "[t]he contrast to the quick and generous American response to Mexico's plight two-and-a-half years earlier implanted an enduring conviction that the United States could not be counted on to respond to crises in East Asia as it would to those in Latin America." The feeling of being left at the mercy of Western interests has created a strong incentive for East Asian countries to increase their formal multilateral economic cooperation in order to limit dependence on future IMF and US support. In the view of Park (2008: 49), the IMF has not regained its credibility in East Asia even a decade after the crisis, "because it has so far refused to engage in frank and constructive dialogue with Asian stakeholders." Ito (2007a: 42) also senses "still widespread, persistent resentment against the IMF in Asia."

The opinion of being let down by the international community and the demand for a regional response was exemplarily expressed by Il Sakong, then President of the Institute for Global Economics in Seoul, during a meeting in Chiang Mai in May 2000 where he stated that "[w]e need to have some kind of defense mechanism. Since not much is

expected to be done at the global level, something should be done at the regional level"
(see Dieter 2000b: 22).

3.4   Initiatives since the Crisis

Already during the Asian crisis attempts were made to establish a regional scheme
for financial cooperation. In August 1997, only weeks after the outbreak of the crisis in
Thailand, the Japanese government proposed the creation of an Asian Monetary Fund
(AMF) as a framework for financial cooperation and policy coordination in the region.
The AMF, which was to be endowed with USD 100 billion of central bank reserves, was
intended as a lender to countries in financial distress and a complementary means of
defense against financial crises in Asia. Kwan (2001: 35) describes the endeavor to build
an AMF "as an attempt by Asian countries to escape domination by Washington and to
achieve financial independence." It is therefore not surprising that the AMF—which was
endorsed by Korea and the ASEAN countries—was averted by the objection of the US
government and the IMF.[27]

The idea of an AMF—even though under a different name—was revived when the
ASEAN finance ministers met with their counterparts of China, Japan, and Korea on
May 6, 2000, in Chiang Mai, Thailand, where they agreed to establish a system of bilateral
short-term financing facilities within the group. This agreement, called the Chiang Mai
Initiative (CMI), provides for mutual assistance consisting of swap arrangements in the
event of a financial crisis.[28] The wording of the declaration of the ASEAN+3 Finance
Ministers (2000: §6) at Chiang Mai diplomatically depicts the region's desire for reducing
dependence on the IMF:

In order to strengthen our self-help and support mechanisms in East Asia through the ASEAN+3
framework, we recognized a need to establish a regional financing arrangement to supplement the
existing international facilities. As a start, we agreed to strengthen the existing cooperative frameworks among our monetary authorities through the "Chiang Mai Initiative."

The CMI consists of an expanded ASEAN Swap Arrangement (ASA) that includes the
ASEAN countries and a network of Bilateral Swap Arrangements (BSAs) among ASEAN+3
countries. As of April 2009 the ASA is USD 2 billion in size, while 16 BSAs have been
successfully concluded with a combined total size of USD 90 billion (table 3.6).

While the amounts available to potential borrowers under the CMI are small in relation
to most East Asian countries' foreign exchange holdings, the swaps nonetheless exceed
borrowers' quotas at the IMF by several multiples (Henning 2005).[29] In May 2008 the
finance ministers of the ASEAN+3 countries agreed on the sidelines of the annual meeting
of the ADB in Madrid to multilateralize the CMI, namely to set up a pool of foreign
exchange reserves (Volz 2008). They decided that at least USD 80 billion of the region's
foreign reserves are to be funneled into a regional fund to protect regional currencies

Table 3.6
Network of bilateral swap arrangements under the Chiang Mai initiative (in billion USD)

From \ To	China	Japan	Korea	Indonesia	Malaysia	Philippines	Singapore	Thailand	Total
China		3.0	4.0	4.0	1.5	2.0		2.0	16.5
Japan	3.0		13.0	12.0	1.0	6.0	3.0	6.0	44.0
Korea	4.0	8.0		2.0	1.5	2.0		1.0	18.5
Indonesia			2.0						2.0
Malaysia			1.5						1.5
Philippines		0.5	2.0						2.5
Singapore		1.0							1.0
Thailand		3.0	1.0						4.0
Total	7.0	15.5	23.5	18.0	4.0	10.0	3.0	9.0	**90.0**

Source: Japan Ministry of Finance (www.mof.go.jp/english/if/CMI_0904.pdf).
Note: Data as of April 2009.

against speculative attacks and provide countries in crisis with liquidity. Of the funds, 20 percent is to be provided by the ASEAN members and the remaining 80 percent by the "Plus Three" countries. In Madrid, other technical details on collateral, repayment schemes, defaults, maturity, and interest rates, among others, were also agreed upon. Substantial progress was made in February 2009, at a special meeting in Phuket, when the ASEAN+3 finance ministers decided in the face of the global financial crisis to increase the funds of the multilateralized CMI to a minimum of USD 120 billion. In Phuket, they also agreed to create an independent regional surveillance unit to monitor and analyze regional economies and support CMI decision-making processes. The final details of the governing mechanisms and the implementation plan for the CMI multilateralization were agreed upon by the ASEAN+3 finance ministers in Bali in May 2009 (Volz 2009). The Bali agreement defines the relationship between each country's share in the reserve pool and its voting rights, which are proportional to individual contributions, but with a bias in favor of the smaller countries. Voting rights are allocated to prevent any of the Plus Three countries, or ASEAN as a group, from holding veto power.[30] The agreement also divides the decision-making mechanism between fundamental issues, which require consensus, and lending issues, which will be subject to majority ruling. Last but not least, the Bali agreement defines the maximum amounts of borrowing for each country, among other details. With the multilateralization of the CMI, ASEAN+3 has effectively established a system for regional cooperation that is self-governed, with a collective decision-making mechanism and the creation of an independent regional surveillance agency. As such, the new reserve pooling arrangement—while stopping short of being a full-fledged AMF—epitomizes the region's commitment to regional financial cooperation.

Another important regional initiative in the field of money and finance is the ASEAN Surveillance Process, which the ASEAN finance ministers agreed on in Washington in October 1998. The objective of the ASEAN Surveillance Process is to strengthen cooperation by (1) exchanging information and discussing the economic and financial development of member states in the region, (2) providing an early warning system and a peer review process to enhance macroeconomic stability and the financial system in the region, (3) highlighting possible policy options and encouraging early unilateral or collective actions to prevent a crisis, and (4) monitoring and discussing global economic and financial developments that could have implications on the region and proposing possible regional and national level actions (ASEAN 1998a). A similar scheme is ASEAN+3's Economic Review and Policy Dialogue (ERPD), which has been in place since May 2000. Under the ERPD, finance ministers and deputies meet semiannually to discuss economic and financial developments in the region. In 2001 the ASEAN+3 finance ministers also agreed to exchange data on capital flows to facilitate an effective policy dialogue. With the multilateralization of the CMI, ASEAN+3 will establish its own independent regional surveillance agency.

A third field of cooperation directly resulting from the crisis experience is the development of regional security markets. For instance, ASEAN+3 countries have developed the Asian Bond Market Initiative (ABMI), which was originally proposed by Japan in 2002. The aim of the ABMI is to develop efficient and liquid bond markets in Asia in order to enable a better utilization of Asian savings for Asian investments and to avoid the currency and maturity mismatches in financing that exacerbated the financial crisis. The ABMI includes efforts to modify existing regulations to facilitate the issuance of and investment in local currency denominated bonds, as well as the development of new securitized debt instruments, credit guarantee and investment mechanisms, foreign exchange transactions and settlement issues, and rating systems. In May 2008 the "New ABMI Roadmap" was endorsed. The four key issues in the New ABMI Roadmap are (1) promoting issuance of local currency-denominated bonds (supply side), (2) facilitating the demand of local currency-denominated bonds (demand side), (3) improving the regulatory framework, and (4) improving related infrastructure for bond markets. These will be addressed by separate task forces (see Schou-Zibell 2008). Complementary activities are the launch of the Asian Bond Funds (ABF) I and II by the Executives' Meeting of East-Asia and Pacific Central Banks (EMEAP).[31]

While the initial focus after the crisis was on financial cooperation, there have been also intensive discussions about exchange rate cooperation. Although no actual steps have been taken in exchange rate coordination hitherto, the ASEAN+3 countries have established research groups to explore the possibility of a regional exchange rate arrangement for East Asia and the possibility of creating regional monetary units (see ASEAN+3 Research Group 2004). Moreover several ASEAN leaders have repeatedly mentioned the option of creating a common currency for ASEAN (e.g., see Estrada 1999; Severino 1999;

Yong 2004; Siazon 2005).[32] At the sidelines of the ADB meeting in Hyderabad in May 2006, the finance ministers of Korea, Japan, and China pledged to enhance the existing cooperation framework to defend regional currencies against speculators and announced that they will "immediately launch discussions on the road map for the system to coordinate foreign exchange policy" (Giridharadas 2006: 12).

The most recent initiative in monetary and exchange rate cooperation was started by the ADB, which proposed the launch of an Asian currency unit (ACU) (see Kawai 2009). The ACU is envisaged as a virtual basket currency similar to the ECU that the Western European countries created in 1979 as part of the EMS. While it is not clear whether the ACU could become a forerunner of a common East Asian currency—indeed it still is unclear if it will be launched—it is undeniable that the region has developed a dynamic in regional integration that cannot be ignored.[33]

As Padoa-Schioppa (2005: 31) notes, "these initiatives are more than just a first step toward greater cooperation, they have also created important fora for an ongoing policy dialogue at the level of finance ministers and central bank governors." And indeed they would have been unthinkable without the changes in East Asian policy makers' attitudes toward regional cooperation brought about by the Asian crisis.

4   The Rise of China

A third factor that has arguably instilled economic cooperation among East Asian countries is the rise of China. The past years have seen what Napoléon Bonaparte allegedly predicted two hundred years ago: "Quand la Chine s'éveillera, le monde tremblera." Like much of the rest of the world, China's neighbors have watched China's transformation and international opening since the 1970s. Since reforms and international opening began in 1978, China has experienced one of the world's fastest growths, with an average annual real growth rate of 9.9 percent between 1978 and 2007 (WEO). China is now already the second largest economy in the world after the United States when measured in purchasing power parity, and the third largest in nominal terms. Moreover it has become the world's second largest exporter, with a share of 8.8 percent in world exports in 2007 (DTS).

China's progress has unsettled many of its neighbors and trading partners. The rise of China is different from that of any other country because of its sheer size. Even for a grouping as large as ASEAN with a population of 570 million, China poses a great challenge with her 1.3 billion people (figure 4.1). According to predictions of the UN Secretariat, China's population might reach as much as 1.5 billion by 2025 (UN Population Division Database). Measured at current prices, China's economy is by now two and a half times larger than that of all ASEAN countries combined and almost three times as large as Korea's (see figure 4.2). While Japan is still a third larger than the Chinese economy, China is catching up rapidly.

China's rise has several implications for East Asian countries. First of all, China is perceived as an economic challenge. In an increasingly competitive and globalized environment, there are deep concerns in East Asian countries that they will be overtaken by China. Like elsewhere, the rest of East Asia fears that China's seemingly unlimited supply of cheap labor will erode its competitiveness. ASEAN countries as well as Japan and Korea worry about losing their competitive edge, especially in high-technology markets (Hale and Hale 2003).

Since 1993, China has been by far the largest recipient of foreign direct investment (FDI) in the Asia–Pacific region, with FDI flows to China amounting to USD 84 billion in 2007 (figure 4.3). There is a growing perception that China's rapidly expanding economy

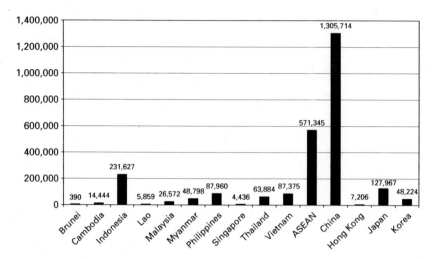

Figure 4.1
Population of East Asian countries (thousand people), 2007

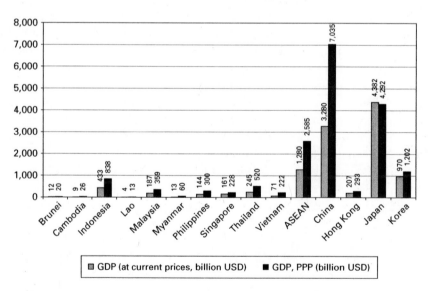

Figure 4.2
GDP of East Asian countries at current prices and PPP (in billion USD), 2007

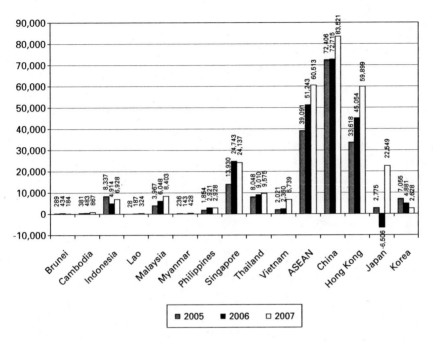

Figure 4.3
FDI flows to East Asian countries (millions of USD), 2005 to 2007

diverts FDI inflows away from the rest of East Asian economies toward China, and that this is hollowing out of their industrial base. The view that "China is grabbing much of the new foreign investment in Asia, leaving its once-glittering neighbors . . . with crumbs" (*New York Times* 2002) is widespread also among East Asian policy makers. For instance, Lee Hsien Loong, today prime minister of Singapore, was quoted in November 2002 by ChinaOnline as saying that "Southeast Asian countries are under intense competitive pressure, as their former activities, especially labor-intensive manufacturing, migrate to China. One indicator of this massive shift is the fact that Southeast Asia used to attract twice as much foreign direct investment as Northeast Asia, but the ratio is reversed" (see Chantasasawat, Fung, and Iizaka 2004: 123). Even though there is no clear empirical evidence of crowding out (Chantasasawat et al. 2004; Mercereau 2005), the fears persist.[1]

Whether or not these fears are well founded—they seem to have nurtured the notion in Southeast Asia that ASEAN countries need to restructure and integrate their economies in order to stay competitive and remain an important growth pole in the global economy.[2] Therefore ASEAN has not only tried to push AFTA. At the 2003 ASEAN Summit in Bali, ASEAN leaders also declared the goal of establishing an ASEAN Economic Community (AEC) by 2020. At ASEAN's annual meeting in January 2007, leaders agreed to speed up the AEC process to 2015, "in response to the growing economic power of China and India" (Burton 2007). The AEC is envisaged as a single market and production base with free flow of goods, services, investments, capital, and skilled labor.[3] Even the possibility of creating a single currency for the AEC has been raised. The rationale for the AEC is that an integrated ASEAN market with a combined population of more than 550 million should keep the region competitive vis-à-vis China—and the other rising giant, namely India.[4] The establishment of an AEC is hoped to strengthen the position of ASEAN member states in relation to China, but also to its other big neighbors Japan, India, and Korea, as well as to international partners like the United States and the European Union and international organizations like the IMF or the World Trade Organization.

China, however, does not only pose an economic challenge to its neighbors but also an opportunity. China is not just a competitor but also a prosperous export market with more than a billion "new capitalists" and consumers. The World Bank (2006: 17) recently asserted that "[t]he rapid growth of China's imports from the rest of East Asia has in effect compensated those economies for their losses in world markets as a result of competitive pressure from China's exports." Table 4.1 shows the trade balance of East Asian countries with Greater China (China and Hong Kong) for the period 2001 to 2007. While the four least developed countries in the region—Cambodia, Lao, Myanmar, and Vietnam—have had persistent trade deficits vis-à-vis China and HK, all others (except Indonesia in 2006 to 2007 and Japan in 2001) have enjoyed surpluses. On the aggregate, China and Hong Kong have been running a growing trade deficit with their neighbors.

China is increasingly becoming the heartbeat of the whole East Asian economy. For all East Asian countries except for Brunei, Indonesia, and Thailand, trade with China and Hong Kong has become more important than trade with Japan. Even more: for all East Asian countries except Brunei, Cambodia, and Malaysia, trade with China is more important now than trade with the United States (see table 5.8 and the analysis in section 5.3). East Asian countries are attempting to further explore trade and investment opportunities with China. For instance, ASEAN and China have signed an accord in November 2004 to create the world's largest free trade area by 2010, with more than 1.8 billion people (ASEAN and China 2004).

The strong intraregional trade ties are also due to extensive investment and production linkages. Since China's opening to foreign investment, Japanese and Korean corporations have been among the biggest investors in China (as they have been in Southeast Asia), taking opportunity of cheap production costs. Multinational corporations have formed regional supply chains, taking advantage of intraregional divisions of labor and promoting the specialization of production by breaking the production process down into different sub-processes within the same industry. The increasing participation of China in regional production networks has created a complex web of economic linkages and given rise to tighter interdependence within the region. This new state of play, which is basically the

Table 4.1
Trade balance of East Asian countries with China and Hong Kong (in million USD), 2001 to 2007

	2001	2002	2003	2004	2005	2006	2007
Brunei	60.07	133.31	145.49	93.30	95.67	55.34	26.51
Cambodia	−182.65	−555.11	−620.92	−737.13	−318.12	−505.01	−1,528.15
Indonesia	1,391.01	1,477.17	1,806.13	1,624.17	2,020.71	−1,477.75	−2,940.72
Japan	−5,038.93	2,179.34	10,490.97	13,372.12	6,014.11	9,225.30	18,996.73
Korea	13,111.54	14,804.26	25,118.88	35,037.22	36,754.79	34,619.58	38,995.45
Lao	−63.09	−56.98	−105.88	−105.41	−100.88	−155.54	−115.66
Malaysia	2,186.92	2,081.16	4,036.38	2,811.71	1,515.90	253.43	416.18
Myanmar	−470.17	−720.32	−867.03	−853.65	−774.37	−1,093.57	−1,496.85
Philippines	62.54	879.47	1,839.61	1,400.52	2,513.96	2,555.73	14,300.09
Singapore	6,168.21	6,626.72	10,392.54	13,175.25	16,587.18	22,739.33	24,517.46
Thailand	1,625.12	1,414.14	2,896.37	2,508.53	2,569.99	3,663.00	5,683.49
Vietnam	−409.17	−1,105.11	−1,877.58	−2,390.20	−3,553.50	−7,050.30	−11,428.21
Sum	18,441.40	27,158.05	53,254.96	65,936.44	63,325.43	62,829.53	85,426.34

Source: DTS.

result of a market-driven integration process, provides a strong incentive to push for the deepening of economic policy cooperation and for exchange rate coordination.

By and large, the Asian financial crisis and the rise of China have created a situation in which East Asian countries have moved closer together and in which they find closer regional economic cooperation a compelling necessity in order to shield off further crises and remain competitive in an increasingly globalized world. As the discussion in the last chapter has shown, the Asian crisis has sharpened the awareness that monetary and financial cooperation needs to be part of this process. Against the backdrop of these developments, the remainder of this study is an attempt at analyzing the costs and benefits of monetary cooperation and integration in East Asia and the best strategy to achieve this.

II Costs and Benefits of Monetary Integration

5   The Standard Approach: The Theory of Optimum Currency Areas

In 1997 Bayoumi and Eichengreen (1997: 761) wrote that "like it or not, the theory of optimum currency areas [OCA] remains the workhorse for analyses of European unification."[1] A decade later, OCA theory still dominates the way most economists think of monetary integration, and now it has become the workhorse for analyses of East Asian monetary integration.[2] OCA theory is basically concerned with an analysis of the costs and benefits of monetary integration, that is, the costs and benefits of flexible exchange rates relative to those of pegged exchange rate regimes or full monetary unification. While an important tool for analysis, OCA theory has several theoretical shortcomings that have led to an overemphasis of the effectiveness of independent monetary and exchange rate policy as stabilization instruments and an undervaluation of the benefits of monetary integration. In particular, its focus is on allocative efficiency and "static, steady-state alternatives" (Collignon 2002: 93). It fails to take into account that monetary integration is an endogenous process in which the criteria that have been developed in the OCA literature to assess the desirability of monetary integration change with the implementation of a policy of integration. As will be shown later in chapter 6, taking a dynamic perspective can turn some of the wisdoms of OCA theory on their head and lead to different conclusions regarding the desirability of fixed exchange rate regimes or monetary union.

Given its prevalence, this chapter will discuss the costs and benefits of monetary integration along the lines of OCA theory and evaluate whether East Asia satisfies the conditions for an OCA. Chapter 6 will then go beyond the conventional, static approach and, after examining the flaws of OCA theory, discuss the changes that monetary integration might bring about. This includes an examination of the effects of monetary integration on trade integration, an empirical investigation of the effects of real and financial integration on output fluctuations in East Asia, as well as an analysis of how a policy of monetary integration could be implemented as a regionwide strategy to establish the macroeconomic conditions and promote the financial market development conducive to sustained growth and development across East Asia. It will also reconsider the costs of monetary integration in terms of a loss of policy autonomy.

5.1   Costs and Benefits in the Optimum Currency Area Theory

Long before monetary integration became a topic of practical importance, the foundations of OCA theory were laid when Robert Mundell (1961: 657) posed the question: "What is the appropriate domain for a currency area?" He acknowledged that "[i]t might seem at first that the question is purely academic since it hardly appears within the realm of political feasibility that national currencies would ever be abandoned in favor of any other arrangement," but he reasoned that "[c]ertain parts of the world are undergoing processes of economic integration and disintegration, new experiments are being made, and a conception of what constitutes an optimum currency area can clarify the meanings of these experiments." (Mundell 1961: 657) Mundell's visionary thinking proved highly influential academically and also became a matter of great political relevance when Western European countries started thinking about monetary integration in the wake of the Bretton Woods crisis (which led to the creation of the snake and the EMS and eventually to the creation of EMU), or when the Soviet Union disintegrated into several currency areas in the 1990s (Tavlas 1993a).

In short, OCA theory examines which countries or regions would be good candidates for a common currency area, or if they would be better off within a system of flexible exchange rates. Mundell (1961: 657) defines a currency area as a "domain within which exchange rates are fixed." In principle, it makes no analytical difference whether one actually deals with monetary unions or exchange rate pegs between currencies, as the main distinction between these two is that the latter are easily reversible while the dissolution of a common currency is more complicated (and costly). Strictly speaking, OCA theory is only concerned with the trade-off between fixed and flexible rates, not whether a fix should be permanent and irrevocable or only temporary.[3]

Frankel (2000: 93) defines an OCA as "a region that is neither so small that it would be better off pegging its currency to a neighbour, nor so large that it would be better off splitting into subregions with different currencies." The OCA literature has developed a number of criteria that influence the costs as well as the benefits of joining or leaving a currency area. We will first discuss the costs and benefits according to the OCA literature in this section and then review the criteria that have been put forward to assess the optimum size of a currency area in section 5.2. Section 5.3 will turn to an empirical examination of the OCA criteria in East Asia.

In a nutshell, the costs and benefits of monetary integration, according to conventional OCA theory, refer to the trade-off between microeconomic efficiency gains brought about by the enlargement of a currency area and macroeconomic losses of economic policy instruments through the sacrifice of policy autonomy. Both will be discussed consecutively.

Benefits

The key benefit of monetary integration, according to conventional OCA theory, is that it will lead to a more efficient allocation of resources within the currency area. The enlargement of a currency area reduces transaction costs and increases price transparency, thereby simplifying economic decisions and facilitating trade in goods and services and financial exchange. Greater transparency also reduces price differentials across the currency area, leading to consumer gains. Because national borders become less important, market forces are allowed to play a freer role, which is supposed to make for more efficient investment, better credit allocation, and increased cross-border holdings of local securities.

Swings in the exchange rate are likely to influence importing and exporting firms' behavior because exchange rate variability exposes foreign trade to uncertainty. With sophisticated financial markets, short-term risk can be hedged relatively easily, but not without cost. Hedging exchange rate risk becomes more expensive and difficult the longer the period that needs to be hedged; in developing countries hedging is often impossible even for shorter periods. If a floating exchange regime leads to significant long-term fluctuations in the exchange rate, the degree of uncertainty increases considerably and so do the costs of insurance (e.g., Ethier 1973; De Grauwe and de Bellefroid 1987).

Exchange rate variability is likely to influence exporting firms' international pricing of goods, as well as firm's international investment behavior (Krugman 1989). Firms usually price their goods or services in the currency of the country they sell them in. Due to competition in the foreign market, they are not able to adjust these prices to exchange rate changes, with the result that the exporting firm has to bear the costs of an appreciation of its home currency, and might even accumulate losses. Krugman's (1989) "sunk cost model" refers to the investment costs that occur when entering and exiting a foreign market, such as costs for market research or the development of a sales network. The larger exchange rate uncertainty, the higher is the risk of a failed investment. This causes potential investors to adopt a wait-and-see attitude toward foreign investment, and because of exchange rate uncertainty exporters will only realize investments with a higher risk premium; that is, they will only undertake investments that can be expected to reap a higher rate on investment than those in the domestic market. As a consequence firms are likely to invest less, which implies opportunity costs and bygone profits.[4] For those engaged in cross-border and foreign currency transactions, predictable or completely fixed exchange rates are therefore of high value, and hence interest groups that prefer fixed over flexible rates can be found especially in sectors exposed to international trade (see Hefeker 1997; Collignon and Schwarzer 2003).

A further benefit of monetary integration is the reduction of barriers to financial integration.[5] As in trade, exchange rate variability and the existence of different currencies segment capital markets and hamper financial integration. A common presumption in the literature on financial integration is that it spurs financial development in the less financially developed regions or countries of the integrating area. The financial systems and their degree of sophistication should therefore assimilate, in the sense that the less developed financial sectors catch up and move toward the standards of the most financially developed sectors. Financial integration should thus increase the supply of finance in the more backward regions and at the same time broaden investment opportunities for agents in the common currency area. This will also encourage international risk diversion through private portfolio diversification.

A well-functioning financial sector is a precondition for the efficient allocation of resources and the exploitation of an economy's growth potential.[6] Improvements in financial intermediation may ameliorate the allocation of resources across investment projects, because a better trading, hedging, and pooling of risk allows the funding of highly profitable, but risky investment projects that would be relinquished otherwise. The more advanced financial systems become, the better they should be able to deal with the problems of asymmetric information that are persistent in financial markets. This would further reduce the cost of financial intermediation. Moreover a more sophisticated financial sector should be more capable of distinguishing between good and bad investment opportunities, increasing the social marginal productivity of capital (Gianetti et al. 2002).[7] Surprisingly, financial sector effects of monetary integration have received relatively little attention in the OCA literature, which has predominantly focused on real economic effects. Section 6.4 will come back to this issue and discuss monetary integration as a way of promoting financial development and of overcoming the problems of (international) asset and liability dollarization in East Asia.

An additional benefit of monetary integration is that central banks, but also commercial banks and companies, forgo or reduce the opportunity costs of holding currency reserves. The main reason for monetary authorities holding international reserves is for defending or managing a peg or managed floating exchange rate regime (Frankel 1983).[8] The build-up of high international liquidity enables a central bank to intervene in the foreign exchange market in support of its own currency in the case of depreciation pressure. It thus gives credibility to the exchange rate regime and provides a line of defense against a sudden reversal of capital flows (see section 10.1). International reserves may hence be viewed as a form of precautionary saving (Aizenman, Lee, and Rhee 2004). While stock-piling international reserves reduces the probability of a liquidity crisis, it is costly, as currency earns no return for the holder, resulting in an opportunity cost for holding it. In practice, international reserves are commonly invested in highly fungible but low return-bearing assets such as US treasury bills. This often implies that they have a negative carry, because the costs of sterilizing foreign exchange interventions by issuing domestic securities exceed the yields earned on reserves. Monetary cooperation and integration may involve the pooling of reserves, which diminishes the need for each individual country to hold large amounts of liquidity. In the case of a monetary union, reserves could be centralized in a common central bank, which would further reduce the need to hold reserves.

Also, as monetary union is likely to take place between countries that had previously stabilized their exchange rates against one another, the main reason to hold reserves, namely to give credibility to a peg, would be removed.

The complete benefits of monetary integration are only enjoyed if full monetary union is achieved, since, by definition, only a single currency eliminates the costs of changing money and the uncertainties about the exchange rate. In the case of a peg or any other fixed exchange rate arrangement short of full monetary unification, the possibility of a revaluation remains, possibly forced by a speculative attack. The existence of different currencies makes cross-border payments comparable to a distortionary tax, as it discriminates against small transactions and prevents fully integrated consumer and financial markets (Collignon 2002).[9] Because the benefits of a currency in its role as medium of exchange—like that of language—are greater, the larger the number of people using it, welfare is disproportionately reduced for small countries using their own money.

It is not clear whether the decision of countries to join a currency area is made based on a cost–benefit analysis as suggested by OCA theory (De Grauwe 2001). It seems that there are several other factors that come into play other than those mentioned by OCA. Besides political motivations, a major factor seems to be the desire to achieve monetary and macroeconomic stability through monetary integration. In conventional OCA analysis, potential benefits such as a gain in monetary credibility and hence lower interest rates or protection from currency crisis are hardly discussed. Only the "new" theory (Tavlas 1993b) acknowledges such benefits, which may be more important than the traditional arguments for monetary integration, as will be discussed in chapter 6.

Costs

The costs of monetary integration, as viewed by OCA theory, refer to the loss of a country's economic policy autonomy. Besides the loss of the exchange rate as an adjustment instrument, countries also have to make concessions with their fiscal policies and give up monetary policy autonomy as a tool to manage the aggregate performance of the economy. The loss of economic policy autonomy is the standard economic argument against monetary integration and a key underlying assumption of OCA theory. This view will be questioned in sections 6.1 and 6.5.

Without capital controls, an exchange rate peg implies that the central bank has to commission its monetary policy to maintain its external target, meaning that it cannot have an internal target, such as price stability, at the same time.[10] If the exchange rate were of no concern, the central bank could initiate expansionary open market policies to stabilize output in the case of a negative shock. With an exchange rate target, however, easing monetary policy would be incompatible, because an increase in domestic money would weaken the external value of the currency. This would require intervention in the foreign exchange market, i.e., buying home currency to stabilize the exchange rate, and causing a contraction of money supply (as well as a loss of international reserves, which might undermine confidence in the exchange rate peg).

If countries go beyond exchange rate stabilization and abandon the national currency by entering a monetary union, they not only lose monetary independence: a common currency implies the complete loss of monetary sovereignty to a common monetary policy-maker for the whole currency area.

From a Keynesian perspective, which Mundell had in mind, monetary policy is not neutral in its effects on the real sector. Given stationary expectations, monetary policy—working through nominal interest rates, the credit channel, and changes in the nominal exchange rate—can be used to influence real economic behavior.[11] Monetary independence hence renders governments or central banks with a powerful policy tool to influence economic cycles. Abandoning this tool would be potentially costly, since monetary policy within a currency area cannot be tailored to the need of any particular country or region in the area. Whether the same interest rate level is appropriate for all countries and regions within a currency area depends on the convergence of economic cycles. If countries or regions within the currency area experience different shocks and cycles, monetary policies directed to each economy's individual disturbances would be appropriate but are precluded. Essentially each member of a currency zone has to accept the common monetary policy, and there is a danger that the common interest rate "will always be some compromise rate, which suits no one country in particular" (Thirlwall 2000: 7).[12]

Moreover a common currency, like a regional exchange rate system, requires a high degree of fiscal coordination (Wyplosz 1991). For example, to secure credibility of the common European monetary policy, the German government pushed through the Stability and Growth Pact (SGP) at the EU summit in Dublin in December 1996. The SGP requires that national governments constrain their budget deficits to 3 percent or less of national GDP. The rationale for curtailing deficits is to avoid ballooning public debt that could induce national governments to pressure the common central bank to lower interest rates, which would reduce the financing costs of their deficits.[13] But also without formal budget constraints, national governments cannot monetize deficits, that is, they cannot (ab)use monetary policy to finance public debt through an inflation tax. Deficit spending on the part of national governments is therefore curtailed. However, since this leads to monetary credibility, it is questionable whether it should be regarded as a cost (Tomann 1997).[14]

A factor that also affects a government's fiscal position is the loss of seignorage. In a country issuing its own currency, the revenues from the difference between the face value of banknotes and their printing cost flow into the government budget. By abolishing the national currency, a country forgoes seignorage as a source of income. But in case of a multilateral monetary union—in contrast to the unilateral adoption of a foreign currency (dollarization or euroization)—the seignorage that falls to the common central bank can be distributed to the member countries so that the loss is compensated.[15]

A cost that only occurs in the case of unilateral monetary unification is the loss of the central bank as a lender of last resort. The role as a lender of last resort enables a central bank to maintain systemic stability of the financial system by being able to provide short-term liquidity to financial institutions that experience liquidity (as opposed to solvency) problems.

5.2 Standard Criteria for an Optimum Currency Area

Given these costs and benefits of monetary integration, the OCA literature has tried to identify the conditions under which countries or regions would be able to adjust to asymmetric supply or demand shocks and restore their internal and external balance without relying on exchange rate adjustments or autonomous monetary policy at equal or lower costs. This is the case if there are alternative mechanisms or instruments for adjustment that help restore equilibrium, or if the exchange rate is not an effective instrument, due to the characteristics of the respective economies. Building on Mundell, several criteria have been developed that should be fulfilled by an OCA. According to these criteria, which partly contradict each other, the benefits are usually weighed against the costs, to determine whether or not monetary integration would have positive effects.

Similarity of Shocks and Business Cycles

The costs of giving up autonomous monetary policies depend to a large degree on the similarity of output fluctuations of the countries or regions in the currency area. If all countries or regions have identical business cycles and experience identical or similar shocks, no individual economic policies are needed to cope with such shocks. If, in contrast, output fluctuations and shocks are highly idiosyncratic or asymmetric, individual policy responses would be appropriate. Asymmetry may result from differences in shocks (impulses) or in economic structures (responses) (Buiter 1997). The more symmetric output cycles, the better countries or regions are therefore suited for a common currency area, as a common policy response will suffice. If, instead, the shocks are negatively correlated, then the case for a common currency area is weakened, as it may be useful to alter the exchange rate for stabilization purposes or to implement independent monetary policies. This is the departure point of the OCA theory as conceived by Mundell (1961).[16]

But there is also a different perspective on the implications of the distribution of macroeconomic disturbances across a currency area, which was also put forward by Mundell. In his less famous article on "uncommon arguments for common currencies," Mundell (1973) abandoned his earlier presumption that asymmetric shocks undermine the case for a common currency area and maintained that, with efficient capital markets, a large currency area that includes many different countries or regions whose macroeconomic disturbances are not symmetric might actually be conducive to interregional or international risk-sharing (see McKinnon 2004; Karlinger 2002). Mundell argued that countries or regions in a common currency area could smooth country- or region-specific shocks by better reserve pooling and portfolio diversification. The international diversification of income sources across the currency area (i.e., residents of a country or region holding claims to dividends, interests, and rental revenue in other countries or regions) can provide an insurance mechanism against domestic shocks. If output across the currency area is imperfectly correlated, such ex ante insurance allows for smoothing both temporary and permanent shocks. Under fixed parities that encourage financial integration, a country suffering an adverse shock can share the loss with a partner if both countries hold claims on each other's output. With flexible rates that inhibit portfolio diversification, in contrast, a country that is devaluing its currency in response to a shock is more or less left alone, being restricted to the (smaller) domestic asset markets, and at the same time facing a lower purchasing power internationally.

Factor Mobility and the Flexibility of Wages and Prices
If business cycles vary across countries or regions of the common currency area, other adjustment mechanisms are needed to cope with country- or region-specific shocks. The most obvious alternative adjustment mechanism would be wage flexibility: in the case of a negative shock, workers would have to lower their nominal wage demands to provide the necessary real wage flexibility. If wages were flexible, labor markets would complete the adjustments without the need for policy interventions. But because nominal wages are typically rigid downward (as are the prices of other input factors such as raw materials and prefabricated goods), they will not help adjust to real economic imbalances.[17] Mundell (1961) therefore regarded high factor mobility (labor and capital) in the countries or regions of the currency area, which could react to real shocks, as a central condition for an OCA. Aside from factor mobility, the flexibility of wages and prices would be an additional adjustment mechanism to country specific shocks. A currency area is thus optimal if all participating countries or regions have flexible wages or mobility of labor and capital. If these criteria are not fulfilled, a system of flexible exchange rates is preferable.[18]

Openness of an Economy
Mundell (1961) assumed that the effects of shocks on the domestic price level and national income could be completely neutralized through exchange rate adjustments. McKinnon (1963) doubted the value of exchange rate policy as an instrument for responding to asymmetric shocks, in particular for economies that are relatively open to international trade, because an open economy is more vulnerable to imported inflation. But the smaller the use of exchange rate policy for fighting asymmetric shocks, the lower are the costs of fixing the exchange rate.

While a devaluation of the national currency increases demand for home products, it also increases the prices of imports, which, depending on the degree of openness and workers' resistance to real wage reductions, will translate into an increase of wages and production costs. This in turn reduces aggregate supply in the domestic economy. In a very open economy a rise of import prices transmits relatively strongly to the domestic price level and leads to an erosion of real purchasing power. Unless unions act under money illusion, they will strive for real wage consistency and demand higher nominal wages to compensate for higher consumer prices.[19] The positive devaluation effect is therefore smaller, and the positive effect on the domestic price level is greater, the more open the economy.

Whether the positive devaluation effect is completely offset depends on the openness of the economy, but also on the behavior of workers and unions. The less money illusion that exists and the more open the economy, the less flexibility can be achieved through changes of the exchange rate level. Empirical studies suggest that devaluation effects are only short-lived (see Emerson et al. 1992: 138–40). An improvement of competitiveness through a currency devaluation is only possible in the short run. Rendering the exchange rate as an instrument for adjusting to shocks is therefore less painful the greater the degree of openness. In a highly open economy, nominal exchange-rate variability ceases to be an adjustment tool.

Product Diversification

Kenen (1969) introduced the degree of product diversification as a criterion for an OCA. In his view, the diversity of a country's product mix and the number of single product regions contained in a single country may be more relevant than labor mobility. He maintained that countries or regions in which output and employment are widely spread across sectors are better suited for a currency area:

Fixed rates, I believe are most appropriate—or least inappropriate—to well-diversified national economies. *Ex ante*, diversification serves to average out external shocks and, incidentally, to stabilize domestic capital formation. *Ex post*, it serves to minimize the damage done when averaging is incomplete. It is also a prerequisite to the internal factor mobility that Mundell has emphasized, because a continuum of national activities will maximize the number of employment opportunities for each specialized variety of labor. (Kenen 1969: 54)

If industry-specific shocks prevail, economies with broadly diversified production structures will have less need for an economywide adjustment brought about by a change of the exchange rate or interest rate. If one tradable goods sector experiences a negative shock while the others boom, resources can be shifted between them without requiring a change in the exchange rate. Indeed, an exchange rate change that alters the price of all traded goods is not helpful at all when some would need to fall and others would need to rise.[20] A highly diversified production and export structure reduces the importance of the exchange rate as an adjustment mechanism, since increasing diversification reduces an economy's dependency on any one export sector, making it less susceptible to exogenous shocks.

Changes in a country's terms of trade via exchange rate changes become less important because fluctuations in demand for certain export products level each other out so that total exports, aggregate demand, and employment remain relatively stable in the face of asymmetric, industry-specific shocks.[21]

Importance and Composition of Intra–Currency Area Trade

As was discussed above, OCA theory sees the primary benefits arising from exchange rate stabilization and monetary union in the reduction of transaction costs. The greater the degree of goods market integration between the countries or regions of a potential currency area, the larger are the benefits that monetary integration is likely to bring about. Hence the share of intra–currency area trade in total trade, as well as in total output of an economy, provide important information about suitable candidates of monetary integration.

The composition of trade is likely to affect the costs and benefits of monetary integration for two reasons. First, the higher the share of trade in manufactures and differentiated goods in which prices are mainly determined by the producer (rather than commodities whose prices are set in international markets), the greater the benefits of exchange rate stability. This is because exchange rate volatility usually affects intraindustry trade in differentiated but substitutable products more than trade in homogeneous products with a well-integrated world market (Bayoumi, Eichengreen, and Mauro 2000). Second, and related to Kenen's argument above, if countries or regions of a currency area posses similar production and export structures, they are likely to be similarly affected by external shocks to these industries, and they are hence well served by a common exchange rate adjustment.

Similarity of Stage of Economic Development and Past Macro Policies

The similarity of economies in terms of their past macroeconomic policies and stage of economic development may also provide information on potential difficulties, and hence cost, of uniform monetary and exchange rate policy (Bayoumi, Eichengreen, and Mauro 2000). In general, it should be easier to integrate countries that have a similar level of economic development, as the stage of development is usually reflected in a country's production structure and financial sector development. Moreover past macroeconomic policies are likely to reflect a country's policy preferences. To the extent that countries have economic priorities similar to those of the other countries in the currency area, there will be less need for a differentiated response to common shocks, strengthening the case for currency integration and reducing the need for monetary independence (Corden 1972).[22] Particularly the similarity of inflation rates has been emphasized as an important condition for an OCA (Fleming 1971), since current account transactions between members of the currency area are more likely to be balanced if inflation rates are similar rather than divergent.

Development and Similarity of Financial Markets

Countries with underdeveloped financial markets are likely to experience relatively high exchange rate volatility. Temporary disturbances that lead some investors to sell assets denominated in domestic currency will cause the exchange rate to plunge if liquidity constraints or other market imperfections prevent other investors from purchasing those assets in anticipation of a subsequent recovery in their value (Eichengreen 1994). In the absence of forward markets it is difficult for firms and households to hedge exchange risk. For countries with underdeveloped financial markets, exchange rate volatility, and hence a floating exchange rate regime, will therefore confer the greatest economic costs, and the benefits of monetary integration will inversely increase.

Moreover the conduct of a common monetary policy is rendered easier if financial systems across the currency area work in a similar manner. As shown by Cecchetti (1999), differences in financial structure are the proximate cause for asymmetries in the monetary policy transmission mechanism.[23] For example, a change in the central bank's interest rate policy would be felt more rapidly in economies where loans are predominantly indexed to short-term interest rates than in countries with fixed interest rate contracts. Financial systems that work in a similar fashion will hence facilitate the conduct of a common monetary policy.

Fiscal Transfer Mechanisms

A further criterion for minimizing the costs of monetary integration is the existence of fiscal transfer mechanisms, which automatically come into play when countries or regions in a common currency area suffer a recession and rising unemployment (Kenen 1969). Such an adjustment mechanism could be, for instance, a unified budget, which automatically redistributes from countries or regions experiencing a strong economy to those suffering from a recession.[24] The importance of fiscal adjustment mechanisms is demonstrated by the US economy, which has a highly federal fiscal system that contributes to regional stabilization in the case of asymmetric shocks.[25] De Grauwe (2000: 10), however, points out that fiscal transfers between countries or regions do not solve the adjustment problem of asymmetric shocks: "They just make life easier in the country (region) experiencing a negative demand shock and receiving transfers from the other countries (regions)." Fiscal transfers are hence only suited to dealing with temporary demand shocks; when the shock is a permanent one, other adjustment mechanisms will be necessary to deal with the problem.[26]

Without fiscal transfer schemes within a currency area, countries still have the option of reacting to asymmetric shocks by implementing structural adjustments designed to improve competitiveness or by using intertemporal adjustment mechanisms, namely anticyclical fiscal policy. Anticyclical fiscal policy, however, would need to be directed to the stabilization of the national or regional economy, which would run contrary to the coordination of unionwide fiscal policies (De Grauwe 2001).

A third financial adjustment mechanism was already mentioned in the context of Mundell's (1973) second take on business cycle convergence in a currency area. International risk-sharing through asset markets provides insurance against region- or country-specific income shocks. Instead of being restricted to local asset markets, the portfolio can be diversified across the whole currency area (or even beyond). The empirical investigations of Asdrubali, Sørensen, and Yosha (1996) suggest that integrated financial markets function similarly to automatic stabilizers of a centralized budget. This would have important implications for the costs and benefits of monetary integration, because monetary integration is likely to stimulate further financial integration within a currency area. Monetary integration would, according to this hypothesis, create its own adjustment mechanisms endogenously.

5.3   Is East Asia an Optimal Currency Area?

Having discussed the theoretical underpinnings of OCA theory and its various criteria, this section turns to the empirical investigation of whether East Asia constitutes such an OCA. This is an issue that a large part of the growing literature on East Asian monetary integration has been concerned with.[27] While it is indeed a useful exercise, as these criteria can help evaluate the readiness of East Asian countries at this point in time to form a currency arrangement, it is insufficient to *only* look at the status quo, as it omits the potential changes that could be induced through a policy process of monetary integration. The discussion in this section should therefore not be regarded as the sole basis for evaluating the pros and cons of monetary integration in East Asia. At least as important as the ex ante evaluation of OCA criteria conducted here is the forward-looking analysis of chapter 6.

Before turning to a more detailed investigation of criteria relating to the similarities of production structures and financial systems of East Asian economies, as well as their patterns of trade, openness to investment, the correlation of macro disturbances across the region, the flexibility of factor markets, and the similarities of economies in terms of past macro policies, we will start off with a broader analysis including the size of East Asian countries, their stages of economic development, and the characteristics of their political and economic systems. For comparison, frequent references will be made to other regions, particularly the European Union and the euro area, both of which are widely regarded as benchmarks for regional (economic and monetary) integration.[28]

General Characteristics: Size and Economic Development

As mentioned earlier, East Asian countries have long been known for their lack of interest in regional (economic) cooperation. While embracing an export-led strategy of development, most East Asian countries were more oriented toward world markets than their regional neighbors. This has mainly been attributed to the region's heterogeneity. And indeed, East Asia represents a smorgasbord in terms of size, stages of economic development, as well as economic and political systems.

Table 5.1 provides an overview of various indicators relating to the size and the stages of economic development of East Asian countries. Columns 2 through 5 show the enormous differences among East Asian countries in terms of population as well as geographic and economic size. In terms of population, the region encompasses countries as small as Brunei (0.4 million people), Singapore (4.4 million), Lao (5.9 million), and Hong Kong (7.2 million); medium-sized countries like the Philippines (88.0 million) and Vietnam (87.4 million); countries as large as Japan (128.0 million) and Indonesia (231.6 million); and of course China with a gigantic population of 1.3 billion. In terms of geographic size, the small territories of Singapore and Hong Kong contrast sharply with the vast land masses of Indonesia and China.

The size of economies, unsurprisingly, also differs widely, albeit with different roles (columns 4 and 5). The three smallest economies of the region—Lao with a GDP of USD 4.1 billion, Cambodia with USD 8.7 billion, and Myanmar with USD 13.5 billion—have only a miniscule fraction of the GDP of the largest regional economy, Japan (0.09 percent in the case of Lao and 0.20 and 0.31 percent in the cases of Cambodia and Myanmar, respectively). Japan, with its USD 4.4 trillion economy, represents 43 percent of the regional GDP. Even all ASEAN countries together, with a cumulative GDP of USD 1.3 trillion, are not much larger than the Korean economy and constitute only 29.2 percent of the Japanese and 39.0 percent of the Chinese GDP, respectively. China, despite its huge population, is only 74.9 percent the economic size of Japan and represents only 32.4 percent of the regional economy. Adjusting for PPP, disparities remain, but the less developed economies tend to "catch up" in these terms. Measured in PPP, the ASEAN countries reach 36.8 percent of the Chinese GDP and 60.2 percent of the Japanese GDP.[29]

Heterogeneity in terms of size does not automatically imply an obstacle to integration, as shown by the European Union. The European Union also encompasses countries as tiny as Malta, with 0.4 million people and a GDP of USD 7.5 billion, or Luxembourg, with a population of 0.5 million and a GDP of USD 49.53 billion, and as large as Germany, with a population of 82.6 million and an economy of USD 3,320.9 billion.[30] Still, the differences are much greater in East Asia than in Europe. This need not be a problem from a purely economic point of view, as, to speak in the words of Mundell (1961), all countries turn into regions when joining a currency area. However, such asymmetry in size potentially makes it more difficult to reach agreements on the apportionment of power within a common currency area. This problem will be discussed later.

East Asian countries also differ widely with respect to economic development. The region includes both affluent industrialized countries and some of the world's poorest nations. Columns 6 and 7 in table 5.1 show the great disparity of income between East Asian countries. GDP per capita ranges from as little as USD 233 in Myanmar,

Table 5.1
General characteristics of East Asian countries

	Population, total, 2007 (thousand people)	Land area (sq km)	GDP (at current prices, billion USD), 2007	GDP, PPP (billion USD), 2007	GDP per capita (at current prices, USD), 2007	GDP per capita, PPP (current int. USD), 2007	Income group, 2007	Energy use (kg of oil equivalent per capita), 2005	Life expectancy at birth, total (years), 2006
Brunei	390	5,270	12.28	19.56	31,879	50,790	High income: non-OECD	7,064.69	77.13
Cambodia	14,444	176,520	8.69	26.06	606	1,817	Low income	n.a.	58.93
China	1,305,714	9,326,410	3,280.22	7,034.84	2,483	5,325	Lower middle income	1,316.33	72.00
Hong Kong	7,206	1,042	207.17	293.31	29,752	42,123	High income: non-OECD	2,653.23	81.63
Indonesia	231,627	1,826,440	432.94	838.48	1,925	3,728	Lower middle income	813.90	68.16
Japan	127,967	374,744	4,381.58	4,292.20	34,296	33,596	High income: OECD	4,151.60	82.32
Korea	48,224	98,190	969.87	1,201.87	20,015	24,803	High income: OECD	4,426.44	78.50
Lao	5,859	230,800	4.11	12.61	669	2,054	Low income	n.a.	63.86

Malaysia	26,572	328,550	186.72	359.27	6,956	13,385	Upper middle income	2,388.77	74.05
Myanmar	48,798	657,740	13.48	59.96	233	1,040	Low income	306.98	61.65
Philippines	87,960	298,170	144.06	299.67	1,626	3,383	Lower middle income	528.49	71.39
Singapore	4,436	683	161.35	228.30	35,162	49,754	High income: non-OECD	6,932.61	79.85
Thailand	63,884	511,770	245.35	519.79	3,732	7,906	Lower middle income	1,587.82	70.24
Vietnam	87,375	325,360	70.94	221.61	828	2,589	Low income	617.24	70.85
Mean	147,175	1,011,549	722.77	1,100.54	12,154	17,306		2,732.34	72.18

Sources: Population data are from UN Population Division Database (estimates); land area from the CIA World Factbook; GDP data from WEO; energy use and life expectancy data are from WDI; income group is from the World Bank country classification.

Note: The World Bank classifies income groups according to 2007 GNI per capita, using the World Bank Atlas method. The groups are: low income, USD 935 or less; lower middle income, USD 936 to USD 3,705; upper middle income, USD 3,706 to USD 11,455; and high income, USD 11,456 or more.

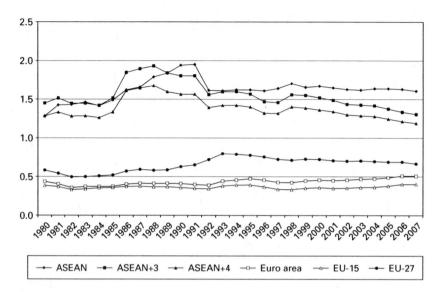

Figure 5.1
Coefficient of variation on per capita income, 1980 to 2007

USD 606 in Cambodia, USD 669 in Lao, and USD 828 in Vietnam, over USD 6,956 in Malaysia, to USD 29,752 in Hong Kong, USD 34,296 in Japan, and USD 35,162 in Singapore.

In terms of per capita income, EU countries are also uneven. For instance, per capita income in Portugal, the poorest of the "old" EU member states, is only 20 percent that of Luxembourg, the richest EU country. This income disparity widened even further with the EU enlargement in 2004; people in Latvia, the poorest EU member country, enjoy on average only 12 percent of Luxemburg's per capita income. But again, the differences are much more pronounced among East Asian countries. The coefficient of variation on per capita income levels is 1.19 for 2007 for the ASEAN+4 countries (figure 5.1). For the same year, the coefficient is even higher for ASEAN+3 and ASEAN with values of 1.31 and 1.61, respectively. This contrasts sharply with values of 0.51 and 0.40 for the euro area and the EU-15, respectively. The much higher values reflect East Asia's far greater diversity in terms of economic development, even when compared to Europe some twenty-five years ago. While the EU enlargement in May 2004 significantly increased income disparities within its borders, the diversity is still much lower than in East Asia, with a coefficient of variation of 0.67 in 2007. In contrast to the European Union, which (even after enlargement) is dominated by developed countries, East Asia includes the full spectrum of low-income, middle-income, and high-income countries (table 5.1, column 8). The regions' diversity in terms of development is also expressed by criteria such as life expectancy and energy use per capita (table 5.1, columns 9 and 10).

Political and Economic System

A further crucial distinction between European and East Asian countries is the latter's disparity with respect to their political and economic systems. While all EU member countries have established democratic societies and free market economies, East Asian countries encompass the full scale of political and economic systems, ranging from free democracies to authoritarian regimes, and from free market economies to centrally planned command economies. Table 5.2 shows the 2008 Freedom House assessment of the state of freedom for East Asian countries. For this index, countries are evaluated based on a checklist of questions on political rights and civil liberties that are derived from the Universal Declaration of Human Rights. Each country is assigned a rating for political rights and for civil liberties based on a scale of 1 to 7, where 1 represents the highest degree of freedom and 7 the lowest. The combined average of each country's political rights and civil liberties ratings determines an overall status of "free," "partly free," or "not free." While, according to this classification, the people of Indonesia, Japan, and Korea live in "free societies" that grant them comprehensive political rights and civil liberties, the societies of Hong Kong, Malaysia, the Philippines, Singapore, and Thailand are only classified as "partly free." Brunei, Cambodia, China, Lao, Myanmar, and Vietnam are classified as "not free."

While economic theory gives no clear explanation why differences in political systems should necessarily imply an obstacle to monetary integration—especially as there is no consensus as to what degree of political integration needs to be associated with monetary

Table 5.2
Freedom rating of ASEAN+4 countries, 2008

Country	Political rights	Civil liberties	Freedom rating
Brunei	6	5	Not free
Cambodia	6	5	Not free
China	7	6	Not free
Hong Kong	5	2	Partly free
Indonesia	2	3	Free
Japan	1	2	Free
Korea	1	2	Free
Lao	7	6	Not free
Malaysia	4	4	Partly free
Myanmar	7	7	Not free
Philippines	4	3	Partly free
Singapore	5	4	Partly free
Thailand	6	4	Partly free
Vietnam	7	5	Not free

Source: Freedom House (2008).

integration—it might at first sight seem obvious that countries with similar political systems, or, maybe more important, with similar political preferences and values, cooperate more easily.[31] On the other hand, it might just as well suffice if government representatives and bureaucrats can agree on the "technical details" of economic and monetary cooperation and treat the choice of political system as an internal affair of the partner country.

Economic freedom also varies greatly between East Asian countries, as shown in table 5.3. From a list of 157 countries included in The Heritage Foundation/Wall Street Journal *Index of Economic Freedom*, Hong Kong ranks first and Singapore second, which sharply contrast to countries such as the Philippines, Cambodia, Indonesia, and China, whose economies are classified as "mostly unfree," or Vietnam, Lao, and Myanmar, whose economies are classified as "repressed."

While Hong Kong and Singapore represent the epitome of capitalism, other countries in the region, such as Vietnam and China, are struggling with a legacy of decades of socialist economic planning. Such differences in economic systems might be of greater concern for monetary integration than differences in political systems. This may be particularly true with respect to differences in financial systems (as will be discussed below). The last decades, however, have seen remarkable changes in the market orientation of East Asian countries, with the Chinese economy being the best example for a gradual move toward a market system and a gradual opening of the economy. Bearing in mind that monetary integration might be a long process, such differences need not be overemphasized.

Table 5.3
Index of economic freedom 2008

Country	Rank (out of 157 countries)	Score (%)	Classification
Hong Kong	1	90.3	Free
Singapore	2	87.4	Free
Japan	17	72.5	Mostly free
Korea	41	67.9	Moderately free
Malaysia	51	64.5	Moderately free
Thailand	54	63.5	Moderately free
Philippines	92	56.9	Mostly unfree
Cambodia	100	56.2	Mostly unfree
Indonesia	119	53.9	Mostly unfree
China	126	52.8	Mostly unfree
Vietnam	135	49.8	Repressed
Lao	137	49.2	Repressed
Myanmar	153	39.5	Repressed
United States	5	80.6	Free

Source: Heritage Foundation/Wall Street Journal (2008).
Note: The definition of scores is: 80 to 100: free, 70 to 79.9: mostly free, 60 to 69.9: moderately free, 50 to 59.9: mostly unfree, 0 to 49.9: repressed. Data for Brunei is not available.

Production Structure: Value Added by Industry

The next criterion is the region's similarity of economic structures. Table 5.4 provides data on the value added by the three principal sectors as a share of each country's GDP. Reflecting the differences in economic development, the least developed countries in the region, namely Cambodia, Lao, Myanmar, and Vietnam, are still heavily dependent on the agricultural sector, with 30, 42, 57, and 20 percent, respectively, of their GDP being produced in this area. Agriculture is also of certain importance for China, Indonesia, Malaysia, the Philippines, and Thailand. On the other side of the development spectrum, Hong Kong (91 percent), Japan (69 percent), Singapore (65 percent), and Korea (57 percent) generate large parts of their GDP in the service sector. But also the upper and lower middle-income economies of China (40 percent), Indonesia (40 percent), Malaysia (41 percent), the Philippines (54 percent), and Thailand (45 percent), as well as the least developed countries Cambodia (44 percent) and Vietnam (38 percent), are engaged in the tertiary sector.

Industry is of greatest importance for Brunei, which generates 73 percent of its GDP in this sector,[32] as well as for Malaysia (50 percent), China (48 percent), Indonesia (47 percent), Thailand (45 percent), and Vietnam (42 percent). Industry also plays a large role

Table 5.4
Value added by sector for ASEAN+4, as percentage of GDP

	Agriculture	Industry	Services, etc.	Sum
Brunei	0.70	73.39	25.91	100
Cambodia	30.10	26.22	43.68	100
China	11.71	48.37	39.91	99.99
Hong Kong	0.06	9.31	90.63	100
Indonesia	12.90	47.05	40.04	99.99
Japan	1.50	29.88	68.61	99.99
Korea	3.25	39.60	57.15	100
Lao	42.01	32.46	25.53	100
Malaysia	8.71	49.94	41.35	100
Myanmar	57.23	9.69	33.07	99.99
Philippines	14.18	31.63	54.19	100
Singapore	0.09	34.74	65.17	100
Thailand	10.70	44.62	44.68	100
Vietnam	20.36	41.56	38.08	100
Mean ASEAN	19.70	39.13	41.17	100
Standard deviation ASEAN	18.38	16.81	12.10	
Mean ASEAN+4	15.25	37.03	47.72	100
Standard deviation ASEAN+4	17.13	16.51	17.92	

Source: WDI.
Note: Data are for 2006, except for Hong Kong and Japan (2005) and for Myanmar (2000). SD stands for standard deviation.

in Cambodia (26 percent), Japan (30 percent), Korea (40 percent), Lao (32 percent), the Philippines (32 percent), and Singapore (35 percent).

On average, both ASEAN and ASEAN+4 countries generate about a third of their GDP in the industrial sector. While many ASEAN countries show a tendency toward the agricultural sector, which on average accounts for 20 percent, China, Hong Kong, Japan, and Korea show a (heavy) tendency toward the service sector. Looking at the sectoral data of the euro area in table 5.5, one sees a much more homogenous picture, with industry accounting for about 27 percent of GDP on average, and services for 71 percent, with significantly lower standard deviation than in the case of East Asia.

The breakdown of activities within the manufacturing sector in table 5.6 does not reveal any fundamental differences among East Asian countries. Chemicals make up about 10 percent of value added in manufacturing, with the only outliers being Hong Kong and Singapore where chemicals account for merely 3 percent of total manufacturing, and Thailand where it accounts for 25 percent. Manufacturing of food, beverages, and tobacco accounts on average for 21 percent, with most countries lying within a 10 percent range. Exceptions here are Japan and Malaysia with 9 percent, the Philippines with 38 percent, and Vietnam with 30 percent. Machinery and transport equipment generates on average about 19 percent of total value added in manufacturing, with China (30 percent), Korea (6 percent), Malaysia (41 percent), the Philippines (8 percent), and Thailand (4 percent) lying outside the 10 percent band. Textiles and clothing accounts for 13 percent on

Table 5.5
Value added by sector for euro area, as percentage of GDP

	Agriculture	Industry	Services, etc.	Sum
Austria	1.72	30.90	67.38	100.00
Belgium	1.01	24.29	74.70	100.00
Finland	2.64	32.45	64.91	100.00
France	2.05	20.75	77.20	100.00
Germany	0.97	29.97	69.06	100.00
Greece	3.28	20.78	75.94	100.00
Ireland	2.08	36.07	61.85	100.00
Italy	2.07	26.57	71.37	100.01
Luxembourg	0.35	14.63	85.02	100.00
Netherlands	2.25	24.55	73.19	99.99
Portugal	2.79	24.98	72.23	100.00
Slovenia	2.32	34.59	63.09	100.00
Spain	3.13	29.70	67.17	100.00
Mean euro area	2.05	26.94	71.01	100.00
Standard deviation euro area	0.86	6.12	6.42	

Source: WDI.
Note: Data are for 2006, except for Ireland (2005). No data available for Cyprus and Malta.

Table 5.6
Value added in manufacturing, as percentage of total value added in manufacturing

	Chemicals	Food, beverages, and tobacco	Machinery and transport equipment	Textiles and clothing	Other manufacturing	Sum
China	12.03	14.39	29.75	11.22	32.61	100.00
Hong Kong	3.29	11.38	24.64	19.61	41.09	100.01
Indonesia	10.41	22.77	21.63	16.90	28.30	100.01
Japan	11.03	9.00	27.04	9.43	43.50	100.00
Korea	9.61	27.37	5.84	20.20	36.98	100.00
Malaysia	8.24	8.83	40.90	3.80	38.24	100.01
Philippines	11.92	38.08	7.87	9.63	32.51	100.01
Singapore	3.48	21.69	12.94	1.58	60.31	100.00
Thailand	24.53	23.07	4.18	13.96	34.26	100.00
Vietnam	6.26	30.19	15.11	20.96	27.48	100.00
Mean ASEAN	10.81	24.11	17.11	11.14	36.85	100.01
Mean ASEAN+3	10.83	21.71	18.36	11.96	37.13	100.00
Mean ASEAN+4	10.08	20.68	18.99	12.73	37.53	100.00

Source: WDI.
Note: Data are for 2003 (Japan, the Philippines), 2002 (Hong Kong, Indonesia, Thailand), 2001 (Malaysia), and 2000 (China and Vietnam).

average, with greater departures from the mean by Singapore (2 percent) and Malaysia (4 percent), Hong Kong (20 percent), Korea (20 percent), and Vietnam (21 percent).[33] Other manufactures on average accounts for 38 percent.

Similarity of Financial Systems

Traditionally all East Asian countries except Hong Kong and Singapore were "bank-based" economies, instead of relying primarily on securities markets for financial intermediation. The strong orientation toward bank lending, which builds on a direct relationship between lender and borrower, and where the lending conditions are negotiable, was heavily criticized after the Asian crisis. It was dismissed as "crony banking" of the Zaibatsu- or Chaebol-type where loans were not extended because of the profitability of investment opportunities but because of personal relationships (Hamada and Lee 2009).

As a result of the crisis, East Asian countries have tried to reduce reliance on banking and instead develop domestic bond and equity markets.[34] Nevertheless, in 11 out of 14 countries the amount of domestic credit extended to the private sector through the banking sector is still much larger than equity or corporate bond markets (figure 5.2). In the least developed countries, Cambodia, Lao, Myanmar, and Vietnam, security markets are still non-existent or negligent. Only in Hong Kong, Korea, and Singapore are local equity markets larger in size than bank lending to the private sector. Leaving aside these three

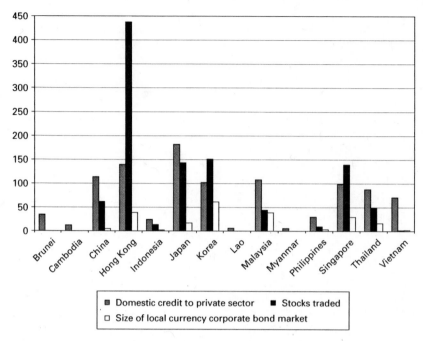

Figure 5.2
Size of financial markets (as percentage of GDP)

countries, the difference in the region lays rather in depth of financial systems (reflecting differences in economic development) than in differences regarding bank, bond, or equity financing.

Patterns of Trade: General Trade Openness

Table 5.7 lists the trade openness of East Asian countries and the euro area, that is, the ratio of total trade (imports plus exports) over GDP, for the period 1980 to 2007.[35] Except for Brunei and Singapore, the ratio increased over this period for all countries, in many cases quite dramatically. On average, total trade of ASEAN+4 countries equals almost 130 percent of GDP in 2007, nearly double that of the euro area, which itself has a relatively high degree of trade openness compared to other countries or regions, such as the United States and Mercosur. If, however, absolute values are used in place of unweighted averages (i.e., the sum of ASEAN/+3/+4 countries' imports and exports divided by the sum of these countries' GDPs), the situation looks different: in this case trade openness of ASEAN is about 130 percent, while the trade openness of ASEAN+3 is just 60 percent.

The lower values for ASEAN+3 are a reflection of Japan's and China's relatively low degree of openness. While China and Japan are the regions' two largest traders, with total trade amounting to USD 2.2 trillion and USD 1.3 trillion, respectively (see annex 2), they also have the largest GDPs.[36] But while Japan has traditionally had low values of trade openness, openness has increased markedly in China over the past 25 years, a development that is likely to continue.[37] Among the ASEAN countries, only Indonesia (56 percent) was below the euro area openness value of 67 percent. In general, one can assert that East Asian countries, with the exception of Japan, are all open economies, making them sensitive to exchange rate fluctuations and reducing the ability of their central banks to influence the domestic price level.[38]

The generally high degree of openness reflects East Asian countries' strong trade orientation. Annex 2 gives a historical perspective on the remarkable export performance of East Asia over the past quarter of a century. The East Asian growth "miracle," as it was famously termed by the World Bank (1993), has been driven to a large degree by buoyant exports.[39] In all countries except Brunei, exports have grown at enormous rates since 1980: in Cambodia, which had almost no exports 25 years ago, nominal exports grew by almost 200,000 percent over this period (imports grew by "only" 6,931 percent); Vietnam (32,658 percent), Lao (7,947 percent), China (6,616 percent), Thailand (2,245 percent), Korea (1,970 percent), Hong Kong (1,646 percent), Singapore (1,434 percent), Malaysia (1,260 percent), the Philippines (1,060 percent), and Myanmar (1,047 percent) all had five- or four-digit nominal export growth. Compared to these figures, the three-digit nominal export growth rates of Japan (447 percent) and Indonesia (489 percent) over this period seem almost nascent. While these nominal growth rates are obviously due to the low levels of exports that many of these countries started with, they reflect the dynamics of the region and the transformation into (highly) open economies that almost all of these countries have gone through over the past decades.

Patterns of Trade: Direction of Trade

Table 5.8 shows trade (i.e., exports plus imports) of the ASEAN+4 countries with their neighbors, as well as with the two most important (US and EU) extra-regional trading partners, as the share of their total trade (world exports plus world imports) for 2007. Exports and imports for the same year are listed separately in tables 5.9 and 5.10 and will be discussed in greater detail below. (Annexes 3 and 4 provide country data for 1980–2007.) The data show that intraregional trade (trade within ASEAN+4) on average accounts for almost 60 percent of total trade. When taking a weighted average for ASEAN+4 instead of an unweighted average, the ratio is still 47 percent, almost the same as the 49 percent for the euro area and higher than the 42 percent for NAFTA, and considerably higher than for other regional groupings such as Mercosur (16 percent), the Economic Community of West African States (ECOWAS, 9 percent), the Commonwealth of Independent States (CIS, 21 percent), the Central American Common Market (CACM, 14 percent), or the Andean Common Market (ANCOM, 9 percent) (figure 5.3).

A look at ASEAN alone reveals the share of trade within this group of countries to be much lower than within ASEAN+4, amounting to a quarter of total trade on a weighted

Table 5.7
Total trade (imports plus exports) as percent of GDP, 1980 to 2007

	1980	1981	1982	1983	1984	1985	1986	1987	1988	1989	1990	1991
Brunei					88.7	87.7	100.6	90.9	92.0	91.8	91.3	96.6
Cambodia							6.9	16.2	11.7	21.0	10.9	5.9
China	12.2	14.8	14.6	14.5	16.4	22.9	25.3	25.7	25.7	25.0	30.1	33.5
Hong Kong	147.4	151.8	139.1	155.6	172.8	171.1	173.2	192.2	213.4	211.5	214.3	224.0
Indonesia	34.3	34.8	35.9	37.9	35.3	28.6	27.5	34.2	33.7	34.5	37.9	39.1
Japan	25.5	25.0	24.7	23.0	24.1	22.5	16.7	15.6	15.3	16.3	17.1	15.9
Korea	61.7	66.3	60.4	59.9	64.2	63.5	59.8	63.1	59.9	52.4	53.9	50.0
Lao	0.0	15.6	17.9	4.9	3.5	3.8	5.8	11.4	26.7	30.7	24.4	23.0
Malaysia	95.4	91.8	89.6	89.7	88.6	87.2	87.9	95.2	106.8	122.6	133.1	142.7
Myanmar	19.2	20.2	12.6	9.8	8.1	8.0	6.7	4.3	3.1	2.1	38.6	67.1
Philippines	43.4	39.8	35.8	38.5	36.9	32.4	33.5	38.1	41.5	44.4	48.0	48.1
Singapore	371.1	350.1	321.1	287.9	281.0	277.4	267.3	298.7	327.8	313.7	308.8	290.8
Thailand	48.6	48.7	42.3	41.6	42.7	42.1	41.9	48.6	58.7	63.1	66.0	69.5
Vietnam	0.0	5.1	3.3	2.2	1.6	16.9	8.7	7.9	16.3	87.5	82.9	61.1
ASEAN	58.7	62.0	58.8	58.7	53.3	55.9	51.3	58.9	71.5	78.0	87.7	89.4
ASEAN+3	29.0	29.9	29.6	28.3	29.1	28.7	22.8	22.6	22.9	24.4	26.9	26.0
ASEAN+4	31.0	32.0	31.7	30.3	31.5	31.1	25.0	25.2	25.8	27.6	30.4	29.8
ASEAN*	61.2	60.6	55.9	51.3	58.6	58.4	58.7	64.5	71.8	81.1	84.2	84.4
ASEAN+3*	54.7	54.8	50.6	46.9	53.2	53.3	53.0	57.7	63.0	69.6	72.5	72.6
ASEAN+4*	61.3	61.7	57.0	54.7	61.7	61.7	61.6	67.3	73.8	79.7	82.7	83.4
euro area	46.4	48.0	47.8	47.1	49.9	50.7	44.1	43.3	43.9	46.4	44.8	42.7

Source: Own calculations with data from DTS and WEO.
Note: * denotes unweighted average.

average as in figure 5.3 (32 percent if taking an unweighted average as in table 5.8). Trade with the "+4" countries is of great importance for all ASEAN countries except Lao (which has 68 percent of its trade with the other ASEAN countries), with an average of 30 percent of ASEAN countries' trade being conducted with China, Hong Kong, Japan, or Korea. On the other side, trade with ASEAN is also important for China, Hong Kong, Japan, and Korea, but at a considerably lower level, with 9, 10, 13, and 10 percent, respectively.

For most countries (Cambodia, Lao, Malaysia, Myanmar, the Philippines, Singapore, Vietnam, and Korea), trade with greater China (China and Hong Kong) has become more important now than trade with Japan. Moreover greater China is a more important trading partner than the United States and the European Union for most East Asian countries, including Japan. Trade with the United States and Europe makes up about 11 percent of their trade, respectively. This rather moderate share of trade with the United States is particularly interesting, as it is commonly claimed that East Asian countries maintain

Table 5.7
(continued)

1992	1993	1994	1995	1996	1997	1998	1999	2000	2001	2002	2003	2004	2005	2006	2007
151.2	162.9	148.0	134.1	140.5	137.1	106.5	84.3	76.5	83.0	86.8	87.9	78.1	76.6	75.2	78.0
37.6	51.4	50.5	56.5	55.3	51.4	66.4	65.1	69.7	69.1	73.9	75.2	79.9	88.5	90.1	109.0
34.7	31.9	42.3	38.6	33.9	34.1	31.8	33.3	39.6	38.5	42.7	51.9	59.8	63.4	66.6	67.2
233.7	228.2	231.2	254.0	238.5	224.9	214.7	216.5	245.7	235.0	249.3	288.0	320.0	331.6	342.9	344.9
40.1	37.3	36.9	38.5	37.0	39.9	72.2	47.0	57.8	54.3	45.2	39.8	45.9	50.1	56.6	56.4
15.1	13.8	14.0	14.8	16.4	17.8	17.3	16.7	18.4	18.4	19.2	20.2	22.1	24.3	28.0	30.5
48.6	47.6	48.1	51.5	51.6	54.8	64.9	59.2	65.0	60.5	57.4	61.3	70.2	68.9	65.1	75.9
30.7	50.7	56.1	50.3	54.2	34.2	79.0	86.3	62.3	61.9	60.6	58.0	63.4	68.1	80.2	81.2
134.3	136.6	156.5	167.9	153.0	155.4	179.9	186.8	192.3	174.1	171.5	170.3	185.0	185.5	186.5	173.3
64.4	68.3	60.1	64.5	77.9	85.8	54.1	46.2	56.4	81.6	84.4	57.3	61.3	59.7	62.2	73.3
46.1	53.2	56.2	60.5	62.1	76.9	88.6	87.0	95.8	91.6	92.0	92.6	96.3	89.8	83.8	95.7
272.9	274.2	282.3	287.8	277.2	269.1	256.7	273.4	294.1	277.8	273.8	318.2	340.2	358.7	374.1	348.6
66.9	68.6	70.1	80.8	72.2	80.8	88.6	88.8	106.6	110.1	105.3	109.5	118.1	129.4	126.3	119.6
60.3	52.4	60.7	67.4	76.0	79.6	76.0	81.2	96.5	96.1	103.7	114.6	128.3	130.5	138.5	154.6
87.7	89.3	94.6	101.6	96.1	102.8	126.5	116.9	132.1	125.7	118.1	120.1	132.1	137.0	137.2	133.1
25.5	24.3	26.2	28.0	30.3	32.6	32.0	31.1	35.2	35.2	37.3	40.9	46.4	50.8	56.1	60.3
29.7	28.4	30.5	32.4	35.1	37.7	37.1	35.6	40.2	40.2	42.4	46.2	51.9	56.5	62.1	66.1
90.4	95.6	97.8	100.8	100.6	101.0	106.8	104.6	110.8	110.0	109.7	112.3	119.7	123.7	127.4	129.0
77.1	80.7	83.2	85.6	85.2	85.9	90.9	88.9	94.7	93.6	93.6	96.7	103.8	107.2	110.3	112.6
88.3	91.2	93.8	97.7	96.1	95.8	99.8	98.0	105.5	103.7	104.7	110.3	119.2	123.2	126.9	129.2
40.5	39.0	42.2	44.4	44.6	48.8	49.7	52.1	59.7	59.4	57.1	56.1	58.9	61.5	65.4	66.6

their (soft) pegs vis-à-vis the US dollar because of the strong US trade ties (e.g., Dooley, Folkerts-Landau, and Garber 2009b). From this direction of trade analysis, it clearly follows that intraregional trade is much more important, and hence, from a trade-perspective, it is more crucial for East Asian countries to maintain intraregional exchange rate stability than to maintain stability toward the dollar. The solution is, of course, that the common dollar pegging also brings about intraregional exchange rate stability.[40] The question is whether intraregional exchange rate stability could not better be achieved by direct exchange rate coordination between East Asian countries rather than by relying on an external anchor. Chapter 8 will come back to this issue.

Figures 5.4 and 5.5 show that there has been a general upward trend of the share of intraregional trade over the past twenty-five years, except for Brunei, Cambodia, China, Lao, and Vietnam. A stagnation or decline in shares of intraregional trade, however, need not necessarily imply a stagnation of or a decrease in regional integration. As can be seen

Table 5.8
Trade of East Asian countries as a percentage of total trade, 2007

	United States	European Union	China	Hong Kong	China+Hong Kong	Japan	Korea	ASEAN	ASEAN+3	ASEAN+4
Brunei	5.55	4.32	2.91	0.35	3.26	24.95	13.19	35.61	76.66	77.01
Cambodia	26.82	11.20	10.27	7.36	17.63	2.65	1.97	29.94	44.83	52.19
China	14.14	16.30		9.52	9.52	10.77	7.35	9.18	27.30	36.83
Hong Kong	9.15	10.23	47.46		47.46	7.33	3.10	9.91	67.80	67.80
Indonesia	7.57	9.84	10.28	1.59	11.87	13.87	6.22	29.32	59.68	61.27
Japan	16.30	12.78	17.74	3.02	20.76		6.10	13.01	36.86	39.88
Korea	11.43	11.95	21.20	2.95	24.15	11.63		10.36	43.19	46.14
Lao	1.03	6.38	7.69	0.45	8.14	1.61	1.34	67.84	78.48	78.93
Malaysia	13.45	12.42	10.63	3.84	14.47	10.88	4.32	25.14	50.97	54.82
Myanmar	0.10	5.73	21.85	1.28	23.13	4.67	2.52	47.14	76.17	77.45
Philippines	12.61	9.26	19.91	6.28	26.19	13.28	4.16	18.51	55.87	62.15
Singapore	10.58	11.52	10.81	6.26	17.07	6.39	4.16	28.60	49.97	56.22
Thailand	9.84	11.31	10.62	3.45	14.08	15.93	2.83	19.68	49.06	52.51
Vietnam	11.52	13.98	14.11	2.97	17.09	10.89	5.37	20.65	51.02	53.99
Mean ASEAN	9.91	9.59	11.91	3.38	15.29	10.51	4.61	32.24	59.27	62.65
Mean ASEAN+3	10.84	10.54	12.16	3.79	15.95	9.81	4.58	27.31	53.85	57.65
Mean ASEAN+4	10.72	10.51	14.68	3.52	18.20	9.63	4.47	26.06	54.85	58.37

Source: Own calculations with data from DTS.
Note: Mean ASEAN, ASEAN+3, ASEAN+4: unweighted average.

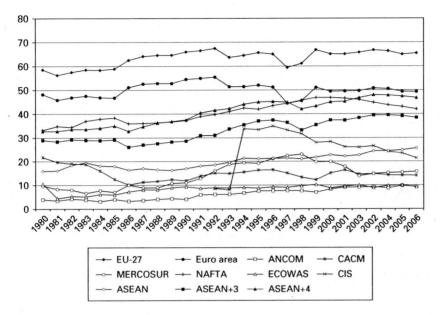

Figure 5.3
Intraregional trade of group as percent of total trade, 1980 to 2006

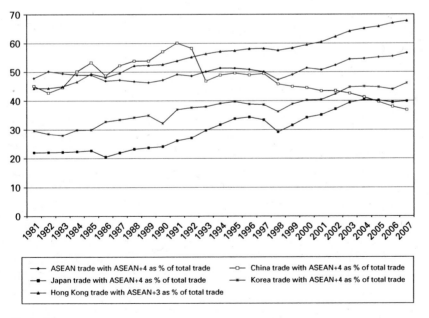

Figure 5.4
Intraregional trade of ASEAN, China, Hong Kong, Japan, and Korea as percent of total trade, 1980 to 2007

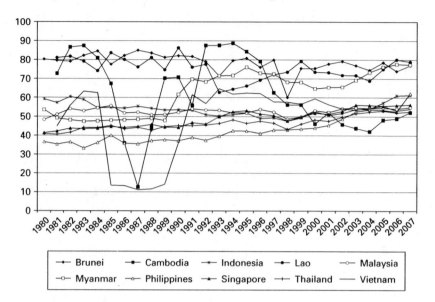

Figure 5.5
Intraregional trade of ASEAN countries as percent of total trade, 1980 to 2007

in figure 5.6, the total trade volume with other ASEAN+4 countries has increased markedly for all countries over the past twenty-five years. The only major declines in trade took place during and following the Asian crisis and from 2000 to 2001, but intraregional trade has increased significantly ever since. For those countries where the share of intraregional trade in total trade has not risen, this is simply due to the fact that their exports with the rest of the world have increased at an even faster rate than their regional exports.[41]

When comparing the intraregional trade of East Asia with that of the European Union, it is noteworthy that in its early stages of economic integration the European Union had fairly high levels of trade protection (Plummer and Click 2009). The European Payments Union, for instance, discriminated in favor of intra-EU imports. Trade integration in East Asia, in contrast, has been essentially a market-driven process, rather than being the result of policy-driven discrimination in favor of intraregional economic interaction. Nevertheless, the degree of trade integration of today's East Asia compares favorably with that of early-stage European Union (or European Economic Community, EEC, as it was called back then). Intraregional trade in today's ASEAN+4 is far higher than the two-fifths traded within the EEC in 1958, the first year of the implementation of the European customs union (Gundlach et al. 1994: 8).

Looking at exports and imports separately, instead of total trade, the patterns of trade become clearer (tables 5.9 and 5.10). Again, while the export and import patterns of East

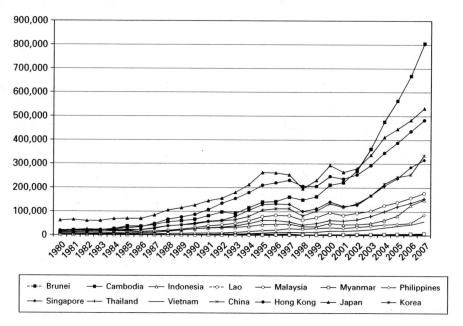

Figure 5.6
Total trade volume (exports plus imports in million USD) with ASEAN+4 countries, 1980 to 2007

Asian countries are obviously different, in most cases they are not fundamentally different. All countries except Brunei, Cambodia, and the Philippines show intraregional exports within 15 percent of the regional (ASEAN+4) average of 51 percent. In the case of Brunei and the Philippines, intraregional exports are high above average, and in the case of Cambodia they are far below average.

With respect to imports, Brunei, Cambodia, Hong Kong, Lao, and Myanmar import considerably more from within the region than the average ASEAN+4 country, while China, Japan, and Korea import much less than average. In general, the share of intraregional imports relative to total imports is even higher than the share of intraregional exports relative to total exports.[42] It is interesting to note that the distribution of China's exports and imports across markets is relatively similar to that of most ASEAN countries. The Japanese trade pattern is also not so different from that of its neighbors.

Summing up, the geographical diversification of trade is generally supportive of regional monetary coordination. Intraregional trade is of utmost importance for all ASEAN+4 countries, and trade shares with the United States and Europe are similar. For the ASEAN countries, as well as for China, Hong Kong, and Korea, overall trade with the United States, the European Union, and Japan is distributed symmetrically, which means that fluctuations in the yen–dollar and the euro–dollar rate are felt similarly, and that none of these three currencies would be a good candidate for a one-sided peg.

Table 5.9
Exports of East Asian countries as a percentage of total exports, 2007

	United States	European Union	China	HK	China+HK	Japan	Korea	ASEAN	ASEAN+3	ASEAN+4
Brunei	5.21	1.42	2.31	0.01	2.32	30.96	16.98	27.99	78.24	78.26
Cambodia	60.64	21.05	1.17	0.44	1.61	3.24	0.10	6.13	10.64	11.08
China	19.52	20.20		14.83	14.83	8.42	4.58	7.65	20.65	35.49
Hong Kong	13.73	13.54	48.67		48.67	4.45	1.97	6.11	61.20	61.20
Indonesia	10.71	12.24	8.62	1.46	10.09	18.50	6.84	19.40	53.37	54.84
Japan	20.38	14.80	15.30	5.45	20.75		7.60	12.20	35.10	40.55
Korea	12.42	13.68	25.84	3.86	29.70	6.88		10.57	43.28	47.14
Lao	1.58	10.36	6.24	0.01	6.24	0.90	1.32	49.90	58.35	58.36
Malaysia	15.62	12.88	8.77	4.62	13.39	9.13	3.80	25.71	47.42	52.04
Myanmar	0.00	6.78	6.84	1.53	8.37	5.65	2.20	49.85	64.54	66.07
Philippines	13.29	10.17	29.27	8.31	37.58	11.77	2.60	16.06	59.70	68.01
Singapore	8.91	10.76	9.67	10.47	20.14	4.81	3.55	31.78	49.81	60.28
Thailand	12.63	13.89	9.73	5.70	15.43	11.89	1.95	21.33	44.89	50.59
Vietnam	22.49	21.09	6.19	1.47	7.66	11.99	2.04	14.24	34.47	35.93
Mean ASEAN	15.11	12.06	8.88	3.40	12.28	10.88	4.14	26.24	50.14	53.55
Mean ASEAN+3	15.65	13.03	10.00	4.47	14.47	9.55	4.12	22.52	46.19	50.66
Mean ASEAN+4	15.51	13.06	12.76	4.15	16.91	9.19	3.97	21.35	47.26	51.42

Source: Own calculations with data from DTS.
Note: Mean ASEAN, ASEAN+3, ASEAN+4: unweighted average.

Table 5.10
Imports of East Asian countries as a percentage of total imports, 2007

	United States	European Union	China	Hong Kong	China+Hong Kong	Japan	Korea	ASEAN	ASEAN+3	ASEAN+4
Brunei	6.64	13.52	4.82	1.41	6.23	5.87	1.17	59.79	71.65	73.06
Cambodia	2.78	4.21	16.73	12.28	29.01	2.24	3.31	46.85	69.12	81.40
China	7.36	11.38		2.84	2.84	13.73	10.84	11.10	35.68	38.51
Hong Kong	4.88	7.13	46.32		46.32	10.02	4.17	13.48	73.99	73.99
Indonesia	4.05	7.14	12.14	1.74	13.87	8.67	5.52	40.43	66.76	68.50
Japan	11.62	10.46	20.54	0.23	20.78		4.39	13.94	38.87	39.11
Korea	10.45	10.23	16.62	2.04	18.67	16.34		10.15	43.11	45.15
Lao	0.71	4.05	8.54	0.71	9.26	2.02	1.35	78.34	90.25	90.96
Malaysia	10.84	11.87	12.86	2.91	15.77	12.98	4.93	24.46	55.24	58.14
Myanmar	0.18	4.75	35.70	1.05	36.75	3.76	2.81	44.64	86.91	87.96
Philippines	11.97	8.40	11.04	4.37	15.41	14.71	5.63	20.84	52.23	56.60
Singapore	12.48	12.38	12.11	1.46	13.57	8.18	4.87	24.99	50.15	51.61
Thailand	6.83	8.52	11.59	1.03	12.62	20.29	3.78	17.90	53.56	54.59
Vietnam	3.37	8.69	20.01	4.09	24.10	10.07	7.84	25.42	63.33	67.42
Mean ASEAN	5.99	8.35	14.55	3.10	17.66	8.88	4.12	38.37	65.92	69.02
Mean ASEAN+3	6.87	8.89	14.05	2.78	16.84	9.14	4.34	32.22	59.76	62.54
Mean ASEAN+4	6.73	8.77	16.36	2.58	18.94	9.21	4.33	30.88	60.77	63.36

Source: Own calculations with data from DTS.
Note: Mean ASEAN, ASEAN+3, ASEAN+4: unweighted average.

Patterns of Trade: Commodity Structure of Trade

Table 5.11 shows data for the composition of East Asian countries' exports, classified by the Standard International Trade Classification (SITC). Several points here are noteworthy. Except for Brunei and Myanmar, manufactured goods is the most important export category for all countries, with an average of 57 percent for ASEAN, 65 percent for ASEAN+3, and 68 percent for ASEAN+4. Exports of manufactured goods are made up of chemical products, machinery and transport equipment, and other manufactured goods. The export of machinery and transport equipment, which for most East Asian countries means electronics,[43] is especially important for the economies of China (47 percent), Hong Kong (54 percent), Japan (64 percent), Korea (59 percent), Malaysia (53 percent), the Philippines (70 percent), Singapore (58 percent), and Thailand (45 percent).

Brunei is almost completely dependent on fuel exports, making up for 96 percent of its total exports. Fuel exports are also important for Indonesia (27 percent), Malaysia (14 percent), Myanmar (47 percent), Singapore (13 percent), and Vietnam (24 percent). Exports of food items and/or agricultural raw materials play a relatively important role for Indonesia (food: 12 percent; agriculture: 6 percent), Malaysia (food: 7 percent), Myanmar (food: 19 percent; agriculture 16 percent), the Philippines (food: 6 percent), Thailand (food: 11 percent; agriculture: 5 percent),[44] and Vietnam (food: 19 percent).

The importance of export manufactures reflects the tremendous changes in the productive structures in general and in trade in particular of almost all East Asian countries. Primary-based exports have fallen in almost all East Asian countries, while exports of manufactured goods (especially electronics, SITC 7) have increased dramatically.[45] In tracking the region's export composition over time, Rahardja (2007) notes that the exports of East Asian countries have become more similar, with average correlation coefficients of export composition and the share of machinery in total exports rising.[46]

Table 5.12 shows an import pattern dominated by manufactures, as is common for industrializing countries. Korea and Japan have lower shares of manufacture imports, but high shares of fuel imports (as has Indonesia). The other two developed economies, Hong Kong and Singapore, also show high manufacture imports, reflecting their role as entrepôt trade hubs for the region. On the whole, the import patterns of East Asian countries are broadly similar.

Finally, table 5.13 displays the concentration and diversification of both exports and imports of East Asian countries, as calculated by UNCTAD. The tables also list some of the EU/EMU core countries, and it shows that these are generally more diversified in their export and import structures than East Asian countries. Brunei is certainly an extreme case of an oil-exporting country that is specialized in one commodity only. As a tendency, the more advanced an economy, and the larger it is, the more diversified are its exports and imports, and accordingly the less concentrated its trade. The snapshot of trade concentration and diversification for the year 2006 suggests that the European countries listed here fulfill Kenen's (1969) diversification criterion much better than the East Asian countries.

Table 5.11
Export structure by main categories (in percent)

	Total value (in million USD)	All food items	Agricultural raw materials	Fuels	Ores and metal, precious tones, and nonmonetary golds	Manufactured goods	Manufactured goods, of which			Unallocated
							Chemical products	Machinery and transport equipment	Other manufactured goods	
Brunei	7,636	0.1	0.0	96.3	0.1	3.3	0.0	1.2	2.1	0.2
Cambodia	3,991	5.7	2.5	0.0	1.7	89.8	0.2	4.7	85.0	0.3
China	968,936	2.9	0.5	1.8	2.4	92.2	4.6	47.1	40.5	0.2
Hong Kong	322,669	0.9	0.5	0.3	5.6	92.5	4.8	53.8	33.9	0.2
Indonesia	100,799	11.6	6.4	27.4	10.5	44.1	5.1	14.0	25.0	0.0
Japan	646,725	0.5	0.5	0.9	2.8	90.6	8.9	63.7	18.0	4.7
Korea	325,457	0.9	0.7	6.4	2.7	89.2	9.8	59.1	20.3	0.1
Malaysia	160,669	7.0	2.7	13.7	1.7	73.4	5.4	52.6	15.4	1.5
Myanmar	4,869	19.2	16.0	47.2	4.4	11.6	0.1	0.4	11.1	1.6
Philippines	47,410	5.5	0.5	2.3	5.1	86.1	1.6	69.5	15.0	0.5
Singapore	271,801	1.6	0.3	13.1	2.1	78.6	11.3	57.7	9.6	4.3
Thailand	130,580	11.2	5.3	5.0	2.8	74.4	8.0	44.7	21.7	1.3
Vietnam	39,826	19.3	4.1	24.4	0.8	51.1	2.0	10.5	38.6	0.3
ASEAN	767,581	9.0	4.2	25.5	3.2	56.9	3.7	28.4	24.8	1.1
ASEAN+3	2,708,699	7.1	3.3	19.9	3.1	65.4	4.8	35.4	25.2	1.3
ASEAN+4	3,031,368	6.6	3.1	18.4	3.3	67.5	4.8	36.8	25.9	1.2

Source: UNCTAD, *Handbook of Statistics* (2008).
Note: Data are for 2006. SITC classification: All food items: SITC 0 + 1 + 22 + 4; agricultural raw materials: SITC 2-22-27-28; fuels: SITC 3; ores and metals: SITC 27, 28, 68, 667 and 971; manufactured goods: SITC 5 to 8 less 68 and 667; chemical products: SITC 5; other manufactured goods: SITC 6 and 8 less 68 and 667; machinery and transport equipment: SITC 7. (Note that "manufactured goods" constitutes of "chemical products," "machinery and transport equip-ment," and "other manufactured goods.")
Figures for ASEAN, ASEAN+3, and ASEAN+4 are unweighted averages.

Table 5.12
Import structure by main categories (in percent)

	Total value (in million USD)	All food items	Agricultural raw materials	Fuels	Ores and metals	Manufactured goods	Manufactured goods, of which			Unallocated
							Chemical products	Machinery and transport equipment	Other manufactured goods	
Brunei	1,676	17.0	0.2	1.6	1.4	79.3	10.5	35.1	33.7	0.5
Cambodia	2,996	7.8	1.3	8.2	0.7	81.1	5.5	20.5	55.0	0.9
China	791,461	2.9	3.6	11.2	9.1	72.9	11.0	45.1	16.8	0.3
Hong Kong	335,754	2.8	0.7	2.9	5.6	87.9	6.0	53.7	28.2	0.1
Indonesia	61,065	8.8	3.5	31.2	3.9	52.7	14.3	25.2	13.2	0.0
Japan	579,064	9.0	2.3	27.9	8.1	51.1	7.1	24.5	19.6	1.6
Korea	309,379	4.2	1.8	28.0	8.5	57.5	8.9	30.0	18.6	0.0
Malaysia	131,127	5.2	1.3	9.0	5.8	77.0	7.8	55.2	14.0	1.7
Myanmar	2,163	14.1	0.6	10.1	1.1	70.4	14.0	23.7	32.7	3.7
Philippines	54,078	6.7	0.8	15.3	2.8	74.3	7.4	56.2	10.8	0.1
Singapore	238,704	2.6	0.4	18.8	3.3	73.0	6.0	54.7	12.4	1.9
Thailand	128,584	3.9	1.8	19.9	7.7	65.7	10.3	36.4	19.0	1.0
Vietnam	44,891	6.0	3.8	14.9	8.5	66.3	14.0	24.0	28.4	0.5
ASEAN	73,920	8.0	1.5	14.3	3.9	71.1	10.0	36.8	24.4	1.1
ASEAN+3	195,432	7.4	1.8	16.3	5.1	68.4	9.7	35.9	22.9	1.0
ASEAN+4	206,226	7.0	1.7	15.3	5.1	69.9	9.4	37.3	23.3	0.9

Source: UNCTAD, *Handbook of Statistics* (2008).
Note: Data are for 2006. For SITC classification, see notes to table 5.18. Figures for ASEAN, ASEAN+3, and ASEAN+4 are unweighted averages.

Table 5.13
Concentration and diversification indexes for exports and imports, 2006

	Exports			Imports		
	Number of commodities exported[a]	Diversification index[b]	Concentration index[c]	Number of commodities imported[a]	Diversification index[b]	Concentration index[c]
Brunei	86	0.838	0.717	204	0.452	0.083
Cambodia	97	0.761	0.365	200	0.544	0.195
China	255	0.442	0.110	257	0.366	0.152
Hong Kong	245	0.512	0.159	248	0.439	0.164
Indonesia	245	0.489	0.129	249	0.427	0.184
Japan	246	0.389	0.147	257	0.293	0.149
Korea	241	0.387	0.156	256	0.330	0.165
Malaysia	254	0.454	0.186	256	0.373	0.221
Myanmar	105	0.821	0.461	214	0.501	0.085
Philippines	225	0.611	0.348	245	0.442	0.319
Singapore	247	0.491	0.271	250	0.366	0.224
Thailand	244	0.390	0.095	255	0.312	0.147
Vietnam	237	0.621	0.210	250	0.415	0.118
Belgium	256	0.367	0.105	257	0.281	0.099
France	257	0.295	0.079	258	0.145	0.076
Germany	256	0.291	0.090	257	0.147	0.070
Luxembourg	221	0.583	0.155	240	0.400	0.108
Netherlands	256	0.373	0.088	257	0.219	0.098

Source: UNCTAD, *Handbook of Statistics* (2008).
a. Number of products (at SITC, Rev. 3, 3-digit group level) exported/imported by country; this figure includes only those products whose figures are greater than USD 100,000 or more than 0.3 percent of the country's total exports.
b. The diversification index, which ranges from 0 to 1, reveals the extent of the differences between the structure of the country's trade and the world average. An index closer to 1 indicates a bigger difference from world average. The diversification index is computed by measuring the absolute deviation of the country share from the world structure (for details, see UNCTAD, *Handbook of Statistics*, 2008).
c. The Herfindahl–Hirschman index is a measure of the degree of market concentration. It has been normalized to obtain values from 0 to 1 (maximum concentration).

But bearing in mind the rapid development the region has gone through, and the fact that trade structures in East Asia have changed quite substantially over the past two or three decades, there is good reason to expect further transformation to most likely result in a further diversification of trade structures in East Asia as countries become more developed.

Openness to Investment

Another aspect of international economic openness relates to direct investment. Figures 5.7 and 5.8 provide data on the inward flow of FDI as a share of gross fixed capital formation and on FDI stocks as share of GDP for East Asian and a few selected European countries. FDI data are generally less robust than trade data since many countries apply different definitions for measuring FDI.

Figure 5.7 shows that FDI as share of gross fixed capital formation compares relatively favorable for most East Asian countries when compared with, say, France or Germany. Hong Kong and Singapore had the highest shares in 2007, with 142.8 and 60.0 percent, respectively, while China, Indonesia, Japan, and Korea have had rather low shares. FDI stocks of East Asian countries as share of GDP are also relatively high (figure 5.8). Again, Hong Kong and Singapore have the highest shares. In 2007 only China, Indonesia, Japan, Korea, and the Philippines had inward FDI stocks lower than Germany, Europe's largest economy.

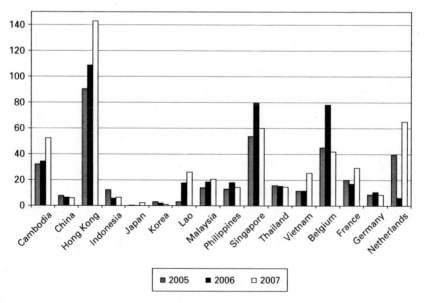

Figure 5.7
Inward FDI flows as percentage of gross fixed capital formation, 2005 to 2007

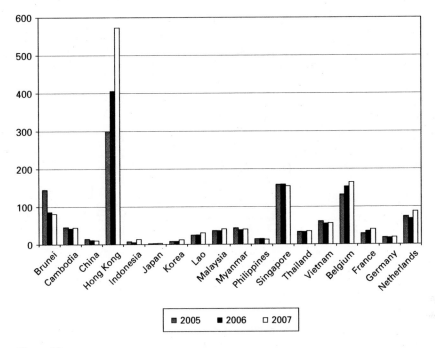

Figure 5.8
Inward FDI stocks as percentage of GDP, 2005 to 2007

Correlation of Macro Disturbances

To analyze macro disturbances, annual data on real GDP and inflation were collected for 14 East Asian and 16 Western European countries. The data are drawn from the IMF's WEO and span the period from 1980 to 2007.[47] Tables 5.14 and 5.15 display simple pairwise correlations of growth rates (measured as the change in the natural logarithm of real output) and inflation rates (measured as the change in the natural logarithm of the GDP deflator) for East Asian as well as Western European countries, respectively. The first observation is that correlations are almost entirely positive and mostly higher among European countries.

A group of countries that displays relatively high positive GDP growth correlations in East Asia consists of Hong Kong, Indonesia, Japan, Korea, Malaysia, the Philippines, Singapore, and Thailand. The correlation coefficients between these countries do not seem much different from those between Western European countries, suggesting that these countries are not much further away from meeting the OCA criterion of high cyclical co-movements than European countries are. Regarding inflation correlations, the same set of countries seems to have moved together, at large, with the exception of Indonesia and Malaysia (table 5.15).

Table 5.14
Growth correlations

	Brunei	Cambodia	China	Hong Kong	Indonesia	Japan
Brunei	1.00					
Cambodia	−0.07	1.00				
China	0.06	0.38	1.00			
Hong Kong	−0.27	0.59	0.11	1.00		
Indonesia	0.14	0.01	0.13	0.61	1.00	
Japan	−0.18	0.05	−0.12	0.41	0.51	1.00
Korea	−0.06	0.23	0.10	0.60	0.72	0.57
Lao	0.21	−0.44	−0.26	−0.16	0.21	−0.12
Malaysia	0.40	−0.10	0.09	0.48	0.82	0.39
Myanmar	0.43	−0.08	−0.04	−0.26	−0.06	−0.59
Philippines	0.12	0.22	−0.36	0.44	0.24	0.02
Singapore	0.25	0.09	0.05	0.57	0.57	0.35
Thailand	0.17	0.06	0.06	0.54	0.82	0.67
Vietnam	0.52	−0.40	0.32	−0.26	0.25	−0.25

	Austria	Belgium	Denmark	Finland	France	Germany	Greece	Ireland
Austria	1.00							
Belgium	0.41	1.00						
Denmark	0.28	0.26	1.00					
Finland	0.04	0.47	0.27	1.00				
France	0.51	0.77	0.15	0.58	1.00			
Germany	0.63	0.64	0.18	−0.10	0.51	1.00		
Greece	0.25	0.49	0.08	0.31	0.38	0.22	1.00	
Ireland	0.24	0.55	0.10	0.41	0.35	0.12	0.50	1.00
Italy	0.19	0.75	0.26	0.42	0.73	0.65	0.20	0.11
Luxembourg	0.56	0.53	0.13	0.14	0.57	0.61	0.39	0.12
Netherlands	0.58	0.72	0.34	0.39	0.58	0.71	0.43	0.55
Portugal	0.47	0.45	−0.21	0.12	0.62	0.53	−0.15	0.26
Spain	0.47	0.78	0.07	0.53	0.81	0.47	0.52	0.51
Sweden	0.21	0.65	0.47	0.78	0.60	0.13	0.43	0.44
Switzerland	0.33	0.52	0.06	0.54	0.56	0.49	0.29	0.23
United Kingdom	0.06	0.41	0.36	0.75	0.46	−0.04	0.20	0.18

Source: Own calculations with data from WEO.

Table 5.14
(continued)

Korea	Lao	Malaysia	Myanmar	Philippines	Singapore	Thailand	Vietnam
1.00							
−0.20	1.00						
0.64	0.05	1.00					
−0.40	0.55	−0.07	1.00				
0.09	−0.07	0.37	0.11	1.00			
0.50	−0.02	0.84	−0.17	0.45	1.00		
0.78	−0.08	0.77	−0.32	0.22	0.59	1.00	
−0.23	0.40	0.36	0.53	0.12	0.21	−0.01	1.00

Italy	Luxembourg	Netherlands	Portugal	Spain	Sweden	Switzerland	UK
1.00							
0.52	1.00						
0.59	0.64	1.00					
0.50	0.37	0.44	1.00				
0.65	0.54	0.65	0.55	1.00			
0.52	0.32	0.51	0.03	0.67	1.00		
0.59	0.47	0.58	0.35	0.44	0.47	1.00	
0.44	0.23	0.37	0.02	0.53	0.71	0.24	1.00

Table 5.15
Inflation correlations

	Brunei	Cambodia	China	Hong Kong	Indonesia	Japan
Brunei	1.00					
Cambodia	−0.30	1.00				
China	−0.23	0.32	1.00			
Hong Kong	−0.28	0.43	0.35	1.00		
Indonesia	−0.05	−0.14	−0.29	−0.15	1.00	
Japan	−0.40	0.64	0.10	0.81	−0.14	1.00
Korea	−0.43	0.58	0.27	0.63	−0.10	0.79
Lao	−0.13	−0.04	−0.35	0.03	0.38	0.17
Malaysia	0.62	−0.07	0.02	0.07	0.44	−0.16
Myanmar	−0.04	0.09	0.09	−0.05	0.31	−0.28
Philippines	−0.03	0.55	0.06	0.63	0.01	0.56
Singapore	0.17	0.48	0.37	0.46	−0.25	0.42
Thailand	−0.15	0.25	0.23	0.43	0.36	0.41
Vietnam	−0.52	0.04	0.15	0.45	−0.22	0.44

	Austria	Belgium	Denmark	Finland	France	Germany	Greece
Austria	1.00						
Belgium	0.66	1.00					
Denmark	0.72	0.76	1.00				
Finland	0.77	0.60	0.83	1.00			
France	0.76	0.82	0.93	0.82	1.00		
Germany	0.76	0.61	0.46	0.47	0.59	1.00	
Greece	0.81	0.72	0.67	0.76	0.73	0.78	1.00
Ireland	0.57	0.68	0.85	0.74	0.87	0.42	0.53
Italy	0.81	0.78	0.90	0.86	0.94	0.68	0.85
Luxembourg	0.36	0.26	0.24	0.16	0.28	0.19	0.10
Netherlands	0.24	0.20	0.35	0.21	0.34	0.19	0.04
Portugal	0.74	0.72	0.73	0.81	0.83	0.61	0.88
Spain	0.82	0.83	0.86	0.79	0.94	0.74	0.85
Sweden	0.78	0.62	0.71	0.82	0.75	0.65	0.87
Switzerland	0.78	0.69	0.64	0.65	0.68	0.75	0.85
United Kingdom	0.77	0.62	0.77	0.76	0.71	0.63	0.77

Source: Own calculations with data from WEO.

Table 5.15
(continued)

Korea	Lao	Malaysia	Myanmar	Philippines	Singapore	Thailand	Vietnam
1.00							
−0.10	1.00						
−0.07	−0.07	1.00					
−0.14	−0.04	0.21	1.00				
0.28	0.18	0.19	−0.35	1.00			
0.54	−0.33	0.39	−0.10	0.05	1.00		
0.60	−0.20	0.34	0.15	−0.01	0.59	1.00	
0.26	0.32	−0.41	−0.13	0.10	0.10	0.11	1.00

Ireland	Italy	Luxembourg	Netherlands	Portugal	Spain	Sweden	Switzerland	United Kingdom
1.00								
0.81	1.00							
0.21	0.26	1.00						
0.54	0.30	0.05	1.00					
0.60	0.86	0.20	−0.01	1.00				
0.77	0.95	0.29	0.23	0.89	1.00			
0.51	0.85	0.21	0.08	0.86	0.83	1.00		
0.48	0.74	0.08	0.18	0.67	0.77	0.82	1.00	
0.55	0.83	0.22	0.17	0.66	0.77	0.83	0.75	1.00

To go beyond basic correlation analysis, we follow Bayoumi and Eichengreen (1994), who have proposed a structural vector autoregression (VAR) approach to estimate underlying aggregate supply and demand shocks.[48] The theoretical framework rests on the aggregate demand / aggregate supply scheme, in which the short-run aggregate supply curve is upward sloping (assuming that capacity utilization can be changed in the short run), while the long-run aggregate supply curve is vertical at the level of full employment and output (see Bayoumi and Eichengreen 1994). Supply shocks, such as changes in technology or productivity, are assumed to have long-run effects and permanently shift the level of production. The aggregate demand curve is downward sloping, reflecting the proposition that lower prices stimulate demand. Demand disturbances, for instance originating from changes in consumption patterns or government expenditure, are assumed to be only temporary, without long-run impact on the level of full employment. Likewise nominal shocks due to changes in the price level or money supply are assumed to have only temporary impact on output and employment.[49] The econometric procedure for distinguishing temporary from permanent shocks builds on Blanchard and Quah (1989) and is explained in detail in Bayoumi and Eichengreen (1994). In short, changes in output and inflation are described in terms of their own past, that is, growth and inflation rates are regressed on lagged values of themselves and of each other.[50]

The results for the correlation of the estimated aggregate supply disturbances are presented in table 5.16. As before, the correlations are generally higher and almost entirely positive for Europe. The supply disturbance correlations generally confirm the group of East Asian countries identified as good OCA candidates based on the simple growth correlations. The results in table 5.16 suggest that Brunei, Cambodia, and Vietnam could also join the group.

Demand disturbances between East Asian countries appear to be less correlated than supply disturbances, and the pattern identified before does not seem to apply here at large (table 5.17). However, as mentioned earlier, supply disturbances can be regarded as generally more important than demand disturbances, so that low or even negative correlations of demand disturbances do not necessarily imply that countries are bad candidates for an OCA. Furthermore, as will be discussed later, inflation rates are dependent on the very nature of the monetary regime, which is likely to change in the process of monetary integration.

On the whole, the historical evidence on macroeconomic disturbances does not indicate that East Asia, or at least a subgroup of countries consisting of Hong Kong, Indonesia, Japan, Korea, Malaysia, the Philippines, Singapore, and Thailand, and maybe also Brunei, Cambodia, and Vietnam, is much behind Europe in satisfying the symmetrical disturbance criterion for an OCA. Goto (2002), who uses a principal component approach, even finds that the confluence of business cycles among Asian countries is stronger than among European countries or NAFTA countries.

Flexibility of Factor Markets

A potentially good indicator for labor market flexibility is long-term unemployment rates as collected in the World Bank's WDI. Unfortunately, such data are only available for Japan and Korea.[51] Data are available, however, for simple unemployment rates, which can be regarded as a rough indicator for labor market flexibility, although it is important to be aware of differences in the definitions of unemployment and the methodologies employed across countries to measure unemployment. Table 5.18 provides such data for East Asian countries as well as the euro area average from 1990 to 2006. The data show that official unemployment in East Asian countries is, with the exceptions of Indonesia, the Philippines, and Singapore, substantially lower than the average rate of unemployment in the euro area, indicating greater flexibility of labor markets and the economy's ability to react to sector- or country-specific shocks. (The figures also illustrate the impact of the Asian crisis, with unemployment rates in Hong Kong and Korea being most affected by the crisis.)

As noted earlier, idiosyncratic shocks can also be mitigated by international labor mobility. Generally speaking, labor mobility between East Asian countries compares favorably with the European Union, which, despite legally free labor mobility under the Single European Act, is often scathed for showing low mobility in comparison to the United States (even with respect to mobility within countries). For instance, workers from Indonesia, Malaysia, the Philippines, and Thailand account for 10 percent of the employment in Singapore; emigration has been as much as 2 percent of the labor force of the sending countries (Madhur 2004: 235). However, as in the European Union, cooperation to bring about a mutual recognition of professional qualifications, university and technical education, and the like, will be needed in East Asia to enable a free flow of (skilled) labor (Plummer and Click 2009). Besides a free flow of goods and capital, this is actually one of the aims of the AEC that ASEAN countries aim to establish by 2015.[52]

With regard to flexibility and freedom of labor markets, a good survey is provided by The Heritage Foundation/The Wall Street Journal's (2008) *Index of Economic Freedom*. To measure the economic freedom indicator discussed above, an evaluation of employment regulations and wage controls is made with grades on a scale ranging from 0 (repressed) to 100 (free). Table 5.19 features The Heritage Foundation/The Wall Street Journal's classification, according to which all East Asian countries except Hong Kong, Japan, Malaysia, Singapore, and Thailand maintain a relatively high level of state control over labor markets, which in part results in inefficiencies. While the level of government intervention in labor markets does not reflect, for instance, the behavior and bargaining power of labor unions, the influence of the latter—if they exist—is rather low in almost all countries of the region. However, employment in the informal sector (which, by definition, is not regulated) is substantial in many of the less developed countries in the region, which contributes to the flexibility of labor markets, although this comes at the cost of partly precarious labor conditions.

Table 5.16
Correlation of supply disturbances

	Brunei	Cambodia	China	Hong Kong	Indonesia	Japan
Brunei	1.00					
Cambodia	0.07	1.00				
China	0.15	0.22	1.00			
Hong Kong	0.08	0.25	0.20	1.00		
Indonesia	0.33	0.16	0.17	0.67	1.00	
Japan	0.09	0.05	0.22	0.44	0.48	1.00
Korea	0.36	0.18	0.19	0.74	0.80	0.60
Lao	0.32	0.41	−0.19	−0.20	0.18	−0.28
Malaysia	0.28	0.02	0.20	0.59	0.86	0.48
Myanmar	0.40	−0.16	−0.36	−0.25	0.03	−0.24
Philippines	0.13	0.29	−0.34	0.55	0.32	0.10
Singapore	0.00	−0.08	0.19	0.63	0.62	0.46
Thailand	0.44	0.27	0.12	0.60	0.73	0.58
Vietnam	0.34	0.16	0.15	−0.06	0.33	0.03

	Austria	Belgium	Denmark	Finland	France	Germany	Greece
Austria	1.00						
Belgium	0.30	1.00					
Denmark	0.31	0.32	1.00				
Finland	0.02	0.40	0.26	1.00			
France	0.43	0.81	0.32	0.56	1.00		
Germany	0.63	0.61	0.44	0.02	0.59	1.00	
Greece	0.03	0.44	0.17	0.28	0.48	0.23	1.00
Ireland	0.02	0.63	0.21	0.34	0.36	0.11	0.02
Italy	0.16	0.78	0.44	0.44	0.76	0.67	0.34
Luxembourg	0.45	0.40	0.28	0.15	0.50	0.46	0.33
Netherlands	0.53	0.54	0.44	0.40	0.62	0.62	0.32
Portugal	0.50	0.43	0.15	0.32	0.53	0.33	−0.27
Spain	0.31	0.69	0.29	0.42	0.71	0.37	0.24
Sweden	0.18	0.57	0.52	0.61	0.63	0.28	0.25
Switzerland	0.47	0.50	0.27	0.60	0.64	0.51	0.16
United Kingdom	0.07	0.11	0.16	0.67	0.36	−0.01	−0.05

Source: Own calculations with data from WEO.

Table 5.16
(continued)

Korea	Lao	Malaysia	Myanmar	Philippines	Singapore	Thailand	Vietnam
1.00							
−0.13	1.00						
0.70	0.06	1.00					
−0.20	0.64	0.09	1.00				
0.25	0.08	0.35	0.05	1.00			
0.57	−0.06	0.86	0.03	0.34	1.00		
0.81	−0.07	0.70	0.02	0.32	0.53	1.00	
−0.06	0.41	0.45	0.31	0.10	0.33	0.04	1.00

Ireland	Italy	Luxembourg	Netherlands	Portugal	Spain	Sweden	Switzerland	United Kingdom
0.31	1.00							
−0.05	0.46	1.00						
0.21	0.48	0.53	1.00					
0.42	0.40	0.08	0.33	1.00				
0.44	0.61	0.33	0.36	0.57	1.00			
0.45	0.60	0.36	0.43	0.28	0.66	1.00		
0.31	0.56	0.33	0.44	0.49	0.32	0.46	1.00	
0.12	0.18	−0.01	0.16	0.30	0.27	0.30	0.37	1.00

Table 5.17
Correlation of demand disturbances

	Brunei	Cambodia	China	Hong Kong	Indonesia	Japan
Brunei	1.00					
Cambodia	0.11	1.00				
China	−0.32	−0.11	1.00			
Hong Kong	−0.05	0.11	0.15	1.00		
Indonesia	−0.28	0.06	−0.16	−0.13	1.00	
Japan	−0.05	0.24	−0.03	0.47	−0.10	1.00
Korea	−0.43	0.34	0.26	0.13	0.08	0.33
Lao	−0.53	0.01	−0.15	−0.29	0.48	−0.07
Malaysia	0.18	0.07	0.28	0.37	0.45	0.15
Myanmar	−0.42	0.06	−0.28	0.26	0.22	0.16
Philippines	−0.31	0.39	0.11	0.64	0.04	0.39
Singapore	0.13	0.16	0.54	0.29	−0.18	0.35
Thailand	−0.37	0.13	0.15	0.26	0.47	0.26
Vietnam	−0.27	−0.35	−0.17	−0.18	−0.23	−0.05

	Austria	Belgium	Denmark	Finland	France	Germany	Greece
Austria	1.00						
Belgium	−0.10	1.00					
Denmark	0.02	0.17	1.00				
Finland	0.47	−0.18	0.10	1.00			
France	0.20	0.36	0.05	0.20	1.00		
Germany	0.30	0.05	−0.46	0.02	0.10	1.00	
Greece	0.31	0.05	−0.09	0.10	0.30	0.16	1.00
Ireland	−0.12	0.27	−0.10	0.22	0.39	0.00	−0.29
Italy	0.19	−0.08	−0.09	0.34	0.25	0.15	0.46
Luxembourg	0.09	0.26	−0.10	−0.09	0.21	−0.17	−0.11
Netherlands	0.23	−0.18	0.04	0.14	0.21	0.02	0.22
Portugal	0.22	0.06	−0.15	0.28	0.40	0.11	0.17
Spain	0.08	0.37	−0.25	−0.09	0.64	0.47	0.39
Sweden	0.14	−0.09	0.11	0.44	0.37	0.04	0.50
Switzerland	0.32	0.00	−0.03	0.07	0.16	0.31	0.77
United Kingdom	0.06	0.06	0.37	0.23	−0.12	−0.06	0.15

Source: Own calculations with data from WEO.

Table 5.17
(continued)

Korea	Lao	Malaysia	Myanmar	Philippines	Singapore	Thailand	Vietnam
1.00							
−0.10	1.00						
0.04	−0.23	1.00					
−0.10	0.28	0.07	1.00				
0.20	−0.09	0.25	−0.24	1.00			
0.42	−0.51	0.45	−0.09	−0.01	1.00		
0.56	0.07	0.38	0.27	−0.02	0.40	1.00	
0.09	0.07	−0.68	−0.18	0.05	−0.17	−0.14	1.00

Ireland	Italy	Luxembourg	Netherlands	Portugal	Spain	Sweden	Switzerland	United Kingdom
1.00								
−0.15	1.00							
−0.04	0.08	1.00						
0.06	0.05	−0.20	1.00					
0.07	0.29	0.41	0.20	1.00				
0.29	0.27	0.18	0.02	0.36	1.00			
−0.02	0.64	0.16	0.08	0.43	0.24	1.00		
−0.22	0.33	−0.16	−0.03	−0.08	0.28	0.54	1.00	
−0.20	0.49	−0.07	−0.11	−0.24	−0.21	0.34	0.27	1.00

Table 5.18
Unemployment as a percentage of total labor force, 1990 to 2006

	1990	1991	1992	1993	1994	1995	1996	1997	1998	1999	2000	2001	2002	2003	2004	2005	2006
Brunei		4.7															
Cambodia									3		2.5	1.7			0.8		
China	2.5	2.3	2.3	2.6	2.8	2.9	3	3	3.1	3.1	3.1	3.6	4	4.3	4.2	4.2	
Hong Kong	1.3	1.8	2	2	1.9	3.2	2.8	2.2	4.6	6.2	4.9	5.1	7.3	7.9	6.8	5.6	
Indonesia	3.9		2.8			8.5	4.4	4.7	5.5	6.3	6.1	8.1	9.1	9.5	9.9	10.3	10.3
Japan	2.1	2.1	2.2	2.5	2.9	3.2	3.4	3.4	4.1	4.7	4.8	5	5.4	5.2	4.7	4.4	
Korea	2.5	2.4	2.5	2.9	2.5	2.1	2	2.6	7	6.3	4.4	4	3.3	3.6	3.7	3.7	
Lao						2.6										1.4	
Malaysia	4.7		3.7	3		3.1	2.5	2.5	3.2	3.4	3	3.5	3.5	3.6	3.5		
Philippines	8.1	9.0	8.6	8.9	8.4	8.4	7.4	7.9	9.6	9.2	10.1	9.8	10.2	10.2	10.9		
Singapore	8.1	9	8.6	8.9	8.4	8.4	7.4	7.9	9.6	9.2	10.1	9.8	10.2	10.2	10.9	7.4	
Thailand	1.7	1.9	2.7	2.7	2.6	2.7	3	2.4	3.2	4.6	2.4	3.4	5.2	5.4	5.3	4.2	
Vietnam	2.2	2.7	1.4	1.5	1.4	1.1	1.1	0.9	3.4	3	2.4	2.6	1.8	1.5	1.5	1.3	
EMU	10.0	8.6	9.5	10.6	11.5	11.2	11.4	11.4	10.8	10.0	8.9	8.0	8.4	8.9	9.1	9.0	

Sources: WDI and ILO.

Table 5.19
Degree of labor freedom

Cambodia: repressed (score: 49.1%)
The labor market operates under inflexible employment regulations that impede employment creation and productivity growth. The nonsalary cost of employing a worker is low, but rigidity of work hours is relatively high. The formal labor market is not fully developed, and the rigidity of the labor market carries with it the risk of an arbitrary dual labor market.

China: moderately free (score: 62.4%)
Restrictive employment regulations hinder employment and productivity growth. The nonsalary cost of employing a worker is high. Dismissing a redundant employee can be relatively costly and may require prior consultation with the local labor bureau and labor union. In general, the capacity to end employment varies according to the location and size of the enterprise.

Hong Kong: free (score: 93.3%)
Highly flexible employment regulations enhance employment opportunities and productivity growth. The labor code is strictly enforced but not burdensome. The nonsalary cost of employing a worker is low, but dismissing a redundant employee can be relatively costly. Regulations on expanding or contracting the number of working hours are very flexible. Hong Kong's labor freedom is one of the highest in the world.

Indonesia: mostly unfree (score: 57.5%)
Restrictive employment regulations impede employment opportunities and productivity growth. The nonsalary cost of employing a worker is moderate, but dismissing a redundant employee can be costly. The difficulty of laying off a worker creates a risk aversion for companies that would otherwise hire more people and grow.

Japan: mostly free (score: 79.8%)
Relatively flexible employment regulations could be further improved to enhance employment opportunities and productivity growth. The nonsalary cost of employing a worker is moderate, and dismissing a redundant employee is not costly. Regulations on the number of work hours remain rigid.

Korea: repressed (score: 49%)
Burdensome employment regulations hinder employment opportunities and productivity growth. The nonsalary cost of employing a worker is low, but dismissing a redundant employee is costly. The high cost of laying off a worker creates a risk aversion for companies that would otherwise hire more people and grow. Regulations related to the number of work hours are not flexible.

Lao: mostly unfree (score: 52.3%)
Employment regulations hinder employment opportunities and productivity growth. The nonsalary cost of employing a worker is low, but dismissing a redundant employee can be both costly and difficult. The difficulty of laying off a worker creates a risk aversion for companies that would otherwise hire more people and grow. Modifying the number of work hours can be difficult.

Malaysia: mostly free (score: 78.7%)
Relatively flexible employment regulations could be further improved to enhance employment opportunities and productivity growth. The nonsalary cost of employing a worker is low, but dismissing a redundant employee can be difficult and costly. There is no national minimum wage, and restrictions on the number of work hours are flexible.

Myanmar: repressed (score: 20%)
Myanmar's formal labor market is not fully developed and remains distorted by state intervention. Regulations regarding wage rates and maximum work hours are not uniformly observed. The government sets public-sector wages and influences wage setting in the private sector. The state uses forced labor to construct military buildings and commercial enterprises.

Philippines: moderately free (score: 61.9%)
Inflexible employment regulations hinder overall productivity growth and employment opportunities. The nonsalary cost of employing a worker is low, but the rigidity of hiring and firing a worker creates a risk aversion for companies that would otherwise employ more people and grow.

Table 5.19
(continued)

Singapore: free (Score: 99%)
Highly flexible employment regulations enhance overall productivity growth and employment opportunities. The non-salary cost of employing a worker is low, and dismissing a redundant employee is not burdensome. Regulations related to the number of work hours are very flexible.

Thailand: free (score: 89.6%)
Flexible employment regulations enhance overall productivity growth and employment opportunities. The nonsalary cost of employing a worker is low, and dismissing a redundant employee is relatively costless. Regulations related to the number of work hours are quite flexible.

Vietnam: mostly unfree (score: 59.5%)
Inflexible employment regulations hinder overall productivity growth and employment opportunities. The nonsalary cost of employing a worker is moderate, but the rigidity of hiring and firing a worker creates a risk aversion for companies that would otherwise employ more people and grow.

United States: free (score: 92.3%)
The labor market operates under highly flexible employment regulations that enhance overall productivity growth and employment opportunities. The non-salary cost of employing a worker is low, and dismissing a redundant employee is not burdensome.

Source: Heritage Foundation/Wall Street Journal (2008).
Note: Information on Brunei is not available. The definition of scores is 80 to 100: free, 70 to 79.9: mostly free, 60 to 69.9: moderately free, 50 to 59.9: mostly unfree, 0 to 49.9: repressed.

On the whole, factor market flexibility appears greater in East Asian countries when compared to the European Union, except maybe for Indonesia, Myanmar, and the Philippines. The overall flexibility of the East Asian economies was also proven by the relatively quick (albeit painful) adjustments and recoveries after the Asian crisis.

Similarity of Economies in Terms of Past Macroeconomic Performance

Table 5.20 provides the averages as well as the standard deviation for annual GDP growth, inflation, current account balance, and government's fiscal balance in relation to GDP of East Asian countries for the period 1980 to 2007. Annual data are presented in annexes 5 through 8.

Average real growth rates over the past twenty-five years were above 5 percent in most cases (columns 2 and 3, annex 5). China and Cambodia were the region's (and, indeed, the world's) top performers, with average annual growth rates of almost 10 and 8 percent, respectively. The only countries with an average growth rate lower than 5 percent were Brunei, Japan, and the Philippines, but the latter has managed to accelerate its performance recently and move closer to the regional mean, with an average growth of 5.1 percent over the period 2000 to 2007. The only two countries that fall out of the regional growth pattern are therefore Japan and Brunei.

The region has managed to establish a generally low level of inflation. Albeit the long-run average inflation rates over the period 1980 to 2007 are quite high for some countries

Table 5.20
Average of past macroeconomic performance, 1980 to 2007

	GDP growth (annual %)		Inflation (annual %)		Current account balance (% of GDP)		Fiscal balance (% of GDP)	
	Mean	SD	Mean	SD	Mean	SD	Mean	SD
Brunei	0.23	5.23	1.88	2.30	53.33	21.47		
Cambodia	8.26	4.24	31.25	55.24	−4.02	11.66	−2.77	2.06
China	9.89	2.85	5.92	6.70	1.90	3.23	−1.76	1.19
Hong Kong	5.10	3.93	4.88	4.94	4.39	5.38	1.17	2.89
Indonesia	5.06	4.07	11.08	9.92	−0.44	3.21	−0.92	1.48
Japan	2.37	1.87	1.24	1.92	2.55	1.24	−3.50	3.07
Korea	6.46	3.82	5.90	5.89	0.64	4.23	−0.02	1.79
Lao	6.33	3.22	35.20	46.29	−9.18	4.51	−3.17	1.15
Malaysia	6.29	3.87	3.18	2.04	1.75	9.37	−4.65	4.85
Myanmar	6.30	5.81	20.22	14.73	−6.05	7.23		
Philippines	3.18	3.60	9.92	8.82	−1.62	3.44	−2.50	1.76
Singapore	7.09	3.84	1.96	2.20	9.47	10.38	6.85	3.89
Thailand	5.90	4.41	4.56	3.93	−1.49	5.85	4.61	7.74
Vietnam	6.62	2.65	68.86	120.49	−3.56	3.90	−2.62	2.12
ASEAN	5.53	4.09	18.81	26.60	3.82	8.10	−0.65	3.13
ASEAN+3	5.69	3.81	15.47	21.57	3.33	6.90	−0.95	2.83
ASEAN+4	5.65	3.82	14.72	20.39	3.41	6.79	−0.77	2.83

Source: Own calculation with data from WDI, WEO, IFS, and ISI Emerging Markets.
Note: Mean and standard deviations are for the period 1980 to 2007 where possible. For full data series, see annexes 5 through 8.

(columns 4 and 5), especially for Cambodia, Lao, Myanmar, and Vietnam (and to a lesser extent for Indonesia and the Philippines), this picture is blurred because of two reasons. First, several countries experienced high, double-digit inflation rates in the early 1980s (see annex 6). Second, during and after the Asian crisis, many countries faced high inflationary pressure, a consequence of a currency devaluation for an open economy. In Indonesia, for instance, inflation went up from 6.2 percent in 1997 to 58 percent in 1998 (and down again to an average of 8.7 percent for the period 2000 to 2007). In Lao, inflation rocketed from 19.5 in 1997 to 90.1 percent in 1998 and 128.4 in 1999, but since then the country managed to bring down inflation to 4.5 percent in 2007. Over the period 2000 to 2007, only Lao (10.8 percent) and Myanmar (23.7 percent) had average inflation rates of over 10 percent. In 2007, Myanmar was the only county in the region with a double-digit inflation rate. On the whole, inflation tends to be quite low, especially for developing countries, and only Indonesia, Lao, Myanmar, and Vietnam continue to struggle with inflation, albeit on a moderate level.[53]

In their current accounts, Cambodia, Lao, and Vietnam have been running sustained deficits over the past quarter of a century (columns 6 and 7, annex 7). Indonesia, Malaysia, Myanmar, the Philippines, and Thailand also had current account deficits before the Asian crisis, but the situation in these countries changed quite dramatically following the crisis. Besides Cambodia, Lao, and Vietnam, the only countries that had current account deficits since 1998 are Myanmar, the Philippines, and Thailand.[54] All other countries have had, partly had very large, surpluses.

With regards to public finances, the historical record is sound for most countries (columns 9–10, annex 8). Albeit the majority of East Asian countries had fiscal deficits over the past twenty-five years, the deficits were rather moderate. The general exception is Japan, which over the past decade had tried to overcome deflation by expansionary fiscal policy (which lead to a downgrading of its sovereign debt rating in 2001), and maybe Malaysia, the Philippines, and Vietnam, where fiscal discipline was a bit loose as well. Otherwise, most countries had either essentially balanced budgets or budget surpluses.

Summary

Most of the indicators show that, while East Asia certainly does not constitute an OCA, it is not faring too badly—also in comparison with Europe. East Asian countries, except China and Japan, are all relatively small and very open economies with somewhat similar (or at least not dramatically different) production structures. Intraregional trade is of utmost importance for all East Asian countries, and trade patterns are also relatively homogenous. Moreover most countries seem to be affected symmetrically by macroeconomic disturbances and factor markets are fairly flexible so as to provide adjustment to idiosyncratic shocks. On the downside, there remain stark differences in economic development that are also reflected in financial systems across the region.

Overall, the results indicate that East Asia is not much further away from optimality than today's euro area was maybe ten or twenty years ago.[55] Bayoumi, Eichengreen and Mauro (2000: 134), who estimate an "OCA index" with East Asian data for 1995, also come to the conclusion that "the Asian economies are not very far from the level of pre-paredness for monetary union of continental Europe in 1987 (only a few years before the Maastricht Treaty was signed and almost a decade after the exchange rate mechanism had been introduced to limit intraregional exchange rate variability and increase monetary cooperation)."[56]

At the beginning of this chapter it was already highlighted that traditional OCA theory—and the analysis of its criteria—is useful for assessing the suitability of countries or regions to form a currency area under current conditions, but that it keeps mum on how these conditions might develop in the future. The prospective development of OCA conditions, however, is what really matters. Rockoff (2003) estimates that it took the United States about 150 years to become an OCA, that is, from 1788 to the mid-1930s. Rockoff's analysis not only indicates that the conditions for optimality of monetary integration are hard to fulfill. His conclusions also suggest that the adjustment of regional economies within a currency area to a policy of monetary integration is an evolutionary process. In this respect the analysis of whether East Asia constitutes an OCA in this chapter tells nothing about its prospects of becoming one and should hence not be the only guide for deciding on the desirability of monetary integration in East Asia. A dynamic perspective that takes account of changes in economic structures will be introduced in the following chapter, which will also reconsider the costs of monetary integration as seen by OCA theory.

6   A Reconsideration of Costs and Benefits

So far the analysis was based in the traditional, mostly static, OCA framework. While OCA theory has to offer important insights, some of its assumptions are misleading or even wrong.[1] Moreover OCA theory fails to take into account that monetary integration is an endogenous process in which the criteria that have been developed in the OCA literature in order to assess the desirability of monetary integration change as a *result* of a policy of integration. Acknowledging these weaknesses of OCA theory and taking a dynamic perspective can turn some of the wisdoms of OCA theory on their head and lead to different conclusions regarding the attractiveness of fixed exchange rate regimes or monetary union.

This chapter will therefore go beyond the conventional, static approach and will discuss the changes that monetary integration might bring about, as well as the costs that it might involve. The next section will develop a critique of OCA theory, which will be followed by empirical and theoretical analyses of the dynamic effects and potential benefits of monetary integration in East Asia in the sections after.

6.1   Critique of the Optimum Currency Area Theory

When I began to work on monetary unions a few years ago it was rare for academics outside Europe to be interested in the subject, and highly unusual to find advocates of monetary union outside a few continental Europeans. Now it is almost the majority view.... Currently there seems to be an emerging consensus in favour of monetary union, at least for many small open economies. What are its roots? At a broad level, there are two: (i) the benefits of floating exchange rates have been over-stated; and (ii) the benefits of monetary union have been understated. (Rose 2001: 193)

Recent developments in economic theory and research on monetary integration have pointed to some important theoretical flaws and weaknesses of the standard OCA theory. Taken seriously, these require a fundamental reconsideration of the costs and benefits of monetary integration.[2] Three insights are of particular importance. First, it has become clear that, in the face of a vertical long-run Phillips curve, countries cannot use flexible exchange rates to realize a chosen combination of inflation and unemployment, and that fine-tuning the real economy through national monetary policy is impossible. Second, modern exchange rate theories tell us that flexible exchange rates are not determined solely or even predominantly by economic fundamentals, which implies that the effectiveness of national exchange rate policy is limited. Third, the Lucas critique has left important marks in the recent literature and challenged the static view of OCA theory. The criticism of OCA theory, together with recent empirical findings, put monetary integration in a much better picture than was previously the case. Building on these insights, the sections after will present East Asia–specific evidence on the prospective costs and benefits of monetary integration.

The "Death of the Phillips Curve"

As noted earlier, Mundell (1961) believed that flexible exchange rates would allow a nation to pursue independent monetary and fiscal policies so as to successfully manipulate aggregate demand to offset private-sector shocks on the supply or demand sides. This understanding of what monetary policy can deliver takes for granted a stable long-term Phillips curve, which is a proposition that governed the theoretical and practical under-standing of economic policy-making in the 1960s and 1970s.[3] The Phillips curve displays a positive relation between inflation and employment and was interpreted at that time as an option for government authorities to increase employment by pursuing expansionary policy. That is, monetary policy was regarded as an instrument to administer a trade-off between inflation and unemployment. In face of such a stable, inverse relation between inflation and unemployment, it would be possible to use exchange rate policy to realize different combinations of inflation and unemployment. Accordingly, a policy of sustained depreciation of the nominal exchange rate could bring about a sustained weakening of the real exchange rate, a lasting improvement in international competitiveness and the current account, and a permanently lower level of unemployment. The loss of independent mon-etary and exchange rate policy would therefore mean the loss of one of a country's most important economic policy tools. Buiter (2000: 245) has termed this common assertion "that monetary policy can be used systematically and effectively to dampen the effect on the real economy of external and/or internal shocks . . . the *fine tuning fallacy*."

This view of a permanent trade-off between inflation and unemployment and a country's ability to choose an optimum point along its Phillips curve has become untenable. The failure was "to distinguish in a consistent way between short-term nominal rigidities and long-term real rigidities," a proposition that has led to a "serious overestimation of the power of monetary policy . . . to influence real economic behaviour" (Buiter 2000: 222).

As was made clear by Phelps (1967) and Friedman (1968), a lowering of unemployment through higher inflation is only possible in the short run and cannot be repeated arbitrarily. The assumed Phillips curve relationship is only valid in the presence of static inflationary expectations or if economic agents live under money illusion, namely if they think in terms of nominal instead of real income. If, instead, price increases are anticipated in wage bargaining, there is no—not even a short-run—trade-off between inflation and unemployment. The long-run Phillips curve is therefore a vertical over the "natural rate of unemployment" (Friedman 1968: 8), namely different inflation rates correspond to the same level of unemployment.

If the long-run Phillips curve is vertical and there is no hysteresis in the natural rate of unemployment, temporary real shocks will have only temporary real effects (Buiter 2000). Whether there is a short-term trade-off depends on nominal rigidities, that is, on expectation formation and the behavior of labor unions and employers. Nominal exchange rate depreciations through expansionary policy therefore have at most a temporary effect on the real exchange rate and on international competitiveness. The transitory real effects will become smaller and shorter-lived if nominal exchange rate depreciations become a frequently and predictably used instrument to boost international competitive advantage.

The "death of the Phillips curve," as Niskanen (2002) has called it, implies that monetary and exchange rate policy will have no significant and permanent impact on the path of an economy's capacity output.[4] This is not to deny that monetary policy can have powerful real effects, but these are only transitory. At the long sight, monetary policy can best contribute to macroeconomic performance and stability by anchoring medium and long-term inflationary expectations and thereby eliminating an important source of uncertainty affecting household and business decisions. To have stabilization ambitions for monetary and exchange rate policy much beyond this, "is likely to lead to greater volatility and instability in the real economy" (Buiter 2000: 246).[5]

An Understanding of the Exchange Rate as an Asset Price
The second fundamental shortcoming of OCA theory is its failure to allow properly for the implications of international capital mobility and the associated disruptive potential of exchange rate flexibility. This has led to an overemphasis on the stabilizing potential of market-determined nominal exchange rates, and a failure to recognize its destabilizing potential (Buiter 2000).

Starting point of the whole OCA framework is the assumption that the members of a currency area lose the exchange rate as an important adjustment instrument. This is based on a view of the exchange rate originating in the flow model of exchange rate determination, according to which the exchange rate provides a speedy and effective adjustment for external disequilibria. Exchange rates are thought to be influenced primarily by changes in economic fundamentals relating to the current account. Exchange rate theory has long parted from such simplistic assumptions.[6] Modern exchange rate theories describe the exchange rate as an asset market variable, which is not only influenced by transactions in the current account but also—or maybe even dominantly—by financial flows and expectations.[7]

The portfolio balance approach to exchange rate determination emphasizes changes in the relative supplies of assets denominated in different currencies as a fundamental cause of exchange rate movements.[8] A central assumption of the portfolio balance model is the imperfect substitutability between domestic and foreign assets. This marks a departure from the proposition of identical substitution elasticities of currencies (an implicit assumption of PPP and interest rate parity theories), which rests on the reduction of money to its role as unit of account and means of transaction in the present (Hauskrecht 2001). But if the functions of money as means of payment for transactions in the future and its function as store of value are considered, this assumption becomes untenable.[9] Currencies differ in their quality as store of value and have different nonpecuniary rates of return. The different valuations of currencies depend, among other factors, on the historical development of nominal exchange rates, a country's international net asset position, the size of the currency area and the investment opportunities therein, and expectations about the currency's future value.

With the exchange rate driven predominantly by asset market developments that are not only based on economic fundamentals and rational behavior, the exchange rate cannot be regarded as a reliable instrument for adjustment to real economic shocks—and hence it cannot be lost as a policy instrument. Quite the opposite, it might itself become a source of instability and distort production, employment, investment, and consumption (Schelkle 2001a).

There are multiple examples of (irrational) exuberance or pessimism in financial markets, such as speculative bubbles, collective mood swings, herd behavior, bandwagon effects, noise trading, panic trading, or trading by agents caught in liquidity shortage in other financial markets that can lead to excessive volatility and persistent misalignments in the foreign exchange markets (Buiter 2000). Other destabilizing phenomena are overshooting exchange rates or self-fulfilling prophecies and speculative attacks that can lead to currency crises. Hence, at times, exchange rate movements may not only *not stabilize* but *need to be stabilized* in order to avoid disturbances in the real economy. So use of other economic policy instruments may be required to stabilize the exchange rate, *reducing* instead of *increasing* domestic policy autonomy. For economies that are strongly affected by such phenomena, in the extreme case, abandoning the exchange rate could therefore mean a benefit and a gain in degrees of freedom of economic policy-making. As Schelkle (2001b: 27) maintains: "taking the exchange rate as an asset price seriously turns the basic message of the OCA approach on its head."

The potential advantages of exchange rate flexibility as a short-term adjustment mechanism or shock absorber therefore need to be weighted against the potential destabilizing role of the exchange rate as a source of shocks and instability. Arguably the globalization of capital and financial markets has increasingly impaired the effectiveness of monetary and exchange rate policy as stabilization instruments.[10] In the view of Cooper (1999: 112), "flexible exchange rates will gradually evolve from being mainly a useful shock absorber for real shocks into being mainly a disturbing transmitter of financial shocks, increasingly troublesome for productive economic activity. Thus a cost–benefit calculation for flexible versus fixed rates will gradually alter the balance against flexibility, even for large countries." Rose (2001: 194) also doubts the value of the exchange rate as a useful economic policy instrument:

Floating exchange rates are said to provide insulation, and to be an additional tool of monetary policy. In practice, they just as often introduce shocks that have to be offset through other tools of economic policy. Rather than being part of the solution, they are frequently part of the problem. That's why so many countries seem to have a "fear of floating" in the memorable phrase of Calvo and Reinhart. [. . .] eliminating exchange rate volatility seems almost to be a free lunch, [. . .]. As a result, thinking about the exchange rate as an extra tool for macro-management is starting to seem unworldly. There are exceptions of course [. . .]. But those cases are . . . exceptions.

The Lucas Critique
The Lucas critique and the time-inconsistency literature pose another challenge to the quintessentially static approach of OCA theory.[11] Lucas's (1976) critique of the then usual way of (econometrically) modeling supposedly structural macroeconomic relations as functions of past policies made clear that such relations cannot be used in simulations designed to predict the effect of a different policy regime. This is because shifts in economic policy often produce a completely different outcome as agents adapt their expectations to the new policy stance.[12] The behavior of economic agents and henceforth also economic structures will respond to economic policy changes. In other words, "[t]he structure of an economy is endogenous to the economic policies applied to it" (Schelkle 2001b: 18).[13]

OCA theory has generally treated the above-discussed criteria as exogenous variables. Yet it is obvious that if economic structures change with economic policies, then the OCA criteria become endogenous instead (Schelkle 2001a). If the economic environment changes in the process of monetary integration, then the convergence of certain parameters need not necessarily be a precondition for successful monetary integration, but rather change could be the desired result. As noted earlier, going back to Fleming (1971), especially the convergence of inflation rates is regarded as precondition for joining a currency area since this is a long-term condition for balanced national accounts within that area. The time-inconsistency argument, however, reverses the order between what can be regarded as precondition and what can be seen as the desired outcome of monetary integration. As an application of the Lucas critique, inflation convergence can be considered as an intended result of monetary integration between countries with different historical inflation histories (Gandolfo 1992; Tavlas 1993b).

Recent contributions have particularly discussed how a stabilization of exchange rates can induce changes in the labor and factor markets or changes in the monetary policy regime that suppress inflationary wage and price setting and that bring about a convergence of inflation rates.[14] The time inconsistency literature was able to show that monetary credibility of a country with high inflation rises through the entry into a currency area because policy makers get their "hands tied." The strategy of tying one's hands (Giavazzi and Pagano 1988) aims at the import of stability, since an exchange rate target (as discussed earlier) requires the subordination of national economic policies and currency devaluations can no longer be used to compensate for inflationary price and wage policies. The assumption is that national governments would not be able to see through such a policy course on their own.

Schelkle (2001a) maintains that especially structural inflation might only be come by with a policy of monetary integration.[15] Indeed structural inflation might have been a main reason for Italy's membership in the EMS, even though it meant a complete departure from past economic policies (see Giavazzi and Pagano 1988).[16] The convergence of interest rates was also one of the Maastricht criteria, and the convergence that was achieved illustrates the structural change in national economic policies that was made possible by the political decision to join EMU. In this light, the monetary convergence that was achieved can be regarded as an endogenous result of the *integration process*, not as a condition that had to be fulfilled ex ante (Tavlas 1993; Schelkle 2001b).

The endogenous change of OCA parameters during the process of monetary integration, however, need not necessarily lead to an optimization of the currency area. The conclusion whether integration will lead to an optimalization or suboptimalization can be ambivalent for single criteria (Schelkle 2001a). As will be discussed later with respect to the effects of real and financial integration on the convergence or divergence of output fluctuations, various transmission channels might exist that work into opposite directions.

Summing up, the Lucas critique makes clear that it is misleading to require certain conditions, which need to be viewed as the desired outcome of monetary integration, to be fulfilled ex ante. The Lucas critique, however, does not invalidate the OCA analysis on East Asia conducted in section 5.3. But it is crucial to be aware that the structures and characteristics of the East Asian economies analyzed there might be subject to change. To fully understand the costs and benefits of monetary integration, it is thus important to overcome the static OCA perspective and also analyze the changes that will be induced by a policy of monetary integration. But the focus should not only be on allocative effects—the development context of monetary integration and the potential accumulative effects also need to be brought to attention. In particular, it is important to consider if and how a strategy of monetary integration can help overcome structures that put a constraint to economic development (Roy and Betz 2000). In this respect the analysis of monetary integration, particularly between developing and emerging countries as in East Asia, also needs to address how it can help create favorable macroeconomic conditions that are conducive to financial market development and to overall economic growth and development.

Building on these insights, the following sections will go beyond the conventional arguments and attempt at analyzing the effects and potential benefits of monetary integration in East Asia. Four different aspects of monetary integration will be analyzed. First, section 6.2 turns to a discussion of the relationship between monetary integration and trade and estimate the trade-creating effects of monetary integration in East Asia. Second comes an empirical investigation of the effects of real and financial integration on output fluctuations in East Asia in section 6.3. This is basically a practical application of the Lucas critique and an attempt to analyze the endogeneity of one of the most important OCA criteria, namely the symmetry of output fluctuations among countries of a currency area. Third, section 6.4 draws attention to the potential role of regional monetary integration in developing regional capital markets and in overcoming the problems of asset and liability dollarization. Fourth, and finally, section 6.5 extends the discussion of the alleged costs of monetary integration and shows that, instead of losing economic policy autonomy, monetary integration might even be a way of (re)gaining some degrees of monetary independence in East Asia.

6.2 Monetary Integration and Trade

As was discussed in section 5.3, over the past few decades, the share of intraregional trade in total trade has reached high levels in East Asia, and the region is set to increase these trading links even more. In addition to trade linkages, intraregional interdependence in FDI has also increased dramatically (Kawai and Urata 2004). Multinational corporations—often from Japan and Korea, but also from Hong Kong, Singapore, the United States, the European Union, and since recently also China—have developed extensive regional production networks in East Asia.[17]

For a region as economically intertwined as East Asia, exchange rate policy spillover effects from one country to another are of great importance. There are numerous problems faced by countries that are close trading partners but follow different exchange rate regimes.[18] First, exchange rate upheavals could lead to reduced exports from the country that loses competitiveness to its partners. This could evoke increased protectionism and even a scaling back or elimination of trade agreements. The country that loses competitiveness as a result of a real exchange rate appreciation vis-à-vis its trading partners may employ anti-dumping or other administrative measures (if tariffs are precluded through trade agreements) to protect domestic firms. The protectionist response may trigger a trade war as well as a round of beggar-thy-neighbor devaluations. Second, investments may be relocated because of severe exchange rate disagreements. Regional trade agreements may spark fierce competition for the location of investment, and swings in the bilateral exchange rates may have important consequences for the location of new investments and might even shift the location of existing investments. Third, and finally, a change of the exchange regime in one of the partner countries may cause an exchange rate crisis in the other. Exchange rate depreciation in one country may reduce the credibility of the partner's commitment to a fixed parity and generate speculative attacks on its currency. A country may thus be forced to abandon its preferred exchange rate policy due to the exchange rate disagreement. All this, in turn, could have repercussions for the country that sparked the crisis (see chapter 3).

Hence the deeper trade relations become and the more comprehensive trade and investment agreements are the more important the question of macroeconomic policy coordination becomes. Increasing intraregional trade turns formerly second-order effects into issues that have to be addressed with first-order preference. In highly integrated areas policy coordination to achieve real exchange rate consistency is therefore essential.

Exchange rate cooperation becomes even more important if countries also compete against one another in third markets, as is the case in East Asia. Hence McKinnon (2005: 5) describes mutual exchange rate stability in East Asia as the "quintessential public good." Because of neighborhood effects, he reasons, a nation's decision to fix or float should not be made independently of other nations' decisions.

While these arguments favor exchange rate coordination over flexible exchange rates, there is no implicit logic for monetary unification. Eichengreen (1998) points out that the need for monetary integration depends on the degree of trade integration that is to be achieved. A free trade area or customs union can be sustained despite the existence of separate national currencies that fluctuate against one another.[19] But deeper integration, including the free movement of goods, services, capital, and people, implies an even greater degree of openness of domestic markets and more intense cross-border competition, making exchange rate changes more disruptive. The European Union has always given great importance to this issue. Indeed, the EU reasoning for monetary union can be described as "one market, one money" (Emerson et al. 1992). If East Asian leaders want to foster deeper integration akin to Europe's single market, they will need to contemplate far-reaching monetary integration like in Europe.

More recently the potential trade-creating effect of a common currency union has gained wide attention in the literature, reinforcing the trade argument for monetary integration. Rose (2000) turned the EU logic upside down and established the case for "one money, one market."[20]

While it is impossible to accurately predict the trade-creating effect of a potential monetary union in East Asia, we can estimate the effect that the similarity of currency regimes had on bilateral trade in the region. To do this, we apply the following gravity model to the trade data from thirteen East Asian countries over the period 1980 to 2003:[21]

$$T_{ijt} = \beta_0 + \beta_1 F_{ijt} + \beta_2 D_{ijt} + \beta_3 I_{1ijt} + \varepsilon_{ijt},$$

where T_{ijt} is an indicator for the level of bilateral trade integration between countries i and j at time t, F_{ijt} is an indicator for the intensity of bilateral FDI, and D_{ijt} is an indicator for the similarity of currency regimes of the two countries in question. I_{1ijt} is a vector comprising the standard variables of the gravity model, and ε_{ijt} is a well-behaved error term.

The gravity model has become standard in the international trade literature, and hence one can draw on a rich body that employs the gravity model.[22] We include the standard variables of the gravity model, namely the product of the natural logarithms of the populations of the two countries under investigation, a variable describing their combined GDP computed as the product of the natural logarithms of each country's GDP, the natural logarithm of the distance between the two countries, and a dummy variable indicating whether the countries share a common land border.[23]

As in Frankel and Rose (1998), bilateral trade integration is measured by computing

$$T_{ijt} = \frac{x_{ijt} + m_{ijt}}{X_{it} + M_{it} + X_{jt} + M_{jt}},$$

where x_{ijt} are the exports from country i to j during period t, m_{ijt} are the imports to country i from j, and X_{it}, M_{it}, X_{jt}, M_{jt} are the total exports/imports of country i/j respectively. A higher value of T_{ijt} thus represents a greater trade intensity between countries i and j. As is common in the literature, we take the natural logarithm of the ratio. The data are from the IMF's Direction of Trade Statistics (DTS). Data for Taiwan are from the Taiwan Statistical Data Book 2004.

Similarly FDI intensity is measured as

$$F_{ijt} = \frac{fdi_{ijt} + fdi_{jit}}{GDP_i + GDP_j},$$

where fdi_{ijt} denotes FDI to country i from country j and fdi_{jit} denotes FDI to country j from i. The bilateral FDI flows are divided by the joint GDP of the two countries. As with the trade measure, F_{ijt} takes a higher value the more integrated the countries are. The bilateral FDI data are taken from the UNCTAD Foreign Direct Investment Statistics and CEIC Asia Database. The GDP data are from IFS and the Taiwan Statistical Data Book 2004.

To measure the similarity of the currency regimes of the two countries in question, hypothetical currency baskets are estimated in order to compute

$$D_{ij} = 1 - |w_{it} - w_{jt}|,$$

where w_{it} is the weight of the US dollar in a hypothetical currency basket of country i. To estimate the weights of the currencies included in the hypothetical currency baskets against which East Asian countries manage their currencies, we follow Frankel and Wei (1994) and regress each East Asian currency e on a constant c, the US dollar, the euro, and the Japanese yen:

$$\Delta \ln\left(\frac{e}{CHF}\right)_t = c + b_1 \Delta \ln\left(\frac{USD}{CHF}\right)_t + b_2 \Delta \ln\left(\frac{EUR}{CHF}\right)_t + b_3 \Delta \ln\left(\frac{JPY}{CHF}\right)_t + \varepsilon_t.$$

The Swiss franc, which can be assumed to be uncorrelated with the three basket currencies as well as with the East Asian currencies, is used as numéraire in order to minimize multicolinearity problems. The β coefficients are the weights of the basket. Δ stands for the first-difference operator and t for time. All variables are in natural logarithms. b_1 is used to compute the above indicator (D_{ij}); that is, $b_1 = w_{it}$. If both countries give the same weight to the dollar in their (hypothetical) currency basket, D_{ij} is one; if one of the countries chooses a hard fix to the dollar ($b_1 = 1$) while the other one chooses a zero dollar weight in its currency basket ($b_1 = 0$), D_{ij} is zero.[24]

The results presented in table 6.1 show a strong trade-creating effect of similar currency regimes in East Asia. The coefficients for the similarity of the currency regime are large and significant. The trade-creating effect gets smaller if China is excluded from the regression, which can be explained by a "Japan effect": Japan is a driving force in intraregional trade but is the only country in the region that does not adhere to the informal "East Asian dollar standard" (McKinnon 2001, 2005). If Japan is omitted from the regression, the currency effect becomes even larger and highly significant. That is, exchange rate stability is beneficial for trade within East Asia.[25]

The coefficients of the other variables are in line with theoretical expectations. Strong FDI links, a shared land border, and larger GDP all increase bilateral trade whereas distance and population have the inverse effect.[26] Given the previous findings in the literature that monetary union has an even larger effect on trade than a hard peg, it is also sensible to expect a significant trade-creating effect of monetary unification in East Asia. In his seminal study, Rose (2000) estimates that two countries that use the same currency trade three times as much than they would with separate currencies.[27] While a reduction of

Table 6.1
Determinants of trade in East Asia

	Full sample	Without China	Without Japan	Without China and Japan
FDI	0.1012***	0.0921***	0.0610	0.0356
	(0.0369)	(0.0367)	(0.0432)	(0.0405)
Similarity of currency regime	1.1036***	0.8280*	2.0410***	1.5680**
	(0.4633)	(0.4633)	(0.6743)	(0.6854)
Distance	−0.5866***	−0.3055*	−0.6808***	−0.2130
	(0.1701)	(0.1813)	(0.2023)	(0.2097)
Common border	0.7391***	1.1925***	0.7495***	1.3917***
	(0.2808)	(0.3283)	(0.2853)	(0.3255)
GDP	0.0210***	0.0199***	0.0239***	0.0229***
	(0.0017)	(0.0018)	(0.0025)	(0.0024)
Population	−0.0062**	−0.0048	−0.0073**	−0.0054
	(0.0028)	(0.0037)	(0.0032)	(0.0039)
Constant	−12.2067***	−13.9071***	−14.0290***	−17.3330***
	(1.4469)	(1.5486)	(1.6989)	(1.8779)
Number of observations	128	104	100	79
R squared	0.5921	0.5951	0.5957	0.6135

Note: *** denotes statistical significance at the 1 percent level, ** at the 5 percent level, and * at the 10 percent level. Standard errors are in parentheses.

exchange rate volatility also has a positive effect on trade, Rose assumes the trade creating effect of a monetary union to be much larger than of a currency area with fixed rates but separate currencies.[28] Rose and van Wincoop (2001) even speak of national currencies as significant barriers to international trade.

While there has been a lot of controversy about the actual magnitude of the trade-creating effect of monetary union, a broad agreement has emerged that a currency union has a significant positive effect on trade.[29] Even though a doubling or tripling of trade as a result of monetary unification deems unreasonably high, these estimates become more plausible when compared with the home market bias in international trade. Rose and Engel (2002) find that members of a currency union are more integrated than countries with separate currencies, but they also find that trade integration is much lower than within countries. Like Rose and Engel, several other studies have revealed that intra-national trade (i.e., trade between regions within a nation) is much larger than between countries. McCallum (1995) shows that trade between Canadian provinces in 1988 was 20 times higher on average than between Canadian provinces and US states. This is remarkable as there are no language, geographic, or tariff barriers to trade. The studies by Helliwell (1998) on trade between Canada and the United States and by Nitsch (2000) on European trade estimate the "home bias" to be around a factor of ten. One possible explanation for this phenomenon is the use of a common currency (Frankel and Rose 2002).

An increase in trade is likely to affect economic growth. To estimate the implications of a common currency on trade and income, Frankel and Rose (2002) proceed in two steps.[30] First, they estimate the effect of a common currency on trade, which (as in Rose 2000) leads to a tripling of trade, without any indication of trade diversion. In the second stage, they estimate that an increase in trade by one percent leads to an increase in per capita income by at least a third of a percent over a period of twenty years. They then combine these two results to estimate the effect of a common currency on income. According to their results, EMU membership of a country like Poland, which conducts half of its total trade with the euro area, would lead to an increase of per capita income of 20 percent.[31]

Indeed, a variety of factors influence international trade, and the choice of exchange rate regime is only one of them. A common language, cultural similarities, a common history, colonial linkages, geographic proximity and shared borders, membership in a free trade area, legal systems, physical infrastructure, and others factors might play a role in explaining trade relations.[32] The discussion on the trade-creating effect of monetary integration should therefore not be misunderstood as denouncing these influences. For sure, the development of physical infrastructure such as roads, bridges, telecommunication, and the like can have an important stimulus on trade between neighboring countries. Particularly in less developed regions, such as the Mekong delta that connects Lao, Cambodia, and Vietnam, such measures will probably have a much greater effect than monetary integration. Nevertheless, the influence of monetary integration, and especially monetary unification, seems to be substantial. Frankel and Rose (2002) even believe it to be as big as the trade-creating effect of a FTA.

6.3   Effects of Real and Financial Integration on East Asian Business Cycles

As discussed in section 5.2, a strong output correlation between potential members of a common currency area is a standard criterion of OCA theory. Traditionally analysis of output cycles was limited to an assessment of the historical record as in section 5.3. More recently, however, the endogenous nature of business cycle correlations has become an important topic of research (basically as an application of the Lucas critique), raising doubts about the explanatory power of a simple ex ante analysis of business cycle correlations when assessing the suitability of countries to form a currency area (Frankel and Rose 1998).

Real and financial integration are both likely to be affected by monetary integration, which may also result in a change in national business cycles (see figure 6.1). The direction of these effects, however, is not clear a priori. Over the past years, particularly the impact of an increase in trade integration on business cycles has received great attention following Frankel and Rose's (1998) seminal paper on the endogeneity of the OCA criteria. Nevertheless, the effects of real and financial integration on output fluctuations have not yet been investigated in a systematic way in the East Asian context, despite its great importance for the discussions about East Asian monetary cooperation and integration.

The analysis in this section aims to fill this gap by building on recent contributions to the literature by Imbs (2004, 2006). A system of simultaneous equations is estimated to analyze whether and how trade and financial linkages influence business cycle

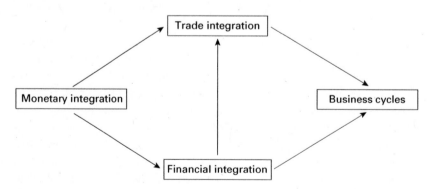

Figure 6.1
Effects of monetary integration on business cycles

synchronization in East Asia, both directly and indirectly. We will first review the theoretical literature and previous empirical findings and then explain the model used for our estimations.

Theoretical Literature and Previous Empirical Findings

From a theoretical angle, the effects of trade and financial integration on business cycles are ambiguous. On one hand, increased intra-industry trade deriving from economies of scale and product differentiation should lead to more synchronized business cycles, a view taken by the European Commission (Emerson et al. 1992) in support of European monetary integration. On the other hand, if classic Ricardian or Heckscher–Ohlin trade prevails, increased trade could result in more specialization of industries, and therefore make countries or regions more vulnerable to idiosyncratic, industry-specific shocks (Kenen 1969; Krugman 1993).

Similarly financial integration could have a divergent effect on business cycles by fostering industrial specialization through the provision of risk insurance across countries/ regions and through the reallocation of capital according to countries' comparative advantage. As financial integration is also likely to have an effect on trade integration, through the provision of trade credit, it could amplify the convergent or divergent effect of trade on output fluctuations (see figure 6.2). Moreover financial linkages could positively affect output co-movement by generating demand-side effects, namely if consumers from different countries have financial investments in each other's countries, they will all enjoy (suffer) a boom (bust) in any of the countries (see section 5.2).

As theory remains ambiguous, the proof of the pudding has to be found in empirical analysis. Following Frankel and Rose (1998), a burgeoning literature on the impact of an increase in trade integration on business cycles has developed. In their paper

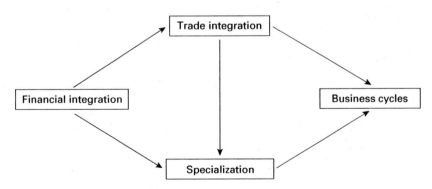

Figure 6.2
Effects of financial integration on business cycles

Frankel and Rose use a panel of bilateral trade and business cycle data spanning twenty industrialized countries over thirty years and find that closer international trade links result in more closely correlated business cycles across countries. Studies by Flandreau and Maurel (2005), Gruben, Koo, and Millis (2003), and others have confirmed this positive relationship. Imbs (2004) also finds the overall effect of trade on business cycle synchronization to be strong, and resulting primarily from intra-industry trade, as predicted by theory.

The empirical results on the link between financial integration and business cycles are less clear to date. One strand of literature finds a divergent effect of financial integration on business cycles. Heathcote and Perri (2004) and Kalemli-Ozcan, Sorensen, and Yosha (2001, 2003), for instance, find that income insurance through financial integration fosters industrial specialization and thus leads to more asymmetric business cycles. On the contrary, Claessens, Dornbusch, and Park (2001) and Imbs (2004, 2006) find that financial integration leads to a synchronization of business cycles.

The studies mentioned so far have all focused on industrial countries. However, a few studies have scrutinized East Asian business cycles as well. Kim, Kose, and Plummer (2003) analyze the business cycles of seven East Asian countries between 1960 and 1996 and compare them with the business cycles of G-7 countries. They find signs of an East Asian business cycle, namely high correlations between individual countries and a constructed East Asian cycle, but they do not analyze the factors that influence the cycles. McKinnon and Schnabl (2003) focus on fluctuations of the yen–dollar exchange rate as a major force affecting the business cycles of the smaller East Asian countries. Moneta and Rüffer (2006) estimate a dynamic common factor model for output growth of ten East Asian countries and find that all countries except China and Japan share a significant common component factor and that a number of external factors, including the yen/dollar rate and the price of oil, play an important role in synchronizing output cycles. Socorro Gochoco-Bautista (2008) finds that the global electronics cycle is a common regional factor that drives industrial output growth within the region.[33]

A few papers have analyzed the effect of trade integration on business cycles in East Asia using simple ordinary least squares (OLS) regressions. Shin and Wang (2003) analyze the business cycles of twelve Asian countries between 1976 and 1997 and find hints that intra-industry trade in East Asia contributes to a convergence of cycles. Using a sample of ten East Asian countries for 1981 to 1995, Choe (2001) finds a positive effect of trade on business cycle correlations. Crosby and Voss (2002) regress business cycles on trade intensity and some macroeconomic variables for thirteen countries for 1980 to 1999 without finding any significant impact of trade on output fluctuations.

The only study so far, to our knowledge, that has also looked at the effects of financial integration on output co-movements in East Asian is by Shin and Sohn (2006), who consider a sample of nine East Asian countries for the period 1971 to 1999/2003. While these authors find that greater trade enhances co-movements of output, they cannot detect any significant effect of financial integration, a result they attribute to the presently low level of financial integration in the region.[34]

Methodology and Data

Most model specifications of the above-mentioned studies (including Frankel and Rose 1998) take a similar form to

$$\rho_{ijt} = \alpha_0 + \alpha_1 T_{ijt} + \alpha_2 F_{ijt} + \alpha_3 S_{ijt} + \alpha C_{ijt} + \varepsilon_{ijt},$$

where ρ_{ijt} denotes bilateral GDP correlations between countries i and j, T_{ijt} stands for bilateral trade integration, F_{ijt} for bilateral financial integration, S_{ijt} for specialization, C_{ijt} for some other control variables, and ε_{ijt} for an error term.

Such single equation models only estimate reduced effects of trade, financial integration, specialization, and so forth, but do not distinguish between direct and indirect effects. The existence of indirect effects in different directions may cause the direct effects to appear small (as they may cancel each other out) in single equation regressions. Furthermore endogeneity is an important concern with such regressions if there are several variables on the right-hand side of the equation; a reason why some researchers have chosen to employ instrumental variables.

To tackle the endogeneity problem and to account for the various indirect effects, such as the effects of financial integration on business cycles through trade and specialization, we choose a simultaneous equations approach, following Imbs (2004, 2006). The specification used here takes the following form:

$$\rho_{ijt} = \alpha_0 + \alpha_1 T_{ijt} + \alpha_2 F_{ijt} + \alpha_3 S_{ijt} + \alpha_4 D_{ijt} + \varepsilon'_{ijt}, \tag{1}$$

$$T_{ijt} = \beta_0 + \beta_1 F_{ijt} + \beta_2 D_{ijt} + \beta_3 I_{1ijt} + \varepsilon^2_{ijt}, \tag{2}$$

$$F_{ijt} = \gamma_0 + \gamma_1 T_{ijt} + \gamma_2 I_{2ijt} + \varepsilon^3_{ijt}, \tag{3}$$

$$S_{ijt} = \delta_0 + \delta_1 T_{ijt} + \delta_2 F_{ijt} + \delta_3 I_{3ijt} + \varepsilon^4_{ijt}, \tag{4}$$

where D_{ijt} is the similarity of currency regimes of the two countries in question, I_{1ijt} the standard variables of gravity model (distance, common language and border, etc.), I_{2ijt} the institutional variables describing the quality of governance, and I_{3ijt} the stage of development of respective countries.

Panel data on thirteen East Asian countries over a time period ranging from 1990 to 2003 are used. The countries are Cambodia, China, Hong Kong, Indonesia, Japan, Korea, Lao, Malaysia, the Philippines, Singapore, Taiwan, Thailand, and Vietnam.[35] The sample is divided into two subsample periods to capture the change over the years: 1990 to 1996 and 1999 to 2003. The crisis years of 1997 and 1998 are excluded.

For all variables, bilateral data are used, as this is argued to be more accurate than aggregate data as used in most studies. While aggregate data are easier to collect, their use is likely to spoil the empirical results because they describe the general openness of an economy with respect to trade, finance, and the like, rather than integration between two economies. The different variables are constructed as follows.

Bilateral GDP Correlations   GDP correlations are measured as

$$\rho_{ijt} = \text{corr}(Y_i, Y_j)_t$$

where Y_i and Y_j are the measures of economic activity of the respective countries, for which we use GDP at constant local prices. Before taking correlations, the data are detrended using first-order differencing.[36] All data are annual and are from WDI and the Taiwan Statistical Data Book 2004.

Bilateral Trade Integration   For bilateral trade integration we can employ the same trade measure already used in the analysis of the trade-creating effects of monetary integration in section 6.2. That is, bilateral trade integration is measured by

$$T_{ijt} = \frac{x_{ijt} + m_{ijt}}{X_{it} + M_{it} + X_{jt} + M_{jt}},$$

where x_{ijt} are the exports from country i to j during period t, m_{ijt} are the imports to country i from j, and $X_{it}, M_{it}, X_{jt}, M_{jt}$ are the total exports/imports of country i/j respectively. The data are from the same sources as in section 6.2.

Bilateral Financial Integration   A more difficult task, which is indeed crucial to this analysis, is to measure financial integration. There are various ways of defining and measuring financial integration. The direct measurement of international financial markets integration has proven, so far, to be an extremely arduous task plagued by ambiguity. This ambiguity results because there is no single mechanism to measure the degree of integration that is free of conceptual and technical difficulties and that is exempted from interpretation problems. The acknowledgment of these difficulties justifies why the literature has developed without pointing to a single measure but rather a set of measures. Financial integration clearly has to be seen as a multi-facetted phenomenon which cannot be captured by any one measure.

The choice of measures that could be used for measuring financial integration in East Asia, however, is restricted due to the characteristics of the financial markets of the region and to the related issue of data availability. As discussed in section 5.3, security markets are weakly developed in the majority of East Asian countries, precluding the use of any measure that makes use of bond or equity indicators. Interest rate parity conditions could be used (as done by De Brouwer 1999), but money markets are also hardly developed in the poorer countries in question.[37] This leaves the banking sector and FDI.[38] While cross-border banking activities would make a potentially useful indicator, there are no data available, effectively reducing the choice to FDI as a measure of financial integration.[39] Choosing FDI, however, also makes sense given the structure of financial linkages of the region, in which it plays a pre-eminent role. To measure financial integration, we thus employ the same FDI measure from section 6.2:

$$F_{ijt} = \frac{fdi_{ijt} + fdi_{jit}}{GDP_i + GDP_j},$$

where fdi_{ijt} denotes FDI to country i from country j and fdi_{jit} denotes FDI to country j from i. The bilateral FDI flows are divided by the joint GDP of both countries. Again, the data are from the same sources cited in section 6.2.

Specialization   To measure specialization, we follow Imbs (2004) in using sectoral real value added to construct

$$S_{ij} = \sum |s_{ni} - s_{nj}|,$$

where s_{ni} is the share of industry n in GDP of country i. The sectoral shares s are computed using one-digit manufacturing value added data from the UN *Statistical Yearbook*.[40] The more similar the sectoral shares of each industry between two countries, the closer this indicator is to zero. If the value added of all sectors is identical for both countries, the indicator takes the value zero.

Similarity of Currency Regimes of the Two Countries in Question   Shin and Wang (2003) suggest employing a number of variables to accommodate for macro policies as possible determinants of business cycle correlations. They use bilateral correlations of government budget deficits as a proxy for fiscal policy coordination and correlations of M2 growth rates as a measure for monetary policy coordination. We argue that such measures of policy coordination are not appropriate for East Asia given that there is actually *no* direct macro policy coordination between these countries. Instead, we propose to use a variable for the similarity of currency regimes. As mentioned before, East Asian countries—except for Japan—basically adhere to the informal East Asian dollar standard; namely they pursue (soft) pegs to the US dollar. The external exchange rate constraint can be expected to have an impact on macro policies and thus on business cycles (despite the widespread existence of capital controls in the region). The currency regimes are interpreted as exogenously determined, in a sense that the current situation constitutes a noncooperative Nash equilibrium and that no single country conforming to the East Asian dollar standard will by itself move away from this regime. Hence the currency regime variable is employed as an exogenous variable in system (1) through (4). As in section 6.2 we use a first measure of currency regime similarity based on the Frankel and Wei estimations and a second one based on bilateral exchange rate volatility.

Instrumental Variables I_{1ijt}, I_{2ijt}, and I_{3ijt} are instrumental variables that contain the vectors of the exogenous determinants of the endogenous variables described above. To instrument trade, we can draw on a rich foundation of literature that employs the gravity model of international trade. I_{1ijt} thus includes the standard variables of the gravity model. These are the product of the natural logarithm of the population of both countries, a variable describing combined GDP computed as the product of the natural logarithm of the GDP of both countries, the natural logarithm of the distance between the two countries, and a dummy variable indicating whether the countries share a common land border. Data sources are the same as in section 6.2.

I_{2ijt} captures institutional variables for financial integration. The variables describe the quality of governance, following Imbs (2006), who first suggested instrumenting financial integration with institutional variables, drawing on the finding of La Porta et al. (1998) that legal institutions are an important determinant of financial development. Especially when considering the specific definition of financial integration used in this paper, namely as bilateral FDI, such instrumental variables are appealing, as one would generally expect FDI to increase with improving governance. The governance indicators used here were developed by the World Bank and include "voice and accountability," "political stability," "government effectiveness," "regulatory policy," "rule of law," and "control of corruption."[41] The "raw" indicators are measured in units ranging from −2.5 to 2.5, with higher values corresponding to better governance outcomes. For the bilateral indicators used here, these indicators are first rescaled by simply adding 2.5 to each value so that the new range is 0 to 5. Then the sum of each pair is taken. The bilateral indicators hence range from 0 to 10, with a higher value indicating better governance in both countries.

Specialization is instrumented by I_{3ijt}, which describes the stage of development of respective countries. More specifically, we employ the natural logarithm of the pairwise difference in GDP per capita, drawing on the finding by Imbs and Wacziarg (2003) that the development of sectoral specialization is related to the development of income per capita.

Instrumental Variable Equation Results First we replicate Frankel and Rose's original regression

$$\rho_{ijt} = \alpha + \beta T_{ijt} + \varepsilon_{ijt} \tag{5}$$

for East Asia, where trade is instrumented with the gravity variables. As in Frankel and Rose, who find a strongly positive and statistically significant effect of greater trade intensity on the correlation of economic activity, the results for East Asia presented in table

Table 6.2
Effect of trade intensity on income correlation (instrumental variable estimates of β)

	Number of observations	β
Whole sample	148	0.0469*
		(0.0263)
Without China	126	0.0333
		(0.0239)
Without Japan	124	0.0492*
		(0.0298)
Without China and Japan	104	0.0213
		(0.0254)

Note: Standard errors in parentheses; * significant at 10 percent level.

6.2 indicate a positive effect of trade integration on output correlations. Also, when the regression is run without China, Japan, and China and Japan, respectively, the effect remains positive, even though it becomes smaller and loses significance when China is omitted. Frankel and Rose note themselves that equation (5) may contain an omitted variable bias, but we may interpret these results as a first hint that increasing trade integration in East Asia has a positive effect on business cycle correlations.[42]

System Equation Results

Table 6.3 depicts the system equation results.[43] As before, we run the regression for the whole sample as well as without China, Japan, and China and Japan, respectively. First, the system equation is estimated as described in equations (1) through (4). The results are presented in columns 2, 4, 6, and 8. To control for a potential world business cycle, a new variable is added to equation (1), namely the natural logarithm of the average US growth (USG) rate over the respective periods. The regression results including this variable are presented in columns 3, 5, 7, and 9. It is noteworthy that the inclusion of the world business cycle variable does not seem to affect the estimation results in a substantial way.

The system equation results substantiate the instrumental variable findings, also indicating a positive direct effect of trade integration on output correlations. However, the results are only statistically significant when China is omitted (column 4). By excluding Japan and including the world business cycle variable, the coefficient even becomes negative. The results for the effect of FDI integration on output fluctuations are more robust: in all regressions we see a positive, partially highly significant effect of FDI integration on output co-movements.

Looking at the whole sample (columns 2 and 3), both trade and financial integration stimulate each other as suggested by positive coefficients for β_l and γ_l in equations (2) and (3). Especially, in view of the close relationship between FDI and intra-industry

Table 6.3
System equation results

	Whole sample		Without China		Without Japan		Without China and Japan	
Number of observations	83		75		65		58	
Column	2	3	4	5	6	7	8	9
GDP correlation								
Trade	0.0511	0.0228	0.1351 *	0.0988	0.0118	-0.0360	0.0432	0.0121
	(0.0626)	(0.0581)	(0.0789)	(0.0671)	(0.0894)	(0.0885)	(0.0921)	(0.0884)
FDI	0.0673	0.0304	0.4122 ***	0.2916 ***	0.2108 **	0.2699 ***	0.3193 ***	0.3520 ***
	(0.0992)	(0.0912)	(0.1185)	(0.1028)	(0.1011)	(0.0987)	(0.1002)	(0.0947)
Specialization	0.0048	-0.0003	0.0082* *	0.0041	0.0035	-0.0021	0.0044	0.0013
	(0.0042)	(0.0041)	(0.0047)	(0.0043)	(0.0045)	(0.0046)	(0.0046)	(0.0044)
Volatility	-0.8704	-0.8153	0.8061	-0.4141	1.8969	2.3528	1.1412	0.7018
	(2.6976)	(2.5143)	(2.6427)	(2.4005)	(2.7363)	(2.5950)	(2.6430)	(2.4359)
USG		12.3690 ***		12.0663 ***		13.7144 ***		13.6499 ***
		(3.4731)		(3.2330)		(4.1261)		(3.7975)
Trade								
FDI	0.0071	0.0177	-0.1054	-0.0734	0.1122	0.0528	-0.4031	-0.4471 *
	(0.1642)	(0.1635)	(0.1965)	(0.1947)	(0.2006)	(0.1973)	(0.2690)	(0.2592)
Volatility	-16.8041***	-16.6761***	-15.5699***	-15.2336***	-11.7497***	-11.6314***	-8.6622 *	-8.2706 *
	(3.9438)	(3.9392)	(4.1644)	(4.1594)	(3.9873)	(4.0134)	(5.0511)	(5.0223)
Distance	-0.3200 *	-0.3178 *	-0.2899	-0.2969	-0.3118	-0.2955	-0.2187	-0.1979
	(0.1768)	(0.1767)	(0.2002)	(0.2002)	(0.2158)	(0.2154)	(0.2733)	(0.2704)
Common border	1.2406 ***	1.2425 ***	1.3040 ***	1.2931 ***	1.2728 ***	1.2729 ***	1.4703 ***	1.4643 ***
	(0.3244)	(0.3241)	(0.3461)	(0.3458)	(0.3258)	(0.3260)	(0.3861)	(0.3851)
Product of GDP	0.0194 ***	0.0195 ***	0.0187 ***	0.0188 ***	0.0224 ***	0.0233 ***	0.0283 ***	0.0289 ***
	(0.0019)	(0.0019)	(0.0021)	(0.0020)	(0.0042)	(0.0042)	(0.0053)	(0.0052)

Product of population	-0.0036 (0.0032)	-0.0038 (0.0032)	0.0001) (0.0040)	-0.0002 (0.0040)	-0.0068 (0.0042)	-0.0075 * (0.0042)	-0.0027 (0.0051)	-0.0029 (0.0051)
FDI								
Trade	0.2686 (0.2126)	0.2750 (0.2122)	0.0383 (0.2570)	0.0601 (0.2595)	0.4897 ** (0.2200)	0.4712 ** (0.2197)	0.3322 (0.2696)	0.3186 (0.2692)
Voice and accountability	0.0721 (0.1886)	0.0690 (0.1868)	0.0901 (0.1797)	0.0876 (0.1881)	0.0257 (0.1658)	0.0299 (0.1671)	0.1057 (0.1924)	0.1069 (0.1917)
Political stability	-0.1782 (0.2082)	-0.1815 (0.2064)	-0.0584 (0.2223)	-0.1143 (0.2308)	-0.0648 (0.1736)	-0.0573 (0.1752)	-0.1538 (0.2287)	-0.1531 (0.2281)
Government effectiveness	0.4171 (0.2738)	0.4034 (0.2715)	0.3248 (0.2727)	0.3971 (0.2835)	0.0771 (0.2627)	0.0493 (0.2648)	0.2256 (0.3312)	0.1673 (0.3300)
Regulatory quality	-0.3243 (0.2906)	-0.2722 (0.2881)	-0.5123 * (0.2893)	-0.5505 * (0.3006)	-0.4541 (0.3406)	-0.5046 (0.3441)	-0.6802 * (0.4126)	-0.6967 * (0.4124)
Rule of law	0.2876 (0.3557)	0.3009 (0.3513)	-0.1428 (0.4518)	-0.0868 (0.4712)	0.1866 (0.3130)	0.1535 (0.3129)	0.0379 (0.4852)	0.0608 (0.4823)
Control of corruption	-0.1619 (0.4149)	-0.1913 (0.4115)	0.2044 (0.4575)	0.1683 (0.4784)	0.1840 (0.3618)	0.2563 (0.3636)	0.4436 (0.4716)	0.4196 (0.4700)
Specialization								
Trade	-9.3979 *** (1.9762)	-9.4689 *** (1.9762)	-10.6799*** (2.2884)	-10.7365*** (2.2897)	-1.3331 (3.0475)	-1.6015 (2.9753)	-3.5038 (3.2056)	-3.6338 (3.1338)
FDI	-9.5745 *** (3.3891)	-9.6792 *** (3.3795)	-12.8857*** (3.8858)	-12.9912*** (3.8803)	-18.2379*** (4.4938)	-17.9886*** (4.3538)	-16.9782*** (4.7090)	-16.5739*** (4.5293)
Difference in GDP per capita	8.9096 *** (1.3215)	9.1306 *** (1.3265)	8.2657 *** (1.4214)	8.6646 *** (1.4340)	11.8377 *** (2.1941)	11.8497 *** (2.1577)	11.2358 *** (2.3531)	10.9767 *** (2.2916)

Note: Standard errors are in parentheses; * significant at 10 percent, ** significant at 5 percent, and *** significant at 1 percent. No constants reported.

trade in East Asia (Fukao, Ishido, and Ito 2003), this is a very plausible result. Declining transportation costs and decreasing trade barriers have brought about an internationalization of production processes, often referred to as production fragmentation or vertical specialization. In East Asia, this has led to the development of extensive regional production networks, as discussed earlier. Over the past decade, China has grown into a manufacturing hub for East Asia, mainly serving as the last segment in the international production chain. It is therefore sensible that β_1 becomes negative when China is omitted from the regression. This might be a manifestation of the special role that China occupies in the regional trade-FDI network.

The results for equation (4) are fairly robust with large coefficients. They suggest that more trade and FDI integration lead to less specialization. This is also consistent with the direction of the estimates for trade and financial integration in equation (1). Indeed, if trade induces less specialization (the European Commission argument) as suggested by the estimates for δ_1, then one should expect a positive effect of trade on output synchronization, namely a positive α_1, which we find. The same holds for FDI integration.

Less clear-cut and somewhat puzzling are the estimates for specialization in equation (1). Theory predicts that specialization leads to less synchronous output (the Krugman argument), so we should expect a negative coefficient for α_3. In table 6.3, however, most estimates for α_3 show a positive sign. But it should be noted that the α_3 coefficients are very close to zero, so that the specialization effect is very small regardless of whether it is positive or negative. The result might also be an indication that the Krugman argument simply does not apply in the case of East Asia, where trade and FDI are very intertwined, as discussed above. Arguably, specialization that is induced by FDI might actually increase synchronization, because of the nature of the regional production networks. This is certainly an issue that needs further investigation in future research.

As regards exchange rate volatility, the effect on output correlation is negative for the whole sample, but the results are not consistent in the other cases. The relationship between exchange rate volatility and trade, however, is straightforward and confirms the gravity model estimations from the last section. In equation (2) we find a very large and significant impact of exchange rate volatility on trade.[44] That is, more volatility significantly reduces trade in East Asia. This finding is important as it provides a strong argument for regional exchange rate coordination, especially considering that intraregional trade accounts for more than half of total trade for the majority of East Asian countries.

The overall effect of trade integration on output fluctuations constitutes the direct effect (α_1) and the indirect effects through the impact of trade on FDI ($\gamma_1 \alpha_2$) and specialization ($\delta_1 \alpha_3$). Accordingly, the overall effect of financial integration on business cycles constitutes the direct effect (α_2), as well as the indirect effects through trade ($\beta_1 \alpha_1$) and specialization ($\delta_1 \alpha_3$). As noted before, the direct effects are positive in both cases ($\alpha_1 > 0$, $\alpha_2 > 0$).[45] Because trade and FDI stimulate each other, their indirect effects on output synchronization are positive as well ($\gamma_1 \alpha_2 > 0$, $\beta_1 \alpha_1 > 0$).[46]

The indirect effects resulting from the impact of trade and FDI integration on specialization are less robust, but most estimates for α_3 show a positive sign, which would imply a negative indirect effect, as both trade and FDI have negative effects on specialization in equation (4). If the overall effects of trade integration on business cycles is calculated for the baseline scenario in column 2, we find the overall effects on output correlations to be positive for both trade integration ($\alpha_1 + \gamma_1\alpha_2 + \delta_1\alpha_3 = 0.0241$) and FDI integration ($\alpha_2 + \beta_1\alpha_1 + \delta_2\alpha_3 = 0.0217$). Calculating the overall effects of trade and FDI integration for the other regression results in columns 3 through 9 also yields positive effects.

Conclusions

Summing up, the system equation results indicate that both trade and FDI integration have a positive direct impact on output fluctuations in East Asia. Moreover the overall effects are positive as well, as trade integration tends to stimulate FDI integration, and vice versa. The estimates for specialization effects are less robust, but in most cases we find a positive—albeit small—effect on output correlations. Furthermore the results suggest that FDI and trade integration reduce specialization, which might be a result of production fragmentation and vertical specialization that has taken place in East Asia over the past decade.

If correct, the results suggest that further economic integration will make output cycles more synchronous in East Asia. In other words, as East Asia becomes more integrated through trade and FDI investment, its output fluctuations will also become more similar. This, in turn, implies that a common macro and exchange rate policy will increasingly suit each individual East Asian country as the need for tailor-made national policies diminishes. Moreover the estimates reconfirm our previous findings that the similarity of exchange rate regimes has a significant positive effect on trade integration in East Asia, underscoring the argument for intraregional exchange rate stabilization. However, a word of caution is warranted: some effects are not always statistically significant, and the quality of the data used for the estimations is not as good as one would wish.

6.4 Monetary Integration, Investment Conditions, and the Development of Regional Capital Markets

In the classic as well as neoclassic traditions, money is regarded as a veil over the real economy.[47] That is to say, money is merely a means of payment on spot markets and a store of value. The neutrality of money implies that the central bank cannot affect the real economy, and money therefore also has no impact on the development of a country's economy. But if money is regarded as a means of deferred payment in an uncertain world with enterprises that finance investment through capital markets, the denomination of debt becomes crucial for production, employment, and growth (Nitsch 2006).

Acknowledging the central role of money in economic development, an analysis of monetary integration between emerging and developing economies, such as those in East Asia, has to address different questions than does an analysis of monetary integration between developed countries, such as those in the euro area. The former has to take into account the specific problems developing countries face.[48] Two of the features that characterize any less developed country are a weak currency status (Schelkle 2000) and a lack of financial maturity (Bordo and Flandreau 2003).[49] As will be argued below, developing countries' lack of an international currency puts a number of constraints on their development prospects and increases financial fragility. This section therefore investigates whether, and to what extent, monetary integration could be used as a strategy to overcome these impediments in order to create favorable macroeconomic conditions, that is, to promote accumulation and to reduce the risk associated with asset and liability dollarization.

The international monetary system is characterized by currency competition and a hierarchy of currencies (figure 6.3). Cohen (1998: 114) likens currency competition to a "vast, three-dimensional pyramid: narrow at the top, where a few popular currencies dominate; increasingly broad below, reflecting varying degrees of competitive inferiority."[50]

Different currencies exhibit different qualities in their function as storage of wealth. In an open economy the central bank has to defend the national currency against competition with other currencies in the portfolios of economic agents. Because of devaluation expectations, an agent holding a weaker currency will demand a higher premium, that is, a higher real interest rate. The international hierarchy of currencies hence sets off a cumulative process by which investments in hard currency countries can be financed most cheaply of all, while market forces cause higher interest rates to be demanded in weaker currency countries, making credits dearer and thus retarding growth and development (Nitsch 1999b). High real interest rates are a problem for some East Asian countries, but not all.

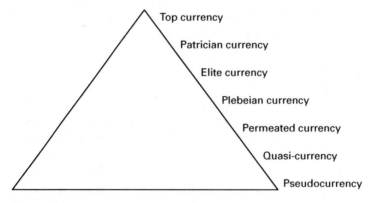

Figure 6.3
The currency pyramid

While least developed countries such as Cambodia (11.2 percent) and Lao (24.2 percent) suffer from relatively high real interest rates, others such as China (2.4 percent), Malaysia (2.3 percent), the Philippines (4.3 percent), and Thailand (2.2 percent) have managed to establish relatively low levels of real interest despite their weak currency status.[51]

Low productive power domestically corresponds to low monetary power internationally. This is demonstrated by the fact that developing countries' currencies are not capable of entering into international contracts (Riese 2004). Weak currency countries are confronted with what Eichengreen and Hausmann (1999) have termed "original sin."[52] They describe original sin as a situation in which the domestic currency cannot be used to borrow long term, even domestically. As a result financial fragility is unavoidable because all domestic investment will have either a currency mismatch (projects that generate domestic currency will be financed with an international currency) or a maturity mismatch (long-term projects will be financed with short-term loans). Both currency and maturity mismatches increase the danger of financial crises. Indeed original sin is widely regarded as one of the causes of the Asian crisis (see the analysis in chapter 3).

Moreover, in a phenomenon McKinnon (2005) has named "conflicted virtue," weak currency countries are unable to lend in their own currencies, forcing creditor countries with weak currencies to cumulate currency mismatches. As most East Asian countries have turned into creditor countries after the Asian crisis, the massive buildup of foreign exchange assets has created a conflicted virtue problem for them. While Brunei, Japan, and Singapore have had current account surpluses for partly more than two decades and China has had more modest current account surpluses since 1994, even the five former crisis economies (Indonesia, Korea, Malaysia, the Philippines, and Thailand), which had current account deficits before 1997, have now accumulated large stocks of liquid dollar assets in both private and public portfolios (see annexes 7 and 9). With mounting dollar claims, non-US holders of dollar assets have to worry more about domestic currency runs, which would cause a domestic currency appreciation and hence a decline of their net wealth. Countries are therefore inclined to avoid large-scale appreciation of their currencies, which might invoke protests from deficit countries about unfair competition through an undervalued currency.[53]

A weak currency status therefore brings with it multiple problems, from retarding financial and real development and increasing the risk of financial crisis to triggering potential trade conflict. A hardening of the currency, or a "pyramid-climbing," is therefore a crucial precondition for creating favorable investment conditions and enabling sustainable economic development and for overcoming the problems of original sin and conflicted virtue. To analyze if and how monetary integration could contribute to a hardening of currencies, it is important to understand what makes a currency an *international* currency.

As Hyman Minsky observed, anyone can create money by issuing IOUs,[54] but the difficult part is to get them to be generally accepted (Kregel 2006). The easiest way to have one's IOUs accepted is to generate liabilities that can only be extinguished through possession of these IOUs. A government can domestically enforce the acceptance of its currency through the fiscal system (and up to a certain degree through its legal system). It can create a tax liability on its citizens that can only be redeemed by rendering the government's IOU in the form of money issued by the government. But this does not work internationally, as a government can only tax its own citizens who are subject to government regulations but cannot force nonresidents to hold claims. The only way to make the currency internationally accepted is by building an expectation that these liabilities will act as perfect substitutes for other countries' monetary authorities' liabilities.

A number of conditions can be identified that contribute to building such expectations. First, the confidence in a currency's future value is dependent on the political stability of the country of origin (Cohen 2000). This is the quintessential precondition for establishing a track record of relatively low inflation and low inflation variability. Second, countries need to develop sound and credible fiscal institutions.[55] In conjunction with noninflationary income policies, an austere fiscal framework lays the groundwork for a noninflationary monetary environment with low nominal as well as real interest rates.

Third, countries need to establish credible monetary regimes. Unpredictable monetary policy makes agents unsure about the future real value of their assets issued in domestic currency and may lead them to denominate them in international currency (Jeanne 2005). Establishing a strong, (de facto) independent central bank with strong inflation aversion and a clear monetary policy objective is an important way to keep down inflationary expectations and to reduce this uncertainty.

Fourth, not running into international debt but instead striving for a surplus in the trade and current account favors national autonomy and employment and helps to create expectations of an appreciation of the national currency (Nitsch 2006). From a long-term development perspective, it is not the short-term stabilization of the exchange rate that is of central importance but rather the durable enhancement of a currency's quality (Fritz 2002). The quality of a nation's currency is undermined when a currency regime is chosen that achieves price and exchange rate stabilization at the cost of an increase in the country's foreign debt. Instead, countries need to develop the ability to generate foreign reserves by generating export surpluses. Such a strategy requires a tendency toward an undervaluation of the currency (Riese 2004). Keeping domestic money scarce represents the necessary condition for securing the undervaluation of the currency because—due to its deflationary effects internally—it allows a country to achieve a price advantage over foreign countries, providing the precondition for the stimulation of exports. Successful examples of this development strategy are Western Germany in the 1950s and Japan in the 1960s and 1970s. The East Asian tiger economies have very successfully followed this strategy more recently.

But developing sound fiscal and monetary institutions and generating export surpluses might not be enough. The literature on the determinants of key currency status points to another factor, namely the size of the economy. Matsuyama, Kiyotaki, and Matsui (1993) explain the international use of currencies and, succinctly, the determinants of key currency status as a function of relative country size and the degree of international economic integration. Because of network externalities and transaction costs, the global portfolio is concentrated in very few currencies. In some ways money is comparable to language, whose usefulness is also dependent on the number of people with whom one can communicate; similarly a currency's utility rises with the number of other market participants using the same currency (Dowd and Greenaway 1993). A currency's attractiveness increases with its transactional liquidity, which in turn is dependent on the existence of well-developed and broad financial markets that offer a wide range of short and long-term investment opportunities as well as fully operating secondary markets (Cohen 2000). Eichengreen, Hausmann, and Panizza (2005) point out that larger countries offer significant diversification possibilities, while smaller countries add fewer diversification benefits relative to the additional costs they imply.

As a result the global portfolio is concentrated in a small number of currencies (those at the top of the international currency pyramid) for reasons partly beyond the control of even the countries that follow sound domestic policies. Developing key currency status is hence a very difficult and maybe even impossible endeavor for small economies.[56] There is also empirical support for this view. Eichengreen et al. (2005) show larger economies to have less of a problem with original sin than smaller ones. Using three different measures of size (log of total GDP, log of total domestic credit, and log of total trade), their estimates suggest that all measures of size are robustly correlated to original sin.

In the face of these constraints, regional monetary integration could be employed by developing nations as a strategy for overcoming their weak currency status and the inability to enter into international contracts with domestic currency. While a hardening of the national currency could, in principle, also be achieved by each country alone through austere monetary and fiscal policies and through the generation of export surpluses, it might not suffice to develop an international currency. Monetary integration, however, could address both issues at the same time. One the one hand, it would place an external constraint on countries participating in the monetary integration process, facilitating the domestic policy adjustment necessary for a hardening of the currency. In the European context Giavazzi and Pagano (1988) have termed this the "advantage of tying one's hands" (see section 6.1). Monetary integration could be used as a disciplinary device for inflation-prone countries by forcing policy makers to pursue more restrictive fiscal and monetary policies than they would otherwise. In return, countries would enjoy potential credibility gains. This strategy worked reasonably well in Europe in the run-up to monetary union.[57]

At the same time monetary integration (monetary union in particular, but also the creation of a basket currency) would address the problems of original sin and conflicted virtue by creating a larger economic entity with vast investment opportunities that would be hard to ignore by international asset managers and that, if backed by austere monetary and fiscal policies, would increase chances of entering the club of international currencies. The underlying logic is that the whole would be equal to more than the sum of its parts. To be sure, size alone is not enough: Russia, Argentina, and Brazil are examples of large emerging economies that, despite their size, face problems of original sin. But, as explained before, good domestic policies are necessary as well, and over most of the past decades these three countries have not been prime examples for prudent economic policy-making.

Bordo, Meissner, and Redish (2005), in an analysis of how five former British colonies (the United States, Canada, Australia, New Zealand, and South Africa) overcame original sin, point to another interesting factor: the role of shocks such as wars and massive economic disruptions. For instance, the onset of World War I essentially closed the London capital market and led Canada, Australia, New Zealand, and South Africa to suspend the gold convertibility of their domestic currencies and raise funds domestically; that is, the disruption of the war basically forced these countries to create domestic bond markets.[58] An interesting parallel can be drawn with East Asia, where the Asian crisis had been such a major shock. As one reaction to the crisis, the region has begun trying to develop regional bond markets (see chapter 3). ABF I and II are first attempts to bundle bond issues by East Asian countries in order to make it more attractive for international investors to include them in their portfolios.

This might be a step in the right direction for East Asia, and pursuing a similar cooperative path in monetary policy could help overcome the problems of original sin and conflicted virtue that are associated with a weak currency status. Individually, most East Asian nations will have little prospect of escaping this trap. For instance, it is hard to imagine how a small developing economy like Vietnam will be ever able to develop its national currency, the dong, into an internationally accepted currency.[59] Yet, united, the region is far too important to be ignored by currency traders. As a possible first move in this direction, in December 2005 the ADB suggested the launch of a currency unit comprised of a basket of regional currencies akin to the ECU. This virtual basket currency could give observers a taste of the kind of standing a regional East Asian currency could achieve in international financial markets. The benefits of such a "parallel currency approach" to monetary integration will be discussed in chapter 11.

6.5   Monetary Integration and the Recovery of Monetary Policy Influence

When you got nothing, you got nothing to lose.
—Bob Dylan in "Like a Rolling Stone," from the album *Highway 61 Revisited* (1965)

In this last section of the chapter, the potential for regional monetary integration to be a way for East Asian nations to (re)gain some degrees of monetary influence in the region is highlighted. Monetary cooperation and integration are not necessarily equivalent to a loss of autonomy, as a country can only lose what it has. This might seem paradoxical at first, as it is usually claimed that monetary integration means a loss of monetary independence (see section 5.1). This equivalence, however, is true only if the participating countries enjoyed monetary autonomy before. In this context it is important to distinguish between sovereignty and policy autonomy: a country might well have the formal right to pursue a certain policy but find itself unable to do so because of policy choices of other nations (DeMartino and Grabel 2003).[60]

In the discourse preceding the creation of EMU, opponents of monetary unification argued that giving up one's own currency would mean losing a forceful policy instrument. However, the discussion in Europe had been somewhat unreal. As Goodhard (1995: 458) pointed out, through their EMS membership EMS countries (except Germany) had already abandoned discretionary monetary policy long before monetary union was finalized, meaning that there would be "virtually no economic cost in doing so formally and completely by moving to a full monetary union."[61] According to De Grauwe (1994: 3) it was "no exaggeration to state that Germany dominates the monetary conditions in Europe."

For a formal test of this hypothesis, the following simple Taylor rule is estimated:

$$r_{ct} = b_1 + b_2 IP_{ct-2} + b_3 \pi_{ct-2} + b_4 r_{Bt-2} + \varepsilon,$$

where r_{ct} is the central bank interest rate of country c at time t, IP_{ct-2} is country c's lagged industrial production, and π_{ct-2} is the lagged inflation rate. r_{Bt-2} is the lagged Bundesbank discount rate.[62] The results for the period ranging from August 1971 to December 1998, namely from the breakdown of the Bretton Woods system to the launch of the euro, are presented in table 6.4.

The estimates show that the monetary policy decisions of all European countries analyzed here, with the exceptions of Greece and Norway (both of which were not members of the EMS),[63] were driven to a large extent by the interest rate policy of the Bundesbank.[64] While domestic inflation and industrial production also seem to have played a role in the conduct of many of these countries' monetary policies, the Bundesbank discount rate had a far greater impact for all countries. US interest rate policy, in contrast, and as one would expect, was not influenced by the Bundesbank.

One can push Goodhard's argument further and argue that the European countries (except Germany) that entered monetary union not only *did not lose* monetary autonomy but actually *(re)gained* some degrees of monetary policy influence through EMU membership. Indeed it is arguable that Germany was the only country that actually lost monetary autonomy. Virtually all other EMU member countries have obtained a voice in monetary policy decisions. Instead of following the Bundesbank's policy stance, all EMU member countries are now represented through their national central bank governors in the ECB's

Table 6.4
Determinants of monetary policy decisions, August 1971 to December 1998

	Bundesbank discount rate	CPI	Industrial production	Observations	R squared
Austria	0.6916*** (0.0463)	0.0597 (0.0385)	−0.0117* (0.0064)	327	0.7776
Belgium[a]	0.9371*** (0.1248)	0.1575*** (0.0497)	−0.0285* (0.0150)	327	0.4310
Denmark	0.7214*** (0.0483)	0.1933*** (0.0379)	−0.0391*** (0.0069)	298	0.7870
Finland	0.3226*** (0.0464)	0.1439*** (0.0226)	−0.0407*** (0.0066)	327	0.6986
France	0.7435*** (0.0785)	0.4341*** (0.0420)	0.0372*** (0.0116)	327	0.6780
Greece	0.2366 (0.1561)	0.1978*** (0.0565)	0.2839*** (0.0261)	327	0.5864
Italy	0.4584*** (0.1462)	0.3403*** (0.0582)	0.0548*** (0.0177)	327	0.3219
Luxembourg[a]	0.9789*** (0.1181)	0.0449 (0.0737)	−0.0842*** (0.0151)	327	0.5000
Netherlands	0.9881*** (0.0594)	−0.0457 (0.0295)	−0.0199** (0.0080)	327	0.7033
Norway	0.1592 (0.1365)	0.3018*** (0.0949)	0.0619*** (0.0160)	327	0.1089
Portugal	0.7889*** (0.2442)	0.5391*** (0.0626)	0.1824*** (0.0206)	327	0.4552
Spain	0.4329* (0.2354)	0.2147** (0.1045)	0.0614** (0.0295)	327	0.0725
Sweden	0.4431*** (0.0968)	0.3301*** (0.0437)	0.0155* (0.0084)	327	0.4673
Switzerland	0.5760*** (0.0674)	0.1695*** (0.0347)		327	0.6292
United Kingdom	0.4792*** (0.1348)	0.2338*** (0.0526)	−0.0039 (0.0260)	327	0.3180
United States	−0.0300 (0.1124)	0.5844*** (0.0692)	0.0016 (0.0121)	327	0.5202

Source: Calculation with data from IFS and Global Financial Data.
Note: Newey West standard errors in parentheses. *** denotes statistical significance at the 1 percent level, ** at the 5 percent level, and * at the 10 percent level.
a. Luxembourg and Belgium had a monetary union, the Belgium–Luxembourg Economic Union, since 1922.

Governing Council, the ECB's monetary policy-making body. Until Slovakia joined EMU as the sixteenth member on January 1, 2009, the central bank governors of each euro area member, along with the six members of the ECB's Executive Board, had the right to vote at each council meeting, providing smaller countries such as Austria and Luxembourg with the same de jure influence on monetary policy as the larger members France, Germany, Italy, and Spain.

With Slovakia's entry the voting rules in the ECB Governing Council have been changed to a rotating system to ensure efficient decision-making in the face of an increase of the Council's current size of twenty-two members to maybe thirty or more in the process of euro area expansion. The new voting scheme gives more weight to the larger euro area economies, but maintains a bias in favor of the smaller countries.[65] In any case, regardless of the distribution of voting rights, the ECB statutes stipulate that national central bank governors sit on the Governing Council in a personal and independent capacity, not as representatives of their own countries.

Among the central banks of the old EU member countries that did not join EMU, the monetary authorities of Denmark and Sweden have basically been forced to shadow ECB policy, without exerting any influence themselves on the policy they have to follow.[66]

A different but also Dylanesque situation applies for most East Asian countries when it comes to the conduct of their monetary policy. As mentioned earlier, the region's exchange rate policy can be described by the East Asian dollar standard, a situation in which all East Asian countries with the exemption of Japan operate more or less tight pegs to the US dollar. The pegs were temporarily lifted during and after the Asian crisis (except in the cases of China, Hong Kong, and Myanmar), but over the last few years there has been a resurrection of the dollar standard (McKinnon 2001; Schnabl 2009), even though most of the countries officially declare their exchange rate regimes as (managed) floats.

Table 6.5 gives an overview of East Asian countries' official and de facto exchange rate regimes. The estimated weights of the US dollar in the hypothetical currency baskets of East Asian countries presented in column 3 show that Cambodia, China, Hong Kong, Malaysia, Myanmar, and Vietnam have basically maintained fixed exchange rates vis-à-vis the dollar.[67] Lao and the Philippines also manage tight pegs to the dollar, with the weights of the dollar in their hypothetical currency baskets above 90 percent. Indonesia, Korea, Singapore (and hence also Brunei, which maintains a currency board vis-à-vis the Singapore dollar), and Thailand allow considerably more flexibility toward the dollar than the previously mentioned countries but nevertheless display a strong dollar orientation in their exchange rate regimes, with dollar weights ranging from 70 to 90 percent. The only exception to this pattern is Japan, with a dollar weight of only 66 percent.

The situation can be illustrated in a stylized manner by the well-known $n - 1$ problem: given n currencies, there are $n - 1$ independent bilateral exchange rates. Maintaining these $n - 1$ bilateral exchange rates fixed ties down as many national money stocks. Hence, there is only one degree of freedom left. In the absence of exogenous rules, the price level is

Table 6.5
De jure and de facto exchange rate regimes in East Asia

	IMF classification	Estimated weight of the USD in hypothetical basket (%)
Brunei dollar	Currency board arrangement(vis-à-vis the Singapore dollar)	72.64
Cambodian riel	Managed floating with no pre-announced path for the exchange rate	98.36
Chinese yuan	Crawling peg: daily fluctuations in the RMB-USD exchange rate are limited to +/–0,3%, against other currencies +/–3%	98.60
Hong Kong dollar	Currency board arrangement(vis-à-vis the US dollar)	98.85
Indonesian rupiah	Managed floating with no pre-announced path for the exchange rate	86.69
Japanese yen	Independently floating	66.07
Korean won	Independently floating	81.35
Lao kip	Managed floating with no pre-announced path for the exchange rate	95.75
Malaysian ringgit	Managed floating with no pre-announced path for the exchange rate	98.88
Myanmar kyat	Managed floating with no pre-announced path for the exchange rate (officially pegged to SDR)	99.18
Philippine peso	Independently floating	90.16
Singapore dollar	Managed floating with no pre-announced path for the exchange rate	73.16
Thai baht	Managed floating with no pre-announced path for the exchange rate	79.08
Vietnamese dong	Managed floating with no pre-announced path for the exchange rate	100.68

Note: The estimates in column 3 were calculated using Frankel and Wei (1994) as presented in section 6.2 with daily exchange rates from 1/1/1999 to 8/14/2008. All dollar weight estimates are significant at the 1 percent level. The yen was regressed only on the dollar and the euro. Data are from Datastream (Reuters and Tenfore). Classifications are from IMF (2008c).

determined by the remaining nth country. In the case of today's East Asia (excluding Japan), this means that East Asian currencies are the $n - 1$ currencies, and the US dollar is the nth currency through which the price level is determined. In other words, policy autonomy rests in the hands of the United States, while East Asian countries more or less have to follow, depending on the degree of rigidity in their exchange regimes.

Although most East Asian countries maintain some form of capital controls that, in principle, should allow for monetary policy autonomy in the face of an exchange rate target, historical evidence suggests quite strongly that capital controls are porous and are easily circumvented.[68] Their effectiveness erodes over time as domestic and international investors and traders find channels, such as "favorable" trade invoicing, to elude them (Edwards 1999).

Furthermore there is a growing amount of empirical literature that puts into doubt even the traditional argument that countries with flexible exchange rates are able to isolate their domestic interest rates from changes in international interest rates. Frankel, Schmukler, and Servén (2004), for instance, find that while floating regimes afford greater monetary independence than fixed regimes, floating regimes offer only temporary monetary independence.[69] That is, while the speed of adjustment of domestic rates toward the long run, one-for-one relation with international interest rates is generally lower under floating than under fixed regimes, even floating regimes cannot exert autonomous monetary policy. Their findings suggest that besides the United States, Germany (now the euro zone) and Japan appear to be the only countries that can independently choose their own interest rates in the long run. Similarly Reade and Volz (2009b) who measure monetary independence across various regions find little monetary independence for smaller nations; even large emerging countries like Brazil, China and India exhibit dependency in their monetary policy whereas big industrialized countries, such as Japan, the United States, and the euro area, do exhibit considerable independence. Fratzscher (2002) also observes that even under flexible exchange rate arrangements it becomes ever more difficult to pursue independent monetary policy.[70] These studies seriously put into doubt the idea that all countries with a national currency automatically enjoy monetary autonomy. This is particularly the case for highly open economies—like those in East Asia (see section 5.3).[71]

Moreover, the underdevelopment of domestic financial markets hampers the conduct of monetary policy, creating a situation wherein the vast majority of East Asian countries have not been able to effectively pursue independent monetary policy. The People's Bank of China (PBC), for instance, did not raise interest rates for more than a decade until October 2004, and even this change was very modest and more symbolic than of practical import.[72] Similarly Malaysia raised its rates in November 2005 for the first time since 1998. The most extreme case of a loss of monetary autonomy in East Asia is Hong Kong. To maintain its currency board vis-à-vis the US dollar, the Hong Kong Monetary Authority has to move in tandem with the Federal Reserve, even though local inflation development has been very different from US inflation over recent years.

To formally investigate the degree of monetary policy independence that East Asian countries have, a cointegration framework is employed. In particular, a vector equilibrium-correction model is used to identify whether East Asian countries belong to steady-state relationships involving interest rates of other countries and whether they adjust to such relationships. If X_t is a vector of money market rates, the model is described as

$$\Delta X_t = \alpha \beta' \Delta X_{t-1} + \sum_{k=1}^{K-1} \Gamma_k \Delta X_{t-k} + \varepsilon_t, \tag{6}$$

where K is the number of autoregressive lags and $\beta' X_{t-1}$ are other cointegrating vectors.[73] To illustrate, assume a big country a and a small country b so that

$$X_t = \begin{pmatrix} r_a \\ r_b \end{pmatrix}. \tag{7}$$

If testing suggests that $r = 1$, there is one cointegrating vector in this system. It is possible to then carry out likelihood-ratio tests to test for the form of the cointegrating vector. Suppose that the restrictions required for the following system are accepted:

$$r_{a,t} = \beta_0 + r_{b,t} + \varepsilon_t. \tag{8}$$

The two countries respond one-for-one in interest rates; if the interest rate of country b rises by 25 basis points, so does the rate of country a. This can be shown in the vector equilibrium-correction model of (6):

$$\begin{pmatrix} \Delta r_a \\ \Delta r_b \end{pmatrix}_t = \begin{pmatrix} \alpha_1 \\ \alpha_2 \end{pmatrix}_t (\beta_0 \, \beta_1 \beta_2) \begin{pmatrix} 1 \\ r_a \\ r_b \end{pmatrix}_{t-1} + \sum_{k=1}^{K-1} \Gamma_k \Delta X_{t-k} + \varepsilon_t. \tag{9}$$

With the restriction $\beta_1 = -\beta_2 = 1$, then

$$\begin{pmatrix} \Delta r_a \\ \Delta r_b \end{pmatrix}_t = \begin{pmatrix} \alpha_1 \\ \alpha_2 \end{pmatrix}_t (r_a - r_b - \beta_0)_{t-1} + \sum_{k=1}^{K-1} \Gamma_k \Delta X_{t-k} + \varepsilon_t. \tag{10}$$

It may be expected that country a would not adjust to this cointegrating vector. As it is a large country, it might be expected to exert monetary policy independence, so $\alpha_1 = 0$. Country b, which is a small country, may be expected to adjust, so $\alpha_2 \neq 0$. Furthermore α_2 describes how much of any disequilibrium is corrected each period, as $\alpha = \Delta X_t / (\beta' X_{t-1})$; hence (ceteris paribus) a speed of adjustment can be calculated. The smaller is this coefficient, the more independent is a country's monetary policy, since it devotes less of its attention to correcting to what other interest rates are doing. As such, the α matrix is very informative about the nature of monetary policy independence. A country not adjusting to a cointegrating vector in which it appears is said to "drive" the system: the level that the country's interest rate is at is not constrained by the cointegrating relationship but in fact dictates what level that cointegrating relationship takes.

Table 6.6 presents estimates of this model for eight East Asian countries (China, Hong Kong, Korea, Thailand, Indonesia, Malaysia, Singapore, and the Philippines). As the large a countries we chose the world's three main currency areas, namely the United States, the euro area, and Japan. The East Asian countries are then the small b countries. We use monthly three-month interbank interest rates from IFS, Datastream, and the Global Financial Database for the periods listed in table 6.6. Along each row are the results relating to each country. Under $\hat{\alpha}_i$ are the estimated speed of adjustment coefficients, followed by the estimated cointegrating vectors under $\hat{\beta}_i$. Underneath each estimated coefficient is its standard error, which indicates whether that particular country enters the cointegrating vector, while bold typeface for the coefficient value denotes that that interest rate adjusts significantly to that particular cointegrating vector. The cointegrating vectors relating to each country b (reported as $\hat{\beta}_1$) show that in each system there was a cointegrating vector relating to that country. Generally there is one steady-state relationship relating to the small country, and a wider cointegrating relationship.

The United States enters all cointegrating vectors. It does not adjust to any of those, which means that it "drives" the system. This suggests that the United States plays a role in determining monetary policy of all the countries considered, to varying extent, depending on the $\hat{\alpha}$ coefficients of the b countries. Japan also enters several cointegrating vectors, while the euro area doesn't seem to affect the monetary policies of East Asian countries at all. Hong Kong has a one-to-one relationship with US rates and each period moves to correct a substantial amount in response to an US move in interest rates. China responds to US interest changes to a lesser extent than Hong Kong, but China's policy is influenced by world interest rates, in particular the US rate. Korea seems to respond quite strongly to changes in both Japanese and US rates. Singapore also moves with US and Japanese interest rates, which is in line with its basket regime in which both the USD and the yen are included. Indonesia, Thailand, and Malaysia respond to US interest rate movements (Indonesia also responds to Japanese rate changes), but rather modestly, suggesting that they do enjoy some monetary policy autonomy.

If the argument is correct and the status quo level of East Asian monetary independence is limited, then the costs of monetary integration in East Asia, at least for the economically small and developing countries, are much lower than commonly assumed. A common agency approach to monetary integration, as pursued in Europe, could pave the way for greater monetary policy flexibility in East Asia. Through the creation of a common monetary arrangement, or even a common currency, which could float freely against the dollar and the euro, East Asian countries could potentially gain some degrees of shared monetary independence. In terms of the $n - 1$ problem, creating a regional monetary arrangement that would take a regional currency or a basket of regional currencies as reference would mean that the one degree of freedom would be shifted to the region. While East Asian

Table 6.6
Cointegrating vectors and adjustments for East Asia

Country	$\hat{\alpha}_1$	$\hat{\beta}_1$					Sample	Lags	Dummies	Impulse	Rank	Normality	Test
		r_b	r_{Ja}	r_{EU}	r_{US}	intercept							
China	−0.11 (0.05)	1	−0.53 (−)	−0.47 (0.12)	−2.03 (0.01)		1998:1–2008:6	6	0	0	2	K(4)	6.58 [0.23]
Hong Kong	−0.26 (0.06)	1			−1		1998:1–2008:8	4	0	0	2	K(4)	11.76 [0.16]
Korea	−0.72 (0.13)	1	−2.80 (0.24)		0.09 (0.02)	−2.66 (0.12)	1998:1–2008:6	4	3	3	2	K(3)	5.70 [0.22]
Thailand	−0.024 (0.007)	1			1.72 (0.6)	−9.29 (2.58)	1998:1–2008:8	4	6	6	2	K(4)	8.94 [0.18]
Indonesia	−0.07 (0.01)	1	0.27 (−)		−1.27 (0.69)	6.32 (2.64)	1998:1–2008:8	4	9	9	2	K(3)	14.98 [0.04]
Malaysia	−0.03 (0.01)	1		−0.68 (0.20)			1998:1–2008:8	6	0	0	2	K(4), AC(1)	12.66 [0.12]
Singapore	−0.14 (0.04)	1	−0.50 (0.06)		−0.50 (0.06)		1998:1–2008:8	6	0	0	2	K(4), AC(1)	9.86 [0.13]
Philippines	−0.19 (0.06)	1	**5.82** **(2.14)**		−1.24 (0.37)	−5.52 (1.41)	1998:1–2008:8	4	0	0	2	K(4)	4.80 [0.31]

Source: Own calculations.
Note: β_1 is the first cointegration vector, α_1 the adjustment of East Asian country b to that vector; only the vector pertaining to that country is reported. A bold typeface reveals a significant parameter. The right panel reports any misspecification issues with the model; K(n) signifies n equations in that model had an excess kurtosis problem, while AC(n) denotes that n equations had problems with autocorrelation. Dummies records how many dummies for identified outliers were required. Test is the test of overidentifying restrictions, with the p-value in square brackets.

countries would still face an external constraint on domestic economic policies, the great difference between a regional currency arrangement or a multilateral monetary union in East Asia and a continued (informal) dollar pegging under the East Asian dollar standard (or even full dollarization) is that the former would give East Asian countries a say in their common monetary and exchange rate policy or policies.[74]

In the case of multilateral monetary union in East Asia, each member country could have a share in the common central bank's policy-making through a pooling of sovereignty. In contrast, continued dollar pegging (or dollarization), while basically requiring the same sacrifices in domestic policy autonomy as monetary union, would mean that all monetary policy influence is abandoned (permanently).[75] One potentially delicate political problem, however, would be the institutional design of a common central bank and the apportionment of power in an East Asian monetary union. A representational structure akin to that of the EMU, with more or less equal rights between all members, would be unrealistic if either China or Japan were involved, making such an arrangement less attractive for the smaller Southeast Asian countries due to the potential dominance of the bigger member countries. Conversely, neither Japan nor China (nor Korea) would be likely to accept the disproportional representation of the economically smaller Southeast Asian member countries the way Germany did in Europe.[76] Even though they are also highly heterogeneous, a solution would probably be easier to reach among ASEAN member nations.

The discussion here and in the preceding sections should therefore not evoke the impression that regional monetary integration—and especially monetary unification—comes without problems and costs. Monetary integration is not a free lunch, and it would be wrong to simply dismiss concerns about the costs of monetary integration—as they are emphasized in traditional OCA theory—and only point at potential trade-creating effects and a likely convergence of business cycles.[77] Especially the surrender of national monetary sovereignty in the case of monetary unification involves uncertainties, not at least regarding the partner countries' future policies. Moreover there would still be the political cost of giving up formal monetary independence, such as the loss of monetary policy autonomy *illusion* and the loss of the national currency as a symbol. Giving up de jure independence could also involve diplomatic costs in the form of political dependency on foreign nations.

But still, the analysis in this chapter showed that the costs of monetary integration in terms of the loss of independent domestic macro policies and the exchange rate policy as a reliable adjustment mechanism are lower than commonly thought, and that the benefits go beyond a mere saving of transaction cost and a better allocation of resources. It tried to highlight monetary integration as a potential strategy to overcoming structures that present obstacles to economic development and to create a stable macroeconomic environment that is conducive to investment and growth. In particular, the chapter drew attention to the potential contribution of monetary integration to developing regional financial markets in East Asia and to overcoming the problems of asset and liability dollarization that are possible sources of macroeconomic instability. Moreover the discussion of the Lucas critique tried to make clear that monetary integration needs to be understood as a dynamic process, in which the criteria for successful monetary integration that were laid out in OCA theory are likely to change through a policy of integration. Rather than being a precondition for successful monetary integration, fulfillment of certain OCA criteria should be regarded as the desired result of integration. In this regard the results of our analysis of the effects of real and financial integration on output movements indicate that further economic integration between East Asian countries would make their output cycles more synchronous, so that the region would increasingly fulfill this important OCA criterion. The overall assessment of the costs and benefits of monetary integration in East Asia that results from this analysis is therefore positive.

This positive conclusion, however, does not imply that a policy of monetary integration in East Asia should necessarily be directed at monetary unification. As was made clear by the definition of monetary integration in chapter 1, different degrees of monetary integration are possible, requiring different degrees of political commitment and entailing different degrees of loss of national autonomy and sovereignty. It is therefore important not to center the discussion about monetary integration in East Asia too narrowly on monetary unification. Indeed, focusing the discussion too much on monetary unification could be counterproductive, as it might evoke the impression that monetary integration is a predetermined path that inevitably leads to monetary union. The following chapters will consider possible exchange rate options for East Asia and, based on an analysis of the European experiences with monetary integration, develop a strategy for monetary integration for East Asia that takes into consideration the specifics of the region.

III Strategies for Monetary Integration in East Asia

7 Current Monetary Arrangements in East Asia

Before turning to a discussion of monetary and exchange rate options for East Asian countries, it is expedient to briefly review the current state of affairs. Table 7.1 provides an overview of the present policy objectives of the region's monetary authorities, their inflation performance over the past decade, the de jure and de facto exchange rate regimes they operate, as well as the degree of capital account openness of East Asian countries.

Column 2 of table 7.1 lists the official policy objectives of East Asian monetary authorities, as declared in their statutes. The only monetary authorities in the region that have price stability explicitly mentioned as their primary monetary objective are those of Japan, Korea, the Philippines, and Singapore ("noninflationary economic growth"). The authorities of Indonesia, Lao, Malaysia, and Thailand have also the external stability of the currency mentioned as a policy goal, in addition to domestic monetary stability. Of the countries with a monetary stability goal, the authorities of Korea, Indonesia, Thailand, and the Philippines have instituted monetary policy arrangements around an inflation objective. Brunei and Hong Kong, both of which operate currency boards, as well as Myanmar, which officially pegs to the IMF's Special Drawing Rights (SDRs), have declared exchange rate targets. The monetary authorities of Cambodia, China, and Vietnam have no predetermined monetary policy goal set out in their statutes; rather, they shall support the government's general policies.

Columns 5 and 6 list the de jure and de facto exchange rate regimes.[1] According to the IMF classification in column 5, three countries (Brunei, China, Hong Kong) follow a pegged exchange rate regime (including currency board and crawling peg regimes); seven countries (Indonesia, Lao, Malaysia, Myanmar, Singapore, Thailand, Vietnam) operate a managed float, whereas the remaining four (Cambodia, Japan, Korea, Philippines) say they are independently floating. However, figure 7.1, which displays the exchange rate movements vis-à-vis the dollar shows that also those countries who classify themselves as managed floaters maintain close links with the dollar. And even among those that describe themselves as free floaters, Cambodia and the Philippines preserve relative stability vis-à-vis the dollar.

Column 6 gives the estimated weights of the dollar, the yen, and the euro in the hypothetical currency baskets of East Asian countries. Annual estimates for the years 1999 to

Table 7.1
Monetary and exchange rate policy of East Asian monetary authorities

Country	Monetary policy objective statement	Central bank independence	Average annual inflation 1999–2007	IMF classification for exchange rate regimes	Estimated basket weights (%)	Capital account openness
Brunei	Brunei Darussalam operates a Currency Board system and has no Central Bank. The Government under the Banking Acts and Finance Companies Act regulates the banking industry. The Ministry of Finance through the Financial Institutions Division closely regulates all banking activities to ensure a stable and fiscally sound business environment. The Brunei Currency Board is responsible for issuing and managing the currency. The Brunei dollar is at par with the Singapore dollar and are both freely traded in the respective countries. Money changer facilities are also available. The banks continue to support local businessmen in their endeavor and thus help in the development of Brunei Darussalam. (Source: http://brunei.gov.bn/about_brunei/economy.htm; for further information, see: http://www.finance.gov.bn/bcb/bcb_index.htm)	na	0.25	Currency board arrangement. Singapore and Brunei have agreed to mutual exchange at par and without charge	USD: 72.64 Euro: 11.68 Yen: 9.13	2.54*

Cambodia	The National Bank of Cambodia shall have the following functions and duties: (i) to determine monetary policy objectives, in consultation with the Royal Government and consideration of the framework of the economic and financial policy of the Kingdom; (ii) to formulate, implement and monitor monetary and exchange policies aimed at the determined objectives; (iii) to conduct regular economic and monetary analysis, make public the results, and submit proposals and measures to the Royal Government; (iv) to license, delicense, regulate and supervise banks and financial institutions and other relevant establishments such as auditors and liquidators; (v) to oversee payments systems in the Kingdom, and to enhance interbank payments; (vi) to act as the sole issuer of national currency of the Kingdom; (vii) to undertake and perform, in the name of the Kingdom, transactions resulting from the participation of the Kingdom in public international institutions in the banking, credit, and monetary spheres; (viii) to establish the balance of payments; (ix) to participate in the management of external debt and claims; (x) to participate in the formation and supervision of the money and financial markets; (xi) to license, delicense, regulate and supervise all those operating in the securities and foreign exchange markets, the market for precious stones and precious metals; (xii) to set interest rates. (Source: http://www.nbc.org.kh/duties-functions-nbc.asp)	n.a.	3.12	Managed floating with no predetermined path for the exchange rate	USD: 98.36 Euro: 2.39 Yen: 3.83	1.27

Table 7.1
(continued)

Country	Monetary policy objective statement	Central bank independence	Average annual inflation 1999–2007	IMF classification for exchange rate regimes	Estimated basket weights (%)	Capital account openness
China	Under the guidance of the State Council, the People's Republic of China (PBC) formulates and implements monetary policy, prevents and resolves financial risks, and safeguards financial stability. The Law of the People's Republic of China on the People's Bank of China provides that the PBC performs the following major functions: issuing and enforcing relevant orders and regulations; formulating and implementing monetary policy; issuing Renminbi and administering its circulation; regulating inter-bank lending market and inter-bank bond market; administering foreign exchange and regulating inter-bank foreign exchange market; regulating gold market; holding and managing official foreign exchange and gold reserves; managing the State treasury; maintaining normal operation of the payment and settlement system; guiding and organizing the anti-money laundering work of the financial sector and monitoring relevant fund flows; conducting financial statistics, surveys, analysis and forecasts; participating in international financial activities in the capacity of the central bank; performing other functions specified by the State Council. (Source: http://www.pbc.gov.cn/english/renhangjianjie/responsibilities.asp)	0.60	1.34	Crawling peg: daily fluctuations in the renminbi-USD exchange rate are limited to +/−0.3%, against other currencies +/−3%	USD: 98.60 Euro: −0.25 Yen: 0.85	−1.13

Hong Kong	The Hong Kong Monetary Authority (HKMA) is the government authority in Hong Kong responsible for maintaining monetary and banking stability. Its main functions are: (i) keeping the Hong Kong dollar stable; (ii) managing the Exchange Fund–Hong Kong's official reserves–in a sound and effective way; (iii) promoting the safety of Hong Kong's banking system; (iv) developing Hong Kong's financial infrastructure to enable money to flow smoothly, freely and without obstruction. The HKMA's policy objectives are: (i) to maintain currency stability, within the framework of the linked exchange rate system, through sound management of the Exchange Fund, monetary policy operations and other means deemed necessary; (ii) to promote the safety and stability of the banking system through the regulation of banking business and the business of taking deposits, and the supervision of authorised institutions; and (iii) to enhance the efficiency, integrity and development of the financial system, particularly payment and settlement arrangements. (Source: http://www.info.gov.hk/hkma/eng/hkma/index.htm)	n.a.	−1.15	Currency board arrangement (backed by reserve currency, since 1983)	USD: 98.85 Euro: 0.24 Yen: 0.48	2.54
Indonesia	In its capacity as central bank, Bank Indonesia has one single objective of achieving and maintaining stability of the Rupiah value. The stability of the value of the Rupiah comprises two aspects, one is stability of Rupiah value against goods and services and the other is the stability of the exchange rate of the Rupiah against other currencies. The first aspect is as reflected by the rate of inflation and the second aspect is as reflected by the development of Rupiah exchange rate against other currencies. (Source: http://www.bi.go.id/web/en/Tentang+BI/ Fungsi+Bank+Indonesia/Tujuan+dan+Tugas/)	0.84	10.04	Managed floating with no predetermined path for the exchange rate	USD: 86.69 Euro: 2.28 Yen: 10.35	1.19

Table 7.1
(continued)

Country	Monetary policy objective statement	Central bank independence	Average annual inflation 1999–2007	IMF classification for exchange rate regimes	Estimated basket weights (%)	Capital account openness
Japan	The Bank of Japan Act sets the Bank's objectives "to issue banknotes and to carry out currency and monetary control" and "to ensure smooth settlement of funds among banks and other financial institutions, thereby contributing to the maintenance of stability of the financial system." The Act stipulates the Bank's principle of currency and monetary control as follows: "currency and monetary control by the Bank of Japan shall be aimed at achieving price stability, thereby contributing to the sound development of the national economy." (Source: http://www.boj.or.jp/en/type/exp/about/expboj.htm)	0.38	−0.33	Independently floating	USD: 66.07 Euro: -3.50	2.00
Korea	The primary purpose of the Bank, as prescribed by the Bank of Korea Act, is the pursuit of price stability. The Bank sets a price stability target in consultation with the Government and draws up and publishes an operational plan including it for monetary policy. (For further information see: http://www.bok.or.kr/template/ eng/html/index.jsp?tbl=tbl_FM000000066_CA000001027)	0.37	2.73	Independently floating	USD: 81.35 Euro: 1.70 Yen: 15.14	−0.09
Lao	The "Role of the Bank: (i) to be the government's chief of staff, responsible for the macro management of the currency, credit and payment accounts of the banks in the whole country. To be a modern centre of command ensuring rapid and efficient services for the commercial banks and other monetary institutions under its authority; (ii) to promote and stabilize the value of the kip within the country and abroad. To raise the efficiency of payment and credit mechanisms in Lao PDR so as to acquire a high degree of effectiveness and transparency; and (iii) to promote, facilitate and control monetary circulation so that it contributes to the economic growth in line with the national socio-economic development plan. (Source: http://www.bol.gov.la/english/boldecree.html)	n.a.	23.84	Managed floating with no predetermined path for the exchange rate	USD: 95.75 Euro: 4.63 Yen: 2.85	−1.13

Malaysia	Bank Negara Malaysia is the central bank for Malaysia. It was established on 26 January 1959, under the Central Bank of Malaya Ordinance, 1958, with the following objectives: (i) to issue currency and keep reserves safeguarding the value of the currency; (ii) to act as a banker and financial adviser to the Government; (iii) to promote monetary stability and a sound financial structure; (iv) to promote the reliable, efficient and smooth operation of national payment and settlement systems and to ensure that the national payment and settlement systems policy is directed to the advantage of Malaysia; and (v) to influence the credit situation to the advantage of the country. (Source: http://www.bnm.gov.my/index.php?ch=7)	0.47	2.08	Managed floating with no predetermined path for the exchange rate	USD: 98.88 Euro: −0.84 Yen: 1.93	−0.09
Myanmar	The Central Bank is responsible to conserve the available Foreign Exchange reserve of the country with the instructions from Ministry of Finance. Exchange management is administered by the controller of Foreign Exchange of the Exchange Management Dept of the Central Bank of Myanmar and the Exchange Management Board. All external payments are subject to authorization, receipt of all export proceeds and invisible use to be declared to Myanmar Foreign Trade Bank. Calculation is pegged to SDR at Ks 9.5084 equal to 1 SDR. 2% margin applied in respect of spot transactions based on fixed SDR-kyat rate. Buying and selling rates of deutsche mark, French francs, Japanese yen, pound sterling, Swiss franc and United States dollars quoted by Myanmar Foreign Trade Bank are determined on the daily calculate of these currencies against the SDR. (Source: http://www.etrademyanmar.com/bank/)	n.a.	22.31	Managed floating with no predetermined path for the exchange rate, officially pegged to SDR	USD: 99.18 Euro: 4.38 Yen: 1.11	−1.8
Philippines	The Bangko Sentral ng Pilipinas' (BSP) primary objective is to maintain price stability conducive to a balanced and sustainable economic growth. The BSP also aims to promote and preserve monetary stability and the convertibility of the national currency. The BSP provides policy directions in the areas of money, banking and credit. It supervises operations of banks and exercises regulatory powers over non-bank financial institutions with quasi-banking functions. (Source: http://www.bsp.gov.ph/about/functions.asp)	0.74	5.14	Independently floating	USD: 90.16 Euro: 3.65 Yen: 6.75	0.14

Table 7.1
(continued)

Country	Monetary policy objective statement	Central bank independence	Average annual inflation 1999–2007	IMF classification for exchange rate regimes	Estimated basket weights (%)	Capital account openness
Singapore	Monetary Authority of Singapore (MAS) is the central bank of Singapore. Our mission is to promote sustained non-inflationary economic growth, and a sound and progressive financial centre. MAS' functions: (i) to act as the central bank of Singapore, including the conduct of monetary policy, the issuance of currency, the oversight of payment systems and serving as banker to and financial agent of the Government; (ii) to conduct integrated supervision of financial services and financial stability surveillance; (iii) to manage the official foreign reserves of Singapore; and (iv) to develop Singapore as an international financial centre. (Source: http://www.mas.gov.sg/about_us/Introduction_to_MAS.html)	0.17	0.85	Managed floating with no predetermined path for the exchange rate (USD is intervention currency)	USD: 73.16 Euro: 15.66 Yen: 7.42	2.54
Thailand	The Bank of Thailand implements monetary policy as specified by the Monetary Policy Committee as follows: mobilizing the deposits, determining the interest rate for loans to financial institutions, trading foreign exchange and exchanging for the future cash flow, borrowing foreign exchange in order to maintain the monetary stability, borrowing money in order to implement the monetary policy, trading securities as necessary and exchanging for the future cash flow in order to control the money supply in the country's financial system, and borrowing or lending the securities with or without returns. . . . Manage the country's foreign exchange rate under the foreign exchange system and manage assets in the currency reserve according to the Currency Act. (Source: http://www.bot.or.th/English/AboutBOT/index/Pages/RolesAndResponsibilities.aspx)	0.21	2.24	Managed floating with no pre-announced path for the exchange rate	USD: 79.08 Euro: 6.83 Yen: 11.15	–0.09

| Vietnam | The State Bank of Vietnam . . . is a ministerial agency of the Government, which performs the State management of monetary and banking activities and acts as the Central Bank of the Socialist Republic of Vietnam; and performs the State management of public services under the jurisdiction of the State Bank. . . . The State Bank shall perform . . . the following specific tasks and powers: . . . (5) To formulate the national monetary plans for the Government to submit to the National Assembly for approval; to utilize interest rates, exchange rates, reserve requirement, open market operations and other instruments in order to implement the national monetary policies; and to submit to the Government schemes on the development of the banking industry and credit institutions; . . . (8) In regard to foreign exchange management: (a) To manage the current transactions, capital transactions and foreign exchange spending in the Vietnamese territory in accordance with law; (b) To manage the State foreign exchange reserves; and to control international reserves; (c) To determine the exchange rates of Vietnam dong versus foreign currencies; to develop foreign currency market; and to develop foreign exchange mechanism to be submitted to the Prime Minister for approval. . . . (14) In regard to the implementation of the functions of the Central Bank: (a) To make arrangement for minting, preservation and transportation of money; and to carry out the operations of issuance, withdrawal, replacement and destruction of money; (b) To carry out refinancing in order to provide short-term credit and payment instruments for the economy; (c) To regulate the money market; and to carry out the open-market operations; | n.a. | 4.57 | Managed floating with no predetermined path for the exchange rate | USD: 100.68 Euro: 2.58 Yen: −0.21 | −1.13 |

Table 7.1
(continued)

Country	Monetary policy objective statement	Central bank independence	Average annual inflation 1999–2007	IMF classification for exchange rate regimes	Estimated basket weights (%)	Capital account openness
	(d) To organize the payment system via banks; to conduct state management of payment activities; to provide payment services; and to pursue the policy of encouraging and strengthening non-cash payment under the approval of the relevant authorities; (d) To act as an agent for, and provide banking services to the State Treasury; (e) To develop the banking information system and provide banking information services; to manage credit information organizations; and to conduct credit rating for Vietnamese enterprises; (g) To perform other functions of the Central Bank. . . . (17) To promote international cooperation in the monetary and banking field in accordance with law. . . . (Source: http://www.sbv.gov.vn/en/home/gtnhiemvu.jsp)						

Sources: Monetary policy objective statements are from central bank homepages as indicated above; IMF classifications are from IMF (2008c); currency weights were estimated using the methodology introduced by Frankel and Wei (1994) as presented in section 5.2 with daily exchange rates from January 1, 1999, to August 14, 2008, from Datastream (Reuters and Tenfore; estimates for Cambodia, Lao, Myanmar and Vietnam are from October, 7, 2003, to August 14, 2008); the capital account openness index is from Chinn and Ito (2008) whose data are available under http://www.ssc.wisc.edu/~mchinn/research.html; the indexes for central bank independence are from Crowe and Meade (2007; http://www.imf.org/external/pubs/ft/wp/2008/data/wp08119.zip) who followed the methodology of Cukierman, Webb, and Neyapti (1992).

Note: Values for central bank independence are for 2003. The Cukierman, Webb, and Neyapti (1992) index ranges from 0 to 1, with a higher value indicating greater independence. Values for capital account openness are for 2006. The Chinn–Ito (2008) index ranges from –2.54 to 2.54 and takes on higher values the more open the country is to cross-border capital transactions. The value for Brunei is not from Chinn and Ito but simply an estimate by the author based on the Brunei government's statement that "[t]here are currently no exchange controls in Brunei."

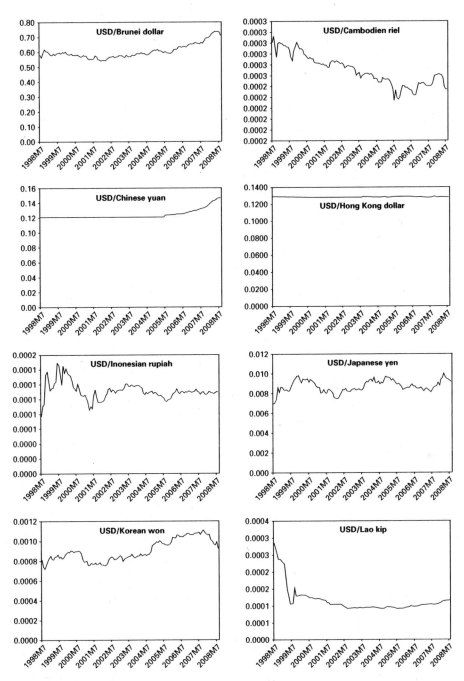

Figure 7.1
Exchange rates of East Asian currencies against the US dollar, July 1998 to October 2008

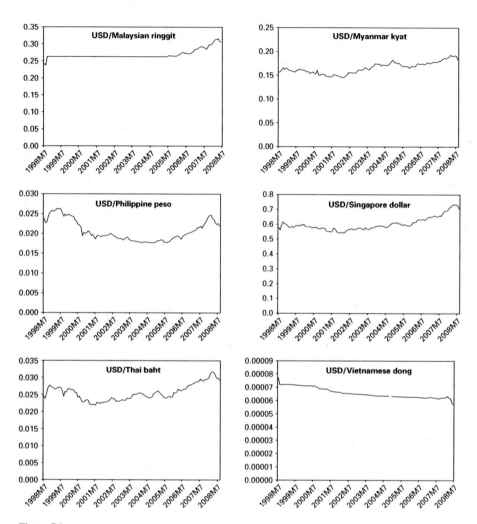

Figure 7.1
(continued)

2008 are presented in annex 9. As discussed earlier (see table 6.5), Cambodia, China, Hong Kong, Malaysia, Myanmar, and Vietnam de facto maintain tight pegs to the USD, with estimated weights of the USD in their hypothetical currency baskets at or close to 100 percent. Lao (96 percent), Indonesia (87 percent), and the Philippines (90 percent) also display a very strong dollar orientation in their exchange regimes. Korea (81 percent) and Thailand (79 percent) have lower but still high dollar weights for the full period 1999 to 2008, implying that they do indeed stabilize their currencies against the dollar, despite their inflation targeting regimes. A look at the annual estimates shows that the weights for the different currencies have shifted over the years, with the dollar losing importance, with weights in 2002, 2005, and 2006 around or below 60 percent for Korea, and below 70 percent for Thailand, respectively. Singapore (and hence Brunei, which has a currency board arrangement with the Singapore dollar) has a dollar weight of 73 percent for the entire period, but in 2004 to 2006 and 2008 was closer to 60 percent. The country that does have a considerably lower dollar weight and that therefore can be described as the only country in the region that does not adhere to the East Asian dollar standard is Japan, with a USD weight of 66 percent for the entire period.

Column 3 presents an index of central bank independence that was constructed by Cukierman, Webb, and Neyapti (1992) from a set of legal characteristics that relate to different aspects of the institution's independence from government and that was recently updated by Crowe and Meade (2007).[2] Of those East Asian countries for which the index is available, the monetary authorities of Indonesia (0.84) and the Philippines (0.74) are ranked the most independent—comparable to the ECB which scores 0.83 out of a possible 1.0. The monetary authorities of China (0.60), Malaysia (0.47), Japan (0.38), and Korea (0.37) have a moderate degree of independence from government, which is somewhat comparable to the score of the Federal Reserve (0.48). Singapore (0.17) and Thailand (0.21) have low levels of central bank independence, something they share with the central banks of Cambodia, Lao, Myanmar, and Vietnam, which were not rated.

Column 4 lists the average inflation performance for the years 1999 to 2007. Except for Lao (24 percent), Myanmar (22 percent), and Indonesia (10 percent), East Asian countries have achieved a remarkably stable monetary environment post-crisis.[3] The relatively low degree of central bank independence for most central banks in the region has thus not resulted in high inflation.

Finally, column 7 presents a measure for capital account openness that was developed by Chinn and Ito (2008). Brunei, Hong Kong, and Singapore have completely liberalized their capital accounts and thus score the maximum on a range from –2.54 to 2.54. Japan's capital account is also very open and was only recently downgraded from 2.54 to 2.0. Cambodia (1.27) and Indonesia (1.19) have relatively open accounts, whereas those of the Philippines (0.14); Korea, Malaysia, and Thailand (–0.09); China, Lao, and Vietnam (–1.13); and Myanmar (–1.8) are fairly closed. Having reviewed the present monetary frameworks of East Asian countries, we now turn to the options for future arrangements.

8   Exchange Rate Options for East Asia

In principle, there are at least three possibilities for future exchange rate policies in East Asia. A first one would be the adoption of freely floating exchange rates throughout the region (or managed floating without cooperation between East Asian countries). This is basically the policy prescribed by the IMF and most North American economists ever since the Asian crisis (e.g., Fischer 2001; Eichengreen 1999). However, given the high degree of economic interdependence within the region, such a unilateral, noncooperative policy would be problematic. As discussed, because East Asia has already reached a very high level of real integration, intraregional exchange rate volatility would have very disruptive effects on the regional economy, and would be aggravated because of poorly developed financial markets and missing hedging opportunities in most of the region. The historical record on floating exchange rates has shown excessive volatility to result and Friedman's (1953) optimism regarding the stabilizing nature of freely floating rates to be unwarranted (see chapter 2). The fact that the East Asian dollar standard recovered after the Asian crisis and still prevails is evidence of East Asian countries' (again, excluding Japan) fear of floating, and it is unlikely that this will change anytime soon. Floating exchange rates, or in general, unilateral exchange rate policies that might go into different directions, would have a highly destabilizing potential for the regional economy. Any monetary and exchange rate policy in East Asia should thus be directed at maintaining relative intraregional exchange rate stability. This leaves two other options.

A second possibility would be a continuation of the current system, which can be referred to as the East Asian dollar standard or the "Bretton Woods II system." In a series of articles McKinnon (2005), McKinnon and Schnabl (2009), as well as Dooley, Folkerts-Landau, and Garber (2003, 2004, 2009a, b) have explained the rationale for East Asian countries to peg their currencies to the US dollar and maintain that this system will continue for years more.[1] The East Asian dollar standard could be managed on an informal or formal basis. That is, East Asian countries could continue just like they do now (basically pegging or soft pegging to the dollar in expectation that the others do the same), or they could develop a more formal Bretton Woods type of arrangement (even though it is unlikely that the United States would give its consent to an official role of the dollar in such a system).[2]

As noted before, pegging to the same external anchor brings about intraregional exchange rate stability, so that an East Asian Bretton Woods II arrangement would be in any case preferable to the free float option.[3] However, there are three serious reservations against a continued reliance on the US dollar. First, maintaining fixed parities with the dollar automatically brings about problems when there are swings in the dollar–euro and dollar–yen rates. As seen before, most East Asian countries (without, of course, Japan) have roughly equal trade shares with the United States, Europe, and Japan, which makes none of these three currencies a good candidate for a single peg. As Mundell (2003b: 2) observes, "[a] major threat to the [current] system arises from gyrations of the major exchange rates. The instability of exchange rates between the large currencies has been enormous." An East Asian Bretton Woods II arrangement, however, would become more sustainable if also Japan were to peg its currency to the dollar, as suggested by McKinnon (2005). This would provide a uniform exchange rate policy for the *whole* region, as well as stability toward the dollar. It would also preclude instability of the dollar–yen rate, the results of which were painfully felt in the Asian crisis. However, a Japanese decision to link the yen to the dollar again is very unlikely.

Second, the risk of maintaining one-sided dollar pegs depends not only on domestic efforts to keep the dollar exchange rate stable[4] but also on the monetary policy in the anchor country and the international value of its currency (Schnabl 2009). The problem is illustrated by the depreciation pressure on the dollar from 2002 until summer 2008, which was in part a result of the historically low US interest rate policy from 2001 up to 2004. To maintain the dollar parity in face of appreciation pressure on their own currencies, East Asian countries were forced to intervene heavily in the foreign exchange market and stockpile dollar reserves. As the scope for sterilization is limited, fast monetary expansion was a result in most East Asian countries, which has led to a fast growth of monetary aggregates, contributed to surging stock and real estate prices (which in some parts of the region had led to financial bubbles that have since burst), and rising inflation.

Rising inflation in the United States and a depreciation of the dollar vis-à-vis other key currencies would erode the international real purchasing power of East Asian countries, especially the commodity exporting countries, as export revenues are mostly earned in dollars while imports are often paid for in euros or other currencies (Schnabl 2009). In addition the international creditor countries in the region face the already mentioned problem of "conflicted virtue," namely balance sheet losses on assets denominated in US dollars as an appreciation of domestic currencies vis-à-vis the dollar reduces the value of these assets in terms of home currencies. The zero interest rate policy and quantitative easing measures that the Fed initiated to end the credit crunch following the collapse of Lehman Brothers in September 2008 has raised serious concerns about the inflationary consequences of this policy. Whether the Fed can withdraw the liquidity quickly enough once the situation changes to prevent the liquidity shortage from turning into a hyperinfla-tion and a free fall of the dollar is of paramount importance for the East Asian creditor countries (Yu 2009). The People's Bank of China, the biggest US creditor, has openly voiced its concerns about the dollar's lasting stability and its unease with a continued reliance on the dollar (Zhou 2009).

Chinn and Frankel (2007) argue that whether or not the dollar will be able to maintain its supremacy as the world's leading international currency depends, besides developments in the euro area, on long-term inflation expectations for the US economy, that is, in the confidence (or lack of it) in US macroeconomic policy.[5] If there is serious doubt about the dollar's future domestic as well as international value, East Asian policy makers will not want to bind their currencies (and indeed economies) to it.[6] While the dollar continues to be the world currency for the time being, the meltdown on Wall Street in September 2008 and the loose US monetary and fiscal policy responses have certainly increased uncertain-ties over the future role of the dollar.[7]

But even if the dollar maintains its strength, the question remains why a region as eco-nomically potent as East Asia should continuously bind itself to an external anchor. As noted earlier, the East Asian dollar standard also constitutes a form of implicit exchange rate coordination. While this system has served the majority of East Asian countries very well (with exception, of course, the period preceding the Asian crisis) we argued earlier that a continued pegging to the dollar involves all the costs, but not all the gains of regional monetary integration.[8] The current dollar pegging might well be feasible for a considerable amount of time as claimed by Dooley et al. (2009a), but as a long-term strategy it is a dead end.

This leads to the third principle choice for exchange rate policies of East Asian coun-tries: to engage in coordinated exchange rate stabilization or at some point even monetary unification. This option could be also described as bloc floating: while intraregional exchange rates would be managed or fixed, the East Asian currencies (or currency) could float freely against outside currencies such as the dollar and the euro. This is the option that will be explored in the remainder of this study.

There are several strategies for exchange rate cooperation aimed at stabilizing intrare-gional exchange rates. Exchange rate coordination based on a dollar anchor was already dismissed (as can be pegging to any other single external currency, such as the euro) as a long-term strategy. This leaves at least five possible future paths for exchange rate coor-dination in East Asia: (1) pegging to a single internal currency such as the yen or yuan, (2) pegging to a currency basket consisting of external currencies, (3) pegging to a cur-rency basket containing regional currencies, (4) creating a regional currency system, and (5) a monetary union with a newly created East Asian currency.

Option 1 is impracticable because East Asia is lacking a regional lead currency that could act as an anchor for regional monetary cooperation in the same way that the German mark fulfilled this function in Europe. Theoretically the yen could perform this function, but Japan's attempts to promote a "yen bloc" throughout the 1980s and 1990s were not successful, and it is unlikely that it would be more successful today. The reasons are only economic in part and also have to do with the fact that the rest of East Asia, and especially China, is not willing to accept a dominant role of Japan and the yen. On the other side, China's financial market impotence and the deficient international status of the yuan preclude an anchor role for the yuan anytime soon. While the Chinese authorities have been pushing for financial market reform, the Chinese financial markets are still in a very early stage of development and far from being able to absorb huge amounts of portfolio investment. Also an East Asian "yuan bloc" is not in sight unless the yuan becomes fully convertible, which will require continued reform of China's foreign exchange market.[9] No other currency in the region, be it the Korean won, the Hong Kong dollar, or the Singapore dollar, will be able to fulfill a regional anchor function.

This leaves options 2 to 5, which will be discussed in greater detail in the following. Before turning to these options for monetary cooperation, however, the next chapter will briefly consider a policy of inflation targeting with free floating, given that this is a policy prescription frequently given by critics of any form of regional monetary cooperation in East Asia. Succinctly, chapter 10 will examine the possibility of a regional monetary system for East Asia, drawing from the European experiences with the EMS. This is followed by an analysis of currency baskets for East Asia in chapter 11. Along the way, we will develop some thoughts also on the long-term possibility of a monetary union in East Asia.

9 Inflation Targeting across the Region

Since quite a number of economists nowadays express a strong preference for floating exchange rates that supposedly allow for monetary policy to be primarily focused on domestic parameters—in contrast to exchange rate targeting in general and regional monetary cooperation in particular—this chapter briefly considers the arguments in favor of floating exchange rates and shows why monetary policies directed at purely domestic targets are problematic for the majority of East Asian countries.

9.1 The Case for Floating Exchange Rates and Inflation Targeting

There are essentially two major arguments in support of floating regimes and against monetary strategies based on an external (i.e., exchange rate) target. First, it is claimed that fixed exchange rate regimes are prone to crisis because they are vulnerable to speculative attacks. This is indeed a serious concern and will be discussed in detail in chapter 10 in the context of a viability of a regional exchange rate system for East Asia.

Second, as discussed before, it is maintained that nonfloating regimes undermine a country's monetary autonomy, at least in a situation without capital account restrictions.[1] In theory, free floaters can use monetary and exchange rate policy to stabilize the domestic economy. The idea is basically that policy makers should keep their own house in order, namely concentrate on achieving domestic price stability and not worry too much about the exchange rate as it will divert attention away from what should be the primary long-run goal of monetary policy: a low and stable inflation rate.

In recent years, inflation targeting has been proposed as a macroeconomic policy framework for emerging market economies by many experts as well as the IMF.[2] In the definition of Bernanke et al. (2001: 4), inflation targeting is "a framework for monetary policy characterized by the public announcement of official quantitative targets (or target ranges) for the inflation rate over one or more time horizons, and by explicit acknowledgement that low, stable inflation is monetary policy's primary long-run goal." According to Svensson (2007), good inflation targeting shares three characteristics: (1) an explicit monetary policy objective in the form of a numerical inflation target, combined with an increasingly explicit concern not only about stability of inflation around the target but also about stability of the real economy;[3] (2) an internal decision process ("forecast targeting") in which projections of the target variables have a prominent role and where the central bank sets the instrument rate in a way that the forecast of the target variables "looks good" relative to the monetary policy objective; and (3) a very high degree of transparency and accountability, with the central bank typically publishing its internal projections and providing detailed motivations of them and of its instrument-rate decisions, in order to both implement the policy effectively and allow detailed external scrutiny of its own performance.

Inflation targeting has received much praise among central bankers and monetary economists (e.g., Bernanke et al. 2001; King 2002; Fracasso, Genberg, and Wyplosz 2003). Several industrialized countries, including Australia, New Zealand, Canada, Israel, Sweden, and the United Kingdom have successfully adopted inflation targeting in one form or another, and the monetary and real stability they have achieved is exceptional from a historical perspective. It is widely agreed that in these countries inflation targeting has led to a more systematic and consistent conduct of monetary policy, a more transparent communication of monetary authorities with the private sector, and a higher degree of accountability.[4] In the view of Bernanke et al. (2001: 308), "inflation targeting is a highly promising strategy for monetary policy . . . that . . . will become the standard approach as more and more central banks and governments come to appreciate its usefulness."

9.2   Problems with Inflation Targeting and Floating in East Asia

Although inflation targeting certainly has its merits, there are also problems with this monetary framework, in particular if applied in developing or emerging economies. As desirable a low and stable inflation rate is, it is typically not the only policy objective these countries have. Other objectives like a balanced current account (or a surplus thereof), stability of the financial sector, and a stable real effective exchange rate might be unattainable if the monetary authority's first and foremost goal is the targeting of a particular level of inflation. Eichengreen (2002) maintains that inflation targeting in emerging markets is difficult because they are typically open, their liabilities are dollarized, and their policy makers lack credibility.

An inflation-targeting strategy is problematic as it essentially requires a floating exchange regime.[5] As Knight (2007) points out, inflation targeting is not consistent with a rigid exchange rate target. In the shorter term there may still be some scope to manage the exchange rate during a transition period—given that the exchange rate management is subordinated to the objective of maintaining low and stable inflation and restricted to managing short-term volatility. But "[i]n the longer term, inflation targeting works best with a fully flexible exchange rate and an open capital account" (Knight 2007: 5).

Park (2006) highlights that models of free floating with inflation targeting (e.g., Svensson 2000) simply assume that current account imbalances are adjusted through changes in the capital account and the exchange rate and thus will not pose any serious policy problems. Take, for instance, an economy with an initially balanced current account hit by an adverse external shock to exports that results in lower income, a fall in the interest rate, a weaker currency, and a deficit of the current account. That economy would face no problems if it is assumed that the (temporary) current account deficit can be financed by borrowing from international capital markets, as long as the currency operates within its debt-servicing capacity. The reality, however, is that most developing and emerging market economies are subject to severe constraints on borrowing from international financial markets. As Park (2006) explains, the inadequacy and poor quality of information, nontransparency of government policies, and political instability often make it difficult to evaluate the long-term debt-servicing capacity of developing and emerging economies.[6] This causes a borrowing constraint, namely developing and emerging economies typically cannot borrow as much as their debt-servicing capacity would allow. Park (2006: 142) thus concludes that "maintaining a current account in balance or its deficit at a manageable level can be an important policy objective, as indeed it is in emerging market economies." An inflation-targeting regime may conflict with such a current account objective.[7]

If developing or emerging economies have access to international capital markets, they often face the restriction that they cannot borrow in their own currency ("original sin," see section 6.4), which creates a currency mismatch problem. As discussed before, a high degree of asset and liability dollarization, as is the case in most East Asian countries, makes countries susceptible to large exchange rate swings vis-à-vis the currency in which the assets and liabilities are denominated. If even a small depreciation of the exchange rate threatens to destabilize balance sheets and output, an inflation- targeting framework would be difficult to sustain (Eichengreen 2002). To avoid balance sheet effects of firms, households, and banks, monetary authorities of economies with high degrees of asset and liability dollarization have a strong rationale to stabilize that particular exchange rate, which is exactly what East Asian monetary authorities did before the Asian crisis, and what they have been doing in less rigid form ever since.

A monetary policy framework that largely disregards exchange rate developments may not only have adverse effects on the stability of the domestic financial sector. Free floating also conflicts with the export-led growth strategy that East Asian countries have followed, and which they are likely to continue to adhere to. Because of the great importance of exports for their growth, East Asian countries have a strong interest in maintaining their export competitiveness, both with respect to their regional neighbors as well as with the rest of the world. Stabilizing the real effective exchange rate might hence be an important policy objective, which is incompatible with inflation targeting as the monetary authority will not be able to freely respond to swings in the nominal exchange rate that could cause misalignment of the real exchange rate.

In addition a high degree of exchange rate volatility may constitute a problem for exporting and importing firms if they have limited or no opportunity to hedge against exchange rate risk, compounding to the fear of floating. Again, this is a factor that complicates a policy of inflation targeting and floating exchange rates for most East Asian countries. Although efforts have been undertaken in the decade since the Asian crisis to overcome institutional deficiencies in foreign exchange markets, these remain shallow, illiquid, and deficient in the market supporting infrastructure in almost all developing and emerging East Asian economies. Currency futures and options are available in some East Asian markets, but markets are typically small and illiquid. For countries with thin capital markets like in developing and emerging East Asia, even moderate capital inflows or outflows can lead to strong movements in the exchange rate, which can be problematic because of the pro-cyclical nature of capital flows.

All this discussion is not to say that it is impossible to successfully implement inflation-targeting regimes in developing and emerging countries. Indeed, there are a couple of emerging economies like Chile and, more recently, Brazil that have established inflation-targeting regimes relatively successfully.[8] Yet the performance of inflation targeters in the developing world at large seems to be less impressive than in industrialized countries (Truman 2003; Fraga, Goldfajn and Minella 2003).[9]

Four East Asian countries—Indonesia, Korea, the Philippines, and Thailand—have introduced some variant of inflation targeting after the Asian crisis. Korea adopted inflation targeting in April 1998, right after the crisis, followed by Indonesia in May 1999, the Philippines in January 2000, and Thailand in May 2000. However, these countries all have pursued rather "flexible" or "soft" versions of inflation targeting with a relatively long target horizon or fairly wide short-run inflation targets, which leave room for monetary policy to pursue also other objectives besides inflation (Rajan 2004).[10] In particular, the central banks of these four countries have all been smoothing exchange rate movements against the dollar. Over the last years, a benign global economic environment with low inflation has enabled monetary policy in these countries to target *both* the level of inflation and the exchange rate. In 2008 inflationary pressure stemming from rising oil and food prices made this inconsistency more evident. It remains to be seen how the underlying conflict between inflation targeting and exchange rate stabilization (or smoothening) can be coped with. Eventually, only one of these two aims can be met. In the case of East Asian countries it is arguable that excessive exchange rate volatility or a strong appreciation of the real effective exchange rate would have too dire consequences for trade as well as for their financial sectors as to completely ignore the exchange rate.

To repeat, East Asia has reached a very high level of real integration where intraregional exchange rate volatility would have very disruptive effects on the regional economy. Floating exchange rates would have a highly destabilizing potential for the region. In theory, according to Friedman (1953), if all East Asian countries were to adopt an inflation-targeting regime that would yield similar inflation rates across the region, intraregional exchange rates should be stable. The experience with floating rates since the demise of the Bretton Woods system, however, has shown that Friedman's prediction of stable exchange rates did not materialize, even if inflation differentials between countries were small.

The fact that the East Asian dollar standard has resurrected after the Asian crisis and still prevails underscores the region's (excluding Japan) fear of floating, and it is unlikely that this will change in the near future.[11] However, as argued before, a continuation of the East Asian dollar standard would be suboptimal. The next two chapters will hence explore two other possible arrangements for regional exchange rate stabilization: the creation of a regional monetary system, and the creation of currency baskets across the region.

10 A Regional Exchange Rate System for East Asia? Lessons of the European Monetary System

One of the lessons that is commonly drawn from the financial crises of the 1990s is that exchange rate pegs should no longer be considered as a sensible option in today's world of highly liberalized and technically sophisticated financial markets. Proponents of the bipolar view argue that "unilateral exchange pegs almost invariably go up in flames at some point" (Rogoff 1998: 169), and recommend that countries should leave the middle ground and instead of following intermediate regimes, choose between either a rigid fix (i.e., monetary unification, full dollarization, or a currency board) or otherwise opt for free floating.[1] With the same line of reasoning, regional exchange rate systems are deemed unsuccessful.

The aim of this chapter is to look once more at the causes of the 1992 to 1993 EMS crisis in order to identify features that contributed to the functioning and eventual collapse of the EMS respectively. In particular, the chapter seeks to analyze the credibility of the system and tries to delineate requirements for successful regional exchange rate regimes in order to examine whether East Asian countries meet these demands and whether the creation of an East Asian Monetary System, as suggested, for example, by Hefeker and Nabor (2005) and Choi (2007), is viable.

The next section dissects the problem of credibility that is inherent to currency pegs. Section 10.2 briefly reviews the literature on the causes of the EMS crisis and assesses the credibility of the EMS using Svensson's (1991) model of target zone credibility. Subsequently, section 10.3 highlights features that enhance the credibility of an EMS-style monetary system to avoid financial crises and investigates whether East Asian countries would be able to meet these requirements in order to create a stable East Asian Monetary System.

10.1 The Problem with Pegs[2]

The sustainability of any exchange rate fix basically depends on its credibility, that is, both foreign and home agents must be convinced that the peg can and will be maintained for a long period of time. This can be demonstrated with a simple monetary model of the exchange rate (see Rogoff 1998):

$$m_t - s_t = \eta\left[i_t - i_t^* \right],$$

$$E_t\left(s_{t+1} - s_t \right) = i_t - i_t^*,$$

where m_t is the log of the domestic money supply, s_t is the log of the exchange rate, i_t is the home nominal interest rate, i_t^* is the foreign nominal interest rate, and $E_t(s_{t+1} - s_t)$ is the expected rate of change of the log of the exchange rate. If the peg is fully credible, then $E_t(s_{t+1} - s_t) = 0$, and thus $i_t = i_t^*$. But if investors, for whatever reasons, believe that the current peg will not be maintained and that the exchange rate will be allowed to depreciate in the near future, then $E_t(s_{t+1} - s_t) > 0$ and $i_t > i_t^*$. This implies that if market participants expect the exchange rate to depreciate in the future, the peg can only be maintained through a rise in domestic interest rates. Theoretically the monetary authorities can infinitely defend the peg by reducing domestic high-powered money supply, by contracting domestic credit, and through intervention in the foreign exchange market (as long as they do not run out of international reserves or credit lines).

Even though an unconditional defense of a fixed exchange rate is always technically feasible, what is relevant for the stability of the exchange rate is not the technical feasibility but rather the perceived costs of defending the parity. A sustained rise in short-term interest rates can have fatal consequences for the domestic banking sector and can sharply dampen aggregate demand and investment activity. As Buiter, Corsetti, and Pesenti (1998: 85) point out, "[i]t is because the authorities care about the side-effects of drastic monetary tightening that speculators can prevail."[3]

There is a threshold point where defending a peg becomes too costly, and investors know this. This is where the speculative element comes in. Models of self-fulfilling currency crises (Obstfeld 1996) have theoretically shown that currency crises can occur even in the absence of balance-of-payments problems (the trigger of a crisis as described in first-generation models following Krugman 1979). Even if "the fundamentals are right," speculative action by market participants could challenge monetary authorities so much that the latter would be forced to adopt austerity policies that would completely choke off the domestic banking sector and economy. Political opposition would become so strong that the costs of keeping the peg become unbearable. Because market participants know that monetary authorities typically have other objectives besides the exchange rate fix, namely the health of the banking system and the economy in general, they know that sustained speculative pressure may eventually cause the monetary authorities to back down and let the currency float, thereby making expectations self-fulfilling. In a situation where the people go to the streets and start banging their saucepans, like in Argentina in 2001, no government will allow its central bank to indefinitely defend a peg.[4] It is the situation of a one-way bet that invites speculators to attack a currency peg: if the peg is abandoned, this results in speculation profits; if it stays, the speculators only bear transaction costs in the form of short-term positions in foreign currency.

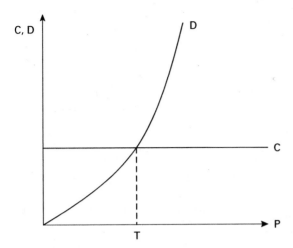

Figure 10.1
Costs of defending a peg

The situation can be described by the following simple graphical model (figure 10.1), which depicts the relationship between the costs D to defend a parity and speculative pressure P. Defense costs (i.e., dampening economic activity through raising interest rates, loss of reserves, debt accumulation) increase exponentially with rising speculative pressure. Defense costs also depend on the size of shocks, output gap, flexibility of labor markets, and so forth. The cost C of giving up the peg is a loss of reputation (political prestige, etc.), which here is assumed to be fixed. As long as $P < T$, the exchange rate peg is credible, since the costs of losing reputation in the case of abandoning the peg exceed the adjustment cost to defend it. If pressure rises beyond the threshold point T where defense costs equal the cost to give up the peg, the peg is no longer credible and thus likely to fail.

Of course, things are not that simple. In reality, the occurrence and timing of a speculative attack are indeterminate, depending on expectations and strategic uncertainty regarding the coordination of the private sector. According to second-generation models of self-fulfilling currency crises, multiple equilibria are possible. If the fundamentals are sufficiently strong, no attack will occur; if the underlying fundamentals become sufficiently weak, uncertainty disappears and there will be only one equilibrium in which an attack will instantly occur. But in the intermediate range an attack is a probabilistic phenomenon. In that respect second-generation models are very similar to first-generation models and predict that countries with weaker fundamentals are more crisis-prone than countries with strong fundamentals. The difference is that seemingly minor random events, or "sunspots" (Obstfeld 1996), could shift the exchange rate peg from a position of credibility into a position where it becomes unsustainable.

In a market in which agents are atomistic (i.e., have small net worth, are credit con-strained, and do not collude), a single speculator would find it impossible to build up enough pressure on her or his own to force the authorities to abandon the peg. A coordi-nated speculative attack is impossible in the absence of common knowledge.[5] No one will attack unless he or she expects a sufficient number of other agents to do the same at the same time. Only if devaluation expectations are sufficiently strong, will joint market action lead to an attack. This will only be the case in a situation where underlying economic or political weaknesses give rise to such expectations.

As Rogoff (1998: 157) points out, "[t]he fine line between a successful currency defense and a costly collapse shows the profound strategic problem facing a monetary authority whose currency is subject to speculative attack." The question then is what defines this fine line; that is to say, what makes an exchange rate fix credible and thus successful? The first and most straightforward answer is: strong fundamentals. If the fundamentals are sufficiently strong, there is no ground for speculation. A second answer refers to the arrangements that determine the credibility of the peg, and this is of particular importance in the case of regional arrangements. To identify the features of successful exchange rate arrangements, the next sections looks at the EMS, widely considered a successful exchange rate arrangement until its *de facto* collapse during the 1992 to 1993 crisis.

10.2   The EMS Crisis and Credibility of the System

Brief Overview of the EMS
The EMS was set up in March 1979[6] with the aim of creating a "zone of monetary stability in Europe."[7] The three main features of the EMS were (1) the exchange rate mechanism (ERM), (2) the ECU, and (3) financing facilities. The ERM consisted of a grid of bilateral exchange rate bands between each of the member currencies. Initially, each currency could fluctuate within a ±2.25 band (±6 percent for the Italian lira as well as for Spain, the United Kingdom, and Portugal, who joined the ERM later) around its assigned bilateral central rate against other members of the ERM. As a reaction to the 1992 to 1993 EMS crisis, the fluctuation margins were widened to ±15 percent in August 1993 (only Germany and the Netherlands agreed to bilaterally maintain their currencies in the ±2.25 percent band). Once two currencies reached the bilateral exchange rate margin, the authorities of both countries were obliged to intervene or take other appropriate measures to keep the exchange rate within the band.

The ECU was a weighted basket currency of the member currencies and served as an "indicator of divergence" within the ERM. Each of the EMS currencies was given a central weight in the ECU basket, reflecting each country's economic importance, its share of intraregional trade and its commitment in the system's financing facilities. To ensure that each member country had the necessary resources to intervene in defense of the bilateral exchange rate parities, extensive financing mechanisms were created. 20 percent of the member countries' gold reserves had to be deposited with the European Monetary Coop-eration Fund in exchange for the equivalent value in ECUs. Furthermore three kinds of credit facilities were created: the very short-term facility, the short-term monetary support, and the medium-term financial assistance. The importance and limits of such support mechanisms will be discussed below.

The institutional setting of the EMS did not change substantially over time. (Annex 10 provides an overview of events in the EMS.) After a turbulent start which was accompa-nied by much skepticism regarding the system's success, and which saw seven realign-ments taking place between the spring of 1979 and the spring of 1983, the EMS entered a period of relative stability. The emphasis was increasingly on nominal and real conver-gence and coordination of monetary policies to support exchange rate stability. The exchange rate as an external anchor proved to have a disciplining effect on national poli-cies, and weak currency members with high-inflation histories successfully used the EMS as a way of importing the Bundesbank's anti-inflationary credibility.[8] The EMS seemed to have reached its aim of being a "zone of monetary stability."

Between 1983 and 1987, only four realignments were required, significantly fewer than in the first four years. After the January 1987 realignment, the EMS entered a new stage with additional participants (reflecting its increasing attractiveness) and without realign-ments for 67 months.[9] Giavazzi and Spaventa (1990) speak of the "new" EMS. The Single European Act of 1986 pushed for liberalizing financial markets, including the removal of capital and exchange controls until July 1990. In the Basle–Nyborg Agreement of Sep-tember 1987, the financing facilities for intervention obligations were substantially aug-mented. Credit facilities were extended for longer periods, and countries were permitted to draw on credits before a currency reached the limits of its EMS band.[10] Interventions were increasingly used to keep exchange rates within the bands to avoid realignments. Interventions to support weak EMS currencies became a regular feature, and the EMS developed into a "quasi-monetary union" (Schiemann 1993: 2). Even at the height of the EMS crisis in September 1992, attempts to avoid a realignment of the peseta, escudo, and punt were made through the introduction of temporary capital controls.[11]

The period of tranquility did not last forever: after five and a half years of nominal exchange rate stability, the EMS tumbled into its most severe crisis in its then fourteen-year history. Following the unexpected rejection of the Maastricht treaty by the Danish voters in a national referendum in June 1992, tensions in the foreign exchange markets increased, and ultimately two of the ten EMS currencies—the Italian lira and the British pound—were driven out of the system, while the Spanish peseta, the Portuguese escudo, and the Irish punt were devalued involuntarily.[12]

Explanations of the Crisis

The debate over the causes of the EMS crisis is centered around two lines of explanations, based on first-generation and second-generation models of currency crises. These two explanations, which stress the importance of fundamentals and the shift in investor sentiments respectively, will be briefly outlined before turning to an assessment of credibility in the ERM.

Fundamentals: First-Generation Models   First-generation models basically view financial crises as a result of weak fundamentals, which antagonize the pursuit of an exchange rate peg. Stable exchange rates must be based on sound economic conditions, that is, authorities must pursue policies consistent with the requirements of a peg. Otherwise, fixed exchange rates will sooner or later become unsustainable and a revaluation will become unavoidable.

Tietmeyer (1998: 47) argues that "unfortunately . . . some European countries did not heed this lesson, especially at the beginning of the nineties. Diverging prices and costs were not sufficiently reduced, whereas exchange rates remained nominally stable. Such differences largely continued to exist, meaning that the currencies of countries with lower inflation rates depreciated in real terms, whereas the currencies of less stability-conscious countries in some cases appreciated sharply in real terms." The persistence (or recurrence) of high inflation and rising labor costs in some EMS countries accordingly eroded their competitiveness and created balance-of-payment problems, eventually leading to crisis.[13]

The Danish referendum, from that perspective, "suddenly made the markets aware of the pent-up problems of divergence" and led to a "rediscovery" of exchange rate risk (Tietmeyer 1998: 49). Seen from this angle, the crisis was purely a result of mounting divergence within the EMS.

Tietmeyer (1998) recalls that the Bundesbank continuously pointed to the growing divergences in the EMS and took a stand against the illusion of de facto monetary union, in which, according to prevailing opinion, no more parity changes would take place. For instance, the Bundesbank wrote in its 1990 annual report:

To the extent that the stability of exchange rates or even the pronounced strength of a number of partner currencies that do not belong to the "hard core" of the EMS can be explained essentially by inflation-induced higher rates of interest, it can be basically justified only if it is consolidated by a domestic economic policy that is durably geared to stability. If success is not achieved in coping with the structural causes of inflation within a reasonable period of time, it will probably become increasingly difficult over the long term to avoid having recourse to exchange rate adjustments. . . . This explains why a currency union that is not based on durable progress in the direction of convergence will remain under the threat of tensions. For this reason, changes in central rates within the EMS should not be excluded in principle during the transitional stages towards bringing about economic and monetary union." (Deutsche Bundesbank 1990: 66)

Eichengreen and Wyplosz (1993) test the Bundesbank view by applying three competitiveness measures (bilateral unit labor costs relative to Germany, multilateral relative unit labor costs adjusted by the business cycle, and the ratio of traded to non-traded goods prices at home) for EMS countries plus Sweden and Finland. They find limited support of real overvaluation. Only for Italy do they find some evidence that wage inflation was inadequately compensated by increases in labor productivity. They conclude that the divergent movement of prices and labor costs played only a limited part in the crisis.

Government deficits and debt to GDP ratios also give no convincing answer to why the Italian, British, Irish, French, Spanish, and Portuguese currencies (to name just the most severely affected ones) came under so much pressure in autumn 2002. As Eichengreen (2001: 13) reasons, "[d]eficits may have been excessive, but this had already been true before the Danish referendum, and there was no change in fiscal stance subsequently."

Speculation and Self-fulfilling Prophecies: Second-Generation Models The second line of explanation emphasizes the role of speculation and self-fulfilling prophecies. Central to this approach is the interpretation of the Danish referendum as a signal to financial markets that concerted speculative pressure could effectuate a demise of currency pegs in the EMS. The weaknesses of fundamentals were known also before the referendum, and the only effective change was in expectations with respect to the realization of a monetary union. Viewed from that angle, the crisis was not the result of fundamental disequilibria, but rather of the market's perception that the Danish referendum had moved the EMS from a position of credibility into a position of vulnerability (Eichengreen 2001).

Markets knew that exchange rate stability within the EMS was not the authorities' sole objective, and that they also cared about the health of the banking system and the economy in general (see section 10.1). With the goal of EMU in sight, the prospective benefits of keeping the exchange rate fixed (one of the Maastricht criteria for qualification for EMU) were high. Monetary authorities were thus expected to be more willing to accept slower growth and higher unemployment as the price for defending the exchange rate and thus their chances of participation in EMU. This calculation changed with the negative outcome of the Danish referendum. When polls for the French referendum also signaled a collapse of the Maastricht treaty, the realization of the EMU suddenly became very uncertain.

In addition slowing economic growth and high unemployment increased the costs of defending the peg. This situation made room for speculators to test the durability of the system. Bad crisis management, namely the inability of policy makers to adequately cope with the situation and convince markets, did the rest of the damage.

Testing EMS Credibility
Having discussed the background of the crisis and the main lines of explanations, this section examines the credibility of the EMS, so as to allow an appraisal of what makes and what undermines the credibility of regional monetary systems.

Most assessments of target zone credibility rely on the analysis of interest rate differentials based on a simple model by Svensson (1991).[14] Assuming the absence of risk premia, the uncovered interest parity condition states that interest rate differentials on similar assets with the same maturity must be equal to the expected rate of currency depreciation over the period so that

$$\left(1+i_t^\tau\right)^{\tau/12} = \left(1+i_t^{*\tau}\right)^{\tau/12}\frac{E\left(S_{t+\tau}\right)}{S_t},\tag{1}$$

where i_t^τ is the domestic-currency interest rate at time t on an asset maturing at $t + \tau$, $i_t^{*\tau}$ is the corresponding rate on an asset denominated in the currency of the foreign currency, S_t denotes the spot exchange rate in period t defined in terms of domestic currency per units of foreign currency, and $E(S_{t+\tau})$ is the expected exchange rate at time $t + \tau$.

If the exchange rate is restricted to a band with lower and upper bounds $\underline{S}$ and $\overline{S}$ so that

$$\underline{S} \le S_t \le \overline{S},\tag{2}$$

this implies that the domestic interest rate i_t^τ will be restricted to a band

$$\underline{i_t^\tau} \le i_t^\tau \le \overline{i_t^\tau}.\tag{3}$$

Rearranging equation (1), the lower and upper bounds of the domestic interest rate band are then given by

$$\underline{i_t^\tau} = \left(1+i_t^{*\tau}\right)\left(\frac{\underline{S}}{S_t}\right)^{12/\tau} - 1 \quad \text{and}\tag{4}$$

$$\overline{i_t^\tau} = \left(1+i_t^{*\tau}\right)\left(\frac{\overline{S}}{S_t}\right)^{12/\tau} - 1.\tag{5}$$

The band can be thus written as

$$\left(1+i_t^{*\tau}\right)\left(\frac{\underline{S}}{S_t}\right)^{12/\tau} - 1 \le i_t^\tau \le \left(1+i_t^{*\tau}\right)\left(\frac{\overline{S}}{S_t}\right)^{12/\tau} - 1.\tag{6}$$

Computing these boundaries for a set of EMS countries vis-à-vis Germany gives the results presented in figures 10.2 though 10.5. The spikes indicate realignments of the respective currencies. As can be seen in figure 10.2, the eurofranc interest rate was outside the credibility boundaries for almost all the time until March 1990 (except for a credibility blip after the April 1986 realignment), implying that the franc–mark parity lacked credibility virtually at all times. Interestingly, it was within the credibility band since March 1990 and remained there (with outliers in December 1990/January 1991 and December 1991) during the months preceding the crisis. Only in August and September 1992, at the height of the crisis, did it again slip outside the credibility boundaries. Except for a brief return to credibility in October 1992, it remained outside the boundaries until February 1993.

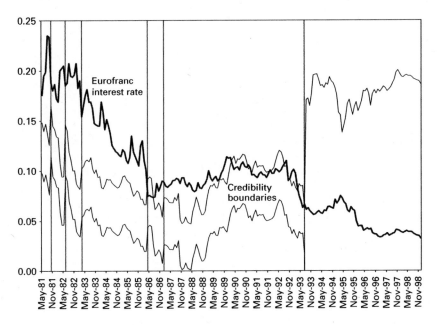

Figure 10.2
Twelve-month eurofranc interest rate and credibility bounds (in percent)

The case of the eurolira interest rate is pretty similar (see figure 10.3): it remained outside the credibility zone for most of the time, and only experienced short periods of credibility (April 1986–April 1997, May 1989–September 1989, February 1990–August 1990, and February 1991–September 1991). From September to November 1991 it remained outside the band until Italy suspended its membership in the ERM on September 17, 1992.

In contrast to the franc and the lira, the Dutch guilder, part of the "hard core" of the EMS, was always credible (figure 10.4). The pound also remained within its credibility boundaries throughout its short ERM membership (figure 10.5). Only in August 1992, just before suspension of its membership, did it lose credibility, suggesting that money markets anticipated a devaluation of the pound.

According to these results the ERM does not appear much less credible (or: not more *noncredible*) in the months before the crisis than before. For France, paradoxically, the crisis occurred when the system, according to this test, was credible for the first time. Also the abrupt swing from credibility to noncredibility in the British case in August 1992 cannot be explained by significant changes in economic conditions. This supports the notion that the crisis was rather caused by a shift of market sentiments and expectations.

Using trend-adjusted measures of realignment expectations, which are also based on interest differentials, Rose and Svensson (1994) similarly find that the credibility of ERM

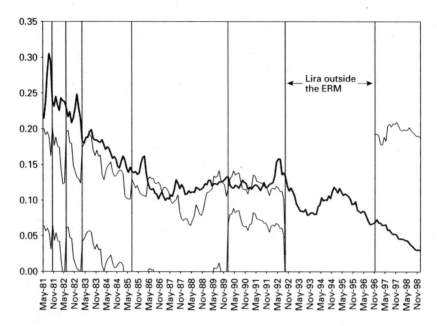

Figure 10.3
Twelve-month eurolira interest rate and credibility bounds (in percent)

Figure 10.4
Twelve-month euroguilder interest rate and credibility bounds (in percent)

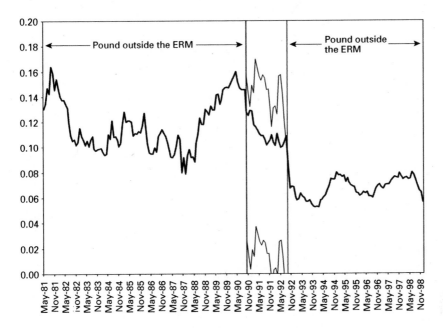

Figure 10.5
Twelve-month europound interest rate and credibility bounds (in percent)

pegs varied significantly over time, mostly for reasons which cannot be well explained by standard macroeconomic variables. While higher inflation differentials vis-à-vis Germany seemed to reduce credibility, realignment expectations generally appeared to be relatively disconnected from macroeconomic phenomena, to "a degree that is disconcerting from an economist's point of view" (Rose and Svensson 1994: 186).[15] Interestingly they find that much credibility seems to be shared by all members of the system, but that this general credibility factor moves significantly over time, frequently reacting to noneconomic events and not moving consistently in response to events that economic theory would consider relevant.[16]

The empirical evidence of credibility within the ERM shows that economic variables only go halfway in explaining the occurrence and timing of the ERM crisis. This suggests that at least part of the success and stability of the EMS/ERM, but also the causes for its eventual collapse, seem to be attributable to its very design and how it was run by policy makers. The following section will therefore discuss the design of the EMS/ERM to identify features that add to or undermine the credibility of such a system in order to understand the challenges for East Asian countries that are contemplating the creation of an East Asian Monetary System.

10.3   Is an EMS-Style System Feasible in Today's East Asia?

What was possible in Europe in the 1980s, a European Monetary System of multilateral exchange rate pegs with periodic realignments, was possible then only because of the widespread maintenance of capital controls. What was possible in Europe in the 1990s, a European Monetary System of somewhat wider bands, was possible only because a credible commitment to move to monetary union in short order anchored expectations. No EMS-style arrangement will be viable elsewhere in today's world of high capital mobility. Eichengreen (1998: 22–23)

This quotation of Eichengreen gives a very clear answer to the question posed above. Yet this section will try to provide a more differentiated answer and identify features that could enhance the viability and credibility of an EMS-style monetary system in today's world. It also analyzes whether East Asian countries can fulfill these conditions. The following aspects will be discussed:

· Cooperation between the monetary authorities of the countries involved

· Independent central banks and robust monetary rules

· Flexibility and the importance of realignments

· Fluctuation margins

· Support funds

· Capital controls

Cooperation between the Monetary Authorities of the Countries Involved
Buiter et al. (1998) highlight the fact that the ERM collapse was a crisis of an exchange rate *system* rather than of a collection of unilateral pegs individually pursued by a number of countries. They see a central cause of the crisis in the lack of coordination of monetary and exchange rate policies within the system. The crisis, they argue, "was in the first instance a conflict among monetary authorities and a failure of the European system as a policy coordination mechanism" (Buiter et al. 1998: 134).

Following German unification, the German government pursued excessive fiscal policy, with the consequence of rising inflation. The Bundesbank responded with a high interest rate policy that increased the strain on the Bundesbank's weak ERM sisters (Bank of England and Banca D'Italia) and ultimately led the lira and sterling to resign from the ERM, because the pursuit of such high interest rate policies would have dampened their economies. In this respect the crisis was the result of the system's inability to find a cooperative response to a shock that increased asymmetries within the system.

A cooperative solution could have been a generalized ERM realignment with a conjunct cut of interest rates by Germany. The Bundesbank's interest rate cut would have given leeway to the United Kingdom and Italy not to raise interest rates further, and a modest realignment involving all ERM currencies would have lowered German import prices, which would have helped to ease inflationary pressures in Germany. Furthermore it would have protected the other ERM countries against the destabilizing shock of exit by the United Kingdom and Italy that left the ERM in troubled waters for another year.

Such a bargain, a German interest rate reduction in return for a general realignment of ERM currencies, had been negotiated at the ministers of finance meeting in Bath on September 5 and 6, 2002, but yielded no positive results (Eichengreen 2001).[17] A cooperative solution was not achieved, and the crisis occurred.

Also Padoa-Schioppa (1994: 14–15) believes:

The difficulties encountered by the ratification process precipitated the crisis of the ERM but were not its underlying cause, which was plainly traceable to what in academic jargon is called a "co-ordination failure." . . . There was the refusal to accept a general realignment and even to call a meeting of the Monetary Committee or of the ministers and central-bank governors when, in September 1992, a general realignment might have calmed the markets. The realignment procedure, once embarked on, did not produce a credible new grid. At various times, and in various ways, through unhelpful declarations that excited markets as well as through policy decisions that caused unnecessary friction, the system was destabilized by its very custodians.

Contradictory statements of the parties involved certainly did not help to convince markets of the continued smooth functioning of the system. This point is illustrated by an episode described by Buiter et al. (1998: 56–57):

In talking to the press [after the Bath summit], the British chancellor [Lamont] referred to a German "commitment" not to raise interest rates. The use of the term "commitment" did not please the president of the Bundesbank. One day later, Schlesinger stated in an interview that the Bundesbank position had in fact not changed since August. According to the reports of the financial press, "Lamont's scuffle with the Bundesbank came at a particular sensitive time and led money managers, corporate treasurers and others in the currency markets to reevaluate their strategies."[18]

Such contradictory statements clearly undermine the credibility of any system and make it more vulnerable to attack. It is the typical situation of a crisis in which tensions arise, and in which the parties involved come under stress. It is therefore important to lay out the rules in order to ensure a cooperative mechanism for finding a solution before a crisis has arrived. Effective policy coordination is an indispensable necessity for gaining and maintaining credibility.

Acknowledging the character of the ERM crisis as a crisis of an exchange rate *system* clearly shifts the focus of attention toward the management of the *system*, which in this case was poor. Speculation was given ground because of the cacophony of the policy makers responsible for defending the system. From this point of view, the characterization of the ERM crisis as a second-generation crisis triggered by self-fulfilling speculation is incomplete.

The major lesson for East Asian countries therefore is that if they consider the creation of a regional exchange rate system similar to the EMS, they need to be sure that cooperation between their monetary authorities can be fully relied upon. Cooperation requires mutual trust and understanding. The institutions involved and their representatives need to develop a common ground from which to tackle conflicting issues in a constructive and solution-oriented way. Moreover national authorities must be willing to subordinate national policy goals, at least at times, for the higher common goal of stability of the common exchange rate system.

This is the most problematic of all issues in East Asia at the present time. Instead of trust, relationships between various countries are tainted with suspiciousness or even distrust. While ASEAN already constitutes a highly heterogeneous group, this is even more the case when dealing with ASEAN+3. The countries involved appear to be driven by differing strategic interests. This is particularly the case for China and Japan, both of which are eager to maintain or increase their sway in the region, and eye each other suspiciously. Squeezed in-between the two giants is Korea, trying to secure its economic position. The ASEAN countries too, fearing competition from China's masses of underemployed labor, try to position themselves as attractive destinations of FDI and seek to maintain their status as thriving export nations.

The close economic relationships that have developed within East Asia should not belie that the diplomatic relations between various countries in the region are strained (see Hamada and Lee 2009). Particularly Japan's relations with its neighbors have experienced serious drawbacks by various instances such as the former Japanese prime minister's visits to the Yasukuni shrine, the Japanese threat to reduce foreign aid to China, and Japan's textbook description of wartime conducts, all of which have generated skepticism of the future course of Japan's diplomatic policy. Conversely, China's alleged operation of submarines within Japan's territorial sea, its opposition to Japan's permanent membership in the UN Security Council, and the benign treatment of students' protest against the Japanese embassy in Beijing have courted resentment in Japan. Furthermore China and Japan still continue their territorial dispute over the Senkaku/Diaoyutai islands north of Taiwan and south of the Ryukyu islands. In the South China Sea with its potentially large natural resources, there are competing territorial claims over various areas such as the Paracel Islands, the Macclesfield Bank, or the Spratly Islands, involving China, Taiwan, Brunei, Malaysia, the Philippines, and Vietnam. It is not hard to envisage other maritime resource disputes developing in the face of East Asia's energy crunch. And, of course, Taiwan and North Korea remain unresolved issues that cast clouds on the regional security. While there is no imminent risk of confrontation, there is always a danger of (unintended) diplomatic or even military escalation that could spill over and distort economic policy cooperation.[19]

While from an economic perspective ASEAN+3 might seem a natural candidate for regional monetary integration (and has indeed taken a few, albeit modest, steps in that direction as discussed before), it is hard to see how the mutual trust and understanding necessary for the creation and maintenance of a regional monetary system could be developed in the short run. Any talk about such a system therefore would need to address the medium term. Countries that struggle even to agree on relatively easy policy issues and that have problems to accomplish already agreed arrangements (think of the ASEAN's struggle to come to terms with AFTA) will find it even more difficult to cooperate in such a sensitive area as exchange rate policy.[20] Chapter 12 will return to this issue and look into the political economy of monetary integration in East Asia to evaluate the prospects of closer cooperation.

Independent Central Banks and Robust Monetary Rules

The long-running debate over rules versus discretion in the conduct of monetary policy has been decided in favor of a rules-based approach, with all major central banks following more or less well-defined monetary rules.[21] Irrespective of an external exchange rate goal, (de facto) central bank independence and a clear monetary objective function are state of the art of modern central banking. Establishing an independent central bank with strong inflation aversion is an important way to keep down inflationary expectations. While beneficial for any economy, this is particularly important for countries with an external anchor, because central bank independence provides credibility to the peg.

The credibility of a peg requires that any exchange rate change, which is in effect a break of the central bank's promise to keep the parity fixed, should only occur in response to extreme disturbances. Devaluations resulting from self-fulfilling speculative attacks must be ruled out. Hence it is not sufficient to preclude balance-of-payment crises through the sound conduct of current and past policies—anticipated future policies matter as well. To preclude speculative attacks, robust monetary policy rules are needed. A robust monetary policy rule is one that obviates changes in monetary and exchange rate policies that are not grounded on fundamentals (see Eichengreen and Wyplosz 1993).

De jure central bank independence is achieved relatively easily; all it needs is a government decree or law. But what really matters is de facto independence from the government. For many (South) East Asian countries, de facto central bank independence still seems a long way off (see table 7.1). Nevertheless, this should not constitute an impediment to forming a regional monetary system. Indeed, the creation of such a system could be used as a strategy to implement strong, independent central banks—similar to the way several European countries used the EMS as a strategy of "tying one's hands" (Giavazzi and Pagano 1988) in order to overcome their inflationary past.

For effective monetary and exchange rate coordination—not only within a regional monetary system—the region will also need a pool of well-trained central bankers who have the technical expertise, as well as the standing to rigorously defend the exchange rate system. Not all East Asian countries, especially the poorer ones, have been able to build up this expertise. Any effort in monetary integration should therefore be accompanied by schemes or institutions aimed at developing the capacities and skills of regional central banks and bankers. Good examples that could be built upon are the South East Asian Central Banks (SEACEN) Research and Training Centre, which was established in 1982 by eight regional central banks and which has now eleven members,[22] and the Center for

Monetary Cooperation in Asia (CeMCoA) which was established by the Bank of Japan in November 2005. Besides technical schooling, such regional training and research centers also provide a forum for exchange of ideas as well as for personal contact between central bankers of different countries—which also helps develop mutual trust and understanding.

Flexibility and the Importance of Realignments

A further, crucial lesson of the ERM crisis is the necessity to incorporate a certain degree of flexibility into the system. Of particular importance is the capacity to undertake relative price adjustments, that is, the possibility of realignments.

Pegged exchange rate systems face difficulties when significant changes are required in the relative prices of domestic and foreign goods, of traded and nontraded goods, and of labor and commodities (Eichengreen and Wyplosz 1993). If the nominal exchange rate is fixed, adjustments have to occur through changes in wages and prices (or the movement of labor). If wages and prices are rigid (at least downward), transitional output losses may result. A revaluation can bring about the needed price adjustments at once and with fewer frictions, because money illusion will make changes in the relative prices less obvious and painful. If labor markets are not sufficiently flexible and prices are sticky, pegged exchange rate systems can only be sustained if nominal exchange rate adjustments, namely revaluations, are allowed for in the case of exceptional shocks.

As Eichengreen (1996) notes, when the EMS was created in 1979, Germany had a third of a century of experience with fixed exchange rate regimes, from the Bretton Woods system and the snake, suggesting that deficit countries would hesitate to adjust. Germany hence acknowledged the necessity of allowing for realignments within the system.

"Adjustments of central rates"[23] was indeed an explicit and frequently used instrument of the EMS until the January 1987 realignment. Jochimsen (1993: 187) observes that these rules "were forgotten during the second half of the 1980s, [when] one mistook the goal of keeping exchange rates stable as already constituting the result of actually holding them stable, without regard to the corresponding exigencies of adjusting domestic fiscal policies and collective bargaining accordingly." Similarly Tietmeyer (1998: 52) suggests that "[m]aintaining unrealistic central rates for too long proved to be the Achilles' heel of the EMS. Thinking in terms of political prestige and national honor played a thoroughly significant role in this."

The literature on exit strategies highlights that realignments can be undertaken without undermining the credibility of the system if they are undertaken only in exceptional circumstances and if the cause can be directly observed or otherwise independently verified.[24] Furthermore moral hazard from the authorities' side must be excluded. The German unification was such a shock, and the Bundesbank indeed argued that it was possible to realign in response to this shock without undermining the credibility of the EMS (Eichengreen and Wyplosz 1993). But conflicting views and national pride hindered a general realignment. This failure to achieve a general realignment led to the crisis and illustrates that it is "absolutely essential to de-politicize the fixing of exchange rates" (Jochimsen 1993: 187). In addition it exemplifies the desirability of generating a discussion on parity changes in good times (Tietmeyer 1998).

Fluctuation Margins

An aspect also related to the flexibility of exchange rate systems is the matter of fluctuation margins. Krugman (1991) shows that a target zone can lead to a "honeymoon" effect: assuming that exchange rates are at least partly determined by the formation of expectations, he demonstrates that the very existence of a target zone can have a stabilizing effect on the exchange rate. When the exchange rate approaches the upper or lower band, market participants will expect the central bank to intervene, so that the exchange rate will move away from the band. These expectations will then suffice to drive the exchange rate away from the band, without need for intervention by the central bank. This honeymoon effect, however, depends on the credibility of the target zone. If it lacks credibility, the market participants will at best take a wait-and-see approach, or otherwise launch an attack, in expectation of an overshooting of the exchange rate, in case that the peg is abandoned. The system could thus cause the crisis it was created to prevent.

In this context, the width of the band is of great importance. Narrow bands allow for risk-free one-way bets, creating incentives for speculative attacks. Wider bands, in contrast, make currency speculations more risk-prone, since they allow for a reversal of exchange rate movements. While wider bands also reduce the stabilizing effects of target zones, they sharpen the awareness of the stability policy response to be borne by the countries themselves, by making convergence deficits in the member countries manifest more easily (Tietmeyer 1998). To reduce the susceptibility of a target zone system, it is hence better to choose wide exchange rate bands than bands that are too narrow.[25]

The built-in flexibility and the width of fluctuation margins relate to the very design of the system, and there is in principle no reason to believe that East Asian countries are not capable of designing a robust monetary system. There is a danger, however, that conflicting interests of the participating countries would lead to murky compromises and result in deficiencies in the design of the system. The rules of the system must be put straight, without room for interpretation. As clearly shown during the EMS crisis, any cracks in the design will lead to a bursting of the system if put under stress.

Support Funds

As discussed in section 10.1, an austere interest rate policy can be used to defend a peg only to a limited extent. The only other means to defend a peg, besides capital controls, is the use of foreign reserves for intervention in the foreign exchange markets. Building up large amounts of foreign reserves can certainly help to increase the credibility of a peg. Having a "war chest" emphasizes a country's ability to forcefully fend off speculative attacks. Holding reserves, however, is costly. Furthermore even a country with a vast amount of reserves can reach its limits in the case of large speculative movements. Fortunately, in the case of a common exchange rate system, common support mechanisms are an additional way of ensuring markets that the peg can and will be defended.

For this reason, and also as a lesson from the experiences with the snake, the French secured a provision in the EMS Act of Foundation, authorizing weak governments to draw unlimited support from their strong-currency partners.[26] In the conviction of Giscard d'Estaing, the French president, a European exchange rate system would only function if the burden was shared equally between the strong and weak currencies (Bernholz 1999).[27]

The EMS was hence established with a very short-term financing facility, providing support that was "unlimited in amount." There is, however, a problem with central banks' mutual assistance. Supporting the weak currency has monetary policy effects on the country with a strong currency. Regardless of whether the central bank intervenes or makes its own currency available to other central banks for intervention purposes, bank liquidity is expanded, and controlling monetary expansion is therefore made more difficult.

It was exactly this reasoning that led the Bundesbank—with reference to the Emminger letter[28]—to curtail interventions during the EMS crisis. After heavy intervention in support of the attacked EMS currencies, it sensed its internal monetary stability under threat. By early September 1992, M3, the Bundesbank's target money aggregate, was rising at an annual rate of almost 10 percent, far above its target of 3.5 to 5.5 percent (Eichengreen and Wyplosz 1993: 110). It is therefore important to understand that while support mechanisms can be an important tool to increase the credibility of a regional exchange rate system, they cannot substitute for economic policies that are consistent with the external exchange rate objective.

Given the amount of official reserves East Asian countries have accumulated since the Asian crisis (see annex 11), it would be easy to create funds to complement a regional exchange rate system. Foreign exchange reserves of East Asian central banks have reached more than USD 3.5 trillion by mid-2008. China's reserves alone exceeded USD 1.9 trillion by September 2008. The reserves of the euro area, in contrast, amount to just USD 226 billion.

The problem, again, lies rather on the political side. No country wants to risk losing money because of the hazardous behavior of its partners, so granting a partner access to one's own reserves involves a great deal of trust that the partner will refrain from cheating. Nevertheless, the region's efforts over recent years to create a network of bilateral lending arrangements under the CMI, and the plans to set up a common reserve pool under the multilateralized CMI (see chapter 3), have demonstrated its capability to constructively cooperate.

Capital Controls

A final point to be raised is the matter of capital controls. Capital controls, for obvious reasons, make things much easier for policy makers who have to guard a pegged exchange rate regime. There has been growing support for the view that EMS-like systems cannot survive in the absence of capital controls. Capital controls, it is argued, played an important role in the functioning of the EMS:

In the 10 years between its creation in 1979 and 1990, when capital accounts were freed, there were 12 realignments, most of them involving several currencies. With few exceptions, these realignments came in the wake of speculative attacks, yet the system survived. The first attack that occurred after capital liberalization was lethal. (Wyplosz 2004: 262)

It is out of question that the handling of the 1992 to 1993 crisis would have been facilitated and that authorities would have had more leeway to come up with solutions if there had still been capital controls. But one can also argue that once the avalanche had been set off, capital controls would not have changed much. As mentioned before, Ireland, Portugal, and Spain actually re-introduced capital controls during the crisis, but this did not prevent the punt, the escudo, and the peseta from remaining under speculative pressure and from facing devaluation in February (punt) and May (peseta and escudo). Also, as argued earlier, a better and more cooperative crisis management could have avoided the crisis, or at least limited its damages. And finally, speculative attacks do not occur entirely out of the blue. If the system is credible, it is also sustainable.

At present, most East Asian countries still retain some form of capital controls (see table 7.1), which would facilitate the establishment of a regional exchange rate system.[29] As a recent IMF survey on financial globalization by Kose et al. (2009) asserts, the empirical evidence that capital controls hamper growth is far from conclusive. Especially for the poorer East Asian countries with less developed financial systems it would therefore seem reasonable to continue using (partial) capital controls as an instrument to facilitate exchange rate stabilization. Capital controls, however, would not be able to make up for a flawed design of the system or compensate for a lack of cooperation between the central banks and other authorities involved.

Conclusion

Just as the EMS was built upon the lessons from the Bretton Woods system and its unsuccessful immediate predecessor, the snake, the experiences with the EMS are worth being borne in mind when considering the desirability and feasibility of similar regional arrangements in today's East Asia.

This chapter has argued that, in contrast to the popular bipolar view on exchange rate choices, intermediate regimes in general and regional exchange rate systems à la EMS in particular should not generally be ruled out even in today's world of highly mobile capital. It has highlighted that the EMS crisis was the crisis of an exchange rate *system*, and not simply the collapse of a collection of unilateral pegs triggered by self-fulfilling speculation. It has tried to show that there exist distinct features that add to the credibility of regional exchange rate systems, and argues that a system that is built upon the lessons of the EMS and which is managed very carefully and cooperatively could be both credible and sustainable even in the twenty-first century. A regional monetary system should hence not be ruled out per se when discussing monetary options for East Asian countries.

Of course, the requirements for successful pegs in general and regional exchange rate systems in particular are very high. A very strong commitment is required from all parties willing to engage in a regional exchange rate system, and the willingness to subordinate internal economic objectives under the objective of exchange rate stability is essential. A crucial precondition for any regional monetary arrangement to be successful is a far-reaching consensus on policy preferences. This is the crux of the matter for East Asia. For the time being, it is hard to see how East Asian countries could develop enough mutual trust and understanding to effectively run a regional exchange rate system and to rule out coordination failure. Creating a regional exchange rate system in East Asia under present conditions would most certainly end in a crisis.

From this assessment of the viability of a regional monetary system it also follows that any talk of monetary *union* is premature at this time. Because the exit costs of a common monetary union are very high, a quick rush into monetary unification is not advisable if the potential partner countries have not had the chance to develop mutual trust as well as an understanding of each other's policy preferences.

Instead of directly creating an exchange rate system (let alone monetary union), East Asian countries should follow a gradual approach to monetary integration (assuming that monetary integration as such is politically desired). This would allow East Asian countries to get to know their potential partners and their policy preferences more closely before the going gets tough. A stepwise approach to monetary integration could first involve the regional (coordinated) adoption of currency baskets, flanked by a strengthening of financing facilities under the CMI and a further enhancement of regional surveillance mechanisms. Over time, the composition of the baskets could be harmonized among East Asian countries, and exchange rate bands could be introduced, developing a more formal regional exchange rate mechanism. Yet another option would be the introduction of a parallel basket currency, which could be used as invoicing currency for trade as well as for the denomination of bonds in a regional bond market. Such a gradual strategy to monetary integration based on currency baskets will be discussed in detail in the following chapter.

11 Basket Strategies for East Asia

As just discussed, directly opting for a full-fledged regional exchange rate system would be premature for East Asia, as the political preconditions are not yet fulfilled for such a demanding endeavor. On the other hand, it would be desirable to escape the "dollar trap." To reach the two goals of securing intraregional exchange rate stability and reducing dependency on the US dollar, a good strategy would be the adoption of currency baskets regionwide.

In general, currency baskets provide an alternative to either freely floating exchange rates or a peg to a single currency. If adopted on a regionwide scale, the stabilizing effect would be somewhat similar to that of a regional exchange rate system, without demanding as much political commitment as the latter. In particular, John Williamson (1999, 2001, 2005, 2009) has advocated the currency basket option for East Asia in a series of articles.[1] In principle, there are two different kinds of currency baskets. The first type of basket, which Williamson promotes, contains international currencies such as the US dollar, the euro, and the yen. The second type of basket consists of regional (i.e., East Asian) currencies. Such a basket would be comparable to the ECU and could be used by East Asian currencies to organize a joint float of their currencies.

Both types of baskets have received considerable attention in East Asia recently. On July 21, 2005, the People's Bank of China officially announced that it had abandoned the eleven-year-old peg to the dollar and instead linked the yuan to an undisclosed basket of currencies.[2] In retrospect, this announcement might be viewed as the starting signal for a fundamental reconsideration of East Asian exchange rate relations. Following the Chinese announcement to drop its currency peg against the dollar, Malaysia instantaneously announced the end of its dollar peg and the ringgit's float against a trade-weighted basket of foreign currencies. While the new Malaysian arrangements differ in detail (the Malaysian central bank stated that it would rely on central bank intervention rather than on a currency trading band to maintain the stability of its managed float), the move epitomizes the role China has attained.[3] China's "new" currency system is also close to that of Singapore, which has used a secret policy band to guide its managed float of the Singapore dollar against a foreign currency basket since the early 1980s. As the Malaysian move demonstrates, it is not inconceivable that other East Asian countries may follow over time and adopt similar currency baskets. The realization of Williamson's proposal for a common basket peg of East Asian countries does not seem unlikely anymore.[4]

The second kind of basket has also gained attention among policy makers. As mentioned earlier, in December 2005 the ADB announced its plan for creating a regional currency basket index, consisting of regional currencies (see Kawai 2009). East Asian governments have signaled considerable interest in such a policy option. In the Joint Message of the 6th Trilateral Finance Ministers' Meeting, which was held on the sidelines of the Annual Meeting of the ADB on May 4, 2006, in Hyderabad, the finance ministers of China, Japan, and Korea stated: "We noted the importance of sharing a long-term vision for financial integration in the region; we agreed on further study of related issues, including the usefulness of regional currency units, through the ASEAN+3 Finance Ministers' Process" (Kawai 2009: 318). In Hyderabad the ASEAN+3 finance ministers also agreed on a joint research project, "[t]oward greater financial stability in the Asian region: Exploring steps to create regional monetary units" (ASEAN+3 2006).[5]

These developments show that regionwide currency baskets have become a realistic policy option for East Asia. The rest of the chapter will hence analyze the suitability of the two types of currency baskets for East Asia. A discussion of the rationale for currency baskets in section 11.1 is followed by a presentation of different hypothetical currency baskets in section 11.2 and their comparison with the actual exchange rate policies conducted. Section 11.3 then sketches a scenario of regional monetary cooperation based on basket strategies.

11.1   Rationale for Currency Baskets

In general, the purpose of a currency basket regime is to stabilize a country's effective exchange rate rather than the bilateral rate to a single currency. The nominal effective exchange rate (NEER) is the weighted average of a country's currency relative to an index or basket of other currencies. The weights are usually chosen to reflect the pattern of trade.[6]

A basket peg with weights that reflect a country's trade structure is especially interesting for countries whose trade is diversified geographically (i.e., for countries whose trade is not heavily concentrated on one particular country or currency area). This is because such a basket regime would help reduce volatility in the NEER compared to a single currency peg, in the case of exchange rate variations among the main trading partner's currencies. Such fluctuations are usually exogenous to a country's own policies and can seriously alter its effective exchange rate and disrupt its macroeconomic balance (Williamson 2009). This is exactly what East Asian countries that were pegged to the dollar experienced in the run-up to the Asian crisis. Fluctuations between the dollar and other major currencies, especially the yen, proved highly destabilizing, eventually contributing to crisis.

Currency baskets hence have particular appeal if the geographic distribution of trade points to no single currency area as an optimal anchor, or if the likely currency is not a good choice as an anchor (e.g., because of macroeconomic or financial instability of that currency area).[7] This is the case for virtually all East Asian countries. It was noted earlier that trade with the United States and the European Union each account for an average of about 11 percent for ASEAN+4 countries. This implies that, from a trade perspective, neither the dollar nor the euro is an optimal choice as an anchor currency for East Asian countries. Furthermore trade with Japan on average accounts for 10 percent, which does not make the yen any more optimal a choice than the dollar or the euro. Finally, trade with China makes up about 15 percent of trade for East Asian countries, only slightly more than trade with the United States, Europe, or Japan. As mentioned before, the Chinese currency is also inapt to fulfill the role of a regional currency anchor because of its inconvertibility and the weakness and shallowness of the Chinese financial markets. Thus, from the point of view of the literature on the optimum peg, no single currency would be a perfect anchor for East Asian countries. Currency baskets would thus be a superior alternative.

There are other reasons why currency baskets have appeal for East Asia. As mentioned, the enormous US "twin deficit" and the monetary policy easing after the 2008 credit crunch have caused increasing doubts about the future international value of the dollar (see chapter 8). The accumulation of huge amounts of dollar reserves to stem the appreciation of domestic currencies has led to a situation where a dollar depreciation would cause significant balance sheet losses, which leads East Asian central banks to further intervene in the market and thus increases reserves even more. To exit this "conflicted virtue circle" abruptly would risk a massive dollar slump or even a full-blown crisis, something all parties wish to avoid.[8] Currency baskets would provide an elegant way out of the dollar dependency: dollar weights could be gradually reduced while the weights of other currencies could be increased. The result would be a diversification of risk without unsettling currency markets.

Moreover currency baskets are an interesting option because they can also be used as a regional strategy for exchange rate cooperation. As discussed, intraregional trade is of utmost importance for East Asia, with a weighted average of intra-ASEAN+4 trade of 47 percent, almost as high as the 49 percent of the euro area (see section 5.3). The regional adoption of broadly similar currency baskets would contribute to intraregional exchange rate stability in the same way the common dollar peg does. Furthermore, as Williamson (2001) points out, a common basket peg would offer the important advantage of ensuring that the exchange rates of East Asian countries in relation to each other are not destabilized by shocks to the dollar/yen/euro rates. This would prevent inadvertent competitive devaluation or the suspicion of instrumented competitive devaluation that could result from different pegging policies.

Because trade structures are broadly similar for most East Asian countries, individual country baskets to stabilize NEER would in most cases include the same currencies with relatively similar weights. In other words, even if all countries in the region adopted baskets tailored to their individual trade structures, the result would be a relatively homogenous exchange rate policy throughout the region, which in effect would result in relative exchange rate stability between East Asian currencies (e.g., Williamson 2001, 2009). Williamson (2001: 104) hence concludes that a regional basket peg would offer "the advantages of the dollar peg without its disadvantages."

A currency basket could thus be a substitute for a peg to an international or regional anchor currency. In addition to supporting regional exchange rate stability, it could provide more flexibility than a full-fledged regional exchange rate system.[9] Another advantage of a currency basket over a regional currency system is that it would require less political commitment, as the former could be maintained by each country individually (although some coordination would be beneficial so as to avoid unintended beggar-thy-neighbor policies). Moreover a virtual basket currency—especially one consisting of regional currencies—could be used as a "parallel currency" for regional trade invoicing and indexing of regional bond issues. This could contribute to further regional integration.

11.2   Constructing Currency Baskets

To illustrate and analyze the effects of currency baskets, three different baskets for East Asian countries are constructed. First, we construct individual country baskets (ICBs), namely currency baskets that are tailored to the trade structure of each individual country. The ICBs consist of the currencies of all trade partners to which at least 3 percent of the country's total exports go, or from where at least 3 percent of the country's total imports come.

The second basket, which we call the DEY, contains the currencies of the G-3 economies, namely the US dollar, the euro, and the Japanese yen. The reason for this choice is simple. First, these are the three most important international currencies. Second, the United States, Europe, and Japan are each important trading partners and investors in East Asia. Third, each of these currency areas has deep and liquid financial markets to invest in. Finally, baskets consisting of the dollar, the euro, and the yen are frequently referred to in the East Asian context, most prominently by John Williamson.

The third basket consists of internal (regional) currencies such as the yen, the Chinese yuan, the Korean won, the Singapore dollar, the Thai baht, and the Malaysian ringgit. In allusion to the European ECU we will call this basket currency the Asian Currency Unit or ACU. For this regional currency basket we choose all ASEAN+4 currencies, because ASEAN+4 (or ASEAN+3) has so far proved to be the most important regional forum concerned with matters of financial and monetary integration. All ASEAN+4 countries have a high degree of regional economic integration in common and have repeatedly expressed concern for regional exchange rate stability. With the CMI, they have also started the first initiative so far which is related to regional monetary cooperation.

The methodology for calculating the three baskets is the same. After a decision has been made which currencies are to be included, one has to decide upon the weights devoted to each currency in the basket and whether to use fixed currency shares or fixed currency units in constructing the baskets. Choosing a fixed number of units of each component currency has the advantage that changes to the basket—such as adding a new currency to the basket, eliminating a currency from the basket, or changing relative basket weights— are easier to administer (Kawai 2009). While the quantity of each constituent currency would remain fixed, its contribution to the value of the basket currency would change with its exchange rate.[10]

There are many possibilities for choosing the weights, such as using total trade shares, export or import trade shares, economic weight, and financial transactions. For the weights of the ICBs and the DEY we simply use total trade shares to reflect the importance of each of the included currency areas for East Asian countries. Also trade shares (as noted before) are responsible for determining the effective exchange rate.[11] Hence, for the ICBs, we take total trade shares of all trade partners to which at least 3 percent of the country's total exports go, or from where at least 3 percent of the country's total imports come, and scale these up to make the sum 100 percent (see annex 12). Accordingly, for the DEY, we take total trade shares of all ASEAN countries, China, Hong Kong, and Korea with the United States, the euro area, and Japan and scale these up to make their sum 100 percent, which yields DEY weights of 36.89 percent for the US dollar, 31.02 percent for the euro, and 32.09 percent for the yen.[12]

In choosing the weights for the ACU, we proceed analogue to the construction of the ECU: each ASEAN+4 currency is given a central weight in the ACU basket, reflecting the country's economic importance in the region (measured by regional GDP share), its share in intraregional trade, and its share in the CMI.[13] The composition of the ACU weights is listed in table 11.1. To avoid dominance of the yen in the ACU basket, we actually take PPP adjusted GDP for measuring regional economic weight.[14] Also, to slightly increase the weights of those countries that did not participate in the CMI so far, we assume a minimum of USD 1 billion of bilateral swaps. Choosing PPP adjusted GDP is certainly somewhat arbitrary, but the construction of the ACU here is more about the principle and the general results are not affected by the choice of these particular measures.

The amounts of each of the participating currencies in the basket are defined in the first period as

$$\{q_1, q_2, \ldots, q_n\} = 1 \text{ ICB} = 1 \text{ DEY} = 1 \text{ ACU}$$

where q_1, q_2, . . ., q_n are the quantities of each currency in the basket. These quantities q_k are calculated by multiplying the central basket weights with the bilateral exchange

Table 11.1
Construction of ACU weights

	(Trade + GDP + CMI shares)/3	Regional trade share	Regional GDP share (PPP terms)	CMI share[a]
Brunei	0.50	0.24	0.13	1.12
Cambodia	0.48	0.16	0.16	1.12
China	30.00	25.79	45.66	18.54
Hong Kong	6.17	15.49	1.90	1.12
Indonesia	4.16	4.79	5.44	2.25
Japan	29.21	17.08	27.86	42.70
Korea	12.92	10.74	7.80	20.22
Lao	0.43	0.08	0.08	1.12
Malaysia	3.23	5.68	2.33	1.69
Myanmar	0.59	0.25	0.39	1.12
Philippines	2.31	2.75	1.95	2.25
Singapore	4.25	10.14	1.48	1.12
Thailand	4.27	4.94	3.37	4.49
Vietnam	1.48	1.87	1.44	1.12
Sum	100.00	100.00	100.00	100.00

Source: Own calculations.
a. A minimum of USD 1 billion of bilateral swaps is assumed for those countries that did not take part in the CMI so far.

rate vis-à-vis any third currency. The formula for calculating the exchange rate of currency j against the, ICBs, the DEY, or the ACU is then

$$S_j = \sum_{k=1}^{n} q_k s_{kj},$$

with S_j being the amount of units of currency j per ICB or DEY or ACU, respectively, q_k being the quantity of currency k in the ICBs, DEY, or ACU, and s_{kj} being the amount of units of currency k per unit of currency j.

Using the above-given weights of national currencies in the DEY and ACU baskets, the hypothetical USD/DEY and USD/ACU exchange rates would look as depicted in figure 11.1, compared to the USD/CNY, the USD/JPY, the USD/KRW, and the USD/THB rates.

The graph exemplifies the effect of the Asian crisis in the movements of the Thai baht and the Korean won. It also shows the instability of the dollar–yen rate that was discussed in chapter 2, and that contributed to the crisis. On the other extreme is the USD/CNY rate, which has been essentially fixed since mid-1995. Only since July 2005 can we see a gradual appreciation of the yuan vis-à-vis the dollar (of 17 percent by September 2008). The graph also illustrates that the hypothetical dollar rates of the ACU and the DEY tend to move between the extremes; excessive movements are smoothed out.

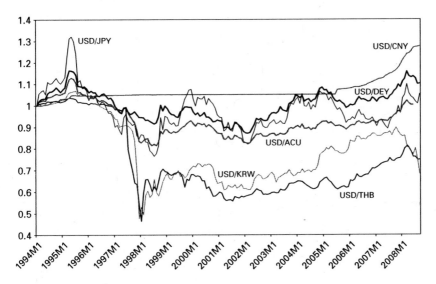

Figure 11.1
Hypothetical DEY and ACU rates vis-à-vis the USD, January 1994 to September 2008

To assess the effect of currency baskets, the behavior of the effective exchange rates of ASEAN+4 countries is compared under four different policy scenarios. First, the NEERs are constructed under the actual policies that were followed. To do this, the NEER weight for each of the ASEAN+4 countries is calculated on the basis of total trade shares. All trading partners are included in the NEER calculation for which either exports or imports account for at least 3 percent of total exports or imports, respectively.[15] The NEER weights are presented in annex 12. The bilateral exchange rates are normalized to 1 for the starting period (January 1994 and January 2000, respectively). The NEER is then calculated as the sum of the bilateral exchange rates times the NEER weights.

Second, NEERs are calculated for the scenario that each ASEAN+4 country uses an ICB which is tailored to its individual trade structure. Third, NEERs are constructed for the scenario that all ASEAN countries, as well as China, Hong Kong, and Korea peg their currencies to the DEY. In this scenario the yen is assumed to float freely. Fourth, the hypothetical NEERs are calculated for the case that all ASEAN+4 countries peg their currencies to the ACU. To compare the volatility of the NEERs under the respective policies, the standard deviation of each country's NEER is computed for the period from January 1994 to September 2008. The results are presented in table 11.2.

The NEERs are considerably less volatile under the basket scenarios than under the policy that was actually followed.[16] That is, collective, regionwide pegging to either type of basket would considerably reduce volatility of East Asian countries' effective exchange rates.[17] The unilateral adoption of country-specific currency baskets would also reduce NEER volatility. Of course, this result (at least for the DEY and ACU

Table 11.2
Standard deviation of NEERs, January 1994 to September 2008

	NEER under actual policy	NEER if ASEAN+4 countries had used individual trade weighted baskets	NEER if ASEAN countries and China. Hong Kong and Korea had used the DEY	NEER if ASEAN+4 countries had used the ACU
Brunei	0.0639	0.1655	0.0114	0.0209
Cambodia	0.1979	0.0180	0.0143	0.0397
China	0.0624	0.0105	0.0035	0.0382
Hong Kong	0.0284	0.0042	0.0015	0.0193
Indonesia	1.3278	0.0107	0.0073	0.0246
Japan	0.0777	0.0508	0.0740	0.0422
Korea	0.2106	0.0073	0.0051	0.0343
Lao	3.9262	0.0171	0.0059	0.1201
Malaysia	0.1261	0.0546	0.0060	0.0303
Myanmar	0.0705	0.0236	0.0151	0.0167
Philippines	0.3579	0.0098	0.0068	0.0238
Singapore	0.0353	0.1031	0.0068	0.0278
Thailand	0.1920	0.0491	0.0051	0.0304
Vietnam	0.1774	0.0119	0.0075	0.0329

Note: NEER is indexed to 1994:01 = 1. Calculations were made with monthly exchange rates from IFS.

scenarios) depends in part on the simplifying assumption that countries fix their currencies one to one to the DEY or the ACU, which implies that intraregional exchange rate volatility is zero (except for the DEY–yen rate under the second scenario). Because East Asian countries have considerable importance in each other's NEER weights (a result of high intraregional trade), this reduces NEER volatility significantly for all countries. However, intraregional exchange rate volatility had been relatively low anyway (except vis-à-vis the yen), so this assumption is not too far-fetched. What the results for the DEY show is that a common exchange rate policy for ASEAN countries (as well as China, Hong Kong, and Korea) able to pay equal attention to movements in the dollar, the yen, and the euro would considerably reduce volatility in the effective exchange rates for all countries involved, compared to the unilateral (soft) dollar pegs that characterized the pre-crisis as well as the current situation. Joint pegging to an ACU would have the same effect also for Japan.

Because the results in table 11.2 include the crisis period, the same estimations were made for the post-crisis period, starting January 2000. As can be seen in table 11.3, the results remain basically unchanged. The only difference is that the standard deviations are on a significantly lower level for most countries than those for the period 1994 to 2008 (which is not surprising given the enormous exchange rate changes for several East Asian currencies during the crisis).

Table 11.3
Standard deviation of NEERs, January 2000 to September 2008

	NEER under actual policy	NEER if ASEAN+4 countries had used individual trade weighted baskets	NEER if ASEAN countries and China, Hong Kong and Korea had used the DEY	NEER if ASEAN+4 countries had used the ACU
Brunei	0.0389	0.0101	0.0103	0.0246
Cambodia	0.0741	0.0058	0.0131	0.0419
China	0.0476	0.0104	0.0060	0.0427
Hong Kong	0.0308	0.0054	0.0037	0.0215
Indonesia	0.1172	0.0054	0.0053	0.0287
Japan	0.0722	0.0075	0.0692	0.0466
Korea	0.0831	0.0069	0.0097	0.0380
Lao	0.1490	0.0038	0.0063	0.1414
Malaysia	0.0371	0.0075	0.0045	0.0350
Myanmar	0.0323	0.0020	0.0035	0.0160
Philippines	0.1085	0.0049	0.0124	0.0260
Singapore	0.0306	0.0081	0.0035	0.0322
Thailand	0.0500	0.0077	0.0094	0.0340
Vietnam	0.1251	0.0065	0.0048	0.0377

Note: NEER indexed to 2000:01 = 1. Calculations were made with monthly exchange rates from IFS.

Even though the results are hypothetical and it is impossible to tell how exchange rates would really have developed if East Asian countries had pegged their currencies to a DEY or ACU, the estimates give reason to assume that pegging to a common basket would contribute to effective and intraregional exchange rate stability and help avoid disruptions resulting from excessive exchange rate movements of key currencies, especially the dollar and the yen.

11.3 A Possible Basket Scenario

The DEY and ACU currency baskets are not necessarily incompatible. In fact a currency basket composed of ASEAN+4 currencies would be equivalent to a G-3 currency basket (or DEY), if each East Asian country uses the G-3 currencies as reference for its exchange rate policy (Kawai, Ogawa, and Ito 2004). A strategy of regional monetary integration that makes use of both kinds of baskets will be outlined in the following.

A first step of such a strategy could be a coordinated move of East Asian countries, including Japan, to adopt currency baskets in line with their trade structures, namely what we called the ICBs. This would create a situation where the East Asian dollar standard would be replaced by an "East Asian basket standard." While such a basket standard would mark a departure from the current regime, the advantage is that it would not require a dramatic change of course. Indeed, dollar weights could be gradually reduced while the shares of other currencies in the baskets could be increased.[18] Each country could administer such a reorientation individually, although a coordinated move would facilitate adjustment. The only country for which the adoption of a basket regime would mean a substantial shift from its current exchange rate policy is Japan.[19] Still, Japan could converge to the other countries' policies gradually, without necessarily making radical policy moves. In general, if countries wish to reap the benefits of relative intraregional and effective exchange rate stability but are reluctant to adhere strictly to a currency basket regime because they want to avoid the risk of pegging and maintain more flexibility than under a basket regime, they could adopt a managed float regime guided by the use of a common basket as numéraire as suggested by Williamson (2009). Compared with other options of maintaining relative regional exchange rate stability, namely a continuation of the East Asian dollar standard or the creation of an East Asian monetary system, this basket option compares favorably, as it would allow for a considerable degree of flexibility. This would not only reduce the risk of currency speculation, but also grant participating countries certain independence in conducting national economic policies.

A second step—which could be made parallel to the adoption of regionwide currency basket regimes—would be the introduction of the ACU as a virtual basket currency. The ACU could fulfill several functions (see Kawai 2009). First, it could be useful as a statistical indicator that summarizes the collective movement of East Asian currencies against external key currencies such as the dollar and the euro. As a regional benchmark index, it could help to monitor regional foreign exchange market developments and help identify the degree of divergence of each component currency from the regional trend.[20] As such, the ACU would only serve as a monitoring device, without requiring any automatic policy reactions such as foreign exchange market interventions.

Second, the ACU could be used as a regionwide "parallel currency" (Eichengreen 2006) to circulate alongside national currencies. Because it would be more stable than any national currency in terms of aggregate regional production and trade, it would be interesting for private corporations and investors to use the ACU for invoicing and settling intraregional trade as well as for regional investment. The ACU could be also useful for developing new tradable financial market instruments and, more generally, for promoting the development of regional capital markets (see section 6.4).

Especially the development of a regional bond market has been given high priority by East Asian policy makers ever since the financial crisis. ACU denominated bonds would be interesting for issuers as well as investors, because the currency risk of basket denominated bonds tends to be lower than that of local currency denominated bonds (Ogawa and Shimizu 2009). Moreover, Ogawa and Shimizu (2009) show that issuing currency basket denominated bonds would, in general, decrease the foreign borrowing costs for bond issuers in all East Asian countries. East Asian governments, as well as private corporations of any nationality investing in the region, would thus have an incentive to issue sovereign or corporate bonds denominated in ACU. On the buying side, ACU-denominated bonds would be attractive for institutional investors not only because of a lower currency risk than of single currency denominated securities, but also because a regionwide ACU bond market, if ever realized, would offer more liquidity and market depth than single national markets. Kawai (2009) points to other possible usage of an ACU. For instance, futures exchanges could offer ACU futures, which would provide hedging instruments for traders even in the absence of onshore derivatives markets for some highly regulated currencies. Finally, commercial banks could accept ACU deposits and make ACU loans, facilitating the financing of regional trade.

Thus there are many ways in which an ACU could be useful for promoting regional trade and finance. When discussing the potential merits of an ACU, however, it is expedient to look at the historical experience with the ECU. As discussed earlier, the ECU was given a prominent role within the EMS (as a means of settlement for monetary authorities, as a denominator for the ERM and for operations under the EMS credit mechanisms, and as a basis for the divergence indicator) and it was also used as unit of account for the EC budget. In addition to its official role, the ECU gained popularity in the private sector, especially in private financial markets, because the ECU exchange rate tended to be more stable than those of its component currencies.[21]

European banks first engaged in ECU trading in order to process deposits of EC institutions and governments, which facilitated the development of an ECU interbank market and stimulated the growth of private ECU deposits. Financial markets basically offered the same financial instruments in ECU that were offered in other major currencies. The biggest success of the private ECU was in the European bond markets, where ECU bonds, at their height, accounted for more than 20 percent of all nondollar eurobonds. Nevertheless, while the ECU gained importance in financial markets, its commercial use was rather limited, with the vast majority of European transactions still being conducted in national currencies (see Eichengreen 2006).[22]

The fact that the ECU never grew into a serious rival to national EC/EU currencies, especially in trade invoicing, need not imply a similar fate for the ACU. Rather, the ECU's limited role in the private sector can be regarded as a result of the strong positions that various national currencies (e.g., the German mark, the French franc, and the British pound) already occupied within the EC/EU economy, leaving only limited room for the ECU.

The East Asian situation is different because national currencies are used almost exclusively for domestic purposes. International (including regional) trade is predominantly invoiced in US dollar (table 11.4), which also dominates East Asian foreign exchange markets (table 11.5).[23] None of the regional currencies has a real advantage of incumbency over the ACU. Instead, the ACU would have to compete with the dollar, the reliance on which—as anchor, reserve, investment, and vehicle currency—is increasingly seen as untenable.

Table 11.4
US dollar use in export and import invoicing of selected East Asian countries

	Invoicing observation	USD share in export invoicing	USD share in import invoicing
Japan	2001	52.8	70.0
Korea	2001	84.9	82.2
Malaysia	1996	66.0	66.0
Thailand	1996	83.9	83.9

Source: Goldberg and Tille (2008: 30).

Table 11.5
Currency shares in foreign exchange markets

	Total (daily averages in billions of USD)	Currency shares (%)[a]			
		USD	Euro	Yen	Other
China	9.3	98.5	0.7	0.7	100.1
Hong Kong	174.6	96.1	12.8	10.4	80.7
Indonesia	2.8	93.0	11.2	8.3	87.5
Japan	238.4	84.6	18.3	71.1	26.0
Korea	33.4	92.2	6.1	11.6	90.1
Malaysia	3.4	97.1	5.9	7.0	90.0
Philippines	2.3	99.2	2.3	2.3	96.2
Singapore	230.6	88.3	27.2	25.1	59.4
Thailand	6.2	94.4	8.8	15.2	81.6
World total	3,988.1	86.8	36.8	17.0	59.4

Source: Own calculations with data from the BIS Triennial Central Bank Survey 2007, table E.4.
Note: Spot, outright forward and foreign exchange swap transactions. Adjusted for local inter-dealer double counting (i.e., "net-gross" basis).
a. Because two currencies are involved in each transaction, the sum of shares adds up to 200 percent.

Table 11.6 shows the currency breakdown of portfolio investment assets for several East Asian countries. Again, the data show a strong dominance of the US dollar for all countries for which data are available, reflecting the preeminent role that the USD still plays in the East Asia region. For all but Japan and Malaysia, the share of the USD in the international portfolio asset investments is above 50 percent.

Provided that one of the main incentives for regional monetary integration is to reduce dominance of and dependency on the dollar (which can be regarded as the current parallel currency for East Asia), the ACU could be a viable alternative. As Williamson (2001: 107) points out, a functioning ACU market would "eliminate the most obvious reason that governments have at the moment for seeking stability in terms of the dollar rather than

Table 11.6
Currency breakdown of portfolio investment assets (in million USD, end 2007)

Currency of denomination	Indonesia	Japan	Korea	Malaysia	Thailand
US dollar	2,081	1,047,293	82,595	4,983	12,030
Euro	13	493,872	8,772	1,138	866
British pound	n.a.	107,941	1,675	189	473
Japanese yen	1	576,976	5,654	201	52
Swiss franc	n.a.	16,571	524	24	32
Other	35	280,915	59,431	6,400	1,240
Total	2,129	2,523,566	158,651	12,935	14,692

Source: IMF Coordinated Portfolio Investment Survey.

their effective exchange rates, which is the microeconomic inconvenience to traders of not being able to use the peg currency for their transactions."

In general, it is only attractive for an economic agent to accept and hold a certain currency—or replace the use of one by another—if the agent expects others to do the same. This is because of the network externalities of money, which were discussed previously. Every network has a tendency for maintaining the status quo. Hence, in order for the ACU to be successful, it will require network participants to be convinced by the general acceptance of the ACU. Whether the ACU would be able to win this acceptance and gain a central role in regional trade and financial markets depends on several factors. Most important, the ACU would need to attain the full endorsement and backing of national governments. East Asian authorities could encourage the use of the ACU in several ways (see Eichengreen 2006). First of all, they could make it more attractive by granting the ACU legal tender status alongside the national currency. Moreover they could try to promote the development of regional ACU security markets by harmonizing regulations and by developing the necessary financial infrastructure, for instance by setting up a regional clearing and settlement system.[24] Governments could also help to create benchmarks by issuing sovereign or quasi-sovereign debt denominated in ACU. This would also make for more liquid secondary markets and encourage issuance by private banks and firms.

To argue that governments could encourage the use of the ACU and the development of a regional ACU bond market, however, does not mean that they should try to force this development at the expense of taxpayers' money. Excessive artificial encouragement of a particular form of bond market will be costly and unlikely to succeed (Hamada and Lee 2009). Indeed, as Eichengreen (2006) points out, one of the main appeals of a parallel currency approach is that it would be market-led and not dictated by politics. Governments should set incentives to create a regionwide ACU market; they should not create it by themselves. Rather, market participants need to be convinced of the seriousness of this idea as well as its advantages.

As mentioned, the ADB has initiated the creation of a regional currency basket index. Encouragingly, the idea has gained the support of both China and Japan, even if the ADB's original plan has not taken off. According to the *Financial Times* (McGregor 2006) both countries have developed "an unusual consensus" in support of an ACU to reduce their reliance on a weakening dollar.[25] This "consensus" between China and Japan illustrates a further advantage of regional currency baskets and the parallel currency approach, namely, that such a strategy circumvents the problem of choosing a single national currency as regional lead currency. Neither China nor Japan would be able to accept dominance of the other, which makes a currency basket a logical choice.

Again, at an early stage of cooperation the ACU would not need to fulfill any official function like the ECU did in the EMS. In the beginning, neither the adoption of a currency basket regime based on trade structures nor the creation of the ACU would require concessions in national sovereignty or a binding commitment to monetary integration. In the longer term, however, as monetary authorities get acquainted with the management of currency baskets, and as markets increasingly rely on the ACU, countries could gradually increase integration efforts and develop the East Asian basket standard into a fully-fledged regional exchange rate system. Gradually, cooperation could be increased and the composition of currency baskets could be harmonized. The ACU could then become the common reference point for exchange rate management of all countries of the region. Over time, when substantial credibility has been accumulated, currency bands could be introduced, developing a formal exchange rate system similar to the EMS, which should then also include intervention obligations in case of deviations from the parity grid. Only if a formal exchange rate system were to be created, would the ACU assume the function of an official unit of account for monetary and exchange rate policy coordination.

Parallel to increasing exchange rate cooperation, authorities would need to intensify monitoring and surveillance of financial markets, for example under the framework of ASEAN+3's ERPD (see chapter 3). Exchange rate coordination would also need to be flanked by financing facilities, such as those under the multilateralized CMI, which could at some point be transformed into a full-fledged regional monetary cooperation fund as in the EMS.

The advantages of such a strategy are at hand. As shown before, currency baskets would help to stabilize NEERs and prevent negative effects of gyrations between major currencies, especially the dollar and the yen. No radical reorientation of exchange rate policies would be required, as most countries in the region have already allowed for more flexibility vis-à-vis the dollar. A gradual reduction of the dollar's weight in regionwide currency baskets would reduce the risk of a dollar crash. At the same time, the ACU could be introduced as a virtual parallel currency to be used for trade invoicing and settling and for developing financial products on a regional capital market. In the early stages political commitment would be very limited, which would make cooperation easier to realize.

Moreover choosing currency baskets and the ACU to guide exchange rate policy circumvents the problem of selecting a regional currency to act as an anchor. Countries could gain experience with regional cooperation and develop trust before moving to more formal cooperation that would require sacrifices to a country's sovereignty. As discussed in the context of the EMS crisis, mutual trust as well as a far-reaching policy consensus is crucial for the success of a regional exchange rate system. A gradual approach to monetary integration in East Asia would allow East Asian countries to get to know their partners more closely and develop a sense of community. If countries are still committed to regional monetary unification after having experienced what close monetary and exchange rate cooperation really means, they could eventually form an East Asian monetary union.[26]

12 Reflections on Monetary Integration in East Asia: Past, Present, and Future

What is the future of money in an increasingly globalized world economy? The question is crucial. Though seemingly technical in nature, the management of money in fact is anything but neutral in its implications for the distribution of wealth and power across the globe. Whoever controls money gains access to real resources—goods and services of all kinds—which in turn are key to attaining economic and political advantage. For citizens of any country it matters greatly whether currency will be governed by recognized state authorities or by others, by friend or by foe, at home or abroad. Will the privilege that money represents be handled responsibly or exploitatively? Will currency be a source of prosperity or conflict? The future of money affects us all. It is our future. (Cohen 2004: xiii)

The general conclusion from the preceding analysis regarding the desirability of and the economic conditions for monetary integration in East Asia is favorable. What matters as well, however, are the political conditions for monetary integration. In the opinion of Mintz (1970), a strong political will might even be the *only* real condition for monetary integration.[1] With respect to this precondition, many observers apparently see dim prospects for East Asian monetary cooperation and integration and dismiss talks of East Asian policy makers about it as pure rhetoric. Particular among Western observers there is a widespread skepticism and disbelief with regard to the viability of monetary integration in East Asia. Critics of the emerging East Asian regionalism frequently argue that:

[T]he region exhibits none of the historical, cultural, or religious commonalities that characterize Europe or North America. . . . Contrary to the claims of some political leaders in the region, there is no "Asian way" that draws these nations together, no common point of view that is intrinsically different from that of the West. (Lincoln 2004: 251)

East Asia, critics like to contend, is lacking a common history that binds the region together and lays the foundation for close political and economic cooperation and integration. Eichengreen (1997: 34–35), for instance, writes: "Proponents of European integration can trace their antecedents back for hundreds of years. . . . The ideal of European integration is intimately connected with the liberal and democratic principles of the European Enlightenment and has roots in centuries of European history. East Asia, in contrast, lacks a comparable tradition of political solidarity. It lacks a Jean Monnet or Paul Henri Spaak to speak for regional integration. In part this reflects the ideological distance between China's communist government and market-oriented regimes elsewhere in East Asia. By contrast, in postwar Western Europe, variants of the social market economy were embraced by virtually all the members of the present-day European Union. At a deeper level, East Asia lacks a Benthamite–Rousseauian–Saint Simonian heritage of collective democratic governance through integration."

Undeniably East Asia is a highly diverse region with more than a thousand languages spoken, more than 300 scripts, and the practice of all kinds of religious convictions. Even a single country like Indonesia has hundreds of sultanats or rajanats in its territory, each of which has its own distinct traditions. But: it is wrong to believe that East Asia is lacking any shared history and therefore a common heritage. Few observers, at least in the West, seem to be aware that East Asia does indeed has a long history of cultural and economic interchange and integration, dating back to ancient times.

To illustrate the close cultural and economic exchange that has flourished in the region for long, the next section will briefly provide an overview of the ancient sinocentric tribute trade system which has arguably shaped modern East Asia. This will be followed by a discussion of the results of a recent survey on regional economic interdependencies among Asian opinion leaders from academia, business, journalism, and politics, which shows that a broad consensus in favor of regional economic integration has already developed in the region. The chapter concludes with some politicoeconomic considerations and predictions regarding the likely future course of East Asian monetary cooperation and integration.

12.1 Brief Review of East Asian Economic Relations

A case in point for the close cultural and economic interchange that has existed in East Asia is the Chinese tribute-trade system, which stretched from Northeast to Southeast Asia for almost a millennium.[2] From the Tang (618–907) through Qing (1644–1911) dynasties of China, the tributary system provided the framework in which the states and other entities of the region operated their relations with China. In essence, the tribute-trade system was "a relationship between two countries, China and the tribute-paying country, with tribute and imperial 'gifts' as the medium, and the Chinese capital as the 'centre.'" (Hamashita 1994: 92) Tributary states regularly sent tribute missions to the Chinese capital, and every time the ruler of one of these states changed, the Chinese emperor dispatched an emissary to officially recognize the new sovereign. Tributary relations were not only centered on China. Japan, Korea, and Vietnam also asserted themselves as "centers" in relation to smaller neighboring states under their sway. The system was sustained by a hierarchical order guided by the Confucian "rule of virtue" (see Hamashita 2003a).

The tributary system not only helped the spread of Confucianism and Chinese culture across the region, it was also closely intertwined with commercial activities. According to Hamashita (1994), the expansion of commercial trade relations between East Asian countries developed in symbiosis with the tribute-trade network.[3] The tribute-trade network also contributed to the penetration of Chinese merchants into Southeast Asia and the emigration of overseas Chinese.

Arguably, the tribute-trade system is the "premise of 'modern' Asia" (Hamashita 1994: 92). Arrighi (1996: 4) maintains that "the present political, economic, and cultural configuration of East Asia is a legacy of the tribute-trade system" and that the emergence of the modern interstate system in the twentieth century "cannot be expected to have displaced, let alone erased, shared understandings . . . that have deep roots in the geography and history of the region. These shared understandings will continue to influence the way in which interstate relations operate in East Asia and between East Asian and non–East Asian states." The lasting existence of widespread Chinese business networks across East Asia is probably the most apparent legacy of the tribute-trade system. These "interstitial business communities," Arrighi (1996: 4–5) asserts, continue to "constitute an "invisible" but powerful connector of the East Asian regional economy."

The history of East Asian tribute-trade relations is not only intriguing because it shows the cultural and economic interconnectedness of the region, it also sets the present rise of China and the emergence of East Asian economic regionalism in a historical perspective. Moreover it includes interesting parallels to the topic of monetary integration in today's East Asia: China's central role in ancient East Asia was reflected in the monetary sphere, with Chinese currency circulating all over the region and at times being the main means of payment or even legal tender in other East Asian countries.

Von Glahn (1996: 89) records that from the twelfth century onward "Chinese coin had become the common currency of the maritime trading world of eastern Asia and served as the domestic currency in a number of foreign lands, including Japan, the Ryukyus, and Vietnam."[4] Japan, for instance, had not minted coins of its own since the tenth century and relied solely on imports of Chinese coin for its medium of exchange for several centuries.[5] By the early fifteenth century, silver coins had achieved a dominant position in the Chinese economy (which had used also copper and bronze coins and sometimes also paper money). Because of the role of Chinese money as "the international currency of eastern Asia" (Von Glahn 1996: 83), the whole region subsequently adopted an East Asian silver standard, with Chinese silver coins as the predominant instrument of exchange in East Asian commerce. The steady expansion of tribute trade and the increasing circulation of silver also led to the absorption of silver from Europe and the Americas, with the tribute-trade zone developing into "an integrated 'silver zone'" (Hamashita 1994: 96).

The existence of a common monetary standard in East Asia's past, of course, gives no reason to expect a similar arrangement in East Asia's future. But it would be wrong to dismiss the prospects for monetary cooperation and integration in East Asia because it allegedly lacks "the historical, cultural, or religious commonalities that characterize Europe or North America" (Lincoln 2004: 251). For sure, East Asia has not yet developed an "integrationist spirit" as in Europe, and the region continues to struggle with political frictions and historical disputes. But also European countries had to cultivate this integrationist spirit. Still today, Europe is far from being the homogeneous group it is often presented as. Like East Asia, Europe is composed of a diverse set of countries, with conflicting views and interests being the rule rather than the exception. Governments still tend to quarrel for what they perceive to be in their national interest. In this context it is worth recalling that European economic integration was a reaction to centuries of wars. From the beginnings of European integration, with the formation of the European Coal and Steel Community in 1951 and the EEC in 1957, economic integration was regarded as much more than a scheme for promoting economic prosperity within Western Europe—it was regarded as a way of building a lasting peace. This has certainly been the greatest and most important achievement of European integration and cannot be measured in economic terms.

12.2   A Survey of Economic Interdependence among Asian Countries

Notwithstanding the apparent political frictions among East Asian nations, the past decade has brought about a notable change in attitude toward regional economic cooperation. In 2007 the ADB conducted a perception survey on "Economic Interdependence among Asian Countries" among 600 opinion leaders of Asian countries (ADB 2008; Capannelli 2007).[6] The results give interesting insights into the views that policy makers, business leaders, academics, and journalists in Asia hold of existing and desirable economic relations among Asian nations, including their opinion about regional cooperation initiatives, the possible creation of new regional institutions, and issues of regional economic identity. The survey also features some questions relating to monetary and financial cooperation.

First of all, the survey results clearly show the awareness that exists among opinion leaders of the economic interdependences in the region. Current economic relations are perceived to be strongest in the area of "trade and investment" (including the creation of regional production networks), where 57 percent of respondents think that relations are strong or very strong. This is followed by relations in "money and finance" (bond markets, equity markets, banking, etc.) with 36 percent of respondents assessing relations to be strong or very strong; "infrastructure" (transport, energy, telecommunication, etc.) with 26 percent; and "health, environment, security and provision of similar public goods" with 19 percent. Ties in trade and investment are perceived to be particularly high by Chinese, Japanese, and Korean respondents, with 75 percent of Northeast Asian respondents seeing strong or very strong relations in this area, as opposed to only 34 percent of South Asian opinion leaders. Relations in the area of money and finance are perceived highest by Southeast Asian respondents.

There seems to be a general consensus that regional economic cooperation as such is favorable. 79 percent of all respondents believe that strengthening economic relations between their countries would provide high or very high benefits in terms of faster and more dynamic economic growth. 75 percent think that strengthening regional economic relations would also lead to a stronger Asian voice in international negotiations; 74 percent believe that fostering regional economic relations will benefit their countries strongly or very strongly by deepening integration with the global economy. 49 percent see high or very high benefits for their countries deriving from strengthening regional economic relations by creating an alternative to global multilateral institutions such as the IMF and the WTO. This view was much stronger among respondents from Southeast and South Asia than among Northeast Asian respondents.

When questioned about the most effective ways to strengthen economic relations, 73 percent considered "implementing regional initiatives for intergovernmental cooperation" to be effective or very effective. 65 percent thought the same of "developing new regional institutions and/or strengthening existing ones," compared with only 42 percent who thought that "just letting market forces operate freely" would be effectual for intensifying regional economic integration.

With respect to the development of regional economic institutions, three quarters of respondents thought that it would be important (44 percent) or very important (32 percent) to develop a regional institution commissioned to facilitating a regional economic policy dialogue and macroeconomic surveillance. 68 percent believed that it would be important (41 percent) or very important (27 percent) to create a regional institution that could provide liquidity and financial support to Asian countries, something the ASEAN+3 finance ministers are currently working on (see chapter 3).[7] There was less enthusiasm, however, for the creation of a regional body concerned with the establishment of a common currency: only 37 percent of the respondents think this would be important (21 percent) or very important (16 percent), with 31 percent being undecided on this issue.

Asked to rate the advantages for their countries from strengthening government-led cooperation through "creating a new mechanism to coordinate monetary and exchange rate policies," a majority was in favor of such a move: 61 percent of respondents rated the advantages as high (44 percent) or very high (17 percent). 26 percent were neutral, while 9 percent saw low, and 2 percent saw very low rewards stemming from regional monetary and exchange rate cooperation (2 percent gave no answer).

Asked about the prospects of a common currency for Asia, 38 percent of all respondents believed that Asian countries will at "some time in the future" create such a currency, which is remarkable if one brings to mind that only a small number of people in Europe actually did believe in the creation of a common European currency even few years before

EMU became a reality. 57 percent, in contrast, do not expect a common currency to be established, saying "no, the economic gap among Asian countries is too wide." Of those respondents who believe that a common currency will be created (226 out of 600), 38 percent think that ASEAN+3 would be the group of countries best positioned for a common currency, followed by 25 percent who think that a subset of ASEAN countries would be best positioned, 17 percent arguing in favor of all of ASEAN, 10 percent for ASEAN+6 (ASEAN+3 plus India, Australia and New Zealand), and 6 percent for all Asian countries.

Opinions on this question differed markedly within the different subregions of Asia: whereas only 28 percent of South Asian respondents believe there will be a common Asian currency in the future, the share is slightly higher among Northeast Asian respondents (31 percent), and much higher among Southeast Asian respondents, of which 54 percent believe that there will be a common currency in the future. The need for monetary integration—culminating in monetary unification—thus seems to be felt more among ASEAN opinion leaders, a policy choice that would be consistent with the establishment of the proposed AEC.

There are stark differences among these subregions also regarding the best-positioned grouping for monetary unification. Of the Northeast Asian respondents who expect a common currency in the future, 51 percent view ASEAN+3 as the best-positioned group. Among ASEAN respondents anticipating monetary unification to happen, 34 percent view ASEAN+3 as the best grouping, 30 percent a subgroup of ASEAN, and 20 percent think ASEAN as a whole would be best suited for a monetary union.

Respondents who believe a common currency will be created were also questioned regarding the time frame they expect this to happen. Of all respondents, 64 percent expect a common currency before the year 2020, the rest believes it will take longer. In South Asia, 84 percent believe that a common currency will be launched before 2020, compared with 59 percent in Southeast Asia and 57 percent in Northeast Asia who think that this time frame is realistic.

Overall, this survey shows clearly that not only regional economic cooperation as such, but also monetary cooperation is considered an important part of the region's current and future policy agenda. This perception seems to be particularly strong in Southeast Asia, where a majority of the interviewed opinion leaders from government, business, academia, and media even expects the creation of a common currency in the future. Few anticipate this to happen quickly, which is in line with the argument that has been made in this book that regional monetary integration, for the time being, should *not* focus on monetary unification and instead should be approached gradually, with less demanding forms of cooperation being pursued first. The survey also shows that no consensus exists as to what forms of regional integration would be optimal and who should be involved. This result points to the need for more public discussion within the region about the future of East Asian political and economic relations.

12.3 The Political Economy of East Asian Monetary Integration

Predicting the future is an impossible task, but one can examine the factors that might influence it. The political economy of East Asian monetary cooperation is a complex matter, yet there are a few trends that have gained force and which can be expected to continue shaping East Asian economic and monetary relations. Part I of this book discussed three factors that have propelled East Asian countries toward considering closer regional monetary and financial cooperation: (1) the instability of the international monetary system, (2) the Asian crisis, and (3) the rise of China. While these three factors have an impact on all East Asian countries, each country is influenced in a different way and has developed its own attitude toward regional cooperation given diverse domestic situations.

Henning (1994) maintains that the disposition of countries toward international monetary matters is jointly determined by private-sector preferences and government institutions. The literature on the political economy of monetary integration highlights the distributional effects of coordination or noncoordination of monetary policies and exchange rates on different groups within an economy (e.g., see Broz and Frieden 2006; Hefeker 1997). Groups involved in foreign trade and investment are generally predicted to have an interest in exchange rate stability as this is commonly assumed to promote trade and investment.[8] Hence internationally oriented corporations that import or export a lot and that are heavily exposed to exchange rate risk are expected to prefer stable exchange rates. Groups whose economic activities are more focused on the domestic economy, in contrast, are assumed to prefer a floating regime that will allow the government to use economic policies to stabilize the domestic economy. The latter group typically includes producers of nontradable goods and firms from the import-competing sector.[9]

The fact that intraregional trade and investment flows in East Asia have increased steadily over the past decades implies that the interest of business communities in the region in stable intraregional exchange rate relations should have increased accordingly. An important characteristic of trade and investment in the region is the fragmentation of production, which is often organized either through a network of small, independent firms or by multinational corporations that use the region as their production base.[10] These production networks, which are driven by FDI from both outside (especially from the United States and EU member states) and inside the region (especially from Japan, Korea, and, since recently, China), are based on a multi-tier division of labor and are binding together the disparate economies of East Asia, integrating them with one another.

Production networks in East Asia are typically vertically integrated and operate by separating a production chain into several sequential production processes which are assigned to the most cost-efficient location. This fragmentation of production is made possible by a combination of rapid improvements in information and communication technology, declining transportation costs, more open markets and a disparity of factor prices within the region. Regional production networks have not only contributed significantly to growth in East Asia, they have led to "an extreme interdependence across East Asian countries" (Haddad 2007: 1). The partly very narrow cost calculations of firms—both subsidiaries of multinational groups or independent, contracting companies—involved in these networks imply that exchange rate swings can seriously affect profit margins and thus drive firms out of business. Indeed, it is arguable that the relative intraregional exchange rate stability under the East Asian dollar standard has been a precondition for these production networks to flourish, especially for those consisting of networks of small, independent firms.[11] Hayakawa and Kimura (2008) maintain that intra–East Asian trade is discouraged by exchange rate volatility more seriously than trade in other regions because of the sensitivity of intermediate goods trade in production networks to exchange rate volatility.

The continuing growth in importance of these production networks, along with the expansion of other commercial and financial ties in the region suggests that a fundamental reorientation of East Asian (again, excluding Japan) exchange rate policies toward freely floating exchange rates is unlikely, in particular for the ASEAN countries, which have formulated their ambitions for creating the AEC by 2015, as mentioned earlier. If fully realized, the AEC would comprise a single market with a free flow of goods, services, investment; freer flow of capital; and free movement of skilled labor. Such a single market would inevitably require a coordination of exchange rates.[12] While it is doubtable that the AEC will be in full operation by 2015, the general political consensus that ASEAN will need to integrate further is there (and was also reflected in the results of the above-mentioned ADB survey), with resulting implications for exchange rate policies.

The situation is different, however, for the "plus three" economies, China and Japan in particular. As highlighted in section 5.3, the openness to trade is significantly greater for the ASEAN economies, making them much more dependent on international—and regional—commerce. Whereas the average trade openness of ASEAN countries in 2007 was 129 percent, it was 76 percent for Korea, 67 percent for China, and 31 percent for Japan.[13] While China has opened up considerably over the past decades, a process that is likely to continue, Japan has traditionally had a relatively closed economy. Still, outward FDI by Japanese multinational corporations to emerging East Asian countries since the yen appreciation that had followed the 1985 Plaza Accord has been a major factor behind the evolution of regional production networks and supply chains and provides the basis for Japan's continuously strengthening economic links with in the region. Moreover Japanese trade openness, which has already increased significantly since the early 1990s, is projected to increase further (METI 2007). A shrinking home market will increasingly force Japanese firms to look for new markets abroad. With rising openness of the economy, and ever growing linkages with China and the rest of East Asia, Japanese corporations are likely to become increasingly interested in government-led regional economic cooperation—which might well include exchange rate coordination—and accordingly convey this interest to the Japanese government.[14]

Given the expected population decline and weak economic prospect in Japan, ADB president Kuroda (2008) predicts that the center of regional economic gravity is likely to shift further away from Japan to China, India, and the ASEAN countries as a group.[15] In Kuroda's (2008: 4) view, "[t]he risk of being marginalized, amid the rapid regional integration process, is real, if Japan does not actively pursue economic cooperation with new regional growth poles." This is a view that is increasingly shared within Japanese business and policy circles. For long Japan has been the undisputed economic leader in East Asia, and as such did not feel the need to seriously engage in regional economic cooperation. A sluggish economic performance since the burst of the bubble and the simultaneous rise of other economies in the region, most significantly China, have increasingly undercut Japan's economic leadership.

China has rapidly developed into a regional economic hub, and is courting Southeast Asian countries with economic partnership agreements (EPAs). The emergence of China as a regional and global power, both politically and economically, constitutes a formidable challenge for Japan, which has prompted it to engage more actively in regional integration processes to avoid marginalization. In trade, Japan has responded to this challenge by signing bilateral EPAs with Singapore, Malaysia, Thailand, Indonesia, and the Philippines as well as a regional agreement with ASEAN. In the financial and monetary spheres, it has been a driving force with the ASEAN+3 finance ministers' meeting, and the CMI and ABMI in particular. As Kenen and Meade (2008) note, Japan has so far sought to lead in fostering monetary cooperation among the East Asian countries and has exercised its influence directly and via the ADB in a defensive attempt to shape the institutional framework for monetary cooperation before China is ready to claim that role. While all this indicates the shift of Japanese policy from what might be called benign neglect toward promoting regional cooperation, and an attempt to assume a leadership position in this process, a clear and coherent Japanese vision regarding East Asian integration and Japan's role therein is lacking to date.

A clear Chinese posture regarding East Asian economic cooperation has not developed yet either.[16] Huang and Zhang (2008) highlight that China has immensely benefited from regional economic integration and that its status as the "world factory" is closely related to the emergence of East Asian production networks in which Chinese firms typically assemble the intermediate products delivered from elsewhere in the region for final export to extra-regional markets. China thus has a firm interest in fostering regional economic cooperation. With growing economic and political strength, China has become increasingly confident in dealing with international affairs, more conscious of its regional responsibilities, and more active in East Asian community building (Zhang 2006). But although the Chinese leadership has repeatedly expressed its commitment to regional economic cooperation, including monetary and financial cooperation, China remains essentially inward-looking, and for the time being it seems unlikely that China would be willing to concede any monetary sovereignty, such as for a regional exchange rate arrangement. But leadership may pass to China even if it does not claim it: if the Chinese economy continues to grow as rapidly as it has done over recent years and the Chinese authorities are capable of maintaining domestic political stability, the ASEAN countries might have to defer to China even if it does not actively seek to exercise leadership in regional monetary matters (Kenen and Meade 2008).

Like Japan, China doesn't seem to have defined a coherent regional strategy. Rather, both countries appear to be involved in a strategic game for regional leadership (Volz and Fujimura 2009). Both China and Japan regard Southeast Asia as their own backyard, and both are eager to maintain or increase their influence in the region. At times the result appears to be a "competition for regional cooperation." For example, China's agreement in November 2004 with ASEAN to create the world's largest FTA by 2010, with more than 1.8 billion people (ASEAN and China 2004), prompted Japan to launch its own formal trade negotiations with ASEAN about a similar ASEAN–Japan FTA.[17] And while the Chinese government was first wary of associating itself with the Japanese AMF-proposal in 1997, it was the Chinese foreign minister who proposed regional financial cooperation to the ASEAN+3 finance ministers two years later (Henning 2005). Indeed, the fear to be preempted or sidelined by the other country seems to be a driving force for both China and Japan to engage in regional cooperation.[18]

The recent consensus that was reached on the multilateralization of the CMI is remarkable and a positive indication for future monetary cooperation as it has demonstrated China's and Japan's ability to effectively collaborate and overcome differing views. The agreement on voting rights that was reached in the Bali Agreement in May 2009—under which China and Japan share joint leadership, while the smaller countries gain a larger weight in the governance structure of the CMI compared to their relative economic size—may indeed signify a precedent for future cooperative initiatives in East Asia.

Nonetheless, the dynamics of regional economic cooperation that has transpired so far cannot obscure that neither China nor Japan has a clear vision or integration agenda. The rivalry between China and Japan runs deep and will no doubt encumber economic, including monetary and exchange rate, cooperation. Both countries remain, despite their regional and international economic exposure, essentially inward-looking. Monetary and exchange rate cooperation is certainly less important for them than for the smaller Southeast Asian economies. Still, if the strategic aspect of regional leadership is added to the storyline, it is not unconceivable that the integration process develops its own momentum.

ASEAN countries are well aware of the Sino–Japanese rivalry and have at times tried to strategically exploit this competition, such as in trade negotiations. Arguing from the perspective of the smaller countries, Kenen and Meade (2008) maintain that few ASEAN countries would want to tie themselves tightly to one of the two countries at the potential expense of its relation with the other. This also explains the attractiveness of the ASEAN+3 grouping for ASEAN.

With its early role played in regional trade liberalization and the current plan for an AEC, ASEAN is certainly to be regarded as a driving force in regional integration. This is not to say that ASEAN member countries all have the same ambitions and vision for regional integration. Indeed motivations appear quite different in part.[19] And yet what all ASEAN countries have in common is their relative economic insignificance if contrasted to the two main regional players China and Japan, or even Korea, and the feeling that regional economic integration is imperative to maintain competitiveness and remain attractive destinations for foreign investment.

Given that the process is still evolving, it is hard to make predictions regarding what form of cooperation among which group of countries might eventually occur. It is likely that ASEAN+3 will remain the core framework for East Asian monetary and financial cooperation, albeit we might see a multi-speed integration process within this grouping. If ASEAN succeeds in building an AEC, ASEAN countries—or possibly a subgroup of ASEAN—can be expected to sooner or later start coordinating their exchange rate policies to guard a smooth functioning of the single market. Most likely this would at first involve an informal and loose exchange rate arrangement based on currency baskets rather than a formalized exchange rate system à la EMS. Such a policy choice would be supported by the analysis in this book, albeit cooperation should ideally involve all ASEAN+3 countries.[20]

One should certainly not expect China or Japan anytime in the near future to enter a formal exchange rate commitment with their East Asian partners. But the fact that China has already opted for a currency basket arrangement, even if not fully operated yet, will facilitate the establishment of an informal East Asian basket standard, which could well comprise the ASEAN countries as well as China and Korea. Japan, which has already been an outsider to the East Asian dollar standard, might join such an informal basket standard at a later stage. Indeed, as was pointed out before, the advantage of pursuing a gradual course of monetary integration that in its first stages would involve relatively little policy commitment and loss of national policy sovereignty is that it would provide countries that are first hesitant to engage in regional exchange rate coordination the opportunity to join at a later stage in the process.

It is evident that East Asian countries are not ready yet to embark on large-scale monetary integration which would involve the creation of a regional monetary system or even a common currency. But as highlighted earlier, monetary integration in East Asia need not—and should not—proceed on the fast track. A gradual approach to monetary integration as was laid out in the last chapter would give East Asian countries time to develop an integrationist spirit before they might move on to more demanding forms of monetary integration. Talks about monetary unification in East Asia are premature at this point in time—not because the economic conditions prohibit it but because the political deter-mination has not yet developed. However, especially for the ASEAN countries monetary union could become a long-term goal, with a prospective ASEAN currency then tied into a regional currency arrangement with China, Japan, and Korea.

So far, economic integration in East Asia has been an essentially market-driven process, but the degree of economic interdependence has reached a level which necessitates also political cooperation to guard the stability of the regional economy. The Asian crisis has shown the danger of financial contagion and has instilled in the heads of East Asia's leaders the necessity to coordinate their exchange rate policies. There are signs that a common political will in favor of monetary integration is developing in East Asia, as reflected in the results of the ADB survey among East Asian opinion leaders cited above. This might be driven more by pragmatism than by love, but the urge to overcome the dependency on the US dollar and escape domination from Washington is a strong binding force.

With the agreement on the multilateralization of the CMI in 2009, the ASEAN+3 countries have effectively established a system for regional cooperation that is self-gov-erned and goes beyond simple information-sharing or peer review. Furthermore it entails a collective decision-making mechanism as well as the creation of an independent unit to conduct regional surveillance. By establishing a common surveillance agency—which might well become a precursor of an AMF or a secretariat for economic cooperation—the ASEAN+3 countries have decided for the first time to institutionalize regionalism. This demonstrates their commitment to regional cooperation, and shows that this heterogeneous batch of countries has found a practical way to work together despite the existing diversity in economic development and differing political systems.

In the quotation at the beginning of this chapter Benjamin Cohen states that "it matters greatly whether currency will be governed by recognized state authorities or by others, by friend or by foe, at home or abroad." It becomes increasingly clear that the region is not intending to continuously subordinate to political and monetary hegemony of the United States—even more after the fallout in the aftermath of the US subprime crisis has tainted the status of the United States as the world's economic superpower. Indeed the 2008 to 2009 global financial crisis is likely to act as a catalyst and speed up the delinking from the dollar. The remarks by Zhou Xiaochuan, the governor of the People's Bank of China, in March 2009 on the need for a new international reserve currency have clearly shown Beijing's unease with a continued reliance on the dollar (Zhou 2009). Once China delinks from the dollar, the other countries in the region will follow. The East Asian dollar standard has served the region well, but the continued growth of the regional economy, the humili-ation of the Asian crisis, US accusations of currency undervaluation against China and other East Asian countries, and uncertainties about the future international value of the dollar have all eroded the appeal of the dollar standard. Even though an "Asian way" may not exist as yet, the region is eager to build one.

The dynamics of East Asian integration should by no means be underestimated. The economic potential of the region and the shared desire since the Asian crisis to reduce dependency on Western financial markets will make it increasingly unlikely that the countries of emerging East Asia will continue to bind their currencies to the US dollar. To draw an analogy to Europe, it is worthwhile remembering that the main impetus for European monetary integration was the collapse of the Bretton Woods system. If we have a Bretton Woods II system today, it will be interesting to see how long the dollar will be able to provide stability to East Asia and if and when the region will emancipate itself from the dollar the way Western Europe did several decades ago.

Notes

Chapter 1

1. The members of ASEAN are Brunei, Cambodia, Indonesia, Lao, Malaysia, Myanmar, the Philippines, Singapore, Thailand, and Vietnam. There are states or territories that will not be considered in this study, even though they also belong to East Asia geographically, most notably Taiwan China and the Democratic Republic of Korea (North Korea). The reason why these two are excluded is that Taiwan and North Korea are politically isolated and not involved in any discussion on regional economic cooperation, let alone monetary cooperation. Also small states or territories such Macao or East Timor are not considered as they are neither included in consultations about regional monetary and financial cooperation, nor have they political or economic weight.

Chapter 2

1. See, for example, Frankel (1998).

2. Cooper (1999) gives a brief but excellent account of exchange rate policy in this period. For a comprehensive treatment of the history of the international monetary system, see Eichengreen (1996).

3. In Nurkse's (1944: 210) view, "[a] system of completely free and flexible exchange rates is conceivable and may have certain attractions in theory; and it might seem that in practice nothing could be easier than to leave international payments and receipts to adjust themselves through uncontrolled exchange rate variations in response to the play of demand and supply. Yet nothing would be more at variance with the lessons of the past."

4. Keynes was an exception who, already in the 1920s, pointed to the advantages for an economy of managed money at the national level, which he regarded to be inconsistent with rigorous adherence to gold standard conventions. Keynes thus proposed the targeting of common inflation rates and a band of floating exchange rates that would leave more scope for independent national monetary policies than a return to the gold standard. See Keynes (1923).

5. Today the IMF has 185 member countries.

6. For a fundamental critique of fixed exchange rates reflecting the tides of time, see Johnson (1969).

7. Triffin (1959) pointed to the problems associated with the gold convertibility of the US dollar and the dollar's role as the world's reserve currency already in the late 1950s and maintained that such a world monetary system was not viable in the long run.

8. For a detailed analysis why the Bretton Woods system collapsed, see Williamson (1977).

9. In practice, it is extremely difficult to prove that a country "manipulates" its exchange rates to gain an unfair competitive advantage, and even if this were evident, there is no clear way of solving this problem (apart from unilateral trade sanctions that could trigger a trade war). The current discussion about global imbalances and the alleged undervaluation of the Chinese yuan is a good illustration. On the yuan debate and the methodological difficulties to empirically determine the degree an exchange rate deviates from its "equilibrium value," see Cheung, Chinn, and Fuji (2009).

10. Exchange rate volatility has increased markedly under the current system as compared to the gold standard or the Bretton Woods regime. See Bordo (1993).

11. Between mid-1995 and April 1997 the yen depreciated by about 50 percent against the dollar. As will be discussed in chapter 3, the yen's depreciation against the dollar had significant impact on the other East Asian countries' export competitiveness, contributing to the Asian crisis.

12. See MacDonald (1999) and Sarno and Taylor (2002: 51ff).

13. De Grauwe, Dewachter, and Embrechts (1993) even make an attempt to model exchange rates making use of chaos theory.

14. Sections 5.1 and 6.2 will come back to the relation between exchange rate volatility and trade.

15. Eichengreen and Hausmann (1999) have termed this phenomenon "original sin." Currency and maturity mismatches as a result of liability dollarization are widely regarded as major factors contributing to the Asian crisis, as will be discussed in the next chapter. McKinnon and Schnabl (2004) have pointed to asset dollarization as a further rationale for exchange rate stabilization. Section 6.4 will discuss regional monetary integration as a potential way of overcoming the problems of asset and liability dollarization in East Asia.

16. The case of the Asian crisis, where financial contagion played an unprecedented role, will be discussed in detail in the next chapter.

17. As Kindleberger and Aliber (2005: 1) record, "[t]he years since the early 1970s are unprecedented in terms of the volatility in the prices of commodities, currencies, real estate and stocks, and the frequency and severity of financial crises."

18. See, for instance, World Bank (1998) and Bordo et al. (2001). On the effects of financial crises on poverty and income distribution see Baldacci, de Mello, and Inchauste (2002).

19. The commission was sponsored by the Council on Foreign Relations. Eleven of the 29 members of the task force, including Fred Bergsten, George Soros, and Paul Volcker urged the G-3 to adopt some form of target zone regime.

20. James (1999) points out that even though the current debate on the international financial architecture has its roots in the crises of the 1990s, the underlying problems have been contested in some form or another since the beginning of globalization some 150 years ago, with a large number of proposals for large-scale reform having been put forward.

21. For conceptual problems to international macroeconomic policy coordination beyond prospects for political realizations, see Frankel (1988) and Rogoff (1985).

22. For a detailed account of the development and implementation of the Plaza and Louvre accords, see Funabashi (1988).

23. According to *The Financial Times*, the United States, Europe and Japan had also discussed the possibility of coordinated currency intervention to support the dollar at the time of the Bear Stearns crisis in March 2008 (Guha 2008).

24. For instance, under the leadership of international financial institutions like the IMF and the World Bank; informal forums a such as the Financial Stability Forum/ Financial Stability Board; central bank committees

such as the Basle Committee on Banking Supervision and the Committee on Payment and Settlement Systems; and private sector entities such as the International Accounting Standards Board. See ECB (2002).

25. In the context of multilateral trade negotiations and frustration with GATT, Baldwin (1997) speaks of a "regionalism-is-easier" attitude.

26. Among other things, intra-European exchange rate flexibility interfered with the Community's Common Agricultural Policy.

27. The EMS and its 1992 to 1993 crisis will be discussed in detail in chapter 10 to delineate lessons for a potential East Asian monetary arrangement.

28. Interest by Denmark and Sweden to finally join the euro area has increased dramatically after their national currencies were severely hit in fall 2008 (Reade and Volz 2009c). Even in the United Kingdom the discussion about EMU membership has been revived.

29. National currencies remained legal tender until they were physically replaced by euro coins and notes in January 2002.

30. This is not to deny problems within EMU, as shown by problems with fiscal policy coordination, persistent growth and inflation differentials in the euro area, and so forth. On whether European monetary integration can serve as a role model for other regions, see, for example, Jørgensen and Rosamond (2002), Angresano (2004), Bridges (2004), and Padoa-Schioppa (2004).

31. See also ECB (2004).

32. The five members of WAMZ are Gambia, Ghana, Guinea, Nigeria, and Sierra Leone. There are further plans to subsequently merge the WAMZ with the already existing West African Monetary Union (WAMU). The WAMU, which currently comprises Benin, Burkina Faso, Guinea Bissau, Côte d'Ivoire, Mali, Niger, Senegal, and Togo, was established in 1962 with a common monetary unit, the franc of the African Financial Community (CFA franc), which is issued by the Central Bank of West African States. On monetary union in West Africa, see Debrun, Masson, and Pattillo (2002) and Masson and Pattillo (2002, 2004a).

33. South Africa, Lesotho, and Swaziland have already been operating a Common Monetary Area since 1986. See Jenkins and Thomas (1997) and Metzger (2006).

34. Apparently Oman and the United Arab Emirates have abandoned plans to join the intended monetary union in the meantime, leaving the realization of the entire project open. See *The Economist* (2009).

Chapter 3

1. This lack of interest in regional cooperation and integration has been commonly attributed to the heterogeneity of the region, both in respect to economic development and political systems. Section 5.3 will return to this in a discussion about whether East Asia constitutes an "optimum currency area."

2. Brunei joined in January 1984, Vietnam in July 1995, Lao and Myanmar in July 1997, and Cambodia in April 1999. For an overview of ASEAN integration, see Plummer and Click (2009).

3. The creation of AFTA can be seen as a reaction to concerns that the emergence of other trade blocs—such as the EU single market, NAFTA, and Mercosur—as well as the rise of China would put ASEAN countries in a disadvantage. As Plummer and Click (2009) note, the original specifics of AFTA were purposefully left ambiguous with a rather loose definition of "free trade" (with tariffs in the range of 0 to 5 percent, rather than the traditional 0 percent), the exclusion of sensitive areas such as rice and automobiles, and a 15-year time frame for implementation. More recently the scope of goods covered by AFTA has been broadened, and the implementation period shortened. AFTA came into full effect for the original ASEAN members and Brunei in 2004, albeit some products are still excluded.

4. APEC not only includes the ASEAN countries, China, Japan, Korea, Taiwan, and the United States, but also Australia, Canada, Chile, Mexico, New Zealand, Papua New Guinea, Peru, and Russia. APEC was established partly as a strategy by the United States to prevent the emergence of an East Asian regionalism that would deliberately exclude the United States. Such tendencies did exist. For instance, the former Malaysian Prime Minister Mahathir Mohammed proposed the creation of an East Asian Economic Caucus, a multilateral grouping of East Asian countries that would exclude countries like the United States and Australia. The United States and Australia were vehemently opposed to this. With American pressure, the Japanese quietly tried to get rid of the idea, while the Australians promoted a more inclusive APEC forum as an alternative (see Fukuyama 2005b).

5. See World Bank (1993) and table 3.3.

6. See, for instance, the IMF's (1997) growth forecasts in its World Economic Outlook of May 1997.

7. Moody's and Standard & Poor's long-term sovereign debt ratings of the later crisis countries remained the same throughout 1996 and the first half of 1997, with the exception of the Philippines and Korea, which were actually upgraded in early 1997. Through the onset of the crisis, the outlook was described as "positive" or "stable" for all crisis countries. The crisis was also unanticipated in the risk assessments of leading investment banks such as Goldman Sachs or the country risk assessments of Euromoney. See Radelet and Sachs (1998: 17–20, tabs. 5–7). The full scale of crisis was not understood even weeks or months after its outbreak. In November 1997, five month after the start of the crisis, US President Bill Clinton described the events in East Asian financial markets at an APEC summit in Vancouver as "a few little glitches in the road" (Goldstein and Hawkins 1998: 1).

8. In the case of Thailand, financial sector problems preceded (and caused) the currency crisis but were then aggravated through the baht devaluation. For an analysis of the Thai case, see Ito and Pereira da Silva (1999). The financial sectors of Cambodia, China, Lao, Myanmar, and Vietnam were less affected through currency devaluations or capital outflows because of limited exposure to external (short-term) capital.

9. International borrowing in foreign currency was also a result of underdeveloped domestic capital markets, a problem that we will come back to in section 6.4. A further incentive to borrow in international currency (in most cases in US dollar) was that international interest rates were generally lower than domestic interest. From the side of international investors, short-term lending to East Asian countries appeared relatively safe because the risk of crisis seemed low.

10. In Indonesia, most international lending was actually to private corporations, which used short-term international credit to finance long-term investment.

11. In Thailand, 56 out of 91 finance companies were liquidated; in Korea, 14 out of 30 merchant banks were closed (Radelet and Sachs 1998: 42).

12. See also Radelet and Sachs (1998: 9, tab. 2).

13. See, for example, Radelet and Sachs (1998), Furman and Stiglitz (1998), Goldstein and Hawkins (1998), Goldstein (1998), Corsetti, Pesenti, and Roubini (1999), Winters (1999), Cheah (2000), Lingle (2000), Ito (2001), Grilli (2002), and Branson and Healy (2009).

14. The empirical evidence for real currency overvaluation before the crisis is mixed, but there is evidence of significant real currency appreciation for Hong Kong, Indonesia, Korea, Malaysia, the Philippines, Singapore, and Thailand in 1996 (Chinn 2000; Furman and Stiglitz 1998; Radelet 1996; Radelet and Sachs 1998; Branson and Healy 2009; Grilli 2002).

15. Kwan (1998) has shown that variations in the dollar–yen exchange rate have a significant effect on output growth in East Asian economies. While a strengthening of the yen depreciates the real effective exchange rates of East Asian countries (given their de facto dollar pegs) and thus accelerates their growth, a weakening of the yen has the opposite effects. For a more recent analysis of the effects of the dollar–yen rate on East Asian countries' business cycles, see McKinnon and Schnabl (2003).

16. Thailand, for instance, had a current account deficit of 8 percent in both years before the crisis. But as Furman and Stiglitz (1998) note, this was not necessarily regarded as unsustainable at the time, since the deficit was used to fund an increase in investment over the high and rising domestic savings rate. From 1990 to 1996 investment in Thailand was at 41 to 42 percent of GDP, while saving was around 35 percent (Branson and Healy 2009: 230).

17. On the mechanisms driving contagion, see also the contributions in Claessens and Forbes (2001).

18. The trade structures of East Asian countries will be analyzed in detail in section 5.3.

19. As Furman and Stiglitz (1998: 3) note, the "depth of the collapse in Indonesia is among the largest peacetime contractions since at least 1960." The vigor of Indonesia's crisis is even more remarkable given the fact that Indonesia had annual real growth rates of 7 to 8 percent of GDP in the years before the crisis, export growth of 10 percent in 1996, and a budget surplus of over 1 percent over the years prior to the crisis. Moreover there were no major corporate bankruptcies and foreign liabilities of banks were moderate (although corporate foreign debts were high).

20. For criticism on the IMF's handling of the Asian crisis, see especially Feldstein (1998), Furman and Stiglitz (1998), and Radelet and Sachs (1998). For a (rather benevolent) IMF self-assessment of its own involvement in the crisis, see Lindgren et al. (1999). For an analysis of allegations of IMF stabilization programs, see Hutchison (2003).

21. For a detailed analysis of the IMF programs, see Radelet and Sachs (1998: 40ff).

22. Contributions by institutions such as the World Bank and the ADB were also largely tied to agreements between the crisis countries and the IMF.

23. Jeffrey Sachs (1998: 10B) even called the IMF "the Typhoid Mary of emerging markets, spreading recessions in country after country."

24. Greenville (2004) even recounts that "one well-qualified candidate for finance minister was recently vetoed because she had spent time at the Fund." In Korea the crisis is still today commonly referred to as the "IMF crisis" (Fukuyama 2005b). At times the IMF acronym was allegedly referred to in Korea as "I'M Fired."

25. Mexico and Turkey were the two other countries whose shares were increased at the Singapore meeting.

26. The term ASEAN+3 is commonly used since May 2000. ASEAN+4 includes Hong Kong.

27. Interestingly Michel Camdessus, the then managing director of the IMF, initially welcomed the AMF proposal (he only disliked that it should be called a "fund"), but later retracted his endorsement in the light of objections of the US Treasury. With European support Washington made considerable efforts to wreck the Japanese proposal, arguing that the AMF would be an agency of potential conflict with the IMF, so Japan, which was unwilling to risk an outright confrontation with its protector, abandoned the plan. The US Treasury also responded to the AMF proposal by providing for faster activation of IMF facilities, offering bilateral funds to crisis countries, and by initiating the IMF's Supplemental Reserve Facility. It should be mentioned that the AMF proposal also failed to get the support of China, which felt that the quick consideration and approval requested was unrealistic and inappropriate. See Henning (2002, 2005)

28. On the CMI, see Henning (2002) and Park and Wang (2005).

29. Since the clash over the AMF, the region has learned its lesson and has been cautious to avoid any overt confrontation on regional matters with Washington and only has pursued small steps that could be hardly criticized by either the US Treasury or the IMF. For instance, to soothe concerns that the IMF's role would be undermined through the CMI, countries agreed to include an "IMF link," which requires that beyond the first 10 percent of each BSA, borrowers must agree to an IMF program and its conditionality. In 2005, however, the nonlinked portion of the swaps was silently increased from 10 to 20 percent (see Henning 2005: 14–6). Once the agreed mechanism for macroeconomic and financial monitoring under the CMI multilateralization becomes

fully functional, the portion of CMI loans that can be disbursed without IMF lending will most likely be increased (Volz 2009).

30. Under the Bali agreement, Japan and China contribute identical shares to the reserve pool (32 percent each), double Korea's share (16 percent). A trick was applied to have equal contributions by China and Japan: China's share comprises the contribution of Hong Kong, which will now join the CMI. The remaining 20 percent are made up by the ASEAN members. Japan and China thus share joint leadership, while the smaller countries gain a larger role in decision-making than their economic size would otherwise warrant. This approach may in practice lay the foundations for future cooperative initiatives in East Asia—joint leadership by the bigger countries, with a positive bias toward the smaller ones (Volz 2009).

31. EMEAP includes Australia, China, Hong Kong, Indonesia, Japan, Korea, Malaysia, New Zealand, the Philippines, Singapore, and Thailand. On the ABFs, see Ma and Remolona (2009).

32. In the Hanoi Plan of Action of December 1998, the ASEAN heads of state and government agreed to "[s]tudy the feasibility of establishing an ASEAN currency and exchange rate system" (ASEAN 1998b: §1.4.1).

33. Chapter 11 will provide a detailed analysis of currency baskets and monetary units for East Asia.

Chapter 4

1. Wu et al. (2002) maintain that China's share of world FDI, relative to its share in world GDP, has not been excessive. They also highlight that official figures on FDI flows to China are distorted, because a significant share of FDI to China consists of "round tripping" of funds that originate from mainland entities. Chinese residents have an incentive to channel funds out of China (often to Hong Kong or Caribbean offshore tax havens) and bring them back in the form of FDI to take advantage of preferential tax treatment. Wu et al. (2002) cite a report of China's Ministry of Foreign Trade and Economic Cooperation according to which Hong Kong and the British Virgin Islands account for about 50 percent of China's FDI inflows since 1998. Estimations by Chantasasawat et al. (2004) suggest that China is not the most important determinant of FDI to the other East Asian economies. They point to other policy and institutional factors such as openness, corporate tax rates, and corruption.

2. In the view of Prime Minister Lee Hsien Loong of Singapore, "Asean has to become more integrated and cohesive. Only thus can we keep up with larger and stronger economies such as China and India." (Burton and Kazmin 2008: 9) Kubny, Nunnenkamp, and Mölders (2008), in contrast, stress that there is actually little empirical evidence that regional integration initiatives improve member countries' attractiveness to FDI.

3. The ASEAN "Vision 2020" of 1997 already declared the goal of creating "a stable, prosperous and highly competitive ASEAN Economic Region in which there is a free flow of goods, services and investments, a freer flow of capital, equitable economic development and reduced poverty and socio-economic disparities" (ASEAN 1997). On the AEC, see Hew and Soesastro (2003) and Plummer and Click (2009).

4. As *The Economist* (2007a) writes about ASEAN: "United, they would be a force to reckon with. Divided, they risk becoming a bunch of also-rans, trailing ever further behind China and India."

Chapter 5

1. Krugman (1994: 18) even stated: "It is arguable that the optimum currency area issue ought to be the centerpiece of international monetary economics."

2. Which is not completely surprising, as it is often the same researchers that worked on European integration who now comment on East Asia.

3. For the costs and benefits of monetary integration, the degree of integration obviously makes a difference, as the full benefits of monetary integration can only be enjoyed in a monetary union. But analytically, the factors affecting the trade-off between a float and peg or a float and monetary union are the same.

4. See also Dixit (1989). Collignon (1999) uses the combination of risk-averse private investors maximizing their wealth and public authorities maximizing aggregate investment to explain the formation of currency blocs. By pegging their currency to an anchor, governments reduce exchange rate risk within the currency bloc, which will stimulate private investment.

5. See Karlinger (2002) for a literature review on the effect of monetary integration on financial markets.

6. While there is still an ongoing debate on the exact transmission channels from finance to economic activity, and its quantitative impact in particular, a large and growing amount of empirical research has documented a robust correlation between finance and growth, as well as a causality running from financial development to economic growth. See Pagano (1993) and Levine (2005).

7. Although the 2008 to 2009 global financial crisis has cast serious doubt on the efficiency of financial markets, the basic message that financial market development is conducive to economic growth still holds.

8. See Flood and Marion (2002) for a literature review.

9. The role of "national money as a barrier to trade" (Rose and van Wincoop 2001) and the potential trade-creating effects of monetary integration will be discussed in section 6.2.

10. Because, in a small open economy, nominal exchange rate fluctuations are likely to translate into fluctuations of the domestic price level, pegging the exchange rate to a stable currency can also stabilize the domestic price level (McKinnon 1963). Hence an external target need not be incompatible with domestic price stability. In practice the import of macroeconomic stability has been a major incentive for small developing and emerging economies to engage in exchange rate stabilization vis-à-vis major stable international currencies like the US dollar, the German mark, or the euro. This, however, does not change the above-noted implication that monetary policy cannot be used as an independent policy instrument for countercyclical policies in face of an external target and free capital flows.

11. Not only did Mundell assume stationary expectations in his theory of optimum currency areas. In what became the standard textbook Mundell–Fleming model, Mundell (1963) maintained this assumption, thereby influencing generations of economists' understanding of the exchange rate as a policy instrument. The assumption of stationary expectations, however, is a problematic one. Section 6.1 will discuss the implications of the "death of the Phillips curve" for OCA theory.

12. As will be discussed later, a further problem in conducting successful monetary policy is the potential existence of differences in transmission mechanisms of monetary policy across the countries of a common currency area, resulting from differences in national financial systems.

13. Moreover large budget deficits of single member countries could induce the ECB to pursue a restrictive monetary policy, under which also countries with prudent fiscal policy would have to suffer. The results of reckless fiscal policies by single member countries are socialized in the whole currency area, as monetary policy is equal for all member countries. There is a danger of moral hazard because the real interest rate and risk premium of a single country with an unsustainable fiscal policy becomes lower than would be the case if it were outside the monetary union. See Buiter, Corsetti, and Roubini (1993).

14. The violations and the recent watering-down of the SGP show how reluctantly the governments of EMU member countries have accepted the loss of fiscal autonomy.

15. Buiter (2000) maintains that a country that joins a monetary union whose currency is used as an international reserve asset and vehicle currency is actually likely to boost its seignorage receipts, because the amount of currency issued by the common central bank will be greater (because of the demand for the currency outside the union) than the sum of currency issued by each individual member country before.

16. This, of course, is a static view as business cycles might change in the process of monetary integration. The effects of real and financial integration on business cycles in East Asia will be analyzed in section 6.3.

17. The assumption of downwardly rigid wages and money illusion was explicitly made by Mundell (1961: 663) for he presumed that "unions bargain for a money rather than a real wage, and adjust their wage demands to changes in the costs of living, if at all, only if the cost of living index excludes imports."

18. This view relates to the "convergence school" of the neoclassical theory of international trade, which maintains that free movement of goods and services will lead to a convergence of income and living standards across countries and regions. Also, an underutilization of resources in economically weak areas is supposed to be alleviated through sufficient wage flexibility (downward) and high mobility of production factors (migration to prosperous regions). See Emerson et al. (1992: 213–15). For criticism on this view, see Thirlwall (2000).

19. The "new macroeconomics revolution" and the introduction of rational expectations have emphasized that nominal rigidities are hardly compatible with rational behavior of economic agents in the long run and have therefore theoretically dismissed money and exchange rate illusion. This, however, does not preclude short-term effects from policy actions (McCallum 1978). Section 6.1 will return to this point.

20. In the pre-OCA discussion, Hayek (1937) actually pointed out that a change in the general price level brought about by exchange rate revaluation is inappropriate to help specific industries adjust to exogenous shocks and might even result in distortions in other sectors that were unaffected at first.

21. The terms of trade describe the relation between import and export prices.

22. Corden (1972) proposed the Phillips curve as an OCA criterion, arguing that countries with different Phillips curves (due to different labor union behavior, differing social preferences between unemployment and inflation, etc.) should not form a currency union. Magnifico (1973) even introduced the concept of "national propensities to inflation." The Phillips curve will be considered in section 6.1.

23. See also Ehrmann et al. (2001). Other important factors affecting the transmission of monetary policy are sectoral specialization and labor market structures. Cecchetti (1999) asserts that differences in financial structures are the result of differing legal structures. These can be harmonized across a currency union so that ex ante differences need not be an obstacle to monetary integration. Section 6.1 will discuss the "endogeneity of OCA criteria" in greater detail.

24. The automatic stabilizers of public budgets help dampen business cycle fluctuations. In a time of recession, public spending for unemployment and social welfare will increase, which will support consumption and aggregate demand. The reverse will be the case in a boom.

25. See Krugman (1993), Sala-i-Martín and Sachs (1992), and von Hagen (1992). A further example is the *Länderfinanzausgleich* between German federal states. See De Grauwe (2005: 11).

26. De Grauwe (2005) points out that if fiscal transfers take on a permanent character, they may even make the adjustment to permanent demand shocks more difficult, as they become a substitute for structural adjustments.

27. See, for instance, Bayoumi and Eichengreen (1994), Bayoumi and Mauro (1999), Eichengreen and Bayoumi (1999), Bayoumi, Eichengreen, and Mauro (2000), Kwack (2004), Yuen (2001), and Ahn, Kim, and Chang (2006).

28. The EMU-member countries, commonly referred to as the euro area, are Austria, Belgium, Cyprus, Finland, France, Germany, Greece, Ireland, Italy, Luxembourg, Malta, the Netherlands, Portugal, Slovakia, Slovenia, and Spain. The EU-15 (the "old" EU members) includes Austria, Belgium, Denmark, Finland, France, Germany, Greece, Ireland, Italy, Luxembourg, the Netherlands, Portugal, Spain, Sweden, and the United Kingdom. The EU-27 includes the EU-15, Cyprus, Czech Republic, Estonia, Hungary, Latvia, Lithuania, Malta, Poland, Slovak Republic, and Slovenia, which all joined the European Union in May 2004, as well as Bulgaria and Romania, which joined in January 2007.

29. It is notable that Japan's GDP is only 61.0 percent of the Chinese GDP if measured in PPP—in contrast to the 133.6 percent when using market exchange rates.

30. Data for European countries are from the same sources as in table 5.8.

31. In Franco–German relations, there has actually been a tendency for governments from the opposite political spectrum to get along better than governments with similar political backgrounds. But the overall political system in this example, obviously, has been the same in both countries.

32. The main industries for Brunei are extraction of petroleum, petroleum refining, liquefaction of natural gas, and construction.

33. Admittedly, it is rather surprising to find high values for textiles and clothing in Hong Kong and Korea. An explanation, at least for Hong Kong, could be that most of its GDP is generated in the service sector (88 percent), so that this relatively high share of textiles and clothing in value added in manufacturing becomes relatively unimportant for the economy as a whole (see table 5.11).

34. As mentioned earlier, they have also started developing a regional bond market.

35. On the patterns and structure of trade in East Asia, see also Kawai and Urata (2004).

36. In 2004, China for the first time exported (and imported) more than Japan, making it the world's third largest exporter behind the United States and Germany. In 2007, it overtook the United States to become the second largest exporter.

37. In the case of Japan, trade openness had actually decreased in the 1980s and early 1990s but has since increased again to 30 percent, a value a bit higher than the 26 percent in 1980.

38. This point will be of relevance when discussing East Asian countries' current degree of monetary policy independence in section 6.5.

39. For a survey of the East Asian model of export-led growth, see World Bank (1993).

40. As will be discussed later, the motivation for stabilizing the dollar exchange rates also stems from the problems associated with underdeveloped capital markets in East Asia.

41. Plummer and Click (2009) point out that economic integration efforts should not only focus on (sometimes misleading) indicators such as shares of intraregional trade and investment, since a successful integration program could theoretically lead to a decrease in these measures.

42. This is a reflection of the intraregional production networks that have developed: intermediate goods are shipped between East Asian countries, assembled, and exported to their final destination, which often lies outside the region, in the United States or the European Union.

43. Transport equipment exports are only important in the case of Korea.

44. Thailand is the world's largest exporter of rice.

45. For a structural change analysis, see Plummer (2003).

46. See also Gill and Kharas (2007: ch. 2).

47. For Brunei and Cambodia data are available only from 1984 onward.

48. Bayoumi and Eichengreen (1994) estimate disturbances for three regions, namely Western Europe, the Americas, and East Asia. Bayoumi and Eichengreen's data cover the period 1960 to 1990 for Europe and 1969 to 1998 for the Americas and East Asia. Other authors that have applied the same methodology for different samples of East Asian and Pacific countries (but with smaller samples and shorter time spans than in this study) are Bayoumi and Mauro (1999), Bayoumi, Eichengreen, and Mauro (2000), Yuen (2001), Kwack (2004), and

Ahn, Kim, and Chang (2006). The results presented in these papers are roughly the same as the results presented here.

49. Aggregate supply shocks can be therefore regarded as more relevant than demand disturbances.

50. A string of restrictions is required to define all elements of the model. For details on the methodology, see Bayoumi and Eichengreen (1994). As in Bayoumi and Eichengreen, lag length was set to 2.

51. The share of long-term unemployed out of total unemployed in 2005 was 33 percent in Japan and 1 percent in Korea, indicating very inflexible and flexible labor markets, respectively. One must point out, however, that the Japanese unemployment is relatively low, although the level today is much higher than a decade ago.

52. In January 2007, ASEAN leaders signed an agreement to regulate migrant workers and improve their legal and social rights in the host country (Economist 2007b). For a collection of case studies examining the labor migration process and related policy issues in East Asia, see Debrah (2002).

53. As a consequence of rising oil and food prices, the whole region experienced inflationary pressure in 2008, but the global recession that started in the second half of 2008 has brought about deflationary tendencies.

54. Thailand had a deficit of 4.3 percent in 2005 after an average surplus of 6.2 percent for the period 1998 to 2004.

55. In the view of Mundell (1961) one can speak of "optimality" and thus an OCA when the benefits of monetary integration outweigh the costs.

56. The index was originally developed for Europe by Bayoumi and Eichengreen (1997) and is derived from the results of a cross-sectional regression that relates observed exchange rate variability to the standard deviation of the difference in growth rates across the two economies, the dissimilarity of the composition of trade, the level of bilateral trade, and the size of the two economies.

Chapter 6

1. One need not necessarily go as far as Buiter (2000: 222) who condemns OCA theory as "one of the low points of post–World War II monetary economics" or as Schelkle (2001b: 2) who describes it as a "dead end for debates on monetary integration."

2. This development is related to the paradigm change in monetary theory that was triggered by Friedman's (1968) essay "The Role of Monetary Policy." The dwindling influence of the Keynesian school of thought since the 1970s and the simultaneous growing prominence of the monetarist school have also strongly changed the thinking about monetary integration, which, as a result, "has shifted from Keynesian-inspired skepticism about monetary integration towards a monetarist-induced sympathy for the cause of monetary union. This shift in intellectual environment has certainly been influential among policy makers and helps to explain the initiatives taken in Europe at the end of the 1980s that ultimately led to monetary union." (De Grauwe 2001: xii)

3. The Phillips curve originates from an analysis by Phillips (1958) on the long-run relationship between unemployment and nominal wage changes in the United Kingdom. Phillips found that high wage rises correspond to low unemployment, and vice versa. Strictly speaking, the relationship between unemployment and inflation refers to the "modified Phillips curve," which was described by Samuelson and Solow (1960). Under certain conditions, the change in price level and nominal wages are identical so that the original meaning remains unchanged (see Bofinger 2001: 97ff).

4. As will be discuss later, the monetary and exchange rate regime, by its influence on the quality of a nation's currency, does have an important impact on financial market development and investment conditions and thereby on economic growth and development. But these effects have nothing to do with "fine-tuning" the economy.

5. On what monetary policy can achieve and what not see also Bernanke et al. (2001: 11–6)

6. As Buiter (2000) points out, the OCA theory was developed in an era when international financial integration was limited and where foreign exchange and capital controls were the norm. At the time Mundell's considerations therefore served their purpose.

7. For an overview of exchange rate theories, see Sarno and Taylor (2002).

8. The seminal contribution to the portfolio balance theory of the exchange rate is Branson (1979). A comprehensive treatment of the portfolio balance model is given in Branson and Henderson (1985).

9. Keynes highlighted the principal uncertainty of the future. In this tradition, the monetarist-Keynesian approach emphasizes the role of money as a bridge between the present and an uncertain future. See Nitsch (1999a).

10. This argument will be developed for East Asian countries in section 6.5.

11. The Lucas critique was given great prominence in the discussion on monetary integration by Frankel and Rose's (1998) article on"The Endogeneity of the Optimum Currency Area Criteria."

12. In the words of Lucas (1976: 42): "In short, it appears that policy makers, if they wish to forecast the response of citizens, must take the latter into their confidence."

13. Examples are reactions to changes in progressive taxation, employment programs, or the central bank's monetary policy (Schelkle 2001b).

14. See Schelkle (2001a). For a comprehensive treatment of the interaction between wage bargaining and monetary policy in the EMU, see Dullien (2004).

15. Structural inflation denotes that the causes of inflation have their roots in structural factors such as the nature of the monetary system (i.e., a lack of independence of the central bank) or the wage bargaining system (i.e., an indexation or fragmentation of wage bargaining). As Buiter (2000: 223) puts it: "[T]he duration of nominal wage and price contracts and . . . the extent to which they are synchronised or staggered is subject to an obvious application of the Lucas critique. These contracting practices are not facts of nature, but the outcomes of purposeful choices. Changes in the economic environment conditioning these choices will change the practices."

16. The disciplining effects of the EMS will be discussed in chapter 10.

17. For an analysis of business networks in East Asia, see Tachiki (2005) and Hamilton-Hart (2005).

18. See Fernández-Arias, Panizza and Stein (2004). These problems are nicely illustrated for Brazil and Argentina in the 1990s by Eichengreen (1998).

19. NAFTA is a case in point.

20. With reference to the European Commission's study "One Market, One Money" (Emerson et al. 1992), Rose (2000) called his article "One Money, One Market: The Effect of Common Currencies on Trade."

21. The countries are Cambodia, China, Hong Kong, Indonesia, Japan, Korea, Lao, Malaysia, the Philippines, Singapore, Thailand, and Vietnam. Taiwan was included to enlarge the sample size. The sample is divided into three subsample periods, 1980 to 1989, 1990 to 1996, and 1999 to 2003, to capture the change over those years, with the crisis years 1997 and 1998 excluded.

22. For an overview of the theoretical foundations of the gravity equation see Frankel (1997: ch. 4).

23. GDP and population data are from WDI, except for Taiwan, which are from the Taiwan Statistical Data Book 2004. Distance was calculated using the distance calculator of the US Department of Agriculture/Agricultural Research Service Phoenix, Arizona (http://www.wcrl.ars.usda.gov/cec/java/capitals.htm).

24. As an alternative measure for the similarity of currency regimes, we compute bilateral exchange rate volatility, namely the standard deviation of the first differences of the natural logarithms of the nominal exchange rate

between the two countries in question. The estimates for the gravity model using this measure, which are not reported here, are almost identical to those in table 6.1, confirming the robustness of the results. For both indicators we use monthly exchange rates from IFS and the Central Bank of China for Taiwan.

25. Using an error correction model, Poon, Choong, and Habibullah (2005) also find that exchange rate volatility has a statistically significant negative impact on real exports in most East Asian countries. The results are also consistent with Baak (2004) who finds a significant negative impact of exchange rate volatility on the volume of trade among Asia Pacific countries. Hayakawa and Kimura (2008) find that intra–East Asian trade is discouraged by exchange rate volatility more seriously than trade in other regions because intermediate goods trade in production networks, which is quite sensitive to exchange rate volatility compared with other types of trade, occupies a significant fraction of trade.

26. Population is expected to control for self-sufficiency and size of the respective countries, because a higher population relates to less dependency on exports and imports due to a larger domestic market and accessible natural resources (see Frankel 1997: ch. 4). As discussed before, the smaller East Asian economies are more open than the large ones. Singapore's share of intraregional trade, for instance, is particularly high due to the fact that it engages considerably in intraregional entrepôt trade.

27. Nitsch (2002) has re-examined Rose's analysis and concluded that a common currency doubles instead of trebles trade. In his response to Nitsch, Rose (2002: 479) sees his general message confirmed: "If I had originally estimated that currency unions leads trade to rise by 'only' 100 percent, I still think that Nitsch would have been provoked to write his paper. The mystery remains."

28. Rose and Engel (2002) point out that since well-integrated countries are more likely to establish a common currency union, the trade effect might be somewhat overestimated. That is, the causality may flow from real integration to monetary unification rather than the reverse.

29. See Rose (2002, 2004), Frankel and Rose (2002), Rose and Engel (2002), Pakko and Wall (2001), Flandreau and Maurel (2005), Nitsch (2002, 2004, 2008), Berger and Nitsch (2008), Baldwin (2006), and Frankel (2006).

30. See also Rose and van Wincoop (2001).

31. Frankel and Rose (2002: 461) point to the tendency of their message: "Our estimates seem very large, and we try not to take them too literally. Rather we hope they shift the terms of the debate on common currencies toward a more serious consideration of the somewhat neglected trade benefit."

32. Some of these factors are usually used as explanatory variables in the gravity model.

33. Several other papers deal with business cycles in East Asia. Girardin (2004), for example, analyzes correlations of East Asian countries' growth with Japan.

34. Arguably, Shin and Sohn's (2006) results are affected by the way they measure financial integration, a rather intricate task that will be discussed in greater detail below and that is differently addressed here.

35. Again, Taiwan is included to increase the sample size.

36. We also tried linear detrending to see if the detrending method affects the estimation results. Moreover, we tried out other measures of economic activity, namely, GDP at constant USD, GDP at PPP, industry value added at constant local prices, and unemployment as a percentage of the total labor force. The results were broadly in line with the ones presented here.

37. Shin and Sohn (2006) construct an indirect measure of financial integration based on the returns on financial assets, namely correlations of monthly interest rates for a given year.

38. One could also use de jure measures of financial integration. Imbs (2004), for instance, uses the IMF's classification of capital account restrictions to construct an indicator of bilateral financial integration. But as he

acknowledges, de jure measures of financial openness say little about effective bilateral financial integration. As a proxy for effective bilateral capital flows, he uses Lane and Milesi-Ferretti's (2001) measure of international financial integration based on aggregate foreign assets and liabilities. But while the use of such measures is very convenient with respect to data availability, they are rather an indicator for international financial openness than for bilateral integration.

39. The BIS actually collects data for cross-border banking activities, but for East Asia only aggregate data are on hand.

40. The industries contained in the UN *Statistical Yearbook* are "agriculture," "mining," "manufacturing," "electricity," "construction," "wholesale," "transport," and "other activities."

41. For information on the indicators, see Kaufmann, Kraay, and Mastruzzi (2005). Data are available at http://www.worldbank.org/wbi/governance/govdata/.

42. For other problems associated with the approach taken by Frankel and Rose, see Kose and Yi (2002).

43. The results presented here were obtained using the second measure for the similarity of currency regimes, namely bilateral exchange rate volatility. When using the Frankel and Wei variable, we obtain almost identical results (except, of course, that the signs of α_4 and β_2 have opposite directions).

44. Note that a negative sign for β_2 in equation (2) in table 6.3 implies that an increase in exchange rate volatility reduces trade. Accordingly, a reduction of volatility should increase trade.

45. Except for trade in case 12.

46. There is, however, an indirect negative effect of FDI on output correlations through the trade channel if China is omitted ($\beta_1\alpha_1 < 0$).

47. This view dates back to the 18th century, when David Hume (1752) initiated the famous "oil-in-the-machine" illustration of the neutrality of money.

48. Fritz and Metzger (2006) hence distinguish "south–south" cooperation from "north–north" cooperation, where "north" refers to a country's ability to accumulate debt in its own currency and "south" refers to its disability to do so.

49. See also Calvo (2001) and Calvo and Mishkin (2003).

50. Similarly Hicks (1969: 89–90) distinguishes "local currency" from "great" currency, which are "widely used in international or distant commerce," whereas the circulation of local currency is "confined to the area which the government controlled."

51. Data are for 2006 and are taken from WDI. The relatively low level of real interest rates in some East Asian countries is due to two factors. First, capital controls make domestic assets imperfect substitutes for foreign assets in private portfolios. Second, directed lending partly outplays the market mechanism. Access to credit, however, remains a problem due to underdeveloped financial markets in most countries, especially for small and medium businesses. For an explanation how the "threat of currency appreciation" has pushed the interest rates of China and several other East Asian countries below the US interest rate level, see McKinnon and Schnabl (2009).

52. The term "original sin" has been criticized by Goldstein and Turner (2004) and Nitsch (2006) because it suggests that it cannot be overcome.

53. Dooley et al. (2009a, b) maintain that East Asian countries keep their currencies pegged to and resist appreciation against the US dollar primarily for mercantilistic reasons, namely to increase domestic growth and employment.

54. An IOU is a promise of money, goods, services, or other items of value, which may be either written or verbal. The name derives from the phonetic pronunciations of the respective letters, which sound like the phrase "I owe you."

55. See, for instance, Corsetti and Mackowiak (2005).

56. Eichengreen et al. (2005) argue that Switzerland and the United Kingdom can be regarded as special cases that achieved key currency status due to their unique historical roles.

57. After entering monetary union, however, the governments of several EMU member countries have manifestly shrugged off fiscal discipline and effectuated a weakening of the SGP.

58. The US case is quite different from that of the other four former colonies. See Bordo et al. (2005).

59. This size argument certainly does not apply to China and Japan (which, in any case, already has an internationally accepted currency), and only to a limited extent to Korea. Korea has tried for quite some time to promote the international use of the won by granting trade credits in won to importers, albeit with rather limited success. In May 2006 Korea announced a strategy for "facilitating the internationalization of the won," which includes a schedule to liberalize the won and capital flows. See Korean Ministry of Finance and the Economy (2006).

60. Mundell (2002) distinguishes between "policy sovereignty" and "legal sovereignty."

61. Goodhard (1995) does mention the costs of losing seignorage, but he argues that the value of seignorage to a stable country with low inflation is small and that the arrangements made under the Maastricht Treaty for returning seignorage to the constituent national central banks suggests that the net loss or gain to most European countries is of secondary importance. One should also highlight the loss of the national central bank's ability to act as a lender of last resort, but in the EMU this function is still fulfilled by the European System of Central Banks with the ECB at the center.

62. Data are monthly and are taken from IFS and Global Financial Data. As is usual for backward-looking Taylor rules, the estimates are obtained using OLS with heteroskedasticity- and autocorrelation-consistent standard errors. See, for instance, Carare and Tchaidze (2005). Changing the lags does not significantly alter the results.

63. The Greek drachma joined the EMS only in March 1998.

64. This result is confirmed by Frankel, Schmukler, and Servén (2004) and Chinn, Frankel, and Philips (1993), who find that interest rates in European countries had become completely insensitive to US interest rates but fully sensitive to German interest rates. Using co-integration analysis, Reade and Volz (2009a) also confirm German monetary hegemony within the EMS.

65. The ECB statutes determine that "from the time when the number of governors of national central banks [NCBs] exceeds 15 and until it reaches 22, the NCB governors will be allocated to two groups, according to a ranking of the size of their Member State's share in the aggregate GDP at market prices and in the total aggregated balance sheet of the monetary financial institutions of the Member States which have adopted the euro. . . . The first group will be composed of five governors with five voting rights and the second group of the remaining governors with the remaining votes." Once the number of NCB governors reaches 22, the governors will be allocated to three groups according to a ranking based on the above criteria. See Article 10.2 of the Statute of the European System of Central Banks and of the European Central Bank.

66. On the Swedish case, see Reade and Volz (2009c). The situation is different for the United Kingdom, where the Bank of England has managed to continue its independent monetary policy tailored to the national economy's needs. This can be attributed to the size of the UK economy as well as its financial sector, which give it a greater pull compared with smaller economies like Denmark and Sweden.

67. On July 21, 2005, the Chinese central bank officially announced that it had abandoned the eleven-year-old peg to the dollar and instead linked the yuan to an undisclosed basket of currencies. Annex 9 presents annual

regression results for all currencies. It shows that in the case of China the dollar weights have gone down since 2004 (when the dollar still had a 100 percent weight) to about 93 percent in 2007 and 2008. The Chinese move was followed by Malaysia. Several of other countries have also loosened their dollar pegs a bit.

68. See table 7.1.

69. This is not inconsistent with Kim and Lee's (2004) finding that the sensitivity of local interest rates to US rates has declined for Korea and Thailand since they moved toward less rigid exchange rate regimes after the Asian crisis.

70. See also Calvo and Reinhart (2001 and 2002).

71. Buiter (1999b: 24) even calls the insistence of "a rather small economy like the UK, quite open to international trade in goods and services and very open to international financial flows" to maintain a national currency "an expensive luxury—a costly way of indulging a taste for national sovereignty."

72. China's rapid accumulation of foreign exchange reserves in recent years demonstrates the constraints that the dollar peg has imposed on its monetary policy. One must note, however, that China has managed to sterilize the large increase of foreign reserve holdings very well and has thus been able to control inflation. The PBC has also made use of other monetary policy instruments, such as reserve requirements for domestic banks and credit ceilings. When announcing the raise of benchmark rates on one-year yuan loans to 5.58 percent from 5.31 percent and the rate on one-year deposits to 2.25 percent from 1.98 percent in October 2004, the PBC said in a statement that "[t]his interest rate rise . . . is to make bigger use of economic measures in resource allocation and macro-adjustment" (Xu 2004), indicating the country's intention to increasingly deploy its macroeconomic policy instruments. Still, even after loosening the dollar peg, Chinese officials acknowledge the monetary restrictions posed by the exchange rate regime. For instance, Yu Xuejun of the China Banking Regulatory Commission was quoted in the Financial Times as saying that the currency system had made the PBC "passive" (McGregor 2007). For a discussion of the domestic and external constraints on Chinese monetary policy, see Goodfriend and Prasad (2006).

73. For details on this methodology, see Reade and Volz (2009b).

74. In a similar fashion, DeMartino and Grabel (2003: 269) argue in a nonmonetary context that "regionalism represents not a further loss to policy autonomy, but a means to recoup it. Working together, states might be able to pursue a policy that each desires but each lacks the ability to achieve independently. In sum, then, regionalism may undermine or enhance policy autonomy, depending on the context and on the policy area at issue." They also maintain that "regionalism *per se* does not entail any sacrifice of state sovereignty" (DeMartino and Grabel 2003: 269).

75. On the advantages of multilateral monetary union over dollarization, see Alexander and von Furstenberg (2000) and Angeloni (2004).

76. On the power structure within the EMU, see Berger and de Haan (2002).

77. As Schelkle (2001a) points out, few would negate Mundell's (1961) assertion that the optimal currency area is not the world. However, Mundell (1968, 2003a) himself later promoted a world currency.

Chapter 7

1. The de jure and de facto exchange rate regimes in table 7.1 are identical with those presented in table 6.5.

2. According to this index, independence is greater when (1) a central bank's officials are insulated from political pressure by secure tenure and independent appointment, (2) the government cannot participate in or overturn its policy decisions, (3) the central bank's legal mandate specifies some price stability goal (whether as a unitary objective or as one of several objectives); and when the central bank's financial independence is ensured by restrictions that limit lending to the government. For more details, see Cukierman, Webb, and Neyapti (1992)

and Crowe and Meade (2007). For a critical perspective on such indexes of central bank independence, see Cargill (1995).

3. In 2008 inflation has soared throughout the region due to high oil and food prices, marking an end to what has become known as the period of great moderation.

Chapter 8

1. Albeit both McKinnon and Dooley et al. argue that the Bretton Woods II system will prevail, they do so with different reasoning. While Dooley et al. direct their attention more to the trade side, McKinnon's argumentation is grounded in the region's financial dependency on the dollar. For a discussion of these two different views, see McKinnon and Schnabl (2009).

2. McKinnon (2005) recommends the formal adoption of dollar pegs throughout the region. He argues that formal "parity commitments" to peg the Chinese and Japanese currencies to the US dollar would encourage the smaller East Asian countries to follow their example so that the result would be "a zone of greater monetary and exchange rate stability for the increasingly integrated East Asian economy." (McKinnon 2005: 52)

3. As was discussed in chapter 2, a global restoration of the Bretton Woods system to include the euro area is unrealistic.

4. The general problem with pegs will be discussed in section 10.1.

5. Chinn and Frankel (2007, 2008) point out that the dollar's supremacy is rivaled, for the first time in postwar history, by another currency, the euro. Galati and Wooldridge (2006) maintain that the introduction of the euro greatly improved the functioning of the euro area financial markets, with liquidity and breadth of the euro financial market fast approaching those of dollar markets. This implies that the traditional argument that there is simply no alternative to the dollar as an investment currency loses value.

6. For a discussion of the implications of a major dollar realignment, see the contributions in Bergsten and Williamson (2004).

7. See, for instance, the comments by Roubini (2009) or Gao (2009) in *The New York Times*.

8. The same is true not only for pegging to the dollar but also full dollarization. While dollarization would not entail the risk of pegging (which will be discussed in detail in the chapter 10), it would mean a complete surrender of both monetary autonomy and sovereignty.

9. See Zhang and Liang (2009). A modest step toward convertibility of the yuan has been made in December 2008, when the Standing Committee of the State Council of the People's Republic of China decided to allow the yuan to be used to settle trade payments with some selected trade partners as a part of a pilot project (see Murase 2009).

Chapter 9

1. See the discussions about the principal trade-off between fixed and floating rates in section 5.1 and the loss of monetary independence in section 6.5.

2. In an evaluation report of the IMF's exchange rate policy advice the IMF's Independent Evaluation Office (IMF IEO 2007: 22) noted that "recent IMF advice on exchange rate policy has mostly been couched in terms of calls for greater exchange rate flexibility." This advice was often linked with a proposed switch to inflation targeting as a nominal anchor. For an IMF assessment of the impact of inflation targeting in emerging markets see IMF (2005).

3. The inclusion of not only an inflation stability objective but also an objective of stabilizing the real economy is usually referred to as "flexible" inflation targeting. The target variables under flexible inflation targeting comprise both inflation and a real variable, such as the output gap.

4. In a recent panel analysis of inflation-targeting countries and a control group of high-achieving industrial countries that do not target inflation Mishkin and Schmidt-Hebbel (2007) find that inflation targeting helps countries achieve lower inflation in the long run, have smaller inflation response to oil price and exchange rate shocks, strengthen monetary policy independence, improve monetary policy efficiency, and obtain inflation outcomes closer to target levels.

5. Mishkin (2000: 109), one of the leading advocates of inflation targeting, acknowledges that "a critical issue for inflation targeting in emerging-market countries is the role of the exchange rate. Emerging-market countries, including those engaging in inflation targeting, have rightfully been reluctant to adopt an attitude of "benign neglect" of exchange-rate movements, partly because of the existence of a sizable stock of foreign currency or a high degree of (partial) dollarization." He thus concludes that "inflation targeting . . . may not be appropriate for many emerging-market countries" (Mishkin 2000: 105).

6. See Calvo and Mishkin (2003) who highlight five fundamental institutional differences for emerging market countries, compared to advanced economies: (1) weak fiscal institutions, (2) weak financial institutions including government prudential regulation and supervision, (3) low credibility of monetary institutions, (4) currency substitution and liability dollarization, and (5) vulnerability to sudden stops (of capital inflows).

7. In the view of Park (2006: 142), "[t]he new macroeconomic framework where inflation targeting is predicated on the assumption that the current account is not a policy concern may therefore be out of touch with the realities of many emerging market economies."

8. Chile has been described as the "poster child" (Mishkin 2004: 15) for inflation-targeting regimes in emerging market countries because it has been successful in lowering inflation to levels found in advanced countries, while at the same time experiencing rapid economic growth. On the Chilean experience with building credibility of its inflation-targeting regime, see Céspedes and Soto (2005).

9. Ball and Sheridan (2005) point out that the adoption of inflation targeting is an endogenous choice and argue that the apparent success of inflation-targeting countries reflects a regression toward the mean: because countries that adopted inflation targeting generally had higher initial inflation rates, their larger decline in inflation merely reflects a general tendency of all countries, both inflation targeters as well as nontargeters, to achieve better inflation and output performance in the 1990s, when inflation targeting was adopted.

10. Bank Indonesia (2008) describes its monetary policy as an "inflation-targeting lite," and given that there appears to be a certain degree of ad hocism in Indonesia's monetary policy, "there are reasons to doubt the degree to which Bank Indonesia is committed to this regime" (Rajan 2004: 8). For problems with inflation targeting in Indonesia, see Chowdhury and Siregar (2004), Alamsyah et al. (2001), and Sarwono (2008).

11. As Park (2006: 141) writes: "Although the IMF has maintained its support for inflation targeting as a nominal anchor, East Asian policymakers have been reluctant to accept such a framework because their financial systems are not mature enough to operate it and even when they are not convinced that it will help ensure price stability with robust growth while avoiding large current account imbalances. Taken together with old and new arguments against free floating, this lack of confidence in the new macroeconomic system [inflation targeting] appears to have been critical in shifting East Asia's emerging economies to managed floating or other intermediate regimes."

Chapter 10

1. An early proponent of such "corner solutions" is Eichengreen (1994: 59), who argued that "[i]ncreases in capital mobility make international monetary arrangements based on exchange rate targets—pegged but

adjustable rates, target zones, and the like—increasingly difficult to operate. International capital flows have already reached very high levels. Insofar as further increases are inevitable, governments may be confronted with a stark choice: to abandon explicit exchange rate targets or contemplate monetary unification." Another influential supporter of the bipolar view is Fischer (2001, 2008). For a critique of the bipolar view, see Frankel (1999) and Williamson (2000).

2. The following draws from Volz (2006).

3. For a model describing the output costs of an interest rate defense of a peg, see Lahiri and Végh (2007).

4. One should mention, however, that the Argentinean crisis was not triggered through self-fulfilling speculation; it would be probably best described by a first-generation model emphasizing the role of fundamentals.

5. The coordinated attack problem is analyzed in Morris and Shin (1997).

6. The EMS succeeded the "snake," a flawed attempt to secure intra-European exchange rate stability in the face of mounting difficulties in sustaining the Bretton Woods system of global fixed exchange rates. The snake was put into operation in April 1972, only four months after the Smithsonian agreement.

7. Resolution of the European Council of December 5, 1978 on the Establishment of the EMS and related matters (reprinted in Gros and Thygesen 1998: 58–63). For details of the EMS, see Gros and Thygesen (1998, chs. 2 and 3), for instance.

8. While average inflation rates between 1979 and 1983 ranged from 4.9 percent in Germany to 17 percent in Italy, they decreased markedly to a range of 1.1 percent in Germany and the Netherlands to 7.1 percent in Italy between 1984 and 1988 (Tietmeyer 1998: 44). The decline in oil prices certainly helped fight inflation, but the main effect can be attributed to stabilization policies.

9. Except for a technical adjustment of the lira in connection with the narrowing of the band width around the lira from 6 to 2.25 percent in January 1990.

10. In fact the Basle–Nyborg Agreement also called for undertaking small realignments more frequently, a recommendation that was never followed. The Agreement is reprinted in Gros and Thygesen (1998: 104–105).

11. Ireland banned foreign exchange trading for foreigners, and Spain required foreigners wishing to move short-term funds into Spain to make 100 percent noninterest bearing deposits at the central bank. Portugal also introduced capital controls (see Schiemann 1993).

12. Finland, which was not an EMS member at that time, was the first to come under pressure and to abandon its unilateral peg, with the result of a depreciation of the markka by 15 percent.

13. The inflation convergence achieved in the mid-1980s indeed widened. The average inflation rate between 1987 and 1992 in the countries with the most stable prices, namely the Netherlands and Germany, were 1.9 and 2.4 percent, respectively, whereas the United Kingdom, Italy, Spain, and Portugal, for example, had rates of 6.0, 5.7, 5.9, and 10.8 percent (see Tietmeyer 1998: 47). This argumentation is often extended by acknowledging that the underlying problems were aggravated through the loose fiscal and tight German monetary policy following German political and monetary unification.

14. See also Marston (1995: 114–19).

15. Eichengreen, Rose, and Wyplosz (1994) also cannot find evidence of significant differences in the behavior of key economic variables between crisis and noncrisis periods in the EMS. (But they do find such evidence for non-ERM observations.)

16. Rose and Svensson (1994) also find a relatively high level of ERM credibility in the months preceding the crisis, which persisted until late August 1992. They conclude that the currency crisis of 1992 does not appear to have been anticipated by financial markets. Other research—such as Eichengreen and Wyplosz (1993), who use the forward exchange rate, or Campa and Chang (1996), who estimate realignment probabilities derived

from option prices to measure market expectations—also indicates that both private-sector agents and policy makers were taken by surprise by the events of mid-September.

17. The British Prime Minister John Major (1999) mentions that Bundesbank President Helmut Schlesinger acknowledged Germany's willingness to cut interest rates in conjunction with a general realignment of ERM currencies but that France refused to go along.

18. Muehring (1992: 11).

19. Hamada and Lee (2009) emphasize the links between economic cooperation and security issues and explore these in a model of nested games.

20. As *The Economist* (2007a) recently wrote about ASEAN's tendency to proclaim new initiatives, "Read the fine print and you will find few significant commitments, let alone concrete targets. ASEAN leaders like the rhetoric of union but not the obligations of it."

21. See, for example, Kydland and Prescott (1977) and Fischer (1990).

22. The members of SEACEN are Central Bank of China (Taiwan), Bank Indonesia, Bank of Korea, Bank Negara Malaysia, Bank of Mongolia, Central Bank of Myanmar, Nepal Rastra Bank, Bangko Sentral ng Pilipinas, Monetary Authority of Singapore, Central Bank of Sri Lanka, and Bank of Thailand.

23. Article 3.2 of the Resolution of the European Council of December 5, 1978, on the establishment of the EMS and related matters (reprinted in Gros and Thygesen 1998: 59).

24. See, for example, Eichengreen et al. (1998).

25. See Cukierman, Spiegel, and Leiderman (2004) for the trade-offs involved in the choice of exchange rate bands.

26. The snake also contained support mechanisms, but as Eichengreen (1996: 159–60) reports, "[t]he European Monetary Cooperation Fund [of the snake] possessed little authority, central bank governors being unprepared to delegate their prerogatives. Meeting separately as the Committee of Central Bank Governors, they were supposed to set guidelines for national monetary policies but did little more than coordinate foreign-exchange market intervention. In the end, there existed no regional analogue to the International Monetary Fund to monitor policies and press for adjustments. The absence of such an institution meant that the strong-currency countries could not be assured that their weak-currency counterparts would undertake policy adjustments. Therefore, the foreign support they were willing to provide was necessarily limited."

27. The details of the envisaged extended support mechanism were indeed the key points mostly discussed when the decisions were being formulated in the second half of 1978 and early 1997 (Bernholz 1999).

28. The Emminger letter refers to a letter which Otmar Emminger, the Bundesbank president who signed the EMS agreement, wrote to the German government to ask for a clause permitting the Bundesbank to opt out from the EMS intervention obligations if they threatened the Bundesbank's mandate to secure price stability. The government acquiesced. The Bundesbank was heavily criticized for limiting its support at some stage. But as Eichengreen and Wyplosz (1993: 109) put it, "it is obvious that no central bank would ever commit unconditionally to unlimited lending."

29. See also McCauley and Ma (2008).

Chapter 11

1. See also Ito (2007b), Kawai (2004, 2009), Kawai, Ogawa, and Ito (2004), Ogawa (2008), Ogawa and Ito (2002), Rajan (2002), and Reisen and van Trotsenburg (1988).

2. As is evident from annex 9, the dollar weight in the new Chinese basket regime is still above 90 percent, so it might be a bit euphemistic to call it a basket peg. However, even this modest change has allowed the Chinese authorities to experiment with operating a basket peg, and the private sector to prepare for more exchange rate flexibility. It is likely that, with growing confidence in the new regime, China will gradually allow for more flexibility in the yuan exchange rate so that the basket regime can come into full force.

3. Already before the Chinese decision to allow more flexibility through the introduction of a currency basket, Ho, Ma, and McCauley (2005) detected a growing orientation of East Asian countries' exchange rate policy toward China. They argue that the rapid expansion of yuan turnover foreshadows a stronger influence of the Chinese currency in regional foreign exchange markets.

4. Williamson (2005) used China's announcement to argue in favor of a "currency basket for East Asia, not just China."

5. On regional monetary units, see Ogawa (2008) and the contributions in Ito (2007b).

6. It is most common to use total trade weights, but weights can be also based on import or export shares. Alternatively, weighting could be based on trade elasticities in order to also include important competitor countries and not only trading partners. The real effective exchange rate (REER) is the NEER adjusted for the effects of inflation. See, for instance, Williamson (2009). On considerations for calculating effective exchange rates for Asian countries that also account for the role of entrepôt trade, see Fung et al. (2006).

7. See Williamson (1982) for a survey of the analysis of the optimal peg.

8. The markets' anxiousness is illustrated by the reaction to the Korean central bank governor's announcement in March 2005 that official reserves would be divested from dollar assets. The dollar plunged immediately after the interview was released, because currency traders feared that other East Asian countries could follow. The consequence was that the Korean central bank immediately had to issue a correction saying that the governor was misinterpreted and that the Bank of Korea only intended to increase its holdings in other currencies but would not reduce its dollar reserves.

9. Even though, as discussed in the previous chapter on the EMS, a regional exchange rate system can also feature relatively wide bands in order to allow for considerable flexibility.

10. That is, a depreciation (appreciation) of a constituent currency will decrease (increase) its weight in the basket currency. The composition of the basket can be revised periodically to respond to changes in the relative importance of participating economies.

11. For the ICBs, the selected basket currencies and their weights actually correspond to those that will be used for the calculation of the NEERs.

12. One could also subsume other regions in these three currency areas. For example, Williamson (2009) adds East Asia's trade with the Middle East and Latin America to trade with the United States, and trade with Sub-Saharan Africa and Eastern Europe to trade with Europe, because these regions predominantly use the dollar and the euro, respectively, for international transactions.

13. The currency weights for the ECU were determined by economic importance in the region, share in intraregional trade, and share in EMS financing facilities. An ACU need not necessarily be constructed analogue to the ECU. For considerations in constructing an ACU and examples of existing currency basket indexes, see Kawai (2009).

14. When taking GDP at market prices, Japan's share in the regional GDP is 44 percent. The yen's weight in the ACU would be 34 percent while the yuan's weight would be 26 percent.

15. Including trading partners with lower trade shares would only complicate calculations without changing the results. The NEER weights are the same for all four scenarios.

16. The only exceptions are Brunei and Singapore, for which the NEER results under the country-tailored basket scenario are a bit higher than under the actual policies followed. Given that Singapore actually does follow a basket regime (and that the Brunei dollar is pegged to the Singapore dollar), this result only suggests that the undisclosed basket that the Monetary Authority of Singapore uses to stabilize its NEER is a bit more sophisticated than the simple basket used here and hence more effective in reducing NEER volatility.

17. This is consistent with the findings of Williamson (2009), who constructs baskets consisting of the dollar and the euro, and the dollar, the euro, and the yen for nine East Asian countries.

18. As mentioned earlier, China and Malaysia have recently made first moves into this direction. Once China allows for more flexibility in its exchange rate and effectively follows its announced basket regime, it is likely that Hong Kong (as well as the other dollar pegging countries in the region) will follow the mainland.

19. Although the yen can be classified as freely floating, Japan has frequently intervened in the foreign exchange market to influence its dollar rate. See Fratzscher (2004).

20. Such divergence analysis can help identify idiosyncratic problems in a particular currency's market and help address vulnerabilities that adversely affect the exchange rate. See Ogawa and Shimizu (2006) and Ogawa (2008).

21. For overviews of the use of the ECU in the private sector see, for instance, Mehnert-Meland (1994) and Johnson (1991).

22. The use of the ECU as invoicing currency remained very limited even after a decade of its existence, with less than 1 percent of Italian, French, and Belgian foreign trade being invoiced in ECU (Jozzo 1989).

23. Japan is an exception insofar that about a third of Japanese exports are denominated in yen. For comparison, the euro is used as invoice currency on 50 to 60 percent of (extra euro area) exports by most euro area countries. US firms invoice more than 90 percent of exports in US dollars. See Goldberg and Tille (2005, 2008).

24. Under the ABMI and the ABF-initiative mentioned in chapter 3, the region has already started the development of regional capital markets.

25. While Japan has been the driving force behind the ACU, China was originally suspicious of proposals for an ACU because it feared domination by the yen. (Both the president of the ADB, Haruhiko Kuroda, and its then head of the Office of Regional Integration, Masahiro Kawai, are former high-level Japanese government officials; Kuroda and Kawai, both former professors of economics, are among the greatest supporters of the ACU.) In the light of expectations of China's continued economic and trade growth, and thus China's growing weight in an ACU, the Chinese concern of potential dominance by the Japanese yen has lessened (McGregor 2006). According to the Financial Times (Guha and Mallet 2006), even the US government signaled that it would not fight efforts to create an ACU, turning the page on over a decade of largely consistent opposition to East Asian monetary and financial integration (see also Volz and Fujimura 2009).

26. As Friedrich Schiller versified in *The Song of the Bell*, "Whoe'er would form eternal bonds should weigh if heart to heart responds."

Chapter 12

1. In Mintz's (1970: 33) own words: "It has often been argued that the conditions under which monetary integration might reasonably be expected to succeed are very restrictive. In fact, these conditions appear no more restrictive than the conditions for the establishment of a successful common market. The major, and perhaps only, real condition for the institution of either is the political will to integrate on part of the prospective members." Similarly Kenen and Meade (2008: 197) emphasize the "primacy of politics." Or as Cohen (2003: 275) puts it, "Monetary unions necessarily imply a measure of *collective* action in the issue and management of money. An alliance requires allies—other states with similar preferences and a disposition to act cooperatively."

2. On the tributary system, see Hamashita (1994, 1997, 2003a, b), Mancall (1968), and Arrighi (1996).

3. Mancall (1968: 77) describes tribute to the Chinese emperor as the sine qua non for commercial activity with China: "At its most . . . fundamental, tribute's relationship to trade can be described as the ritual appropriate to commercial activities in the universe. Tribute was, in this sense, a 'sanction' for commercial activity, but it was not a specific sanction for a specific act, nor was it a permissive sanction. Rather, it was the *sine qua non*: trading activity within the Chinese world required the presentation of tribute to the emperor by someone at some point in time, and preferably, though not necessarily, by the representative of the chief of the power trading with China. . . . In this sense, the presentation of tribute and the receipt of gifts were ceremonial barter cosmologically required as a basis for trade."

4. For a detailed account of China's monetary history including the use of Chinese coins across East Asia, see Von Glahn (1996).

5. At times the dependency on Chinese coinage also brought about problems for the countries that had adopted Chinese money. Von Glahn (1996: 88ff) reports of episodes during which the supply of Chinese coin throughout the East Asian trading world was disrupted, either because the Chinese stopped minting or because they tried to restrict the outflow of money from China. This sometimes caused sharp contractions in the other regional economies, especially in Japan, which "had become utterly dependent on Chinese coin" (Von Glahn 1996: 88–89).

6. For the ADB's "Economic Interdependence among Asian Countries" survey, 600 opinion leaders from twelve Asian countries were questioned between August and November 2007. The survey sample is divided into three subregions: Northeast Asia (244 respondents from Japan, China, and Korea), Southeast Asia (198 respondents from Indonesia, Malaysia, Thailand, Philippines, Singapore, and Vietnam), and South Asia (158 respondents from India, Pakistan, and Sri Lanka). Unfortunately, only the aggregate results by regions are available; that is, the country-by-country data that would provide information on the differences between countries were not disclosed. Unless mentioned otherwise, the results presented here refer to the whole survey sample; stark subregional differences are mentioned if they exist. The results presented here draw on ADB (2008) and Capannelli (2007). Some additional information was kindly provided to the author by the ADB's Office of Regional Economic Integration which conducted this survey.

7. Note that the survey was conducted before the multilateralization of the CMI was officially agreed upon in May 2008.

8. Using firm-level data from the World Bank's World Business Environment Survey, Broz, Frieden, and Weymouth (2008) present cross-national evidence that confirm the theoretical expectations about the relationship between economic positions of firms and their preferences for currency policy.

9. Similarly banks and other financial institutions without substantial international business or foreign asset portfolio will be usually most concerned about domestic inflation, as rising inflation typically reduces the positive spread between the cost of funds and the return on assets, threatening to lower their profitability. They will thus have a preference for the central bank having a strong focus on inflation, i.e., exchange rate policy will not be a primary concern for them (Henning 1994). Banks engaged in international business will typically find it easier than manufacturers to cope with volatile exchange rates, although banks with heavy long-term commitment in foreign fixed assets, such as foreign subsidiaries, might as well be adversely affected by exchange rate volatility.

10. Chapter 3 of ADB (2008) provides a good overview of production networks in East Asia. For an analysis of production fragmentation and intra-industry trade in East Asia, see Ando (2006) and Hiratsuka (2008), as well as the contributions in Hiratsuka (2006).

11. It is typically more difficult and costly for small firms to hedge against exchange rate risk than for large firms. For instance, Japanese multinationals, who are important players in regional production networks in East Asia, have their own financial infrastructures, including banks, and financial know-how to hedge exchange rate risk, making Japanese (and regional) exchange rate policy a matter of secondary importance to them (Volz and Fujimura 2009). However, as Japanese firms' involvement in East Asia production networks often takes the form

of joint ventures (often in minority ownership), production sharing (through subcontracting) and nonequity arrangements (e.g., long-term contracting), the exchange rate risk is often passed on to the smaller partner in Southeast Asia or China.

12. This reminds of Europe, where the European Commission maintained that one market needs one money (Emerson et al. 1992). In the context of Mercosur, Eichengreen (1998: 33) argues that for a region adopting a far-reaching integration initiative that involves the creation of a true single, integrated market, "exchange rate swings will become more politically disruptive, and monetary unification becomes not only feasible but essential."

13. Indonesia, the largest ASEAN economy, is also the least open economy in Southeast Asia, with a trade to GDP ratio of 56 percent in 2007 (see table 5.7).

14. For an analysis of the political economy of Japanese monetary and exchange rate policy with an emphasis on regional monetary cooperation, see Volz and Fujimura (2009). A comprehensive analysis of the political economy of Japanese monetary policy is provided by Cargill, Hutchison and Ito (1997, 2000).

15. It should be noted that China, as well as Korea, are also facing severe problems of population aging. See Eberstadt (2004).

16. Yu (2007) reminds of the Chinese leadership's preference for gradualism when it comes to policy reform, epitomized in Deng Xiaoping's slogan "Crossing the river by feeling the stones." In the context of regional monetary cooperation Yu predicts that the Chinese authorities are likely to prefer a series of small steps in the direction of greater monetary cooperation, where at each step they will wait and evaluate the benefits before proceeding. The Chinese preference for gradualism, which is in line with the approach put forward in this book, implies that monetary integration in East Asia is likely to be a drawn-out process.

17. See *Wall Street Journal Europe* (2004) and Jopson (2004). A trading arrangement is also being negotiated between ASEAN and Korea. These arrangements are envisaged as building blocks for the possible establishment of an East Asia Free Trade Area (EAFTA) involving all ASEAN+3 countries. On the race for FTAs in East Asia, see Munataka (2006: ch. 7).

18. Nabers (2008) also highlights that rivalry between China and Japan has led Tokyo to come up with innovative proposals each time Beijing has approached ASEAN bilaterally.

19. The ASEAN Charter that ASEAN leaders signed at the 13th ASEAN Summit in Singapore in November 2007 exposed the sharp divisions persisting among the signatories (e.g., Arnold 2007).

20. In the assessment of Kenen and Meade (2008), the most probable outcome concerning East Asian monetary integration is the use of a currency basket by the ASEAN countries.

References

ADB. 2008. *Emerging Asian Regionalism. A Partnership for Shared Prosperity*. Manila: Asian Development Bank.

Ahn, Changmo, Hong-Bum Kim, and Dongkoo Chang. 2006. Is East Asia fit for an optimum currency area? An assessment of the economic feasibility of a higher degree of monetary cooperation in East Asia. *Developing Economies* 44 (3): 288–305.

Aizenman, Joshua, Yeonho Lee, and Yeongseop Rhee. 2004. International reserves management and capital mobility in a volatile world: Policy considerations and a case study of Korea. Working paper 10534. National Bureau of Economic Research, Cambridge, MA.

Alamsyah, Halim, Charles Joseph, Juda Agung, and Doddy Zulverdy. 2001. Towards implementation of inflation targeting in Indonesia. *Bulletin of Indonesian Economic Studies* 37 (3): 309–24.

Al-Mansouri, Abdulrahman, and Claudia Helene Dziobek. 2006. Providing official statistics for the Common Market and Monetary Union in the Gulf Cooperation Council (GCC) countries: A case for "Gulfstat." Working paper 06/38. International Monetary Fund, Washington, DC.

Alexander, Volbert, and George M. von Furstenberg. 2000. Monetary integration—A superior alternative to full dollarization in the long run. *North American Journal of Economics and Finance* 11 (2): 205–25.

Ando, Mitsuyo. 2006. Fragmentation and vertical intra-industry trade in East Asia. *North American Journal of Economics and Finance* 17 (3): 257–81.

Angeloni, Ignazio. 2004. Unilateral and multilateral currency unions: Thoughts from an EMU perspective. In Volbert Alexander, Jacques Melitz, and George M. von Furstenberg, eds., *Monetary Unions and Hard Pegs*. Oxford: Oxford University Press, 41–50.

Angresano, James. 2004. European Union integration lessons for ASEAN+3: The importance of contextual specificity. *Journal of Asian Economics* 14 (6): 909–26.

Arnold, Wayne. 2007. Historic Asean Charter reveals divisions. *International Herald Tribune*, November 20.

Arrighi, Giovanni. 1996. The rise of East Asia and the withering away of the interstate system. *Journal of World Systems Research* 2 (15): 1–35.

Asdrubali, Pierfederico, Bent E. Sørensen, and Oved Yosha. 1996. Channels of interstate risk sharing: United States 1963–1990. *Quarterly Journal of Economics* 111 (4): 1081–1110.

ASEAN. 1997. ASEAN Vision 2020. Kuala Lumpur, December 15, http://www.aseansec.org/1814.htm.

ASEAN. 1998a. Terms of understanding on the establishment of the ASEAN surveillance process. Washington, DC, October 4, http://www.aseansec.org/739.htm.

ASEAN. 1998b. Hanoi Plan of Action. http://www.aseansec.org/10382.htm.

ASEAN+3. 2006. The Joint Ministerial Statement of the 9th ASEAN+3 Finance Ministers' Meeting. Hyderabad, May 4, http://www.aseansec.org/18390.htm.

ASEAN+3 Finance Ministers. 2000. The Joint Ministerial Statement of the ASEAN+3 Finance Ministers Meeting. Chiang Mai, May 6, http://www.aseansec.org/635.htm.

ASEAN+3 Research Group. 2004. ASEAN+3 Research Group Studies 2003-2004. http://www.mof.go.jp/jouhou/kokkin/ASEAN+3research.htm.

ASEAN and China. 2004. Agreement on Trade in Goods of the Framework Agreement on Comprehensive Economic Cooperation between the Association of Southeast Asian Nations and the People's Republic of China. November 29, http://www.aseansec.org/16646.htm.

ASEAN and Korea. 2006. Agreement on Trade in Goods under the Framework Agreement on Comprehensive Economic Cooperation among the Governments of the Member Countries of the Association of Southeast Asian Nations and the Republic of Korea. August 24, http://www.aseansec.org/AKFTA%20documents%20signed%20at%20aem-rok,24aug06,KL-pdf/TIG%20-%20ASEAN%20Version%20-%2022August2006-final.pdf.

Baak, Saang Joon. 2004. Exchange rate volatility and trade among the Asia Pacific countries. *Journal of International Economic Studies* 8 (1): 93–116.

Balassa, Bela. 1961. *The Theory of Economic Integration*. Homewood, IL: Irwin.

Baldacci, Emanuele, Luiz de Mello, and Gabriela Inchauste. 2002. Financial crises, poverty, and income distribution. Working paper 02/4. International Monetary Fund, Washington, DC.

Baldwin, Richard E. 1997. The causes of regionalism. *World Economy* 20 (7): 865–88.

Baldwin, Richard E. 2006. The Euro's trade effects. *Proceedings of the June 2005 Workshop on What Effects Is EMU Having on the Euro Area and Its Member Countries?* Working paper 594. European Central Bank, Frankfurt am Main.

Ball, Laurence, and Niamh Sheridan. 2005. Does inflation targeting matter? In Ben S. Bernanke and Michael Woodford, eds., *The Inflation-Targeting Debate*. Chicago: University of Chicago Press, 249–76.

Bank for International Settlements. 2007. *Triennal Central Bank Survey. Foreign Exchange and Derivatives Market Activity in 2007*. Basel: BIS.

Bank Indonesia. 2008. Inflation targeting framework (ITF). http://www.bi.go.id/web/en/Moneter/Inflation+Targeting/Inflation+Targeting+Framework/.

Bayoumi, Tamim, and Barry J. Eichengreen. 1994. One money or many? Analyzing the prospects for monetary unification in various parts of the world. In *Princeton Studies in International Finance*, no. 76. Princeton: Princeton University.

Bayoumi, Tamim, and Barry J. Eichengreen. 1997. Ever closer to heaven? An optimum-currency-area index for European countries. *European Economic Review* 41 (3–5): 761–70.

Bayoumi, Tamim, Barry J. Eichengreen, and Paolo Mauro. 2000. On regional monetary arrangements for ASEAN. *Journal of the Japanese and International Economies* 14 (2): 121–48.

Bayoumi, Tamim, and Paolo Mauro. 1999. The suitability of ASEAN for a regional currency arrangement. Working paper 99/162. International Monetary Fund, Washington, DC.

Bénassy-Quéré, Agnes, and Maylis Coupet. 2005. On the adequacy of monetary arrangements in Sub-Saharan Africa. *World Economy* 28 (3): 349–73.

Berger, Helge, and Jacob de Haan. 2002. Are small countries too powerful within the ECB? *Atlantic Economic Journal* 30 (3): 263–80.

Berger, Helge, and Volker Nitsch. 2008. Zooming out: The trade effect of the euro in historical perspective. *Journal of International Money and Finance* 27 (8): 1244–1260.

Bergsten, C. Fred 2000. Toward a tripartite world. *The Economist* (July 15): 23–25.

Bergsten, C. Fred, and John Williamson 1983. Exchange rates and trade policy. In William R. Cline, ed., *Trade Policy in the 1980s*. Washington, DC: Institute for International Economics, 99–120.

Bergsten, C. Fred, and John Williamson 1994. Is the time ripe for target zones or the blueprint? In Bretton Woods Commission, ed., *Bretton Woods: Looking into the Future*. Washington, DC: Bretton Woods Commission, C21–30.

Bergsten, C. Fred, and John Williamson, eds. 2004. *Dollar Adjustment: How Far? Against What?* Special report 17. Washington, DC: Institute for International Economics.

Bernanke, Ben S., Thomas Laubach, Frederic S. Mishkin, and Adam S. Posen. 2001. *Inflation Targeting: Lessons from the International Experience*. Princeton: Princeton University Press.

Bernholz, Peter. 1999. The Bundesbank and the process of European monetary integration. In Deutsche Bundesbank, ed., *Fifty Years of the Deutsche Mark. Central Bank and the Currency in Germany Since 1948*. Oxford: Oxford University Press, 731–89.

Blanchard, Olivier Jean, and Danny Quah. 1989. The dynamic effects of aggregate demand and supply disturbances. *American Economic Review* 79 (4): 655–73.

Bofinger, Peter, and Christina Gerberding. 1988. EMS: A model for a world monetary order? *Intereconomics* (September/October): 212–19.

Bofinger, Peter. 2001. *Monetary Policy. Goals, Institutions, Strategies, and Instruments*. Oxford: Oxford University Press.

Bonpasse, Morrison. 2007. *The Single Global Currency. Common Cents for the World*. Newcastle, ME: Single Global Currency Association.

Bordo, Michael D. 1993. The gold standard, Bretton Woods and other monetary regimes: An historical appraisal. Working paper 4310. National Bureau of Economic Research, Cambridge, MA.

Bordo, Michael D., Barry J. Eichengreen, Daniela Klingebiel, and Maria Soledad Martinez-Peria. 2001. Is the crisis problem growing more severe? *Economic Policy* 16 (32): 51–82.

Bordo, Michael D., and Marc Flandreau. 2003. Core, periphery, exchange rate regimes, and globalization. In Michael D. Bordo, Alan M. Taylor, and Jeffrey G. Williamson, eds., *Globalization in Historical Perspective*. Chicago: University of Chicago Press, 417–72.

Bordo, Michael D., Christopher M. Meissner, and Angela Redish. 2005. How original sin was overcome: The evolution of external debt denominated in domestic currencies in the United States and the British dominions, 1800–2000. In Barry J. Eichengreen and Ricardo Hausmann, eds., *Other People's Money: Debt Denomination and Financial Instability in Emerging Market Economies*. Chicago: University of Chicago Press, 122–53.

Branson, William H. 1979. Exchange rate dynamics and monetary policy. In Assar Lindbeck, ed., *Inflation and Unemployment in Open Economies*. Amsterdam: North-Holland, 189–224.

Branson, William H., and Conor N. Healy. 2009. Monetary and exchange rate policy coordination in ASEAN+1. In Koichi Hamada, Beate Reszat, and Ulrich Volz, eds., *Towards East Asian Monetary and Financial Integration*. Cheltenham: Elgar, 222–64.

Branson, William H., and Dale W. Henderson. 1985. The specification and influence of asset markets. In Ronald W. Jones and Peter B. Kenen, eds., *Handbook of International Economics*, vol. 2. Amsterdam: North-Holland, 749–805.

Bretton Woods Commission. 1994. Bretton Woods: Looking to the future. Commission report. *Staff Review Background Papers.* Washington, DC: Bretton Woods Commission.

Bridges, Brian. 2004. Learning from Europe. Lessons for Asia Pacific regionalism? *Asia Europe Journal* 2 (3): 387–97.

Browne, Christopher, and David Orsmond. 2006. Pacific island countries: Possible common currency arrangement. Working paper 06/234. International Monetary Fund, Washington, DC.

Broz, J. Lawrence, and Jeffrey A. Frieden. 2006. The political economy of exchange rates. In Barry R. Weingast, ed., *Handbook of Political Science.* Oxford: Oxford University Press, 587–97.

Broz, J. Lawrence, Jeffrey A. Frieden and Stephen Weymouth. 2008. Exchange rate policy attitudes: Direct evidence from survey data. *IMF Staff Papers* 55 (3): 417–44.

Buiter, Willem H. 1997. The economic case for monetary union in the European Union. *Review of International Economics* 5 (4, special suppl.): 10–35.

Buiter, Willem H. 1999a. The EMU and the NAMU: What is the case for North American Monetary Union? *Canadian Public Policy* 25 (3): 285–305.

Buiter, Willem H. 1999b. Price of independence. *Financial Times* (June 17): 24.

Buiter, Willem H. 2000. Optimal currency areas: Why does the exchange rate regime matter? With an application to UK membership in EMU. *Scottish Journal of Political Economy* 47 (3): 213–50.

Buiter, Willem H. 2008. Economic, political, and institutional prerequisites for monetary union among the members of the Gulf Cooperation Council. *Open Economies Review* 19 (5): 579–612.

Buiter, Willem H., Giancarlo Corsetti, and Paolo A. Pesenti. 1998. *Financial Markets and European Monetary Cooperation. The Lessons of the 1992–93 Exchange Rate Mechanism Crisis.* Cambridge: Cambridge University Press.

Buiter, Willem H., Giancarlo Corsetti, and Nouriel Roubini. 1993. Excessive deficits: Sense and nonsense in the Treaty of Maastricht. *Economic Policy* 8 (16): 58–90, 99–100.

Burton, John. 2007. ASEAN to debate tighter integration rules. *Financial Times* (January 9).

Burton, John, and Amy Kazmin. 2008. Discomfort zone: A divided ASEAN is struggling to match dreams with reality. *Financial Times* (November 11): 9.

Calvo, Guillermo A. 2001. Capital markets and the exchange rate, with special reference to the dollarization debate in Latin America. *Journal of Money, Credit and Banking* 33 (2, pt. 2): 312–34.

Calvo, Guillermo A., and Frederic S. Mishkin. 2003. The mirage of exchange rate regimes for emerging market countries. *Journal of Economic Perspectives* 17 (4): 99–118.

Calvo, Guillermo A., and Carmen M. Reinhart. 2001. Fixing for your life. In Susan Collins and Dani Rodrik, eds., *Brookings Trade Forum 2000.* Washington, DC: Brookings Institution, 1–39.

Calvo, Guillermo A., and Carmen M. Reinhart. 2002. Fear of floating. *Quarterly Journal of Economics* 117 (2): 379–408.

Campa, José Manuel, and Kevin P.H. Chang. 1996. Arbitrage-based tests of target zone credibility: Evidence from ERM cross-rate options. *American Economic Review* 86 (4): 726–40.

Capannelli, Giovanni. 2007. *Increasing economic interdependence in Asia: A perception survey. Mimeo.* Office of Regional Economic Integration, Asian Development Bank, Manila.

Carare, Alina, and Robert Tchaidze. 2005. The use and abuse of Taylor rules: How precisely can we estimate them? Working paper 05/146. International Monetary Fund, Washington, DC.

Cargill, Thomas F. 1995. The statistical association between central bank independence and inflation. *Banca Nazionale del Lavoro Quarterly Review* 48 (193): 159–72.

Cargill, Thomas F., Michael M. Hutchison, and Takatoshi Ito. 1997. *The Political Economy of Japanese Monetary Policy.* Cambridge: MIT Press.

Cargill, Thomas F., Michael M. Hutchison, and Takatoshi Ito. 2000. *Financial Policy and Central Banking in Japan.* Cambridge: MIT Press.

Cecchetti, Stephen G. 1999. Legal structure, financial structure, and the monetary policy transmission mechanism. *Federal Reserve Bank of New York Economic Policy Review* 5 (2): 9–28.

Céspedes, Luis F., and Claudio Soto. 2005. Credibility and inflation targeting in an emerging market: Lessons from the Chilean experience. *International Finance* 8 (3): 545–75.

Chantasasawat, Busakorn, K. C. Fung, Hitomi Iizaka and Alan Siu. 2004. The giant sucking sound: Is China diverting foreign direct investment from other Asian economies? *Asian Economic Papers* 3 (3): 122–40.

Cheah, Hock-Beng. 2000. The Asian economic crisis: Three perspectives on the unfolding of the crisis in the global economy. In Frank-Jürgen Richter, ed., *Economic Growth, Institutional Failure and the Aftermath of the Crisis.* Houndmills, Basingstoke: Palgrave Macmillan, 97–116.

Cheung, Yin-Wong, Menzie D. Chinn, and Eiji Fujii. 2009. The illusion of precision and the role of the Renminbi in regional integration. In Koichi Hamada, Beate Reszat, and Ulrich Volz, eds., *Towards East Asian Monetary and Financial Integration.* Cheltenham: Elgar, 325–56.

Chinn, Menzie D. 2000. Before the fall: Were East Asian currencies overvalued? *Emerging Markets Review* 1 (2): 101–26.

Chinn, Menzie D., and Jeffrey A. Frankel. 2007. Will the euro eventually surpass the dollar as leading international reserve currency? In Richard Clarida, ed., *G7 Current Account Imbalances: Sustainability and Adjustment.* Chicago: University of Chicago Press, 283–322.

Chinn, Menzie D., and Jeffrey A. Frankel. 2008. Why the euro will rival the dollar. *International Finance* 11 (1): 49–73.

Chinn, Menzie D., Jeffrey A. Frankel, and Steve Philips. 1993. Financial and currency integration in the European monetary system: The statistical record. In Francisco Torres and Francesco Giavazzi, eds., *Adjustment and Growth in the European Monetary Union.* Cambridge: Cambridge University Press, 270–306.

Chinn, Menzie D., and Hiro Ito. 2008. A new measure of financial openness. *Journal of Comparative Policy Analysis* 10 (3): 309–22.

Choe, Jong-Il. 2001. An impact of economic integration trough trade: On business cycles for 10 East Asian countries. *Journal of Asian Economics* 12 (4): 569–86.

Choi, Gongpil. 2007. Toward an exchange rate mechanism for emerging Asia. In Duck-Koo Chung and Barry J. Eichengreen, eds., *Toward an East Asian Exchange Rate Regime.* Washington, DC: Brookings Institution Press, 121–36.

Chowdhury, Anis, and Hermanto Siregar. 2004. Indonesia's monetary policy dilemma—Constraints of inflation targeting. *Journal of Developing Areas* 37 (2): 137–53.

Claessens, Stijn, Rüdiger W. Dornbusch, and Yung Chul Park. 2001. Contagion: Why crises spread and how this can be stopped. In Stijn Claessens and Kristin J. Forbes, eds., *International Financial Contagion*. Boston: Kluwer Academic, 19–42.

Claessens, Stijn, and Kristin J. Forbes, eds. 2001. *International Financial Contagion*. Boston: Kluwer Academic.

Cohen, Benjamin J. 1998. *The Geography of Money*. Ithaca: Cornell University Press.

Cohen, Benjamin J. 2000. *Life at the Top: International Currencies in the Twenty-first Century*. Essays in International Economics, vol. 221. Princeton: Princeton University.

Cohen, Benjamin J. 2003. Are monetary unions inevitable? *International Studies Perspectives* 4 (3): 275–92.

Cohen, Benjamin J. 2004. *The Future of Money*. Princeton: Princeton University Press.

Collignon, Stefan. 1999. Bloc floating and exchange rate volatility: The causes and consequences of currency blocs. In Stefan Collignon, Jean Pisani-Ferry, and Yung Chul Park, eds., *Exchange Rate Policies in Emerging Asian Countries*. London: Routledge, 285–322.

Collignon, Stefan. 2002. *Monetary Stability in Europe*. London: Routledge.

Collignon, Stefan, and Daniela Schwarzer. 2003. *Private Sector Involvement in the Euro: The Power of Ideas*. London: Routledge.

Commission on the Future International Financial Architecture. 1999. *Safeguarding Prosperity in a Global Financial System: The Future International Financial Architecture Report of an Independent Task Force*. Washington, DC: Council on Foreign Relations.

Cooper, Richard N. 1984. A monetary system for the future. *Foreign Affairs* 63 (1): 166–84.

Cooper, Richard N. 1999. Exchange rate choices. In Jane Sneddon Little and Giovanni P. Olivei, eds., *Rethinking the International Monetary System*. Boston: Federal Reserve Bank, 99–123.

Corden, W. Max 1972. *Monetary integration. Essays in International Finance*, vol. 32. Princeton: Princeton University.

Corsetti, Giancarlo, and Bartosz Mackowiak. 2005. A fiscal perspective on currency crises and original sin. In Barry J. Eichengreen and Ricardo Hausmann, eds., *Other People's Money: Debt Denomination and Financial Instability in Emerging Market Economies*. Chicago: University of Chicago Press, 68–94.

Corsetti, Giancarlo, Paolo Pesenti, and Nouriel Roubini. 1999. The Asian crisis: An overview of the empirical evidence and policy debate. In Pierre-Richard Agénor, Marcus Miller, David Vines, and Axel Weber, eds., *The Asian Financial Crisis. Causes, Contagion and Consequences*. Cambridge: Cambridge University Press, 127–63.

Crosby, Mark, and Graham Voss. 2002. Business cycles in Asia–Pacific. Mimeo. Universities of Melbourne and Victoria.

Crowe, Christopher, and Ellen E. Meade. 2007. Evolution of central bank governance around the world. *Journal of Economic Perspectives* 21 (4): 69–90.

Cukierman, Alex, Yossi Spiegel, and Leonardo Leiderman. 2004. The choice of exchange rate bands: Balancing credibility and flexibility. *Journal of International Economics* 62 (2): 379–408.

Cukierman, Alex, Steven B. Webb, and Bilin Neyapti. 1992. Measuring the independence of central banks and its effect on policy outcomes. *World Bank Economic Review* 6 (3): 353–98.

De Brouwer, Gordon. 1999. *Financial Integration in East Asia*. Cambridge: Cambridge University Press.

De Carvalho, Fernando J. Cardim. 2006. Perspectives for a monetary union between Argentina and Brazil. In Barbara Fritz and Martina Metzger, eds., *New Issues in Regional Monetary Coordination. Understanding North–South and South–South Arrangements.* Houndmills, Basingstoke: Palgrave Macmillan, 98–115.

De Grauwe, Paul. 1994. *Alternative Strategies towards Monetary Union in Europe.* Vorträge, Reden und Berichte Nr. 35. Saarbrücken: Europa-Institut, Universität des Saarlandes.

De Grauwe, Paul. 2000. *Economics of Monetary Union,* 4th ed. Oxford: Oxford University Press.

De Grauwe, Paul, ed. 2001. *The Political Economy of Monetary Union.* Cheltenham: Elgar.

De Grauwe, Paul. 2005. *Economics of Monetary Union.* 6th ed. Oxford: Oxford University Press.

De Grauwe, Paul, and Bernard de Bellefroid 1989. Long-run exchange rate variability and international trade. In Sven W. Arndt and J. David Richardson, eds., *Real Financial Linkages among Open Economies.* Cambridge: MIT Press, 193–212.

De Grauwe, Paul, Hans Dewachter, and Mark Embrechts. 1993. *Exchange Rate Theory: Chaotic Models of Foreign Exchange Rates.* Oxford: Blackwell.

Debrah, Yaw A., ed. 2002. *Migrant Workers in Pacific Asia.* London: Frank Cass.

Debrun, Xavier, Paul R. Masson, and Catherine Pattillo. 2002. Monetary union in West Africa: Who might gain, who might lose, and why? Working paper 02/226. International Monetary Fund, Washington, DC.

DeMartino, George, and Ilene Grabel. 2003. Globalization, regionalism and state capacity in developing countries: A note. In Philip Arestis, Michelle Baddeley, and John McCombie, eds., *Globalisation, Regionalism and Economic Activity.* Cheltenham: Elgar, 266–73.

Bundesbank, Deutsche. 1990. *Annual Report 1990.* Frankfurt am Main.

Dieter, Heribert. 2000a. Nach den Krisen der 90er Jahre: Re-Regulierung der internationalen Finanzmärkte. *PROKLA Zeitschrift für kritische Sozialwissenschaft* 30 (1): 39–59.

Dieter, Heribert. 2000b. Monetary regionalism: Regional integration without financial crises. Working paper 52/00. Centre for the Study of Globalisation and Regionalisation, University of Warwick, Coventry.

Dieter, Heribert, and Richard Higgot. 2003. Exploring alternative theories of economic regionalism. From trade to finance in Asian cooperation? *Review of International Political Economy* 10 (3): 430–55.

Dixit, Avinash. 1989. Hysteresis, imports penetration, and exchange rate pass-through. *Quarterly Journal of Economics* 104 (2): 205–27.

Dooley, Michael, David Folkerts-Landau, and Peter Garber. 2003. An essay on the revived Bretton Woods system. Working paper 9971. National Bureau of Economic Research, Cambridge, MA.

Dooley, Michael, David Folkerts-Landau, and Peter Garber. 2004. The Revived Bretton Woods system: The effects of periphery intervention and reserve management on interest rates and exchange rates in center countries. Working paper 10332. National Bureau of Economic Research, Cambridge, MA.

Dooley, Michael, David Folkerts-Landau, and Peter Garber. 2009a. Bretton Woods II still defines the International Monetary System. Working paper 14731. National Bureau of Economic Research, Cambridge, MA.

Dooley, Michael, David Folkerts-Landau, and Peter Garber. 2009b. East Asia's role in the revived Bretton Woods system. In Koichi Hamada, Beate Reszat, and Ulrich Volz, eds., *Towards East Asian Monetary and Financial Integration.* Cheltenham: Elgar, 141–58.

Dowd, Kevin, and David Greenaway. 1993. Currency competition, network externalities and switching costs: Towards an alternative view of optimum currency areas. *Economic Journal* 103 (420): 1180–89.

Dullien, Sebastian. 2004. *The Interaction of Monetary Policy and Wage Bargaining in the European Monetary Union: Lessons from the Endogenous Money Approach*. Houndmills, Basingstoke: Palgrave Macmillan.

Eberstadt, Nicholas. 2004. Power and population in Asia. *Policy Review* 123 (February/March): 3–27.

ECB. 2002. Recent developments in international co-operation. *ECB Monthly Bulletin* (February): 53–65.

ECB. 2004. Economic integration in selected regions outside the European Union. *ECB Monthly Bulletin* (October): 67–84.

The Economist. 2007a. Close call: ASEAN talks of integration. *The Economist* (January 17).

The Economist. 2007b. Wandering workers. *The Economist* (January 18).

The Economist. 2009. Monetary union in the Gulf. Disunited Arab Emirates. *The Economist* (May 21).

Edwards, Sebastian. 1999. How effective are capital controls? *Journal of Economic Perspectives* 13 (4): 65–84.

Ehrmann, Michael, Leonardo Gambacorta, Jorge Martínez-Pagéz, Patrick Sevestre, and Andreas Worms. 2001. Financial systems and the role of banks in monetary policy transmission in the euro area. Discussion paper 18/01. Deutsche Bundesbank, Frankfurt am Main.

Eichengreen, Barry J. 1994. *International Monetary Arrangements for the 21st Century*. Washington, DC: Brookings Institution.

Eichengreen, Barry J. 1996. *Globalizing Capital. A History of the International Monetary System*. Princeton: Princeton University Press.

Eichengreen, Barry J. 1997. International monetary arrangements. Is there a monetary union in Asia's future? *Brookings Review* 15 (2): 33–35.

Eichengreen, Barry J. 1998. Does Mercosur need a single currency? Working paper 6821. National Bureau of Economic Research, Cambridge, MA.

Eichengreen, Barry J. 1999. *Toward a New Financial Architecture. A Practical Post-Asia Agenda*. Washington, DC: Institute for International Economics.

Eichengreen, Barry J. 2001. The EMS crisis in retrospect. Discussion paper 2704. Centre for Economic Policy Research, London.

Eichengreen, Barry J. 2002. Can emerging markets float? Should they inflation target? Working paper series 36. Banco Central do Brasil, Brasília.

Eichengreen, Barry J. 2006. The parallel-currency approach to Asian monetary integration. *American Economic Review* 96 (2, AEA Papers and Proceedings): 432–36.

Eichengreen, Barry J., and Tamin Bayoumi. 1999. Is Asia an optimum currency area? Can it become one? Regional, global, and historical perspectives on Asian monetary relations. In Stefan Collignon, Jean Pisani-Ferry, and Yung Chul Park, eds., *Exchange Rate Policies in Emerging Asian Countries*. London: Routledge, 347–66.

Eichengreen, Barry J., and Ricardo Hausmann. 1999. Exchange Rates and Financial Fragility. In *Proceedings, Federal Reserve Bank of Kansas City*, August, pp. 329–368.

Eichengreen, Barry J., Ricardo Hausmann, and Ugo Panizza. 2005. The Mystery of Original Sin. In *Other People's Money: Debt Denomination and Financial Instability in Emerging Market Economies*, ed. Barry J. Eichengreen and Ricardo Hausmann. Chicago: University of Chicago Press, 233–65.

Eichengreen, Barry J., Paul R. Masson, Hugh Bredenkamp, Barry Johnston, Javier Hamann, Esteban Jadresic, and Inci Ötker. 1998. Exit strategies: Policy options for countries seeking greater exchange rate flexibility. Occasional paper 168. International Monetary Fund, Washington, DC.

Eichengreen, Barry J., Andrew K. Rose, and Charles Wyplosz. 1994. Speculative attacks on pegged exchange rates: An empirical exploration with special reference to the European Monetary System. Discussion paper 1060. Centre for Economic Policy Research, London.

Eichengreen, Barry J., Andrew K. Rose, and Charles Wyplosz. 1996. Contagious currency crises. Working paper 5681. National Bureau of Economic Research, Cambridge, MA.

Eichengreen, Barry J., and Charles Wyplosz. 1993. The unstable EMS. *Brookings Papers on Economic Activity* 24 (1993-1): 51–143.

Emerson, Michael, Daniel Gros, Alexander Italianer, Jean Pisani-Ferry, and Horst Reichenbach. 1992. *One Market, One Money. An Evaluation of the Potential Benefits and Costs of Forming an Economic and Monetary Union.* Oxford: Oxford University Press.

Estrada, Joseph Ejercito. 1999. Welcome remarks at the Third ASEAN Informal Summit. http://www.aseansec. org/5299.htm.

Ethier, Wilfred J. 1973. International trade and the forward exchange market. *American Economic Review* 63 (3): 494–503.

Feldstein, Martin. 1998. Refocusing the IMF. *Foreign Affairs* 77 (2): 20–33.

Fernández-Arias, Eduardo, Ugo Panizza, and Ernesto Stein. 2004. Trade agreements, exchange rate disagreements. In Volbert Alexander, Jacques Mélitz, and George M. von Furstenberg, eds., *Monetary Union and Hard Pegs: Effects on Trade, Financial Development, and Stability.* Oxford: Oxford University Press, 135–50.

Fischer, Stanley. 1990. Rules versus discretion in monetary policy. In Benjamin M. Friedman and Frank H. Hahn, eds., *Handbook of Monetary Economics.* Amsterdam: North-Holland, 1155–84.

Fischer, Stanley. 2001. Exchange rate regimes: Is the bipolar view correct? *Journal of Economic Perspectives* 15 (2): 3–24.

Fischer, Stanley. 2008. Exchange rate systems, surveillance, and advice. *IMF Staff Papers* 55 (3): 367–83.

Flandreau, Marc, and Mathilde Maurel. 2005. Monetary union, trade integration, and business cycles in 19th century Europe. *Open Economies Review* 16 (2): 135–52.

Fleming, J. Marcus. 1971. On exchange rate unification. *Economic Journal* 81 (323): 467–88.

Flood, Robert P., and Nancy P. Marion. 2002. Holding international reserves in an era of high capital mobility. In Susan M. Collins and Dani Rodrik, eds., *Brookings Trade Forum 2001.* Washington, DC: Brookings Institution Press, 1–68.

Flood, Robert P., and Andrew K. Rose. 1999. Understanding exchange rate volatility without the contrivance of macroeconomics. *Economic Journal* 109 (459): F660–72.

Fracasso, Andrea, Hans Genberg, and Charles Wyplosz. 2003. *How Do Central Banks Write? An Evaluation of Inflation Reports by Inflation Targeting Central Banks.* Geneva Reports on the World Economy. Special report 2. London: Centre for Economic Policy Research.

Fraga, Arminio, Ilan Goldfajn, and André Minella. 2003. Inflation targeting in emerging market economies. Working paper 10019. National Bureau of Economic Research, Cambridge, MA.

Frankel, Jeffrey A. 1983. International liquidity and monetary control. In George M. von Furstenberg, ed., *International Money and Credit: The Policy Roles.* Washington, DC: International Monetary Fund, 65–109.

Frankel, Jeffrey A. 1988. *Obstacles to International Macroeconomic Policy Coordination. Princeton Studies in International Finance 64.* Princeton: Princeton University.

Frankel, Jeffrey A. 1997. *Regional Trading Blocs in the World Economic System*. Washington, DC: Institute for International Economics.

Frankel, Jeffrey A., ed. 1998. *The Regionalization of the World Economy*. Chicago: University of Chicago Press.

Frankel, Jeffrey A. 1999. No single currency regime is right for all countries or at all times. Working paper 7338. National Bureau of Economic Research, Cambridge, MA.

Frankel, Jeffrey A. 2000. Impact of the euro on members and non-members. In Robert Mundell and Armand Clesse, eds., *The Euro as a Stabilizer in the International Economic System*. Boston: Kluwer Academic, 93–111.

Frankel, Jeffrey A. 2006. Comments on Richard Baldwin's "The Euro's Trade Effects." *Proceedings of June 2005 Workshop on What Effects Is EMU Having on the Euro Area and Its Member Countries?* Working paper 594. European Central Bank, Frankfurt am Main, 76–90.

Frankel, Jeffrey A., and Andrew K. Rose. 1998. The endogeneity of the optimum currency area criteria. *Economic Journal* 108 (449): 1009–25.

Frankel, Jeffrey A., and Andrew K. Rose. 2002. An estimate of the effect of common currencies on trade and income. *Quarterly Journal of Economics* 117 (2): 437–66.

Frankel, Jeffrey A., Sergio L. Schmukler, and Luis Servén. 2004. Global transmission of interest rates: Monetary independence and currency regime. *Journal of International Money and Finance* 23 (5): 701–33.

Frankel, Jeffrey, and Shang-Jin Wei. 1994. Yen bloc or dollar bloc? Exchange rate policies of the East Asian economies. In Takatoshi Ito and Anne Krueger, eds., *Macroeconomic Linkages: Savings, Exchange Rates, and Capital Flows. NBER East Asia Seminar on Economics*. vol. 3. Chicago: University of Chicago Press, 295–329.

Fratianni, Michele, and Andreas Hauskrecht 2002. A centralized monetary union for Mercosur: Lessons from EMU. Paper prepared for the conference on Euro and Dollarization: Forms of Monetary Union in Integrated Regions. Fordham University and CEPR, New York, April 5–6.

Fratzscher, Marcel. 2002. The euro bloc, the dollar bloc, and the yen bloc: How much monetary policy independence can exchange rate flexibility buy in an interdependent world? Working paper 154. European Central Bank, Frankfurt am Main.

Fratzscher, Marcel. 2004. Exchange rate policy strategies and foreign exchange interventions in the group of three economies. In C. Fred Bergsten and John Williamson, eds., *Dollar Adjustment: How Far? Against What?* Special Report 17. Washington, DC: Institute for International Economics, 259–71.

Freedom House. 2008. *Freedom in the World 2008. The Annual Survey of Political Rights and Civil Liberties*. Lanman, MD: Rowman and Littlefield.

Friedman, Milton. 1953. The case for flexible exchange rates. In Milton Friedman, ed., *Essays in Positive Economics*. Chicago: University of Chicago Press, 157–203.

Friedman, Milton. 1968. The role of monetary policy. *American Economic Review* 58 (1): 1–17.

Fritz, Barbara. 2002. *Entwicklung durch wechselkurs-basierte Stabilisierung? Der Fall Brasilien*. Marburg: Metropolis Verlag.

Fritz, Barbara, and Martina Metzger, eds. 2006. *New Issues in Regional Monetary Coordination. Understanding North–South and South–South Arrangements*. Houndmills, Basingstoke: Palgrave Macmillan.

Fukao, Kyoji, Hiraki Ishido, and Keiko Ito. 2003. Vertical intra-industry trade and foreign direct investment in East Asia. *Journal of the Japanese and International Economies* 17 (4): 468–506.

Fukuyama, Francis. 2005a. Re-envisioning Asia. *Foreign Affairs* 84 (1): 75–80.

Fukuyama, Francis. 2005b. All quiet on the eastern front? *Wall Street Journal* (March 1): 18.

Funabashi, Yoichi. 1988. *Managing the Dollar: From the Plaza to the Louvre*. Washington, DC: Institute for International Economics.

Fung, San Sau, Marc Klau, Guonan Ma, and Robert N. McCauley. 2006. Estimation of Asian effective exchange rates: A technical note. Working paper 217. Bank for International Settlements, Basel.

Furman, Jason, and Joseph E. Stiglitz. 1998. Economic crises: Evidence and insights from East Asia. *Brookings Papers on Economic Activity* 29 (1998-2): 1–135.

G-20. 2009. The Global Plan for Recovery and Reform. April 2, www.londonsummit.gov.uk/resources/en/PDF/final-communique.

Galati, Gabriele, and Philip Wooldridge. 2006. The euro as a reserve currency: A challenge to the pre-eminence of the US dollar? Working paper 218. Bank for International Settlements, Basel.

Gandolfo, Giancarlo. 1992. Monetary unions. In John Newman, Murray Milgate, and Peter Eatwell, eds., *The New Palgrave Dictionary of Money and Finance*. London: Macmillan, 765–70.

Gao, Victor Zhikai. 2009. China's heart of gold. *New York Times*, May 13.

Gianetti, Mariassunta, Luigi Guiso, Tullio Jappelli, Mario Padula, and Marco Pagano. 2002. *Financial Market Integration, Corporate Financing and Economic Growth. European Commission economic papers 179*. Brussels: European Commission.

Giavazzi, Francesco, and Marco Pagano. 1988. The advantage of tying one's hands: EMS discipline and central bank credibility. *European Economic Review* 32 (5): 1055–82.

Giavazzi, Francesco, and Luigi Spaventa. 1990. The "new" EMS. In Paul De Grauwe and Lucas Papademos, eds., *The European Monetary System in the 1990s*. New York: Longman, 65–85.

Gil, Indermit, and Homi Kharas. 2007. *An East Asian Renaissance. Ideas for Economic Growth*. Washington, DC: World Bank.

Girardin, Eric. 2004. Regime-dependent synchronization of growth cycles between Japan and East Asia. *Asian Economic Papers* 3 (3): 147–76.

Giridharadas, Anand. 2006. Asian finance ministers talk of united currency. China, Japan and South Korea huddle. *International Herald Tribune* (May 5): 12.

Glick, Reuven, and Andrew K. Rose. 1999. Contagion and trade. Why are currency crises regional? *Journal of International Money and Finance* 18 (4): 603–17.

Goldberg, Linda S., and Cédric Tille. 2005. "Vehicle currency use in international trade. Working paper 11127. National Bureau of Economic Research, Cambridge, MA.

Goldberg, Linda S., and Cédric Tille. 2008. Macroeconomic interdependence and the international role of the dollar. Working paper 13820. National Bureau of Economic Research, Cambridge, MA.

Goldfajn, Ilan, and Rodrigo Valdés. 1996. Balance of payment crises and capital flows: The role of liquidity. Working paper 5650. National Bureau of Economic Research, Cambridge, MA.

Goldstein, Morris. 1998. *The Asian Financial Crisis: Causes, Cures, and Systemic Implications. Policy Analyses in International Economics 55*. Washington, DC: Institute for International Economics.

Goldstein, Morris, and John Hawkins. 1998. The origin of the Asian financial turmoil. Research discussion paper 9805. Economic Research Department. Reserve Bank of Australia, Sydney.

Goldstein, Morris, and Philip Turner. 2004. *Controlling Currency Mismatches in Emerging Markets*. Washington, DC: Institute for International Economics.

Goodfriend, Marvin, and Eswar Prasad. 2006. A framework for independent monetary policy in China. Working paper 06/111. International Monetary Fund, Washington, DC.

Goodhard, Charles. 1995. The political economy of monetary union. In Peter B. Kenen, ed., *Understanding Independence. The Macroeconomics of the Open Economy*. Princeton: Princeton University Press, 448–505.

Gordon, Lincoln. 1961. Economic regionalism reconsidered. *World Politics* 13 (2): 231–53.

Goto, Junichi. 2002. *Economic preconditions for monetary integration in East Asia*. Mimeo. Kobe University.

Greenville, Stephen. 2004. Good advice gets bad name in South-East Asia. *Financial Times* (November 14).

Grilli, Enzo. 2002. The Asian crisis: Trade causes and consequences. *World Economy* 25 (2): 177–207.

Gros, Daniel, and Niels Thygesen. 1998. *European Monetary Integration*, 2nd ed. Harlow: Addison Wesley Longman.

Gruben, William C., Jahyeong Koo, and Eric Millis. 2003. How much does trade affect business cycle synchronization. Working paper 0203. Research Department, Federal Reserve Bank of Dallas.

Guha, Krishna. 2008. Report of US currency rescue plan. *Financial Times* (August 28).

Guha, Krishna, and Victor Mallet. 2006. US drops opposition to Asian currency unit. *Financial Times* (June 16).

Gundlach, Erich, Ulrich Hiemenz, Rolf J. Langhammer, and Peter Nunnenkamp. 1994. *Regional Integration in Europe and Its Effects on Developing Countries*. Tübingen: Mohr.

Haddad, Mona. 2007. Trade integration in East Asia: The role of China and production networks. Policy research working paper 4160. World Bank, Washington, DC.

Hale, David, and Lyric Hughes Hale. 2003. China takes off. *Foreign Affairs (Council on Foreign Relations)* 82 (6): 36–43.

Hamada, Koichi, and Inpyo Lee. 2009. International political conflicts and economic integration. In Koichi Hamada, Beate Reszat, and Ulrich Volz, eds., *Towards East Asian Monetary and Financial Integration*. Cheltenham: Elgar, 61–84.

Hamashita, Takeshi. 1994. The tribute trade system and modern Asia. In A. J. H. Latham and Heita Kawakatsu, eds., *Japanese Industrialization and the Asian Economy*. London: Routledge, 91–107.

Hamashita, Takeshi. 1997. The intra-regional system in East Asia in modern times. In Peter J. Katzenstein and Takashi Shiraishi, eds., *Network Power: Japan and Asia*. Ithaca: Cornell University Press, 113–35.

Hamashita, Takeshi. 2003a. Ryukyu networks in maritime Asia. *Kyoto Review of Southeast Asia* 3 (2), http://kyotoreview.cseas.kyoto-u.ac.jp/issue/issue2/index.html.

Hamashita, Takeshi. 2003b. Tribute and treaties: Maritime Asia and treaty port networks in the era of negotiation, 1800–1900. In Giovanni Arrighi, Takeshi Hamashita, and Mark Selden, eds., *The Resurgence of East Asia. 500, 150 and 50 Year Perspectives*. London: Routledge, 17–50.

Hamilton-Hart, Natasha. 2005. The regionalization of Southeast Asian business: Transnational networks in national contexts. In T. J. Pempel, ed., *Remapping East Asia. The Construction of a Region*. Ithaca: Cornell University Press, 170–91.

Hauskrecht, Andreas. 2001. Ärmste Entwicklungsländer und das geeignete Wechselkursregime—gibt es eine universelle Empfehlung? In Renate Schubert, ed., *Entwicklungsperspektiven von Niedrigeinkommensländern—Zur Bedeutung von Wissen und Institutionen.* Berlin: Duncker und Humblot, 13–28.

Hayakawa, Kazunobu, and Fukunari Kimura. 2008. The effect of exchange rate volatility on international trade: The implication for production networks in East Asia. Discussion paper 156. Institute of Developing Economies, Chiba.

Hayek, Friedrich A. 1937. *Monetary Nationalism and International Stability.* London: Longmans Green.

Heathcote, Jonathan, and Fabrizio Perri. 2004. Financial globalization and real regionalization. *Journal of Economic Theory* 119 (1): 207–43.

Hefeker, Carsten. 1997. *Interest Groups and Monetary Integration. The Political Economy of Exchange Regime Choice.* Boulder: Westview Press.

Hefeker, Carsten, and Andreas Nabor. 2005. China's role in East-Asian monetary integration. *International Journal of Finance and Economics* 10 (2): 157–66.

Helleiner, Eric. 2006. *Towards North American Monetary Union? A Political History of Canada's Exchange Rate Regime.* Montreal: McGill-Queen's University Press.

Helliwell, John F. 1998. *How Much Do National Borders Matter?* Washington, DC: Brookings Institution Press.

Henning, C. Randall. 1994. *Currencies and Politics in the United States, Germany, and Japan.* Washington, DC: Institute for International Economics.

Henning, C. Randall. 2002. *East Asian Financial Cooperation.* Policy Analyses in International Economics 68. Washington, DC: Institute for International Economics.

Henning, C. Randall. 2005. Systemic contextualism and financial regionalism: The case of East Asia. Mimeo. American University and Institute for International Economics, Washington, DC.

The Heritage Foundation/Wall Street Journal. 2008. *2008 Index of Economic Freedom. The Link between Economic Opportunity and Prosperity.* Washington, DC: Heritage Foundation.

Hew, Denis, and Hadi Soesastro. 2003. Realizing the ASEAN Economic Community by 2020: ISEAS and ASEAN-ISIS approaches. *ASEAN Economic Bulletin* 20 (3): 292–96.

Hicks, John. 1969. *A Theory of Economic History.* Oxford: Clarendon Press.

Hiratsuka, Daisuke, ed. 2006. *East Asia's De Facto Economic Integration.* Houndmills, Basingstoke: Palgrave Macmillan.

Hiratsuka, Daisuke. 2008. Production fragmentation and networks in East Asia characterized by vertical specialization. In Daisuke Hiratsuka and Yoko Uchida, eds., *Vertical Specialization and Economic Integration in East Asia.* Tokyo: JETRO, 91–116.

Ho, Corinne, Guonan Ma, and Robert N. McCauley. 2005. Trading Asian currencies. *BIS Quarterly Review* (March): 49–58.

Yanghua, Huang, and Zhang Yongsheng. 2008. East Asian economic integration and its impact on the Chinese economy. Revision of paper presented at the Conference on Regional Economic Integration beyond Europe. German Development Institute, Bonn, December 19–20, 2007.

Hume, David. 1752. Of money. Reprinted in David Hume (1754), *Essays: Moral.* London: Political and Literary.

Hutchison, Michael M. 2003. A cure worse than the disease? Currency crises and the output costs of IMF-supported stabilization programs. In Michael P. Dooley and Jeffrey A. Frankel, eds., *Managing Currency Crises in Emerging Markets*. Chicago: University of Chicago Press, 321–54.

ILO. 2005. *Yearbook of Labor Statistics 2005*. Geneva: International Labor Organization.

Imbs, Jean. 2004. Trade, finance, specialization and synchronization. *Review of Economics and Statistics* 86 (3): 723–34.

Imbs, Jean. 2006. The real effects of financial integration. *Journal of International Economics* 68 (2): 296–324.

Imbs, Jean, and Romain Wacziarg. 2003. Stages of diversification. *American Economic Review* 93 (1): 63–86.

IMF. 1997. *World Economic Outlook. Globalization: Opportunities and Challenges*. Washington, DC: International Monetary Fund.

IMF. 2001. IMF managing director congratulates Korea on early repayment of 1997 stand-by credit. In *News Brief No. 01/82*, August 22. Washington, DC: International Monetary Fund.

IMF. 2005. *World Economic Outlook. Building Institutions*. Washington, DC: International Monetary Fund.

IMF. 2006. IMF Executive Board recommends quota and related governance reforms. Press Release 06/189, September 1. International Monetary Fund, Washington, DC.

IMF. 2008a. The GCC monetary union—Choice of exchange rate regime. Middle East and Central Asia Department. International Monetary Fund, Washington, DC, August 28.

IMF. 2008b. IMF quotas: A factsheet (September), http://www.imf.org/external/np/exr/facts/quotas.htm.

IMF. 2008c. *Annual Report on Exchange Arrangements and Exchange Restrictions*. Washington, DC: International Monetary Fund.

IMF IEO. 2007. *IMF Exchange Rate Policy Advice*. Washington, DC: Independent Evaluation Office of the International Monetary Fund.

Institute of International Finance. 1998. Capital flows to emerging market economies. January 29. Washington, DC.

Ito, Takatoshi. 2001. Growth, crisis, and the future of economic recovery in East Asia. In Joseph E. Stiglitz and Shahid Yusuf, eds., *Rethinking the East Asian Miracle*. Oxford: Oxford University Press, 55–94.

Ito, Takatoshi. 2007a. Asian currency crisis and the International Monetary Fund, 10 years later: Overview. *Asian Economic Policy Review* (2): 16–49.

Ito, Takatoshi, ed. 2007b. *A Basket Currency for Asia*. London: Routledge.

Ito, Takatoshi, and Luiz Pereira da Silva. 1999. The credit crunch in Thailand during the 1997–98 crisis: Theoretical and operational issues of the JEXIM survey. *EXIM Review* 19 (2): 1–40.

James, Harold. 1999. A historical perspective on international monetary arrangements: Opening address. In Jane Sneddon Little and Giovanni P. Olivei, eds., *Rethinking the International Monetary System*. Boston: Federal Reserve Bank, 33–40.

Jeanne, Olivier. 2005. Why do emerging economies borrow in foreign currency? In Barry J. Eichengreen and Ricardo Hausmann, eds., *Other People's Money: Debt Denomination and Financial Instability in Emerging Market Economies*. Chicago: University of Chicago Press, 190–217.

Jenkins, Carolyn, and Lynne Thomas. 1997. Is Southern Africa ready for regional monetary integration? Research paper 10. Centre for Research into Economics and Finance in Southern Africa, LSE, London.

Jochimsen, Reimut. 1993. A German perspective. In Paul Temperton, ed., *The European Currency Crisis. What Chance Now for a Single European Currency?* Cambridge: Probus, 175–89.

Johnson, Christopher. 1991. *ECU. The Currency of Europe*. London: Euromoney Books.

Johnson, Harry G. 1969. The case for flexible exchange rates, 1969. *Federal Reserve Bank of St. Louis Review* 51 (6): 12–24.

Jopson, Barney. 2004. Japan and Asean target free trade agreement. *Financial Times* (September 5).

Jørgensen, Knud Erik, and Ben Rosamond. 2002. Europe: Laboratory for a global polity? In Morten Ougaard and Richard Higgott, eds., *Towards a Global Polity*. London: Routledge, 189–206.

Jozzo, Alfonso. 1989. The use of the ECU as invoicing currency. In Paul De Grauwe and Theo Peeters, eds., *The ECU and European Monetary Integration*. Houndmills, Basingstoke: Macmillan, 148–90.

Kalemli-Ozcan, Sebnem, Bent E. Sorensen, and Oved Yosha. 2001. Economic integration, industrial specialization, and the asymmetry of macroeconomic fluctuations. *Journal of International Economics* 55 (1): 107–37.

Kalemli-Ozcan, Sebnem, Bent E. Sorensen, and Oved Yosha. 2003. Risk sharing and industrial specialization: Regional and international evidence. *American Economic Review* 93 (3): 903–18.

Kaminsky, Graciela, and Carmen Reinhart. 1999. The twin crises: The causes of banking and balance-of-payment problems. *American Economic Review* 89 (3): 473–500.

Karlinger, Liliane. 2002. The impact of common currencies on financial markets: A literature review and evidence from the euro area. Working paper 2002–35. Bank of Canada, Ottawa.

Katzenstein, Peter J. 2005. *A World of Regions. Asia and Europe in the American Imperium*. Ithaca: Cornell University Press.

Kaufmann, Daniel, Aart Kraay, and Massimo Mastruzzi. 2005. *Governance matters IV: Governance indicators for 1996–2004*. Mimeo. World Bank, Washington, DC.

Kawai, Masahiro. 2004. The case for a tri-polar currency basket system for emerging East Asia. In Gordon de Brouwer and Masahiro Kawai, eds., *Exchange Rate Regimes in East Asia*. London: Routledge, 360–83.

Kawai, Masahiro. 2009. The role of an Asian currency unit. In Koichi Hamada, Beate Reszat, and Ulrich Volz, eds., *Towards East Asian Monetary and Financial Integration*. Cheltenham: Elgar, 304–22.

Kawai, Masahiro, Eiji Ogawa, and Takatoshi Ito. 2004. *Developing new regional financial architecture: A proposal*. Mimeo. Tokyo University and Hitotsubashi University.

Kawai, Masahiro, and Shujiro Urata. 2004. Trade and foreign direct investment in East Asia. In Gordon de Brouwer and Masahiro Kawai, eds., *Exchange Rate Regimes in East Asia*. London: Routledge, 15–102.

Kenen, Peter B. 1969. The theory of optimum currency areas: An eclectic view. In Robert A. Mundell and Alexander K. Swoboda, eds., *Monetary Problems of the International Economy*. Chicago: University of Chicago Press, 41–60.

Kenen, Peter B., and Ellen E. Meade. 2008. *Regional Monetary Integration*. Cambridge: Cambridge University Press.

Keynes, John Maynard. 1923. *A Tract on Monetary Reform*. Published for the Royal Economic Society 1971. The Collected Writings of John Maynard Keynes. vol. IV. Cambridge: Cambridge University Press.

Kim, Sunghyun Henry, M. Ayhan Kose, and Michael G. Plummer. 2003. Dynamics of business cycles in Asia: Differences and similarities. *Review of Development Economics* 7 (3): 462–77.

Kim, Chang-Jin, and Jong-Wha Lee. 2004. Exchange rate regimes and monetary independence in East Asia. In Gordon de Brouwer and Masahiro Kawai, eds., *Exchange Rate Regimes in East Asia*. London: Routledge, 302–19.

Kindleberger, Charles P., and Robert Z. Aliber. 2005. *Manias, Panics, and Crashes: A History of Financial Crises*, 5th ed. Hoboken, NJ: Wiley.

King, Mervin A. 2002. The inflation target ten years on. *Bank of England Quarterly Bulletin* 42 (4): 459–74.

Knight, Malcolm D. 2007. Inflation targeting in emerging market economies. Speech at a Seminar on Inflation Targeting, Bank of Morocco, April 4, www.bis.org/speeches/sp070405.htm.

Korean Ministry of Finance and the Economy. 2006. The foreign exchange liberalization plan of the Korean Ministry of Finance and the economy. Seoul, May 19.

Kose, M. Ayhan, Eswar Prasad, Kenneth S. Rogoff, and Shang-Jin Wei 2009. Financial globalization: A reappraisal. *IMF Staff Papers* 56 (1): 8–62.

Kose, M. Ayhan and Kei-Mu Yi 2002. The trade comovement problem in international macroeconomics. Staff report 155. Federal Reserve Bank of New York.

Kregel, Jan. 2006. Chances and limits of South–South monetary coordination. In Barbara Fritz and Martina Metzger, eds., *New Issues in Regional Monetary Coordination: Understanding North–South and South–South Arrangements*. Houndmills, Basingstoke: Palgrave Macmillan. 42–53.

Krugman, Paul R. 1979. A model of balance-of-payment crises. *Journal of Money, Credit and Finance* 11 (3): 311–25.

Krugman, Paul R. 1989. *Exchange-Rate Instability*. Cambridge: MIT Press.

Krugman, Paul R. 1991. Target zones and exchange rate dynamics. *Quarterly Journal of Economics* 106 (3): 669–82.

Krugman, Paul R. 1993. Lessons of Massachusetts for EMU. In Francisco Torres and Francesco Giavazzi, eds., *Adjustment and Growth in the European Monetary Union*. Cambridge: Cambridge University Press, 241–61.

Krugman, Paul R. 1994. Six skeptical propositions about EMU. In Anthony Courakis and George S. Tavlas, eds., *Financial and Monetary Integration*. Cambridge: Cambridge University Press.

Kuroda, Haruhiko. 2008. A vision for Asian economic integration and Japan. Speech given at the ADB-ADBI Joint-Conference on Emerging Asian Regionalism: The Challenges of Economic Integration, September 12, Tokyo, http://www.adbi.org/speeches/2008/09/12/2686.keynote.address.kuroda.emerging.asian.regionalism/.

Kwack, Sung Yeung. 2004. An optimum currency area in East Asia: feasibility, coordination, and leadership role. *Journal of Asian Economics* 15 (1): 153–69.

Kwan, Chi Hung. 1998. The yen, the yuan, and the Asian currency crisis: Changing fortune between Japan and China. Occasional paper, Asia/Pacific Research Center, Stanford University.

Kwan, Chi Hung. 2001. *Yen Block: Toward Economic Integration in Asia*. Washington, DC: Brookings Institution Press.

Kydland, Finn E., and Edward Prescott. 1977. Rules rather than discretion: The inconsistency of optimal plans. *Journal of Political Economy* 85 (3): 473–91.

Kubny, Julia, Peter Nunnenkamp, and Florian Mölders. 2008. Regional integration and FDI in emerging countries. Working paper 1418. Kiel Institute for the World Economy, Kiel.

LaRouche. 2008. New Bretton Woods: Sarkozy calls for reestabilshment of fixed-exchange rates. LaRouche Political Action Committee, October 22, http://www.larouchepac.com/news/2008/10/22/new-bretton-woods-sarkozy-calls-for-reestablishment-fixed-exchan.html.

La Porta, Rafael, Florencio Lopez-de-Silanes, Andrei Shleifer, and Robert Vishny. 1998. Law and finance. *Journal of Political Economy* 106 (6): 1113–55.

Lahiri, Amartya, and Carlos A. Végh. 2007. Output costs, currency crises and interest rate defence of a peg. *Economic Journal* 117 (516): 216–39.

Lane, Philip R., and Gian Maria Milesi-Ferretti. 2001. The external wealth of nations: Measures of foreign assets and liabilities for industrial and developing countries. *Journal of International Economics* 55 (2): 263–94.

Leahy, Chris. 2004. Indonesia starts to set its own course. *Euromoney* (March): 62–65.

Levine, Ross. 2005. Finance and growth: Theory and evidence. In Philippe Aghion and Steven Durlauf, eds., *Handbook of Economic Growth*. Amsterdam: Elsevier, 865–934.

Lincoln, Edward. 2004. *East Asian Economic Regionalism*. Washington, DC: Brookings Institution.

Lindgren, Carl-Johan, Tomás J. T. Baliño, Charles Enoch, Anne-Marie Gulde, Marc Quintyn, and Leslie Teo. 1999. Financial sector crisis and restructuring: Lessons from Asia. Occasional paper 188. International Monetary Fund, Washington, DC.

Lingle, Christopher. 2000. Institutional basis of Asia's economic crisis. In Frank-Jürgen Richter, ed., *Economic Growth, Institutional Failure and the Aftermath of the Crisis*. Houndmills, Basingstoke: Macmillan, 53–70.

Lucas, Robert E., Jr. 1976. Economic policy evaluation: A critique. In ed. Karl Brunner and Allan H. Meltzer, eds., *The Phillips Curve and Labor Markets*. Carnegie Conference Series on Public Policy. Amsterdam: North-Holland, 19–46.

Ma, Guonan, and Eli M. Remolona. 2009. Learning by doing in market reform: Lessons from a regional bond fund. In Koichi Hamada, Beate Reszat, and Ulrich Volz, eds., *Towards East Asian Monetary and Financial Integration*. Cheltenham: Elgar, 87–103.

MacDonald, Ronald. 1999. Exchange rate behaviour: Are fundamentals important? *Economic Journal* 109 (459): F673–91.

Madhur, Srinivasa. 2004. Costs and benefits of a common currency for the ASEAN. In Suthiphand Chirathivat, Emil-Maria Claassen, and Jürgen Schröder, eds., *East Asia's Monetary Future: Integration in the Global Economy*. Cheltenham: Elgar, 231–42.

Magnifico, Giovanni. 1973. *European Monetary Integration*. London: Macmillan.

Major, John. 1999. *The Autobiography*. London: HarperCollins.

Mancall, Mark. 1968. The Ch'ing tribute system: An interpretative essay. In John King Fairbank, ed., *The Chinese World Order. Traditional China's Foreign Relations*. Cambridge: Harvard University Press, 63–89.

Marston, Richard C. 1995. *International Financial Integration*. Cambridge: Cambridge University Press.

Masson, Paul R. 2008. Currency unions in Africa: Is the trade effect substantial enough to justify their formation? *World Economy* 31 (4): 533–47.

Masson, Paul R., and Catherine Pattillo. 2002. Monetary union in West Africa: An agency of restraint for fiscal policies? *Journal of African Economies* 11 (September): 387–412.

Masson, Paul R., and Catherine Pattillo. 2004a. *The Monetary Geography of Africa*. Washington, DC: Brookings Institution.

Masson, Paul R., and Catherine Pattillo. 2004b. A single currency for Africa? *Finance and Development* (December): 9–15.

Matsuyama, Kiminori, Nobuhiro Kiyotaki, and Akihiko Matsui. 1993. Toward a theory of international currency. *Review of Economic Studies* 60 (2): 283–307.

McCallum, Bennet T. 1978. Price level adjustments and the rational expectations approach to macroeconomic stabilization policy. *Journal of Money, Credit, and Banking* 10 (4): 418–36.

McCallum, John. 1995. National borders matter: Canada–U.S. regional trade patterns. *American Economic Review* 85 (3): 615–23.

McCauley, Robert, and Guonan Ma. 2008. Resisting financial globalisation in Asia. Paper prepared for the Bank of Thailand International Symposium 2008, Bangkok, November 7–8.

McGregor, Richard. 2006. China and Japan support launch of ACU. *Financial Times* (August 29).

McGregor, Richard. 2007. Manipulation fuels critics' fire. *Financial Times* (November 7): 7.

McKinnon, Ronald I. 1963. Optimum currency areas. *American Economic Review* 53 (4): 717–25.

McKinnon, Ronald I. 1984. *An International Standard for Monetary Stabilization. Policy Analyses in International Economics, no. 8.* Washington, DC: Institute for International Economics.

McKinnon, Ronald I. 1988. Monetary and exchange rate policies for international financial stability: A proposal. *Journal of Economic Perspectives* 2 (1): 83–103.

McKinnon, Ronald I. 2001. After the crisis, the East Asian dollar standard resurrected: An interpretation of high-frequency exchange rate pegging. In Joseph E. Stiglitz and Shahid Yusuf, eds., *Rethinking the East Asian Miracle*. Oxford: Oxford University Press, 197–246.

McKinnon, Ronald I. 2004. Optimum currency areas and key currencies: Mundell I versus Mundell II. *Journal of Common Market Studies* 42 (4): 689–715.

McKinnon, Ronald I. 2005. *Exchange Rates under the East Asian Dollar Standard. Living with Conflicted Virtue.* Cambridge: MIT Press.

McKinnon, Ronald I., and Gunther Schnabl. 2003. Synchronized business cycles in East Asia, and fluctuations in the yen/dollar exchange rate. *World Economy* 26 (8): 1067–88. Reprinted in Ronald I. McKinnon. 2005. *Exchange Rates under the East Asian Dollar Standard: Living with Conflicted Virtue*. Cambridge: MIT Press, 53–76.

McKinnon, Ronald I., and Gunther Schnabl. 2004. The East Asian dollar standard, fear of floating, and original sin. *Review of Development Economics* 8 (3): 331–60. Reprinted in Ronald I. McKinnon. 2005. *Exchange Rates under the East Asian Dollar Standard: Living with Conflicted Virtue*. Cambridge: MIT Press, 13–52.

McKinnon, Ronald, and Gunther Schnabl. 2009. Current account surpluses and conflicted virtue in East Asia: China and Japan under the dollar standard. In Koichi Hamada, Beate Reszat, and Ulrich Volz, eds., *Towards East Asian Monetary and Financial Integration*. Cheltenham: Elgar, 159–91.

Meese, Richard, and Kenneth S. Rogoff. 1983. Empirical exchange rate models of the seventies: Do they fit out of sample? *Journal of International Economics* 14 (1–2): 3–24.

Mehnert-Meland, Ralph J. 1994. *ECU in Business: How to Prepare for the Single Currency in the European Union*. London: Graham and Trotman.

Mercereau, Benoît. 2005. FDI flows to Asia: Did the dragon crowd out the tigers?" Working paper 05/189. International Monetary Fund, Washington, DC.

METI. 2007. *White Paper on Economy and International Trade* [Tsusho Hakusho]. Ministry of Economy and International Trade, Tokyo.

Metzger, Martina. 2006. The common monetary area in southern Africa. In Barbara Fritz and Martina Metzger, eds., *New Issues in Regional Monetary Coordination: Understanding North–South and South–South Arrangements*. Palgrave Macmillan. Houndmills, Basingstoke: Macmillan, 147–64.

Mintz, Norman. 1970. *Monetary Union and Economic Integration*. New York: New York University Press.

Mishkin, Frederic S. 2000. Inflation targeting in emerging-market countries. *American Economic Review* 90 (2): 105–09.

Mishkin, Frederic S. 2004. Can inflation targeting work in emerging market countries? Working paper 10646. National Bureau of Economic Research, Cambridge, MA.

Mishkin, Frederic S., and Klaus Schmidt-Hebbel. 2007. Does inflation targeting make a difference? Working paper 12876. National Bureau of Economic Research, Cambridge, MA.

Moneta, Fabio, and Rasmus Rüffer. 2006. Business cycle synchronisation in East Asia. Working paper 671. European Central Bank, Frankfurt am Main.

Morris, Stephen, and Hyun Song Shin. 1997. Approximate common knowledge and coordination: Some lessons from game theory. *Journal of Logic Language and Information* 6 (2): 171–90.

Morris, Stephen, and Hyun Song Shin. 2004. Liquidity black holes. *Review of Finance* 8 (1): 1–18.

Muehring, Keith. 1992. Currency chaos: The inside story. *Institutional Investor* (October): 11–15.

Munataka, Naoko. 2006. *Transforming East Asia. The Evolution of Regional Economic Integration*. Washington, DC. Brookings Institution Press.

Mundell, Robert A. 1961. A theory of optimum currency areas. *American Economic Review* 51 (4): 657–65.

Mundell, Robert A. 1968. A plan for a world currency. Joint Economic Committee Hearings, September, Washington, DC.

Mundell, Robert A. 1973. Uncommon arguments for common currencies. In Harry G. Johnson and Alexander K. Swoboda, eds., *The Economics of Common Currencies*. Cambridge: Harvard University Press, 114–32.

Mundell, Robert A. 2000. Currency areas, exchange rate systems and international monetary reform. *Journal of Applied Econometrics* 3 (2): 217–56.

Mundell, Robert A. 2002. Monetary unions and the problem of sovereignty. *Annals of the American Academy of Political and Social Science* 579 (January): 123–52.

Mundell, Robert A. 2003a. The international monetary system and the case for a world currency. Lecture delivered at Leon Kozminski Academy of Entrepreneurship and Management, Warsaw, October 23.

Mundell, Robert A. 2003b. Prospects for an Asian currency area. *Journal of Asian Economics* 14 (1): 1–10.

Murase, Tetsuji. 2009. China makes a step forward towards a RMB currency area. CEAC Commentary 56. Council on East Asian Community, Tokyo, http://www.ceac.jp/e/commentary/090422.pdf.

Mussa, Michael. 1995. Panel: One money for how many? In Peter B. Kenen, ed., *Understanding Interdependence. The Macroeconomics of the Open Economy*. Princeton: Princeton University Press, 98–104.

Nabers, Dirk. 2008. China, Japan and the quest for leadership in East Asia. Working paper 67. German Institute of Global and Area Studies, Hamburg.

New York Times. 2002. Economic juggernaut: China is passing US as Asian power. *New York Times* (June 29).

Niskanen, William A. 2002. On the death of the Phillips curve. *Cato Journal* 22 (2): 193–98.

Nitsch, Manfred. 1999a. Vom Nutzen des monetär-keynesianischen Ansatzes für Entwicklungstheorie und -politik. In Renate Schubert, ed., *Neue Wachstums- und Außenhandelstheorie. Implikationen für die Entwicklung-*

stheorie und -politik, Schriften des Vereins für Socialpolitik, Neue Folge, vol. 269. Berlin: Duncker and Humblot, 183–214.

Nitsch, Manfred. 1999b. Entwicklungstheorie unter Unsicherheit. Das Investitionsrisiko als Motor und Störquelle von Entwicklung. In Rheinold E. Thiel, ed., *Neue Ansätze zur Entwicklungstheorie*. Bonn: DSE, 312–20.

Nitsch, Manfred. 2006. Comment on Perspectives for a Monetary Union Between Argentina and Brazil. In Barbara Fritz and Martina Metzger, eds., *New Issues in Regional Monetary Coordination. Understanding North–South and South–South Arrangements*. Houndmills, Basingstoke: Palgrave Macmillan, 116–25.

Nitsch, Volker. 2000. National borders and international trade: Evidence from the European Union. *Canadian Journal of Economics* 33 (4): 1091–1105.

Nitsch, Volker. 2002. Honey, I shrunk the currency union effect on trade. *World Economy* 25 (4): 457–74.

Nitsch, Volker. 2004. Comparing apples and oranges: The effect of multilateral currency unions on trade. In Volbert Alexander, Jacques Mélitz, and George M. von Furstenberg, eds., *Monetary Union and Hard Pegs. Effects on Trade, Financial Development, and Stability*. Oxford: Oxford University Press, 89–100.

Nitsch, Volker. 2008. Monetary integration and trade: What do we know? Revised version of a paper prepared for the Conference on Regional Economic Integration Beyond Europe. German Development Institute, Bonn, December 15–16, 2007.

Nurkse, Ragnar. 1944. *International Currency Experience*. Geneva: League of Nations.

Obstfeld, Maurice. 1996. Models of currency crises with self-fulfilling features. *European Economic Review* 40 (3–5): 1037–47.

Ogawa, Eiji. 2008. Currency baskets for East Asia. Revised version of a paper prepared for the Conference on Regional Economic Integration Beyond Europe. German Development Institute, Bonn, December 15–16, 2007.

Ogawa, Eiji, and Takatoshi Ito. 2002. On the desirability of a regional basket currency arrangement. *Journal of the Japanese and International Economies* 16 (3): 317–34.

Ogawa, Eiji, and Junko Shimizu. 2006. AMU deviation indicators for coordinated exchange rate policies in East Asia and their relationship with effective exchange rates. *World Economy* 29 (12): 1691–1708.

Ogawa, Eiji, and Junko Shimizu. 2009. Currency denomination in Asian bond markets. In Koichi Hamada, Beate Reszat, and Ulrich Volz, eds., *Towards East Asian Monetary and Financial Integration*. Cheltenham: Elgar, 104–37.

Padoa-Schioppa, Tommaso. 1994. *The Road to Monetary Union in Europe: The Emperors, the Kings, and the Genies*. Oxford: Clarendon Press.

Padoa-Schioppa, Tommaso. 2004. East Asian monetary arrangements: A European perspective. *International Finance* 7 (2): 311–23.

Padoa-Schioppa, Tommaso. 2005. Regional economic integration in a global framework. In Julie McKay, Maria Oliva Armengol, and Georges Pineau, eds., *Regional Economic Integration in a Global Framework*. Frankfurt am Main: European Central Bank, 27–34.

Pagano, Marco. 1993. Financial markets and growth: An overview. *European Economic Review* 37 (2–3): 613–22.

Pakko, Michael R., and Howard J. Wall. 2001. Reconsidering the trade-creating effects of a currency union. *Federal Reserve Bank of St. Louis Review* (September/October): 37–45.

Park, Yung Chul. 2006. *Economic Liberalization and Integration in East Asia: A Post-crisis Paradigm*. Oxford: Oxford University Press.

Park, Yung Chul. 2008. East Asia's self-managed reserve pooling arrangement and the global financial architecture. In Barry J. Eichengreen and Richard Baldwin, eds., *What G20 Leaders Must Do to Stabilise Our Economy and Fix the Financial System*. London: Centre for Economic Policy Research, 49–51.

Park, Yung Chul, and Yunjong Wang. 2005. The Chiang Mai initiative and beyond. *World Economy* 28 (1): 91–101.

Phelps, Edmund S. 1967. Phillips curves, expectations of inflation and optimal unemployment over time. *Economica* 34 (105): 254–81.

Phillips, Alban W. 1958. The relation between unemployment and the rate of change of money wage rates in the United Kingdom, 1861–1957. *Economica* 25 (100): 283–99.

Pilbeam, Keith. 1998. *International Finance,* 2nd ed. Houndmills, Basingstoke: Macmillan.

Plummer, Michael G. 2003. Structural change in a globalized Asia: macro trends and U.S. policy challenges. *Journal of Asian Economics* 14 (2): 243–81.

Plummer, Michael G., and Reid W. Click. 2009. The ASEAN economic community and the European experience. In Koichi Hamada, Beate Reszat, and Ulrich Volz, eds., *Towards East Asian Monetary and Financial Integration*. Cheltenham: Elgar, 13–40.

Poon, Wai-Ching, Chee-Kong Choong, and Muzafar Shah Habibullah. 2005. Exchange rate volatility and exports for selected East Asian countries. *ASEAN Economic Bulletin* 22 (2): 144–59.

Radelet, Steven. 1996. Measuring the real exchange rate and its relationship to exports: An application to Indonesia. Development discussion paper 229. Harvard Institute for International Development, Cambridge, MA.

Radelet, Steven, and Jeffrey D. Sachs. 1998. The onset of the East Asian financial crisis. Working paper 6680. National Bureau of Economic Research, Cambridge, MA.

Rahardja, Sjamsu. 2007. Big dragon, little dragons: China's challenge to the machinery exports of Southeast Asia. Policy research working paper 4297. World Bank, Washington, DC.

Rajan, Ramkishen S. 2002. Exchange rate policy options for post-crisis Southeast Asia: Is there a case for currency baskets? *World Economy* 25 (1): 137–63.

Rajan, Ramishken S. 2004. Inflation targeting frameworks in Asia. *Business Times* (March 24): 8.

Reade, J. James and Ulrich Volz. 2009a. Leader of the pack? German monetary dominance in Europe prior to EMU. Discussion paper 419. Department of Economics, University of Oxford.

Reade, J. James and Ulrich Volz. 2009b. Measuring monetary policy independence across regions. Mimeo. University of Oxford and German Development Institute, Bonn.

Reade, J. James and Ulrich Volz. 2009c. Too much to lose, or more to gain? Should Sweden join the Euro? Discussion paper 442. Department of Economics, University of Oxford.

Reisen, Helmut, and Axel van Trotsenburg. 1988. Should the Asian NICs peg to the yen? *Intereconomics* (July/August): 172–77.

Riese, Hajo. 2004. Development strategy and economic theory: Comments on a neglected topic. In Jens Hölscher and Horst Toman, eds., *Money, Development and Economic Transformation. Selected Essays by Hajo Riese*. Houndmills, Basingstoke: Palgrave Macmillan, 84–113.

Rockoff, Hugh. 2003. How long did it take the United States to become an optimal currency area? In Forrest H. Capie and Geoffrey E. Wood, eds., *Monetary Unions: Theory, History, Public Choice*. London: Routledge, 76–103.

Rogoff, Kenneth S. 1985. Can international monetary policy cooperation be counterproductive? *Journal of International Economics* 18 (3–4): 199–217.

Rogoff, Kenneth S. 1996. The purchasing power parity puzzle. *Journal of Economic Literature* 34 (2): 647–68.

Rogoff, Kenneth S. 1998. The risk of unilateral exchange rate pegs. In Bank of Korea, ed., *The Implications of Globalization of World Financial Markets*. Conference Proceedings, Seoul, 153–70.

Rose, Andrew K. 2000. One money, one market: The effect of common currencies on trade. *Economic Policy* 15 (30): 9–45.

Rose, Andrew K. 2001. What should academics tell policy-makers about monetary union? In David Gruen and John Simon, eds., *Future Directions for Monetary Policies in East Asia*. Sydney: Reserve Bank of Australia, 193–97.

Rose, Andrew K. 2002. Honey, the currency union effect on trade hasn't blown up. *World Economy* 25 (4): 475–79.

Rose, Andrew K. 2004. The effect of common currencies on international trade: A meta-analysis. In Volbert Alexander, Jacques Mélitz, and George M. von Furstenberg, eds., *Monetary Union and Hard Pegs: Effects on Trade, Financial Development, and Stability*. Oxford: Oxford University Press, 101–12.

Rose, Andrew K., and Charles Engel. 2002. Currency unions and international integration. *Journal of Money, Credit and Banking* 34 (4): 1067–89.

Rose, Andrew K., and Lars E.O. Svensson. 1994. European exchange rate credibility before the fall. *European Economic Review* 38 (6): 1185–1216.

Rose, Andrew K., and Eric van Wincoop. 2001. National money as a barrier to international trade: The real case for currency union. *American Economic Review* 91 (2): 386–90.

Roubini, Nouriel. 2009. The almighty Renminbi? *New York Times* (May 13).

Roy, Tobias, and Karl Betz. 2000. Währungskooperation im Mercosur. Diskussionsbeiträge des Fachbereich Wirtschaftswissenschaft 2000/15. Volkswirtschaftliche Reihe. Free University of Berlin.

Sachs, Jeffrey D. 1998. With friends like IMF. . . . *Cleveland Plain Dealer* (June 6): 10B.

Sala-i-Martín, Xavier, and Jeffrey Sachs. 1992. Fiscal federalism and optimum currency areas: Evidence for Europe from the United States. In Matthew B. Canzoneri, Vittorio Grilli, and Paul R. Masson, eds., *Establishing a Central Bank: Issues in Europe and Lessons from the US*. Cambridge: Cambridge University Press, 195–219.

Samuelson, Paul A., and Robert M. Solow. 1960. Problem of achieving and maintaining a stable price level—Analytical aspects of anti-inflation policy. *American Economic Review* 50 (2): 177–94.

Sarno, Lucio, and Mark P. Taylor. 2002. *The Economics of Exchange Rates*. Cambridge: Cambridge University Press.

Sarwono, Hartadi. 2008. Monetary policy in emerging markets: The case of Indonesia. In Luiz de Mello, ed., *Monetary Policies and Inflation Targeting in Emerging Economies*. Paris: OECD.

Schelkle, Waltraud. 2000. Regional integration among less developed economies: Discordant variations on an evergreen. In Martina Metzger and Birgit Reichenstein, eds., *Challenges for International Organizations in the 21st Century*. Houndmills, Basingstoke: Macmillan, 65–88.

Schelkle, Waltraud. 2001a. *Monetäre Integration. Bestandsaufnahme und Weiterentwicklung der neueren Theorie.* Heidelberg: Physica-Verlag.

Schelkle, Waltraud. 2001b. *The optimum currency area approach to European monetary integration: Framework of debate or dead end? South Bank European paper 2/2001.* South Bank University, London.

Schiemann, Jürgen. 1993. *Erfolgsbedingungen für eine Kern-Wechselkursunion in Europa im Lichte der Krise des Europäischen Währungssystems im Herbst 1992. Ein Vorschlag zur Reform des EWS. Discussion paper in economic policy 29.* Hamburg: Institute for Economic Policy of the University of the Federal Armed Forces.

Schnabl, Gunther. 2009. Capital markets and exchange rate stabilization in East Asia: Diversifying risk based on currency baskets. In Koichi Hamada, Beate Reszat, and Ulrich Volz, eds., *Towards East Asian Monetary and Financial Integration.* Cheltenham: Elgar, 267–89.

Schou-Zibell, Lotte. 2008. Regional cooperation and development of bond markets: The Asian experience. In Ulrich Volz, ed., *Financial Innovation and Emerging Markets. Opportunities for Growth vs. Risks for Financial Stability.* Berlin: InWEnt, 127–44.

Severino, Rodolfo C. 1999. An emerging East Asian community: Reality or mirage?" Address at the regional Conference on Common Currency for East Asia: Dream or Reality. August 5, http://www.aseansec.org/3444.htm.

Shin, Kwanho, and Chan-Hyun Sohn. 2006. Trade and financial integration in East Asia: Effects on co-movements. *World Economy* 29 (12): 1649–69.

Shin, Kwanho, and Yunjong Wang. 2003. Trade integration and business cycle correlation in East Asia. *Asian Economic Papers* 2 (3): 1–20.

Siazon, Domingo L., Jr. 2005. ASEAN and the formation of an East Asian community. Speech at the Japan National Press Club, April 6, http://www.jnpc.or.jp/cgi-bin/pb/pdf.php?id=139.

Sneddon Little, Jane and Giovanni P. Olivei. 1999. Why the interest in reform. In Jane Sneddon Little and Giovanni P. Olivei, eds., *Rethinking the International Monetary System.* Boston: Federal Reserve Bank, 41–88.

Socorro Gochoco-Bautista, Maria. 2008. Output movements in East Asia: Is there a regional factor? *World Economy* 31 (6): 738–62.

Steil, Benn. 2007. The end of national currency. *Foreign Affairs* 86 (3): 83–96.

Stewart, Michael. 1984. *The Age of Interdependence. Economic Policy in a Shrinking World.* Cambridge: MIT Press.

Stiglitz, Joseph E. 2000. What I learned at the world economic crisis: The insider. *New Republic* (April 17), http://www.mindfully.org/WTO/Joseph-Stiglitz-IMF17apr00.htm.

Sturm, Michael, and Nikolaus Siegfried. 2005. Regional monetary integration in the member states of the Gulf Cooperation Council. Occasional paper 31. European Central Bank, Frankfurt am Main.

Svensson, Lars E.O. 1991. The simplest test of target zone credibility. *IMF Staff Papers* 38 (3): 655–65.

Svensson, Lars E.O. 2000. Open-economy inflation targeting. *Journal of International Economics* 50 (1): 155–83.

Tachiki, Dennis. 2005. Between foreign direct investment and regionalism: The role of Japanese production networks. In T. J. Pempel, ed., *Remapping East Asia. The Construction of a Region.* Ithaca: Cornell University Press, 149–69.

Tavlas, George S. 1993a. The theory of optimum currency areas revisited. *Finance and Development* 30 (2): 32–35.

Tavlas, George S. 1993b. The "new" theory of optimum currency areas. *World Economy* 16 (6): 663–67.

Thirlwall, Anthony P. 2000. *The Euro and "Regional" Divergence in Europe.* London: New Europe Research Trust.

Tietmeyer, Hans. 1998. Financial crisis management in the EU/ERM. In Scheherazade S. Rehman, ed., *Financial Crisis Management in Regional Blocs.* Boston: Kluwer Academic, 39–54.

Tomann, Horst. 1997. *Stabilitätspolitik. Theorie, Strategie und europäische Perspektive.* Berlin: Springer.

Triffin, Robert. 1959. Testimony before the Joint Economic Committee of Congress, October 28, 1959. Reprinted in Robert Triffin. 1961. *Gold and the Dollar Crisis.* New Haven: Yale University Press, 3–14.

Truman, Edwin M. 2003. *Inflation Targeting in the World Economy.* Washington, DC: Institute for International Economics.

UNCTAD. 2004. *Trade and Development Report: Policy Coherence, Development Strategies, and Integration into the World Economy.* United Nations Conference on Trade and Development, Geneva.

UNCTAD. 2006. *World Investment Report 2006.* United Nations Conference on Trade and Development, Geneva.

UNCTAD. 2007. *World Investment Report 2007.* United Nations Conference on Trade and Development, Geneva.

UNCTAD. 2008. *World Investment Report 2008.* United Nations Conference on Trade and Development, Geneva.

UNCTAD. 2008. *Handbook of Statistics 2008.* United Nations Conference on Trade and Development, Geneva.

Volz, Ulrich. 2006. On the feasibility of a regional exchange rate system for East Asia: Lessons of the 1992–93 EMS crisis. *Journal of Asian Economics* 17 (6): 1107–27.

Volz, Ulrich. 2007. Integration? What integration? In Françoise Nicolas, ed., *Korea in the New Asia: East Asian Integration and the China Factor.* London: Routledge, 69–92.

Volz, Ulrich. 2008. Asian monetary fund, take two. *Far Eastern Economic Review,* Forum, June, http://feer.com/economics/2008/june/an-asian-monetary-fund-second-try.

Volz, Ulrich. 2009. A new era of financial cooperation. *Far Eastern Economic Review.* Forum, June, http://www.feer.com/economics/2009/june53/A-New-Era-of-Financial-Cooperation.

Volz, Ulrich, and Manabu Fujimura. 2009. The political economy of Japanese monetary and exchange rate policy: With special reference to regional monetary cooperation in East Asia. *Economic Review* 1 (1): 3–46.

Von Glahn, Richard 1996. *Fountain of Fortune: Money and Monetary Policy in China, 1000–1700.* Berkeley: University of California Press.

Von Hagen, Jürgen 1992. Fiscal arrangements in a monetary union: Evidence from the US. In Donald E. Fair and Christian de Boissieu, eds, *Fiscal Policy, Taxation and the Financial System in an Increasingly Integrated Europe.* Boston: Kluwer Academic, pp. 337–59.

Wall Street Journal Europe. 2004. China, Asean sign accord to lift tariffs by 2010. *Wall Street Journal Europe* (November 30): 3.

Wang, Qishan. 2009. China and Britain must join hands over the crisis. *Financial Times* (May 8): 9.

Williamson, John. 1977. *The Failure of World Monetary Reform, 1971–74.* New York: New York University Press.

Williamson, John. 1982. A survey of the literature on the optimal peg. *Journal of Development Economics* 11 (1): 39–61.

Williamson, John. 1985. *The Exchange Rate System,* rev. ed. Policy Analyses in International Economics 5. Washington, DC: Institute for International Economics.

Williamson, John. 1999. The case for a common basket peg for East Asian currencies. In Stefan Collignon, Jean Pisani-Ferry, and Yung Chul Park, eds., *Exchange Rate Policies in Emerging Asian Countries.* London: Routledge, 327–43.

Williamson, John. 2000. *Exchange Rate Regimes for Emerging Markets: Reviving the Intermediate Option. Policy Analyses in International Economics 60.* Washington, DC: Institute for International Economics.

Williamson, John. 2001. The case for a basket, band and crawl (BBC) regime for East Asia. In David Gruen and John Simon, eds., *Future Directions for Monetary Policies in East Asia.* Sydney: Reserve Bank of Australia, 97–111.

Williamson, John. 2005. *A currency basket for East Asia, not just China. Policy brief in international economics PB05–1.* Institute for International Economics, Washington, DC.

Williamson, John. 2009. East Asian currency baskets. In Koichi Hamada, Beate Reszat, and Ulrich Volz, eds., *Towards East Asian Monetary and Financial Integration.* Cheltenham: Elgar, 290–303.

Williamson, John, and Marcus H. Miller. 1987. *Targets and Indicators: A Blueprint for the International Coordination of Economic Policy. Policy Analyses in International Economics 22.* Washington, DC: Institute for International Economics.

Winters, Jeffrey A. 1999. The determinants of financial crisis in Asia. In T. J. Pempel, ed., *The Politics of the Asian Economic Crisis.* Ithaca: Cornell University Press, 79–97.

Wolf, Martin. 2004. We need a global currency. *Financial Times (*August 3).

World Bank. 1993. *The East Asian Miracle: Economic Growth and Public Policy.* Oxford: Oxford University Press.

World Bank. 1998. *Global Economic Prospects and the Developing Countries 1998/99: Beyond Financial Crisis.* Washington, DC: World Bank.

World Bank. 2000. East Asia update, special focus: Poverty during crisis and recovery. Washington, DC: East Asia and Pacific Publications, World Bank.

World Bank. 2006. East Asia update. November 2006. Managing through a global downturn. Washington, DC: World Bank.

Worrell, DeLisle. 2003. A currency union for the Caribbean. Working paper 03/35. International Monetary Fund, Washington, DC.

WTO. 2008. *International Trade Statistics 2008.* Geneva: World Trade Organization.

Wu, Friedrich, Poa Tiong Siaw, Yeo Han Sia, and Puah Kok Keong. 2002. Foreign direct investments to China and Southeast Asia: Has ASEAN been losing out? *Economic Survey of Singapore* (third quarter): 96–115.

Wyplosz, Charles. 1991. *European Economy* (special Issue: Monetary Union and Fiscal Policy Discipline): 165–84.

Wyplosz, Charles. 2004. Regional exchange rate arrangements: Lessons from Europe for East Asia. In Asian Development Bank, ed., *Monetary and Financial Integration in East Asia: The Way Ahead,* vol. 2. Houndmills, Basingstoke: Palgrave Macmillan, 241–84.

Xu Binlan. 2004. Bank rates raised for first time in a decade. *China Daily* (October 29).

Yong, Ong Keng. 2004. Towards ASEAN financial integration. Remarks of the Secretary-General of ASEAN at the Economix 2004 Conference. University of Indonesia, Jakarta, February 18, http://www.aseansec.org/16013 .htm.

Yu, Yongding. 2007. Toward East Asian monetary and financial cooperation: A Chinese perspective. In Duck-Koo Chung and Barry J. Eichengreen, eds., *Toward an East Asian Exchange Rate Regime*. Washington, DC: Brookings Institution, 49–66.

Yu, Yongding. 2009. The road map of the reform of the international monetary and financial system: Some thoughts on current international financial crisis and East Asia's responses. Paper prepared for the Commission of Experts of the President of the United Nations General Assembly on Reforms of the International Monetary and Financial System, http://www.un.org/ga/president/63/commission/refdocmembers.shtml.

Yuen, Hazel Phui Ling. 2001. Optimum currency areas in East Asia. A structural VAR approach. *ASEAN Economic Bulletin* 18 (2): 206–17.

Zhang, Jikang, and Liang Yuanyuan. 2009. Institutional and structural problems of China's foreign exchange market and the RMB's role in East Asia. In Koichi Hamada, Beate Reszat, and Ulrich Volz, eds., *Towards East Asian Monetary and Financial Integration*. Cheltenham: Elgar, 357–86.

Zhang, Xiaoming. 2006. The rise of China and community building in East Asia. *Asian Perspective* 30 (3): 129–48.

Zhou, Xiaochuan. 2009. Reform the International Monetary System. People's Bank of China, Beijing, http://www.pbc.gov.cn/english//detail.asp?col=6500&ID=178.

Annexes

Annex 1

Chronology of the Asian crisis, March 1997–July 1999

1997

March 3	Thailand	First official announcement of problems in two unnamed finance companies, and a recapitalization program.
March–June	Thailand	66 finance companies secretly receive substantial liquidity support from the Bank of Thailand. Significant capital outflows.
April	Malaysia	Bank Negara Malaysia imposes limits on bank lending to the property sector and for the purchase of stocks.
June 29	Thailand	Operations of 16 finance companies suspended and a guarantee of depositors' and creditors' funds in remaining finance companies announced.
July 2	Thailand	Baht is floated and depreciates by 15–20%. IMF negotiations begin.
Early July	Indonesia	Pressure on the rupiah develops.
July 8–14	Malaysia	Bank Negara Malaysia intervenes aggressively to defend the ringgit: efforts to support the ringgit are abandoned; ringgit is allowed to float.
July 11	Indonesia	Widening of the rupiah's band.
July 11	Philippines	Peso is allowed more flexibility.
July 13	Korea	Several Korean banks are placed on negative credit outlook by rating agencies.
July 14	Philippines	The Philippines extends and augments its existing IMF-support program of 1997, and arranges a stand-by facility in 1998. IMF offers the Philippines USD 1.1 bn loan package.
July 24	All	"Currency meltdown"—severe pressure on rupiah, baht, ringgit, and peso.
August 5	Thailand	Measures adopted to strengthen financial sector. Operations of 42 finance companies suspended.
August 14	Indonesia	Authorities abolish band for rupiah, which plunges immediately.
August 20	Thailand	IMF approves a USD 3.9 3-year stand-by arrangement. The plan assumes a positive growth of 2.5% in 1997 and 3.5% in 1998. It calls for maintaining gross financial reserves at the equivalent of 4.2 months of imports in 1997 and 4.4 months in 1998; limiting the end-period rate of inflation to 9.5% in 1997 and 5% in 1998; targeting a small overall fiscal surplus by 1998 through an increase in the rate of the value-added tax and selective expenditure cuts; initiating a credible and upfront restructuring of the financial sector, focused on the identification and closure of unviable financial institutions (56 finance companies).

Annex 1
(continued)

1997		
August 25	Korea	Government guarantees banks' external liabilities; withdrawal of credit lines continues.
October 8	Indonesia	Government agrees to request help from the IMF.
October 14	Thailand	Financial sector restructuring strategy announced; Financial Sector Restructuring Agency and asset management company established; blanket guarantee strengthened; new powers to intervene in banks.
October 24	Thailand	Emergency decrees to facilitate financial sector restructuring.
October 31	Indonesia	IMF announces a USD 23 bn multilateral financial package involving the World Bank and Asian Development Bank to help Indonesia stabilize its financial system. Bank resolution package announced; 16 commercial banks closed; limited deposit insurance for depositors in other banks; other bank closures to follow.
November 5	Indonesia	IMF approves a USD 10 bn 3-year stand-by credit and releases a disbursement of USD 3 bn. Measures include financial sector restructuring, with the closure of 16 insolvent banks; structural reforms to enhance economic efficiency and transparency, with the liberalization of foreign trade and investment, the dismantling of monopolies, and privatization; stabilizing the rupiah through a tight monetary policy; implementing fiscal measures equivalent to 1% of GDP in 1997–8 and 2% in 1998–99, to yield a 1% of GDP surplus in both years.
Mid-November	Thailand	Change in government. Significant strengthening of economic reform program.
November 19	Korea	Exchange rate band widened. Won falls sharply.
November 21	Korea	Government requests IMF assistance.
November 25	Thailand	In light of larger that expected depreciation of the baht, a second IMF package for Thailand is approved. The new plan includes additional measures to maintain the target fiscal surplus of 1% of GDP, the establishment of a timetable for financial sector restructuring, and plans to protect the weaker sectors of society.
November	Korea	Korea Asset Management Corporation's (KAMCO) nonperforming asset fund is established.
December 4	Korea	IMF approves a USD 21 bn 3-year stand-by arrangement and releases a disbursement of USD 5.6 bn. The initial program assumes GDP growth in 1998 of 2.5% and features comprehensive financial sector restructuring, including central bank independence, strong market and supervisory discipline, and the suspension of 9 insolvent banks. Fiscal measures equivalent to 2% of GDP make room for the costs of financial restructuring, consistently with a balanced budget. The plan calls for efforts to dismantle the non-transparent and inefficient ties among government bank and business; for the implementation of trade and capital account liberalization measures, as well as for labor market reforms; for the publication and dissemination of key economic and financial data. Rollover of short-term debt continues to decline.
December 8	Thailand	IMF disbursement of USD 810 m. 56 suspended finance companies are permanently closed.
Mid-December	Indonesia	Deposit runs on banks, accounting for half of banking system assets.
December 16	Korea	Government allows won to float.

1997		
December 18	Korea	New government is elected; commitment to program is strengthened. IMF disburses USD 3.5 bn.
December 24	Korea	Government issues a letter of intent pointing at the need for an acceleration of the program as the situation deteriorates. The plan includes further monetary tightening, the abolition of the daily exchange rate band, and the lifting of all capital account restrictions. Financial sector reform and market liberalization, as well as trade liberalization, are expedited. The IMF also announces that a debt rescheduling by international banks is critical to Korea's recovery. Foreign private bank creditors agree to maintain exposure temporarily.
December 29	Korea	Legislation passed strengthening independence for Bank of Korea and creating Financial Supervision Commission.
December 30	Korea	IMF disbursement of USD 2 bn.
December 31	Thailand	Bank of Thailand intervention in 1 commercial bank; shareholders' stakes eliminated.
December	Korea	14 merchant banks are suspended and 2 large commercial banks taken over by the government.

1998		
January 1	Malaysia	Measures announced to strengthen prudential regulations.
January 15	Indonesia	Second IMF-supported program announced. The plan allows for a relaxation of the previous fiscal targets, that is now a budget deficit equal to 1% of GDP. Previous IMF conditions not fulfilled but reiterated in the second package include: dismantling of government monopolies, postponing infrastructure projects, and closing insolvent banks. Indonesian Bank Restructuring Agency (IBRA) established and blanket guarantee announced.
January 15	Korea	IMF disbursement of USD 2 bn.
January 16	All	International lenders agree on plan to officially roll over short-term debt.
January 20	Malaysia	Bank Negara Malaysia announces blanket guarantee for all depositors.
January 23	Thailand	Bank of Thailand intervenes in 2 commercial banks; shareholders eliminated.
January 26	Indonesia	Indonesian Bank Restructuring Agency (IBRA) established and blanket guarantee announced.
January 28	Korea	Agreement with external private creditors on rescheduling of short-term debt.
January	Korea	10 of 14 suspended merchant banks closed; 20 remaining merchant banks are required to submit rehabilitation plans.
February 7	Korea	Government agrees to third IMF program. GDP growth projections are lowered to 1%. The letter of intent includes additional measures to target fiscal deficit to 1% of GDP, increasing the amount of financial instruments available to foreign investors, and broadening the financial sector reform strategy o accommodate stabilization of short-term debt payments.
February 15	Korea	New president and government take office.
February 17	Korea	IMF disbursement of USD 2 bn.
February 24	Thailand	Further modification of IMF plan: the fiscal policy target is adjusted from a surplus of 1% to a deficit of 2% of GDP.
February	Indonesia	President Suharto reelected. Doubts about future of financial sector program grow stronger amid political uncertainty. Rupiah depreciates further and currency board is debated.

1998		
March 4	Thailand	IMF disbursement of USD 270 m.
March 11	Thailand	One commercial bank purchased by foreign strategic investor.
March 25	Malaysia	Program to consolidate finance companies and to recapitalize commercial banks is announced.
March 31	Thailand	New loan classification and loss provisioning rules introduced.
March	Philippines	3-year stand-by arrangement agreed with IMF.
April 4	Indonesia	IBRA closes 7 banks and takes over 7 others.
April 10	Indonesia	Government issues a Supplementary Memorandum of Economic and Financial Policies on additional measures. These include strong monetary policy, accelerated bank restructuring, and a comprehensive agenda of structural reforms. The IMF allows the government to continue its fuel and power subsidies. In the light of the failure of the first two packages, the IMF announces a stricter enforcement of provisions.
End-April	Korea	4 of 20 merchant banks' rehabilitation plans rejected; banks are closed.
May 2	Korea	Authorities update the program of economic reforms. Growth forecasts for 1998 are further revised downward to -2%. The letter of intent includes the accommodation of a larger fiscal deficit of about 2% of GDP in 1998, measures to strengthen and expand the social safety net, the loosening of restrictions on foreign exchange transaction, and the formation of an appraisal committee to evaluate recapitalization plans by undercapitalized banks.
May 4	Indonesia	IMF disbursement of USD 1 bn.
May 18	Thailand	Bank of Thailand intervention in 7 finance companies; shareholders eliminated.
Mid-May	Indonesia	Widespread riots. Rupiah depreciates, deposit runs intensify, and Bank Indonesia must provide liquidity.
May 21	Indonesia	President Suharto steps down.
May 26	Thailand	Government agrees 4th IMF program. The main priority is to prevent any further slowdown of the economy and foster an early recovery. The modified program calls for cautious and gradual reductions of interest rates, higher monetary growth rates, a looser fiscal deficit target at 3% of GDP, and accelerated corporate debt restructuring with financial sector reform.
May 29	Korea	IMF disbursement of USD 2 bn.
May 29	Indonesia	1 major private bank taken over by IBRA.
June 5	Indonesia	International lenders and Indonesian companies agree on corporate debt rescheduling.
June 10	Thailand	IMF disbursement of USD 135 m.
June 24	Indonesia	Government agree additional IMF reforms in light of changing political climate and worsening economic situation. Provisions include an increase in social expenditures (7.5% of GDP); a budget deficit target of 8.5% of GDP; the closure, merging, or recapitalization of weak banks; and the establishment of a bankruptcy system.
June 29	Korea	For the first time, government closes commercial banks (5 small ones). 2 merchant banks are closed and 2 merged with commercial banks.
June 30	Korea	New loan classification and loss provisioning rules introduced.
June	Malaysia	Danaharta, an asset management company, is established.

Annex 1
(continued)

1998

July 15	Korea	A new letter of intent by the government announces a further easing of macroeconomic policies. The letter includes the accommodation of a larger fiscal deficit for 1998 (5% of GDP), and measures to bolster the social expenditure program.
July 15	Indonesia	IMF disbursement of USD 1 bn. The IMF increases financing by USD 1.4 bn.
Mid-July	Indonesia	Authorities allow market-determined interest rates on Bank Indonesia bills.
July 29	Indonesia	Government requests the cancellation of the existing arrangements with the IMF and its replacement with a new extended arrangement, including new measures on bank and corporate restructuring and improvements in the distribution system.
August 14	Thailand	Comprehensive financial sector restructuring plan announced, including facilities for public support of bank recapitalization. Intervention in 2 banks and 5 finance companies; shareholders' stakes eliminated.
August 25	Indonesia	IMF disbursement of USD 1 bn. IMF approves an extended facility with a longer repayment period.
August 25	Thailand	The Thai program is modified to incorporate a more comprehensive approach to bank and corporate restructuring. The fiscal deficit target is still at 3% of GDP for both 1998 and 1999, but this target excludes the costs of financial sector restructuring.
August 25	Korea	IMF disburses USD 1 bn.
August 30	Thailand	Majority ownership in 1 medium-sized commercial bank by foreign strategic investor.
August	Malaysia	Danamodal (bank restructuring and recapitalization agency) is established.
September 23	Indonesia	Indonesia's bilateral external debt to official creditors refinanced.
September 30	Indonesia	Bank Mandiri created through merger of the 4 largest state-owned banks. Plans announced for joint government-private sector recapitalization of private banks.
September	Malaysia	Capital controls introduced, exchange rate pegged, disclosure requirements relaxed, and measures to stimulate bank lending adopted.
October 6	Indonesia	Amended Banking Law passed, which included strengthening of IBRA.

1999

February 15	Malaysia	Capital controls replaced with declining exit levies.
March 13	Indonesia	Government closes 38 banks and IBRA takes over 7 others. Eligibility of 9 banks for joint recapitalization with government announced.
April 21	Indonesia	Closure of 1 joint-venture bank.
April	Indonesia	Government announces a plan to recapitalize the 3 other state banks (all insolvent).
June 30	Indonesia	Eight private banks recapitalized jointly through public and private funds.
July 5	Indonesia	Government announces plan for resolution of IBRA banks.
July 31	Indonesia	Legal merger of component banks of Bank Mandiri.
July	Thailand	1 small private bank intervened and put up for sale; 1 major bank announces establishment of an asset management company.

Sources: Adapted from Lindgren et al. (1999, Box 1) and Corsetti et al. (1999, Box 4.1).

Annex 2

Exports and imports of East Asian countries (in million USD), 1980–2007

		1980	1981	1982	1983	1984	1985	1986	1987	1988	1989	1990	1991	1992
Brunei	X	4,589	4,001	3,786	3,367	3,183	2,934	1,798	1,901	1,707	1,882	2,212	2,466	3,913
	I	573	589	732	724	622	606	653	641	744	859	1,000	1,111	2,416
Cambodia	X	0	2	5	2	4	5	3	10	8	21	42	57	165
	I	0	78	51	52	49	· 27	11	13	24	52	56	62	751
China	X	18,139	21,476	21,866	22,096	24,825	27,331	31,370	39,465	47,664	52,914	62,760	71,967	85,621
	I	19,505	21,631	18,920	21,313	25,953	42,480	43,275	43,223	55,352	59,141	53,810	63,877	81,872
Hong Kong	X	19,747	21,843	20,922	21,979	28,351	30,221	35,492	48,551	63,285	73,237	82,272	98,728	119,661
	I	22,401	24,770	23,455	24,007	28,560	29,703	35,363	48,465	63,905	72,154	82,490	100,283	123,444
Indonesia	X	21,916	23,810	22,354	21,195	21,896	18,602	14,810	17,178	19,379	21,940	25,683	29,189	33,982
	I	10,837	13,270	16,859	16,352	13,880	10,275	10,725	12,855	13,489	16,470	22,005	25,929	27,280
Japan	X	130,473	151,540	138,479	147,013	169,816	177,257	210,821	231,404	265,057	274,693	287,839	315,018	339,997
	I	141,291	142,874	131,570	126,525	136,147	130,523	127,663	150,912	187,495	209,641	235,334	236,658	232,908
Korea	X	17,439	21,271	21,827	24,460	29,259	30,291	34,799	47,316	60,705	60,527	67,815	72,378	77,340
	I	22,063	26,154	24,250	26,196	30,628	31,058	31,734	41,026	51,812	60,210	74,405	81,826	82,951
Lao	X	0	15	24	24	11	17	14	23	56	95	64	82	103
	I	0	72	76	26	40	54	60	80	102	129	149	154	258
Malaysia	X	12,961	11,773	12,044	14,128	16,563	15,408	13,977	17,935	21,098	25,051	29,421	34,406	40,710
	I	10,832	11,591	12,419	13,250	14,068	12,311	10,836	12,710	16,569	22,590	29,173	36,754	39,935
Myanmar	X	415	446	391	378	301	303	288	219	147	215	409	527	684
	I	785	823	409	268	239	283	304	268	244	194	668	1,068	1,046
Philippines	X	5,787	5,721	5,020	4,935	5,343	4,614	4,808	5,696	7,044	7,755	8,195	8,846	9,835
	I	8,295	8,477	8,262	7,863	6,262	5,351	5,212	6,937	8,662	11,171	12,994	12,946	14,569
Singapore	X	19,509	21,094	20,931	21,967	24,216	22,982	22,622	28,811	39,456	44,788	52,804	59,248	63,499
	I	24,017	27,577	28,179	28,164	28,671	26,239	25,514	32,627	43,870	49,695	60,959	66,269	72,177
Thailand	X	6,501	7,027	6,935	6,368	7,414	7,123	8,864	11,564	15,910	20,182	23,072	28,875	32,473
	I	9,218	9,956	8,536	10,283	10,415	9,271	9,184	13,014	20,302	25,376	33,414	37,957	40,686
Vietnam	X	0	141	179	205	250	693	789	854	1,038	2,472	2,525	2,189	2,918
	I	0	566	435	408	525	1,842	2,155	2,455	2,757	3,032	2,842	2,483	3,027

Source: DTS

Note: Imports (I) and exports (X) are valued at current prices.

Annex 2
(continued)

1993	1994	1995	1996	1997	1998	1999	2000	2001	2002	2003	2004	2005	2006	2007
3,632	3,290	3,388	3,670	3,973	1,980	2,552	3,162	3,336	3,440	4,422	4,510	5,633	6,699	7,351
3,055	2,760	2,960	3,516	3,154	2,334	1,328	1,427	1,315	1,630	1,341	1,640	1,668	2,000	2,314
267	243	357	293	626	934	1,040	1,123	1,296	1,489	1,771	2,188	3,014	3,562	3,897
981	1,152	1,573	1,632	1,116	1,129	1,243	1,424	1,456	1,675	1,732	2,075	2,548	2,985	5,484
91,696	120,869	148,959	151,168	182,920	183,746	194,936	249,208	266,709	325,744	438,364	593,358	762,337	969,284	1,218,170
103,628	115,706	13?,164	138,949	142,163	140,385	165,718	225,175	243,567	295,440	412,836	561,422	660,218	791,793	967,346
135,120	151,533	173,556	180,530	187,870	173,693	173,793	202,249	190,081	200,320	224,040	259,423	289,509	316,819	344,738
138,605	161,781	192,765	198,551	208,623	184,602	179,650	213,328	201,474	208,024	232,580	271,458	299,967	334,691	368,223
36,840	40,069	45,453	49,892	53,444	48,851	48,661	62,118	56,318	57,154	61,013	71,550	85,623	113,582	129,043
28,328	32,013	40,629	42,902	41,698	27,349	24,003	33,515	30,962	31,289	32,549	46,524	57,700	92,581	115,017
362,831	395,317	443,292	411,614	421,466	388,040	419,456	478,361	403,517	416,789	471,906	565,811	594,887	646,787	714,254
241,713	274,323	336,141	349,664	338,709	280,867	310,774	379,577	349,081	337,172	382,953	454,809	515,194	578,696	621,870
85,816	101,358	131,330	137,683	144,102	132,780	143,881	172,257	150,436	162,308	193,806	253,741	284,337	296,680	360,973
86,630	102,348	135,110	150,157	144,635	93,372	119,741	160,481	141,098	152,125	178,826	224,460	261,211	281,859	365,439
241	300	311	321	192	371	463	391	376	386	438	535	697	1,133	1,207
432	564	589	690	409	645	809	690	719	722	809	1,056	1,270	1,639	2,064
47,130	58,750	73,726	78,218	78,909	73,471	84,551	98,154	88,201	93,387	104,968	126,509	140,977	160,664	176,207
45,628	59,562	77,633	78,458	79,059	58,338	65,502	82,204	73,358	79,513	82,735	104,304	113,609	130,477	146,982
864	940	1,198	1,183	1,132	1,139	1,393	1,980	2,625	2,753	2,768	3,159	3,702	4,378	4,762
1,280	1,538	2,342	2,678	2,862	2,358	2,528	3,039	2,663	2,969	3,226	3,452	3,569	3,788	5,159
11,268	13,442	17,379	20,562	25,238	29,505	35,487	38,216	32,150	35,208	36,231	39,680	41,215	46,976	67,120
17,642	22,544	28,297	31,867	39,142	29,531	30,753	34,491	33,057	35,427	37,505	44,039	47,414	51,532	70,875
74,103	96,911	118,221	125,190	125,403	109,915	114,754	138,046	121,826	125,219	160,073	198,694	229,447	272,057	299,173
85,386	102,642	124,397	131,338	132,601	101,612	111,074	134,633	116,020	116,483	136,327	172,697	200,197	238,797	263,325
37,330	46,138	58,701	56,478	58,431	55,392	58,492	68,963	65,113	68,850	80,318	96,214	110,158	130,555	152,459
46,192	55,092	77,085	74,939	63,466	43,703	50,350	61,924	62,057	64,721	75,824	94,407	118,143	130,605	141,346
2,985	4,054	5,621	7,463	9,484	9,307	11,541	14,483	15,020	16,705	20,144	26,485	32,447	38,377	46,189
3,924	5,826	8,359	11,285	11,875	11,310	11,742	15,637	16,217	19,745	25,255	31,969	36,761	46,104	62,093

Annex 3
Exports of ... to ... (as percent of total exports), 1980–2007

Brunei	1980	1981	1982	1983	1984	1985	1986	1987	1988	1989	1990	1991	1992
USA	8.60	10.69	12.75	8.10	5.54	7.33	6.09	1.62	2.06	4.92	3.41	1.06	0.93
EU	0.02	1.41	2.90	0.72	2.32	0.04	0.13	0.18	0.08	0.14	0.24	0.51	0.23
Euro Area	0.01	1.39	2.89	0.70	2.28	0.00	0.04	0.12	0.03	0.09	0.12	0.18	0.04
China	0.00	0.00	0.00	0.00	0.00	0.00	0.00	0.00	0.32	0.41	0.14	0.14	0.19
Hong Kong	0.02	0.01	0.00	0.00	0.01	0.00	0.04	0.02	0.02	0.01	0.01	0.01	0.02
China+HK	0.02	0.01	0.00	0.00	0.01	0.00	0.04	0.02	0.33	0.42	0.15	0.15	0.21
Japan	70.88	68.97	67.73	67.72	68.43	61.24	66.86	61.74	65.05	58.15	58.10	62.58	55.15
Korea	0.00	0.00	4.27	7.53	5.43	0.00	7.36	9.74	10.39	13.14	12.37	10.30	12.07
ASEAN	12.74	13.79	10.98	13.16	16.10	20.82	16.95	22.84	17.81	18.85	20.93	19.81	25.92
ASEAN+3	83.62	82.76	82.97	88.41	89.96	82.06	91.17	94.33	93.56	90.55	91.54	92.84	93.32
ASEAN+4	83.64	82.77	82.97	88.41	89.97	82.06	91.21	94.35	93.58	90.56	91.55	92.85	93.35

Cambodia	1980	1981	1982	1983	1984	1985	1986	1987	1988	1989	1990	1991	1992
USA		19.16	0.00	4.31	2.29	5.66	16.95	1.89	4.33	1.42	0.00	0.00	0.05
EU		3.83	28.61	14.23	2.52	5.25	11.12	7.89	4.11	4.29	5.01	37.20	19.02
Euro Area		0.00	26.75	5.60	0.23	0.00	5.65	2.18	4.01	2.97	4.43	36.93	18.85
China		45.98	48.30	12.93	6.88	11.33	0.00	0.00	2.17	4.44	0.39	0.76	0.10
Hong Kong		0.00	0.00	0.00	0.00	0.00	2.83	0.00	0.00	0.00	0.81	0.32	0.31
China+HK		45.98	48.30	12.93	6.88	11.33	2.83	0.00	2.17	4.44	1.19	1.08	0.41
Japan		19.16	9.29	12.93	4.59	3.78	5.65	5.68	14.07	9.74	7.58	8.68	5.13
Korea		0.00	0.00	0.00	0.00	0.00	0.00	0.00	0.00	0.00	0.00	0.00	0.00
ASEAN		1.15	3.72	37.51	60.12	28.88	2.83	5.97	37.02	64.88	74.56	44.31	67.44
ASEAN+3		66.28	61.30	63.37	71.59	43.99	8.48	11.65	53.26	79.07	82.52	53.75	72.67
ASEAN+4		66.28	61.30	63.37	71.59	43.99	11.30	11.65	53.26	79.07	83.33	54.07	72.98

China	1980	1981	1982	1983	1984	1985	1986	1987	1988	1989	1990	1991	1992
USA	5.42	7.01	8.07	7.75	9.32	8.55	8.39	7.68	7.13	8.34	8.47	8.61	10.04
EU	17.83	15.02	12.79	14.11	11.33	11.14	16.06	13.11	12.38	11.27	10.57	10.26	9.72
Euro Area	9.95	10.11	8.56	8.67	7.66	6.96	8.14	8.59	8.61	8.04	8.58	8.54	7.90
Hong Kong	24.00	24.50	23.69	26.23	26.53	26.15	31.16	34.88	38.27	41.42	43.28	44.66	43.81
Japan	22.23	22.10	21.98	20.44	20.77	22.29	16.19	16.20	16.88	15.86	14.68	14.25	13.66
Korea	0.00	0.00	0.00	0.00	0.00	0.00	0.00	0.00	0.00	0.00	0.69	3.03	2.85
ASEAN	6.59	6.64	6.02	5.32	8.02	10.40	6.12	6.04	6.21	6.06	6.61	6.19	5.45
ASEAN+3	28.82	28.74	28.00	25.76	28.79	32.69	22.31	22.24	23.09	21.92	21.98	23.46	21.96
ASEAN+4	52.82	53.24	51.69	51.99	55.32	58.84	53.47	57.12	61.36	63.34	65.26	68.12	65.77

Annex 3
(continued)

1993	1994	1995	1996	1997	1998	1999	2000	2001	2002	2003	2004	2005	2006	2007
0.61	1.39	1.97	2.08	2.45	10.29	15.32	11.96	11.55	8.09	7.75	8.65	9.52	7.80	5.21
0.40	0.85	0.77	1.05	1.17	14.39	2.09	3.62	1.51	1.86	0.33	2.60	1.09	1.95	1.42
0.24	0.35	0.50	0.66	0.58	0.32	0.43	0.28	0.15	0.43	0.13	0.12	0.09	0.02	0.07
0.00	0.00	0.01	0.00	0.00	0.00	0.43	1.76	4.04	6.39	6.67	4.50	3.35	2.92	2.31
0.05	0.11	0.14	0.03	0.03	0.17	0.14	0.03	0.02	0.01	0.05	0.05	0.01	0.02	0.01
0.05	0.11	0.14	0.03	0.03	0.17	0.57	1.79	4.06	6.40	6.72	4.56	3.36	2.94	2.32
61.15	54.65	55.57	53.29	53.06	47.19	42.02	40.67	46.20	40.04	40.96	38.14	36.83	30.85	30.96
11.17	13.73	15.67	18.48	18.14	15.59	11.27	12.88	12.33	12.21	11.19	13.97	12.70	15.01	16.98
22.82	26.16	22.20	21.36	20.86	9.32	25.08	23.16	16.66	19.29	20.18	17.22	25.23	25.82	27.99
95.14	94.54	93.44	93.13	92.06	72.11	78.80	78.47	79.23	77.93	79.00	73.84	78.11	74.60	78.24
95.19	94.64	93.58	93.15	92.09	72.28	78.94	78.50	79.25	77.94	79.05	73.89	78.12	74.62	78.26

1993	1994	1995	1996	1997	1998	1999	2000	2001	2002	2003	2004	2005	2006	2007
0.17	0.41	1.42	1.40	13.69	31.38	22.67	65.89	64.22	64.51	63.61	59.97	52.93	53.32	60.64
14.68	11.09	14.54	38.56	11.26	14.06	14.09	20.62	24.88	19.43	19.58	27.02	16.78	18.23	21.05
13.86	9.38	10.75	26.49	6.07	11.11	8.41	12.45	14.39	10.52	11.48	18.51	12.30	13.28	15.36
0.41	0.37	1.46	2.13	7.28	4.52	0.86	2.12	1.29	0.56	0.37	0.58	0.47	0.44	1.17
0.27	1.59	3.14	4.69	2.04	2.87	3.68	0.65	0.35	0.40	0.28	0.24	17.95	15.23	0.44
0.69	1.96	4.60	6.82	9.32	7.39	4.53	2.77	1.64	0.96	0.64	0.81	18.42	15.67	1.61
29.38	3.28	1.87	2.05	1.01	0.85	0.89	0.96	1.03	1.27	1.22	1.15	2.08	0.96	3.24
0.00	0.00	0.00	0.00	0.18	0.06	0.05	0.00	0.08	0.10	0.08	1.15	0.07	0.09	0.10
51.13	77.06	63.12	39.50	59.83	42.41	30.30	6.78	5.87	6.09	5.55	3.78	4.73	6.75	6.13
80.92	80.72	66.45	43.68	68.30	47.84	32.10	9.86	8.27	8.02	7.22	6.65	7.36	8.23	10.64
81.19	82.31	69.60	48.37	70.34	50.71	35.78	10.51	8.61	8.42	7.50	6.89	25.30	23.46	11.08

1993	1994	1995	1996	1997	1998	1999	2000	2001	2002	2003	2004	2005	2006	2007
18.51	17.72	16.61	17.68	17.90	20.68	21.55	20.93	20.39	21.51	21.13	21.09	21.43	21.04	19.52
14.05	13.57	13.76	13.98	13.94	16.37	16.55	16.47	16.74	16.25	18.05	18.31	19.11	19.59	20.20
10.75	10.17	10.63	10.63	10.51	12.29	12.49	12.28	12.25	11.91	13.45	13.79	14.62	14.37	14.97
24.07	26.78	24.17	21.77	23.94	21.11	18.92	17.86	17.44	17.95	17.40	17.00	16.33	16.04	14.83
17.21	17.78	19.11	20.43	17.40	16.17	16.62	16.71	16.90	14.88	13.56	12.39	11.03	9.47	8.42
3.12	3.62	4.49	4.98	4.99	3.41	4.01	4.53	4.70	4.76	4.58	4.69	4.61	4.60	4.58
5.83	5.93	7.03	6.83	6.94	6.00	6.30	6.96	6.96	7.24	7.05	7.23	7.28	7.36	7.65
26.16	27.33	30.63	32.24	29.33	25.59	26.92	28.20	28.57	26.88	25.19	24.31	22.92	21.42	20.65
50.22	54.11	54.80	54.01	53.28	46.69	45.85	46.07	46.00	44.84	42.60	41.31	39.25	37.46	35.49

Annex 3
(continued)

Hong Kong	1980	1981	1982	1983	1984	1985	1986	1987	1988	1989	1990	1991	1992
USA	26.12	27.73	28.87	32.16	33.17	30.77	31.30	27.83	24.79	25.27	24.09	22.68	23.05
EU	24.96	20.59	19.51	17.78	15.76	13.65	16.04	17.37	17.08	16.80	18.78	19.08	17.28
Euro Area	15.60	12.23	11.93	10.82	9.48	8.46	10.34	11.59	11.51	11.48	13.50	14.05	12.51
China	6.33	8.99	9.27	11.35	17.74	26.00	21.27	23.26	26.91	25.69	24.71	27.08	29.59
Japan	4.60	4.68	4.50	4.40	4.41	4.23	4.65	5.09	5.84	6.18	5.69	5.38	5.23
Korea	1.15	1.32	1.52	1.73	1.74	1.80	2.34	2.62	2.64	2.62	2.32	2.14	1.62
ASEAN	11.40	11.71	12.44	11.09	8.40	6.64	6.73	6.31	6.22	6.77	7.36	6.60	6.58
ASEAN+3	23.48	26.69	27.73	28.56	32.29	38.67	35.00	37.27	41.60	41.26	40.07	41.20	43.03

Indonesia	1980	1981	1982	1983	1984	1985	1986	1987	1988	1989	1990	1991	1992
USA	19.64	18.31	15.86	20.13	20.57	21.72	19.59	19.49	16.19	15.84	13.10	12.02	13.00
EU	6.74	5.10	4.27	4.95	5.47	6.77	9.91	9.54	11.61	11.12	12.29	13.41	14.76
Euro Area	5.71	4.23	3.52	3.69	4.31	5.22	8.01	7.75	9.27	8.86	9.73	10.51	11.64
China	0.00	0.03	0.06	0.13	0.04	0.45	0.94	2.00	2.54	2.44	3.25	4.08	4.11
Hong Kong	0.69	0.62	0.65	0.86	1.19	1.87	2.33	2.44	2.86	2.41	2.41	2.41	2.59
China+HK	0.69	0.65	0.71	0.98	1.23	2.33	3.27	4.44	5.40	4.85	5.65	6.49	6.70
Japan	49.25	47.94	50.07	45.66	47.28	46.20	44.86	43.04	41.73	42.17	42.53	36.89	31.67
Korea	1.34	1.24	2.73	1.54	2.72	3.53	2.40	3.92	4.38	4.14	5.31	6.67	6.13
ASEAN	12.60	11.95	15.67	16.41	11.38	10.71	10.46	10.08	10.86	11.18	9.95	11.48	13.43
ASEAN+3	63.18	61.17	68.54	63.74	61.41	60.88	58.66	59.03	59.51	59.93	61.04	59.12	55.33
ASEAN+4	63.88	61.79	69.19	64.59	62.61	62.76	60.99	61.48	62.37	62.34	63.45	61.52	57.93

Japan	1980	1981	1982	1983	1984	1985	1986	1987	1988	1989	1990	1991	1992
USA	24.46	25.66	26.39	29.48	35.59	37.62	38.86	36.74	34.05	34.20	31.66	29.27	28.45
EU	15.78	14.56	14.50	14.86	13.27	13.39	16.49	18.54	19.98	19.47	20.76	20.70	20.01
Euro Area	11.45	10.19	9.95	10.28	9.22	9.44	11.91	13.44	14.58	14.33	15.78	16.12	15.46
China	3.92	3.35	2.53	3.35	4.24	7.10	4.71	3.60	3.58	3.09	2.13	2.73	3.52
Hong Kong	3.67	3.49	3.40	3.60	3.85	3.70	3.42	3.87	4.42	4.18	4.55	5.19	6.11
China+HK	7.58	6.84	5.93	6.94	8.09	10.81	8.14	7.47	8.00	7.26	6.69	7.92	9.63
Korea	4.13	3.72	3.52	4.09	4.25	4.04	5.01	5.77	5.83	6.00	6.08	6.38	5.23
ASEAN	10.38	10.31	11.04	10.49	8.49	6.60	5.99	6.96	8.22	9.52	11.61	12.08	12.22
ASEAN+3	18.43	17.38	17.08	17.92	16.97	17.74	15.71	16.32	17.63	18.61	19.82	21.19	20.97
ASEAN+4	22.10	20.87	20.48	21.52	20.83	21.45	19.14	20.19	22.05	22.79	24.37	26.38	27.09

Annex 3
(continued)

1993	1994	1995	1996	1997	1998	1999	2000	2001	2002	2003	2004	2005	2006	2007
23.06	23.22	21.81	21.25	21.80	23.43	23.88	23.28	22.31	21.40	18.65	16.95	16.06	15.11	13.73
16.38	15.43	15.31	15.28	15.11	16.19	16.50	15.65	14.91	13.84	13.76	14.02	14.56	14.01	13.54
11.96	11.10	11.04	10.79	10.53	11.06	11.11	10.50	10.09	9.23	9.40	9.54	10.12	9.65	9.37
32.33	32.78	33.34	34.33	34.91	34.45	33.37	34.48	36.88	39.31	42.62	44.01	45.00	46.98	48.67
5.15	5.57	6.11	6.55	6.08	5.25	5.42	5.54	5.92	5.36	5.40	5.32	5.27	4.89	4.45
1.67	1.59	1.62	1.63	1.49	1.03	1.58	1.89	1.75	1.95	2.04	2.18	2.14	2.11	1.97
6.22	6.65	6.88	6.87	6.63	5.61	5.98	6.08	5.76	6.29	6.05	6.15	5.86	5.82	6.11
45.37	46.59	47.94	49.38	49.10	46.34	46.34	47.99	50.31	52.91	56.10	57.67	58.27	59.80	61.20

1993	1994	1995	1996	1997	1998	1999	2000	2001	2002	2003	2004	2005	2006	2007
14.20	14.55	13.91	13.62	13.39	14.42	14.20	13.67	13.78	13.25	12.11	12.28	11.55	11.48	10.71
14.94	15.47	15.33	15.96	15.55	16.53	15.12	14.41	14.29	14.47	13.72	12.73	12.10	12.21	12.24
11.56	12.05	12.07	12.57	10.98	11.41	11.79	11.23	11.02	11.34	10.93	10.14	9.91	9.79	9.98
3.39	3.30	3.83	4.12	4.17	3.75	4.13	4.46	3.91	5.08	6.23	6.44	7.78	7.70	8.62
2.44	3.30	3.65	3.26	3.34	3.82	2.73	2.50	2.29	2.17	1.94	1.94	1.74	1.54	1.46
5.84	6.60	7.48	7.38	7.51	7.57	6.86	6.96	6.20	7.25	8.17	8.37	9.52	9.24	10.09
30.33	27.28	27.03	25.83	23.36	18.66	21.37	23.21	23.10	21.07	22.30	22.31	21.08	19.38	18.50
6.03	6.47	6.42	6.58	6.48	5.26	6.82	6.95	6.70	7.19	7.09	6.75	8.28	6.45	6.84
13.59	14.93	14.25	15.41	17.06	19.13	17.01	17.52	16.88	17.38	17.58	18.17	18.48	20.31	19.40
53.33	51.97	51.53	51.94	51.07	46.80	49.33	52.13	50.59	50.72	53.19	53.66	55.62	53.83	53.37
55.78	55.27	55.18	55.19	54.41	50.62	52.06	54.64	52.88	52.89	55.13	55.60	57.36	55.38	54.84

1993	1994	1995	1996	1997	1998	1999	2000	2001	2002	2003	2004	2005	2006	2007
29.46	30.02	27.53	27.50	28.09	30.85	31.04	30.10	30.41	28.84	24.87	22.73	22.86	22.76	20.38
16.85	15.69	16.12	15.62	15.97	18.92	18.23	16.85	16.54	15.31	16.01	15.80	14.63	14.55	14.80
12.80	11.73	12.19	11.82	11.85	14.22	13.88	12.80	12.66	11.53	12.17	11.95	10.75	10.87	11.04
4.78	4.73	4.95	5.30	5.15	5.20	5.59	6.35	7.67	9.59	12.18	13.06	13.45	14.35	15.30
6.29	6.51	6.27	6.16	6.47	5.79	5.28	5.68	5.76	6.10	6.34	6.26	6.05	5.63	5.45
11.07	11.24	11.21	11.46	11.61	10.99	10.87	12.03	13.43	15.69	18.52	19.32	19.50	19.98	20.75
5.29	6.16	7.06	7.14	6.19	3.97	5.50	6.42	6.27	6.86	7.38	7.82	7.85	7.78	7.60
13.92	15.48	17.58	17.86	16.61	12.03	12.99	14.32	13.45	13.38	12.98	12.90	12.79	11.82	12.20
24.00	26.37	29.58	30.30	27.95	21.20	24.09	27.09	27.39	29.83	32.54	33.78	34.09	33.94	35.10
30.29	32.88	35.85	36.46	34.42	26.98	29.37	32.77	33.15	35.93	38.88	40.04	40.14	39.57	40.55

Annex 3
(continued)

Korea	1980	1981	1982	1983	1984	1985	1986	1987	1988	1989	1990	1991	1992
USA	26.52	26.74	28.80	33.78	35.98	35.62	40.00	38.85	35.38	33.38	28.64	25.71	23.48
EU	16.93	14.21	14.42	13.75	12.39	12.04	13.47	15.73	14.87	13.18	14.99	15.35	13.32
Euro Area	12.53	10.05	8.88	8.65	8.07	8.13	9.69	11.14	10.55	9.28	10.83	11.36	9.95
China	0.00	0.00	0.00	0.00	0.00	0.00	0.00	0.00	0.00	0.00	0.00	1.38	3.43
Hong Kong	4.72	5.43	4.14	3.34	4.38	5.17	4.86	4.66	5.87	5.54	5.57	6.59	7.64
China+HK	4.72	5.43	4.14	3.34	4.38	5.17	4.86	4.66	5.87	5.54	5.57	7.97	11.07
Japan	17.43	16.47	15.60	13.83	15.75	15.01	15.59	17.83	19.77	21.75	18.64	17.07	15.00
ASEAN	6.59	5.45	6.24	5.84	4.84	5.08	3.84	4.19	5.06	6.34	7.52	10.13	11.70
ASEAN+3	24.02	21.92	21.84	19.67	20.60	20.09	19.43	22.02	24.83	28.09	26.16	28.59	30.13
ASEAN+4	28.74	27.34	25.99	23.01	24.98	25.26	24.29	26.68	30.70	33.63	31.73	35.18	37.77

Lao	1980	1981	1982	1983	1984	1985	1986	1987	1988	1989	1990	1991	1992
USA		6.62	6.01	10.60	17.57	2.75	1.93	3.91	5.21	0.82	0.14	2.44	5.62
EU		1.20	3.42	2.08	10.78	6.86	4.63	16.42	10.25	3.38	9.38	26.85	29.62
Euro Area		0.60	1.50	0.00	6.39	4.39	1.93	9.50	1.23	1.04	8.49	25.29	25.48
China		51.16	25.53	17.42	42.33	52.17	62.46	41.44	28.80	12.00	9.08	2.46	3.24
Hong Kong		4.21	4.13	0.00	0.80	3.29	0.00	1.17	0.49	0.63	0.00	0.13	0.52
China+HK		55.38	29.66	17.42	43.13	55.46	62.46	42.62	29.29	12.63	9.08	2.60	3.76
Japan		23.48	4.51	9.47	5.59	6.59	9.01	5.86	11.07	7.60	7.08	4.92	10.49
Korea		0.00	0.00	0.00	0.00	0.00	0.00	0.00	0.00	0.00	0.00	0.00	0.00
ASEAN		11.92	51.18	59.27	8.15	16.03	9.08	23.26	38.81	44.59	68.41	55.95	43.51
ASEAN+3		86.56	81.22	86.16	56.07	74.79	80.55	70.57	78.68	64.18	84.57	63.33	57.24
ASEAN+4		90.77	85.35	86.16	56.87	78.09	80.55	71.74	79.17	64.81	84.57	63.47	57.76

Malaysia	1980	1981	1982	1983	1984	1985	1986	1987	1988	1989	1990	1991	1992
USA	16.35	13.06	11.62	13.19	13.47	12.78	16.44	16.57	17.36	18.70	16.95	16.88	18.65
EU	18.58	16.64	15.84	15.53	13.54	14.89	15.02	14.86	15.04	15.96	15.52	15.26	15.37
Euro Area	14.74	12.81	12.23	12.19	10.35	11.77	11.00	11.05	10.89	11.62	10.98	10.36	10.85
China	1.67	0.75	0.92	1.11	0.99	1.05	1.17	1.56	1.97	1.92	2.10	1.86	1.90
Hong Kong	1.88	2.02	1.92	1.73	1.42	1.34	2.22	2.82	3.39	3.07	3.17	3.35	3.81
China+HK	3.55	2.77	2.83	2.84	2.41	2.39	3.39	4.38	5.36	4.99	5.28	5.20	5.70
Japan	22.82	21.14	20.34	19.69	22.76	24.56	23.30	19.54	16.96	16.03	15.31	15.86	13.27
Korea	2.02	3.65	3.66	4.68	5.00	5.88	5.16	5.31	4.79	5.01	4.62	4.40	3.41
ASEAN	22.71	26.88	30.48	28.59	26.66	25.94	21.99	24.24	24.48	25.59	29.45	29.44	29.87
ASEAN+3	49.23	52.41	55.40	54.08	55.41	57.42	51.63	50.64	48.19	48.55	51.49	51.56	48.45
ASEAN+4	51.11	54.43	57.31	55.81	56.83	58.76	53.85	53.46	51.58	51.62	54.66	54.91	52.26

Annex 3
(continued)

1993	1994	1995	1996	1997	1998	1999	2000	2001	2002	2003	2004	2005	2006	2007
21.23	20.43	18.54	15.92	15.16	17.38	20.57	21.95	20.84	20.30	17.73	16.96	14.60	13.33	12.42
12.53	12.04	13.60	12.77	13.33	15.67	15.41	14.45	14.16	14.76	14.07	15.14	15.60	15.29	13.68
9.36	9.18	10.07	8.62	8.62	10.85	10.18	10.29	10.87	11.03	10.64	11.26	11.76	11.04	9.31
6.00	6.12	6.96	8.26	9.42	9.02	9.51	10.71	12.09	14.63	18.12	19.61	21.78	21.33	25.84
7.49	7.91	8.13	8.08	8.14	6.99	6.29	6.22	6.28	6.25	7.56	7.14	5.46	5.86	3.86
13.50	14.03	15.10	16.35	17.56	16.01	15.80	16.93	18.37	20.89	25.68	26.76	27.24	27.19	29.70
13.48	13.34	12.98	11.45	10.25	9.23	11.02	11.88	10.97	9.33	8.91	8.55	8.45	8.13	6.88
11.78	12.32	13.69	14.75	14.13	11.56	12.31	11.69	10.94	11.34	10.45	9.47	9.65	9.79	10.57
31.26	31.78	33.63	34.46	33.80	29.82	32.85	34.28	34.00	35.30	37.48	37.63	39.87	39.24	43.28
38.75	39.69	41.77	42.55	41.94	36.80	39.13	40.50	40.29	41.55	45.04	44.78	45.34	45.10	47.14

1993	1994	1995	1996	1997	1998	1999	2000	2001	2002	2003	2004	2005	2006	2007
4.45	1.66	1.70	0.84	3.63	5.39	2.73	2.25	0.97	0.68	0.91	0.63	0.59	0.75	1.58
12.27	10.49	10.89	7.30	41.52	25.87	22.13	26.20	29.36	29.95	28.76	28.91	19.70	10.45	10.36
12.27	10.19	10.60	5.24	33.79	22.08	17.93	23.14	25.94	25.21	23.16	21.66	17.05	9.41	8.80
10.60	2.70	2.83	0.25	0.15	1.94	1.88	1.49	1.80	2.27	2.33	2.12	3.33	3.98	6.24
0.00	0.00	0.00	0.00	0.00	0.02	0.01	0.11	0.03	0.02	0.03	0.00	0.00	0.03	0.01
10.60	2.70	2.83	0.25	0.15	1.96	1.89	1.60	1.83	2.29	2.36	2.13	3.34	4.02	6.24
3.66	1.63	1.70	0.53	3.49	4.80	2.66	2.79	1.68	1.58	1.53	1.36	1.05	1.00	0.90
0.79	0.00	0.00	0.16	0.35	0.00	0.24	0.13	0.12	0.03	0.03	0.24	0.28	1.13	1.32
40.79	52.76	54.98	79.54	18.09	40.18	51.64	42.69	38.26	37.02	34.96	32.23	43.98	55.72	49.90
55.84	57.09	59.51	80.48	22.08	46.91	56.41	47.11	41.86	40.90	38.85	35.95	48.64	61.83	58.35
55.84	57.09	59.51	80.48	22.08	46.93	56.42	47.22	41.89	40.92	38.88	35.96	48.65	61.87	58.36

1993	1994	1995	1996	1997	1998	1999	2000	2001	2002	2003	2004	2005	2006	2007
20.33	21.19	20.77	18.22	18.44	21.62	21.92	20.54	20.20	20.16	19.57	18.77	19.69	18.79	15.62
14.93	14.48	14.42	13.94	14.57	16.58	16.07	14.01	14.15	12.82	12.60	12.61	11.79	12.78	12.88
10.32	10.13	9.78	9.94	10.70	12.31	11.70	10.17	10.76	9.79	9.62	9.36	9.13	9.88	10.07
2.55	3.29	2.56	2.41	2.35	2.71	2.74	3.09	4.33	5.63	6.49	6.69	6.60	7.25	8.77
4.12	4.62	5.35	5.89	5.52	4.64	4.47	4.52	4.61	5.68	6.46	5.97	5.85	4.95	4.62
6.67	7.91	7.91	8.30	7.87	7.36	7.21	7.61	8.94	11.31	12.95	12.65	12.44	12.20	13.39
12.97	11.93	12.48	13.42	12.65	10.50	11.64	13.02	13.34	11.28	10.69	10.10	9.35	8.86	9.13
3.42	2.80	2.73	3.05	3.19	2.28	2.94	3.30	3.36	3.36	2.90	3.50	3.36	3.61	3.80
28.41	27.92	27.56	28.52	28.10	24.32	23.81	26.56	25.09	26.00	24.82	25.09	26.08	26.06	25.71
47.36	45.94	45.33	47.40	46.30	39.81	41.13	45.96	46.12	46.27	44.90	45.38	45.39	45.79	47.42
51.48	50.56	50.67	53.29	51.82	44.45	45.59	50.48	50.73	51.95	51.36	51.34	51.23	50.74	52.04

Annex 3
(continued)

Myanmar	1980	1981	1982	1983	1984	1985	1986	1987	1988	1989	1990	1991	1992
USA	0.48	0.75	0.75	0.75	0.75	0.75	0.75	0.75	0.75	0.75	2.29	5.05	5.53
EU	12.77	8.94	8.94	8.94	8.94	8.94	8.94	8.94	8.94	8.94	6.86	7.07	6.16
Euro Area	8.40	7.11	7.11	7.11	7.11	7.11	7.11	7.11	7.11	7.11	5.09	4.63	4.20
China	1.18	1.22	1.22	1.23	1.22	1.22	1.22	1.22	1.22	1.22	8.14	18.27	17.46
Hong Kong	7.55	9.14	9.14	9.14	9.14	9.14	9.14	9.14	9.14	9.14	5.60	6.40	6.53
China+HK	8.73	10.36	10.36	10.36	10.36	10.36	10.36	10.36	10.36	10.36	13.74	24.67	23.98
Japan	9.95	8.37	8.37	8.37	8.37	8.37	8.37	8.37	8.37	8.37	6.94	8.52	6.29
Korea	0.20	5.33	5.33	5.33	5.33	5.33	5.33	5.33	5.33	5.33	2.20	0.84	0.80
ASEAN	27.32	20.15	20.15	20.15	20.15	20.15	20.15	20.15	20.15	20.15	28.21	19.01	18.43
ASEAN+3	38.65	35.08	35.08	35.08	35.08	35.08	35.08	35.08	35.08	35.08	45.49	46.64	42.97
ASEAN+4	46.21	44.22	44.22	44.22	44.22	44.22	44.22	44.22	44.22	44.22	51.09	53.04	49.50

Philippines	1980	1981	1982	1983	1984	1985	1986	1987	1988	1989	1990	1991	1992
USA	27.54	30.95	31.64	36.32	38.03	35.94	35.55	36.17	35.66	37.84	37.87	35.63	39.08
EU	18.11	17.07	15.69	17.52	14.42	14.52	18.72	19.49	18.13	17.55	18.54	19.20	19.53
Euro Area	14.88	13.11	11.25	12.25	9.68	10.35	13.42	14.63	12.93	12.76	13.74	14.34	14.30
China	0.78	1.37	2.10	0.45	1.13	1.75	2.10	1.54	0.95	0.65	0.75	1.44	1.16
Hong Kong	3.32	3.88	3.94	3.21	4.38	4.04	4.58	4.86	4.88	3.89	4.03	4.43	4.71
China+HK	4.10	5.24	6.04	3.66	5.51	5.80	6.68	6.41	5.83	4.54	4.79	5.87	5.87
Japan	26.61	21.92	22.89	19.93	19.36	18.95	17.71	17.21	20.10	20.39	19.79	20.02	17.75
Korea	3.51	3.47	3.02	3.01	1.85	1.62	2.34	1.73	2.28	2.07	2.80	2.58	1.79
ASEAN	6.73	7.42	7.30	7.27	9.69	11.41	7.25	8.90	7.08	7.00	7.27	7.21	5.61
ASEAN+3	37.62	34.17	35.30	30.67	32.02	33.74	29.40	29.38	30.40	30.11	30.61	31.26	26.30
ASEAN+4	40.94	38.04	39.24	33.88	36.41	37.79	33.97	34.24	35.28	34.00	34.64	35.68	31.02

Singapore	1980	1981	1982	1983	1984	1985	1986	1987	1988	1989	1990	1991	1992
USA	12.43	13.13	12.48	18.00	19.92	21.02	23.24	24.30	23.75	23.29	21.24	19.70	21.10
EU	13.65	11.62	10.24	10.09	10.62	11.15	11.83	13.05	13.89	14.61	15.64	15.29	16.21
Euro Area	10.15	8.52	7.51	7.22	7.45	7.83	8.52	9.48	10.30	10.36	11.51	11.36	12.63
China	1.58	0.85	1.15	0.97	1.00	1.45	2.52	2.56	3.02	2.68	1.51	1.45	1.75
Hong Kong	7.67	8.71	8.37	6.74	6.14	6.33	6.46	6.30	6.23	6.30	6.49	7.19	7.82
China+HK	9.24	9.55	9.51	7.71	7.15	7.78	8.99	8.86	9.25	8.98	8.01	8.64	9.57
Japan	8.00	10.07	10.81	9.14	9.31	9.34	8.54	9.02	8.60	8.55	8.74	8.66	7.60
Korea	1.48	1.39	1.51	2.08	1.58	1.22	1.43	1.64	1.95	1.93	2.22	2.35	2.05
ASEAN	22.89	23.38	25.39	25.98	23.59	22.66	20.99	21.23	21.49	21.86	22.34	23.64	22.46
ASEAN+3	33.94	35.68	38.86	38.17	35.48	34.68	33.48	34.45	35.06	35.01	34.81	36.11	33.87
ASEAN+4	41.61	44.39	47.23	44.91	41.63	41.00	39.95	40.75	41.29	41.32	41.31	43.30	41.68

Annex 3
(continued)

1993	1994	1995	1996	1997	1998	1999	2000	2001	2002	2003	2004	2005	2006	2007
5.27	7.02	6.60	8.93	9.91	13.96	15.95	22.36	17.38	12.54	9.71	0.00	0.00	0.00	0.00
7.46	7.29	6.10	8.66	12.60	14.09	15.31	16.70	15.47	13.19	13.79	15.84	8.48	7.43	6.78
4.79	4.24	4.45	6.53	9.45	10.97	11.79	12.37	11.20	9.11	9.61	11.20	6.36	6.02	5.35
17.32	13.81	11.35	10.56	5.90	4.92	6.62	5.73	4.65	4.52	5.57	5.94	6.74	5.25	6.84
6.48	5.32	4.87	4.97	4.06	3.63	2.44	1.45	0.96	0.82	0.94	1.16	1.19	1.12	1.53
23.81	19.13	16.22	15.54	9.95	8.55	9.06	7.18	5.60	5.34	6.51	7.10	7.92	6.36	8.37
7.52	7.32	7.14	7.94	7.95	7.14	6.62	5.48	3.53	3.64	4.58	5.18	4.99	5.15	5.65
1.51	1.04	1.00	1.38	1.35	1.05	1.02	1.04	1.75	1.86	0.96	0.87	1.38	1.93	2.20
19.42	23.03	30.27	25.38	20.64	15.53	19.18	21.29	35.59	37.56	36.43	45.20	51.30	54.40	49.85
45.78	45.21	49.76	45.26	35.83	28.65	33.43	33.54	45.52	47.58	47.54	57.18	64.41	66.72	64.54
52.26	50.53	54.63	50.23	39.89	32.28	35.87	34.99	46.48	48.40	48.48	58.34	65.60	67.84	66.07

1993	1994	1995	1996	1997	1998	1999	2000	2001	2002	2003	2004	2005	2006	2007
38.53	38.52	35.77	33.88	35.09	34.38	29.57	29.85	27.98	24.68	20.08	18.17	18.03	18.32	13.29
17.83	17.58	17.70	15.92	18.23	20.57	19.44	18.11	19.52	18.47	16.64	17.19	17.00	18.54	10.17
12.66	12.46	12.05	11.23	13.54	14.22	13.87	13.70	16.03	15.30	14.25	15.03	15.36	17.07	7.57
1.48	1.22	1.20	1.60	0.97	1.16	1.62	1.74	2.47	3.85	5.92	6.69	9.89	9.83	29.27
4.85	4.84	4.73	4.22	4.64	4.49	5.49	4.99	4.91	6.70	8.54	7.93	8.10	7.82	8.31
6.33	6.06	5.93	5.82	5.61	5.66	7.11	6.73	7.38	10.55	14.46	14.61	17.99	17.65	37.58
16.08	15.03	15.76	17.84	16.62	14.34	13.13	14.68	15.73	15.03	15.92	20.12	17.48	16.48	11.77
1.96	2.17	2.55	1.80	1.73	1.72	2.91	3.07	3.25	3.80	3.63	2.80	3.38	3.00	2.60
7.04	10.64	13.59	13.10	13.76	12.95	14.06	15.65	15.51	15.71	18.17	17.23	17.34	17.31	16.06
26.55	29.05	33.10	34.34	33.08	30.18	31.72	35.13	36.95	38.39	43.63	46.84	48.08	46.61	59.70
31.40	33.89	37.83	38.56	37.72	34.68	37.21	40.13	41.87	45.09	52.17	54.77	56.18	54.44	68.01

1993	1994	1995	1996	1997	1998	1999	2000	2001	2002	2003	2004	2005	2006	2007
20.34	18.67	18.25	18.42	18.44	19.88	19.22	17.31	15.40	15.26	12.85	11.72	10.41	10.15	8.91
15.04	13.82	13.88	13.47	14.32	16.38	15.80	14.00	14.06	13.34	12.82	13.09	12.06	11.26	10.76
11.52	10.66	10.87	10.25	10.64	12.56	11.68	11.03	11.26	10.56	9.36	9.34	8.73	8.02	7.50
2.57	2.16	2.33	2.71	3.23	3.70	3.42	3.90	4.37	5.48	6.33	7.75	8.61	9.75	9.67
8.67	8.65	8.57	8.15	9.60	8.39	7.68	7.85	8.88	9.16	9.01	8.88	9.40	10.13	10.47
11.24	10.81	10.90	10.87	12.83	12.09	11.09	11.75	13.26	14.64	15.34	16.63	18.01	19.88	20.14
7.46	6.98	7.80	8.19	7.06	6.57	7.42	7.54	7.67	7.14	6.06	5.82	5.46	5.46	4.81
2.78	2.61	2.74	3.77	2.95	2.33	3.10	3.56	3.85	4.16	3.78	3.72	3.51	3.21	3.55
24.85	29.83	30.33	29.24	27.78	23.93	25.83	27.36	26.96	27.15	32.37	31.55	31.37	30.85	31.78
37.66	41.59	43.20	43.91	41.02	36.53	39.76	42.35	42.85	43.92	48.54	48.83	48.96	49.27	49.81
46.33	50.24	51.77	52.06	50.62	44.92	47.44	50.21	51.73	53.09	57.55	57.71	58.36	59.40	60.28

Annex 3
(continued)

Thailand	1980	1981	1982	1983	1984	1985	1986	1987	1988	1989	1990	1991	1992
USA	12.66	12.89	12.70	14.97	17.17	19.68	18.12	18.71	20.12	21.59	22.71	21.01	22.49
EU	26.85	23.03	24.46	22.53	21.65	20.01	22.59	23.64	22.04	20.35	23.37	24.03	21.86
Euro Area	24.00	20.21	21.58	19.23	18.23	16.45	18.12	18.70	17.18	15.53	17.67	17.94	16.14
China	1.90	2.65	4.42	1.68	2.46	3.80	3.11	3.35	2.98	2.68	1.16	1.16	1.19
Hong Kong	5.07	4.80	4.93	4.97	3.79	4.04	3.99	4.22	4.47	4.31	4.50	4.67	4.64
China+HK	6.97	7.45	9.35	6.66	6.26	7.84	7.10	7.57	7.45	6.99	5.66	5.83	5.83
Japan	15.10	14.17	13.71	15.08	13.02	13.36	14.22	14.98	15.99	16.95	17.20	17.78	17.51
Korea	0.76	2.15	1.17	1.43	1.65	1.86	2.75	1.32	1.60	1.49	1.71	1.59	1.64
ASEAN	17.79	15.29	16.20	16.35	14.77	14.92	14.84	14.18	12.15	11.94	11.92	12.03	13.52
ASEAN+3	35.55	34.25	35.51	34.55	31.90	33.94	34.92	33.83	32.73	33.06	31.99	32.57	33.86
ASEAN+4	40.62	39.05	40.44	39.52	35.70	37.98	38.91	38.06	37.20	37.37	36.49	37.23	38.50

Vietnam	1980	1981	1982	1983	1984	1985	1986	1987	1988	1989	1990	1991	1992
USA		0.06	0.00	0.00	0.04	0.00	0.00	0.00	0.00	0.00	0.00	0.00	0.00
EU		30.08	21.27	25.23	18.85	9.83	9.88	10.95	11.70	8.96	9.39	6.13	8.89
Euro Area		10.05	6.04	9.44	7.10	2.48	2.95	3.61	3.20	3.77	6.68	5.39	7.35
China		0.00	0.00	0.00	0.00	0.00	0.00	0.00	0.00	0.01	0.31	0.88	3.28
Hong Kong		21.41	41.38	31.24	32.00	6.87	5.76	5.81	6.29	3.19	9.63	10.20	6.91
China+HK		21.41	41.38	31.24	32.00	6.87	5.76	5.81	6.29	3.20	9.94	11.08	10.19
Japan		23.98	18.23	16.89	18.58	4.66	4.31	5.99	5.84	10.56	13.48	32.86	28.58
Korea		3.28	0.00	1.38	0.00	2.24	2.56	0.46	0.68	1.01	1.06	2.34	3.21
ASEAN		9.91	14.45	19.59	21.74	6.38	9.00	7.69	7.06	5.38	13.81	23.96	19.74
ASEAN+3		37.16	32.68	37.85	40.33	13.28	15.86	14.13	13.58	16.96	28.65	60.05	54.80
ASEAN+4		58.57	74.06	69.10	72.33	20.15	21.62	19.94	19.87	20.16	38.29	70.25	61.72

Source: DTS.

Annex 3
(continued)

1993	1994	1995	1996	1997	1998	1999	2000	2001	2002	2003	2004	2005	2006	2007
21.44	20.65	17.17	17.75	19.09	21.98	21.66	21.32	20.34	19.64	17.02	16.10	15.39	15.03	12.63
19.76	16.99	16.39	16.49	16.47	17.99	17.30	16.30	16.67	15.35	15.23	14.92	13.58	13.84	13.89
13.91	11.86	11.27	11.98	11.67	12.98	12.58	11.69	12.00	10.85	10.94	10.64	9.86	9.84	9.89
1.15	2.02	2.80	3.31	2.98	3.19	3.18	4.07	4.40	5.16	7.11	7.38	8.27	9.05	9.73
5.25	5.17	4.98	5.74	5.83	5.03	5.09	5.04	5.07	5.37	5.39	5.12	5.56	5.53	5.70
6.40	7.19	7.77	9.05	8.81	8.22	8.28	9.11	9.46	10.53	12.50	12.49	13.82	14.57	15.43
16.88	16.75	16.14	16.60	14.95	13.50	14.12	14.74	15.30	14.53	14.19	13.98	13.60	12.63	11.89
1.24	1.24	1.37	1.79	1.73	1.13	1.56	1.83	1.89	2.03	1.98	1.93	2.04	2.06	1.95
17.16	20.27	20.30	20.40	20.99	17.24	18.58	19.34	19.35	19.71	20.60	22.01	21.99	20.83	21.33
36.42	40.28	40.61	42.09	40.65	35.06	37.44	39.99	40.93	41.43	43.87	45.30	45.89	44.57	44.89
41.67	45.45	45.58	47.83	46.48	40.09	42.54	45.02	46.00	46.80	49.27	50.41	51.45	50.09	50.59

1993	1994	1995	1996	1997	1998	1999	2000	2001	2002	2003	2004	2005	2006	2007
0.00	2.34	3.02	2.74	3.02	5.04	4.37	5.06	7.10	14.69	19.56	18.97	18.26	21.95	22.49
8.76	10.76	12.67	12.36	18.15	23.38	23.03	20.62	21.13	19.94	20.03	18.76	16.98	20.46	21.09
6.89	8.52	10.34	9.04	13.33	17.65	17.40	15.61	15.94	14.79	14.61	13.57	12.56	15.19	15.68
4.55	7.29	6.44	4.56	5.00	4.73	6.47	10.61	9.44	9.09	9.35	10.95	9.95	5.89	6.19
5.66	4.86	4.57	4.17	4.54	3.42	2.04	2.18	2.11	2.04	1.83	1.44	1.09	1.48	1.47
10.21	12.15	11.00	8.73	9.54	8.15	8.51	12.79	11.55	11.13	11.18	12.38	11.04	7.36	7.66
31.39	29.09	25.99	20.72	17.67	16.27	15.48	17.78	16.71	14.59	14.44	13.37	13.38	12.69	11.99
3.33	2.13	4.19	7.48	4.40	2.46	2.77	2.43	2.70	2.81	2.44	2.30	2.05	1.98	2.04
21.53	22.02	19.79	23.82	21.32	21.71	21.80	18.09	17.01	14.59	14.66	15.26	17.70	13.42	14.24
60.80	60.54	56.40	56.58	48.39	45.17	46.52	48.91	45.86	41.07	40.89	41.88	43.07	33.98	34.47
66.46	65.39	60.97	60.75	52.93	48.59	48.56	51.09	47.98	43.11	42.72	43.32	44.16	35.46	35.93

Annex 4

Imports (c.i.f.) of ... from ... (as percent of total imports), 1980–2007

Brunei	1980	1981	1982	1983	1984	1985	1986	1987	1988	1989	1990	1991	1992
USA	20.06	18.70	16.98	19.52	15.21	15.57	12.22	12.07	12.58	12.67	15.28	13.67	18.38
EU	20.66	15.80	15.27	16.93	17.05	17.88	24.23	22.72	19.38	20.42	18.09	19.71	21.10
Euro Area	9.89	5.55	7.19	7.85	7.30	7.94	15.30	13.31	10.50	10.20	10.35	9.45	14.26
China	1.84	2.18	1.84	1.88	1.99	1.99	1.89	2.29	2.11	2.30	2.70	2.88	2.07
Hong Kong	1.41	1.15	1.34	1.10	1.46	1.49	1.35	1.32	1.14	1.16	1.57	1.77	1.86
China+HK	3.25	3.33	3.18	2.98	3.46	3.48	3.24	3.61	3.25	3.46	4.27	4.65	3.93
Japan	23.69	22.39	23.60	19.13	19.98	19.80	17.69	14.39	15.95	14.72	14.57	15.77	15.47
Korea	0.20	0.50	4.39	0.65	0.98	0.00	0.89	1.54	1.49	1.03	0.62	0.63	0.85
ASEAN	26.14	31.97	27.86	30.80	32.53	32.34	35.61	37.72	39.78	41.67	41.89	36.16	35.53
ASEAN+3	51.86	57.04	57.70	52.46	55.48	54.13	56.08	55.93	59.33	59.72	59.78	55.45	53.92
ASEAN+4	53.27	58.19	59.03	53.57	56.94	55.62	57.43	57.25	60.48	60.88	61.34	57.21	55.78

Cambodia	1980	1981	1982	1983	1984	1985	1986	1987	1988	1989	1990	1991	1992
USA		16.28	3.46	5.07	2.46	0.00	1.00	0.83	0.00	0.07	0.00	0.00	2.36
EU		5.56	6.97	6.44	8.20	15.92	30.48	29.05	10.05	9.16	25.71	16.74	3.76
Euro Area		5.14	5.24	3.99	5.92	11.61	16.38	22.00	6.50	7.15	23.97	15.23	3.30
China		0.42	1.08	1.27	0.00	2.01	1.00	1.65	1.84	2.78	5.91	3.85	1.87
Hong Kong		4.35	1.08	4.65	0.67	0.00	13.98	0.00	0.46	3.16	3.22	9.48	3.30
China+HK		4.77	2.16	5.92	0.67	2.01	14.98	1.65	2.30	5.93	9.13	13.33	5.17
Japan		14.60	11.47	6.97	12.10	6.83	16.98	9.10	22.13	7.60	8.99	11.93	33.51
Korea		0.00	0.00	0.00	0.00	0.00	0.00	0.00	0.00	0.00	0.00	0.00	0.00
ASEAN		53.55	75.47	75.47	68.93	62.65	11.19	2.48	16.53	53.24	43.27	32.24	52.14
ASEAN+3		68.56	88.03	83.71	81.03	71.50	29.16	13.23	40.50	63.62	58.17	48.02	87.52
ASEAN+4		72.92	89.11	88.35	81.70	71.50	43.14	13.23	40.96	66.78	61.39	57.50	90.82

China	1980	1981	1982	1983	1984	1985	1986	1987	1988	1989	1990	1991	1992
USA	19.64	21.65	22.75	12.92	14.78	12.24	10.90	11.19	11.98	13.30	12.25	12.54	10.87
EU	20.00	17.34	15.45	19.92	16.88	18.08	22.81	21.18	18.24	18.40	18.27	15.21	13.75
Euro Area	12.21	12.66	10.39	13.14	11.41	13.13	16.23	15.33	13.59	14.01	13.68	12.40	11.28
Hong Kong	2.92	5.72	6.95	8.02	10.90	11.21	12.88	19.52	21.69	21.20	27.07	27.46	25.09
Japan	26.50	28.58	20.62	25.78	31.04	35.73	28.80	23.34	19.98	17.81	14.23	15.70	16.72
Korea	0.00	0.00	0.00	0.00	0.00	0.00	0.00	0.00	0.00	0.00	0.44	1.67	3.20
ASEAN	3.35	2.74	4.86	3.18	3.23	2.78	3.58	5.00	5.78	6.37	5.82	6.17	5.39
ASEAN+3	29.85	31.32	25.48	28.97	34.28	38.51	32.38	28.34	25.76	24.18	20.49	23.55	25.31
ASEAN+4	32.77	37.04	32.42	36.99	45.18	49.73	45.25	47.86	47.45	45.38	47.56	51.01	50.40

Annex 4
(continued)

1993	1994	1995	1996	1997	1998	1999	2000	2001	2002	2003	2004	2005	2006	2007
25.08	11.34	8.84	17.46	10.00	5.80	13.07	10.78	8.69	3.14	11.39	3.31	3.28	2.65	6.64
27.02	18.29	16.42	16.00	17.92	38.79	11.27	15.79	12.66	10.84	10.66	15.54	9.76	14.59	13.52
22.27	9.76	9.12	8.15	10.97	18.49	5.94	7.62	5.21	4.48	6.84	7.11	4.25	5.87	4.41
1.25	1.78	3.00	2.61	2.46	0.43	1.45	1.18	1.44	1.42	4.82	3.06	3.51	5.48	4.82
1.64	1.04	2.74	3.50	3.64	1.22	3.96	4.19	4.29	3.91	6.50	3.78	2.11	1.59	1.41
2.88	2.82	5.74	6.11	6.11	1.64	5.41	5.38	5.73	5.33	11.31	6.84	5.61	7.07	6.23
9.36	10.09	8.80	7.91	11.18	2.90	7.99	4.72	4.64	21.55	9.90	7.24	6.91	5.57	5.87
0.87	0.95	1.42	1.51	1.80	0.85	1.22	1.12	1.38	1.81	2.33	2.12	4.05	1.09	1.17
30.17	47.74	50.30	42.70	45.51	44.37	54.27	57.65	62.56	53.24	46.66	60.18	63.69	58.25	59.79
41.64	60.55	63.53	54.73	60.95	48.55	64.93	64.67	70.02	78.02	63.71	72.60	78.15	70.38	71.65
43.28	61.59	66.27	58.23	64.59	49.76	68.90	68.87	74.31	81.93	70.20	76.38	80.26	71.98	73.06

1993	1994	1995	1996	1997	1998	1999	2000	2001	2002	2003	2004	2005	2006	2007
2.04	0.71	1.88	1.44	2.40	3.45	3.06	2.30	1.14	0.93	0.94	1.12	1.42	0.85	2.78
4.40	6.70	7.00	7.75	12.03	13.51	7.56	6.60	1.97	4.54	2.87	4.95	8.91	4.08	4.21
3.74	5.68	6.46	6.85	10.07	11.83	5.45	5.12	1.56	3.64	2.53	4.38	8.37	3.57	3.76
2.28	3.37	3.61	4.27	5.07	8.48	6.91	7.92	5.97	11.81	12.90	16.48	16.62	17.55	16.73
3.45	3.08	2.73	3.03	6.01	11.50	14.94	17.85	8.03	22.19	23.60	19.91	17.65	18.06	12.28
5.73	6.44	6.34	7.30	11.08	19.98	21.85	25.78	14.00	34.00	36.50	36.39	34.27	35.61	29.01
5.59	6.16	5.37	3.81	7.50	6.30	5.95	4.10	1.35	3.82	4.32	4.03	3.93	4.34	2.24
0.00	0.00	0.00	0.00	10.29	8.49	6.42	5.39	3.41	5.66	4.66	4.80	5.91	4.89	3.31
78.07	77.56	75.97	73.65	29.36	25.90	38.91	38.92	71.77	35.55	35.47	33.99	31.02	34.33	46.85
85.93	87.09	84.95	81.73	52.22	49.16	58.20	56.34	82.50	56.83	57.35	59.31	57.49	61.12	69.12
89.38	90.16	87.68	84.76	58.23	60.66	73.14	74.19	90.53	79.03	80.95	79.22	75.14	79.18	81.40

1993	1994	1995	1996	1997	1998	1999	2000	2001	2002	2003	2004	2005	2006	2007
10.26	12.08	12.20	11.64	11.46	12.11	11.76	9.94	10.77	9.22	8.22	7.97	7.42	7.49	7.36
16.00	16.66	16.49	14.57	13.65	14.87	15.60	13.70	14.98	13.49	13.32	12.56	11.20	11.45	11.38
12.72	13.60	13.64	11.75	10.97	11.69	12.03	10.67	12.13	11.18	11.16	10.55	9.42	9.67	9.51
10.13	8.20	6.51	5.64	4.92	4.75	4.16	4.19	3.87	3.65	2.69	2.10	1.85	1.36	2.84
22.49	22.75	21.95	21.01	20.39	20.16	20.38	18.44	17.58	18.10	17.96	16.81	15.22	14.63	13.73
5.17	6.32	7.78	8.98	10.47	10.70	10.40	10.31	9.61	9.67	10.45	11.09	11.64	11.34	10.84
6.06	6.20	7.49	7.82	8.69	9.00	9.01	9.85	9.54	10.56	11.46	11.22	11.36	11.31	11.10
33.72	35.27	37.22	37.82	39.55	39.87	39.78	38.60	36.72	38.34	39.87	39.11	38.22	37.28	35.68
43.86	43.47	43.73	43.46	44.48	44.61	43.94	42.78	40.59	41.99	42.57	41.22	40.08	38.64	38.51

Annex 4
(continued)

Hong Kong	1980	1981	1982	1983	1984	1985	1986	1987	1988	1989	1990	1991	1992
USA	11.84	10.45	10.82	10.99	10.93	9.48	8.43	8.55	8.30	8.22	8.07	7.55	7.39
EU	12.83	12.20	12.76	12.26	11.91	12.24	12.22	11.83	11.13	10.66	10.44	9.80	10.12
Euro Area	7.36	7.12	7.34	7.35	7.35	7.93	8.11	7.96	7.86	7.78	7.75	7.26	7.66
China	19.64	21.28	23.01	24.35	24.97	25.48	29.58	31.05	31.20	34.94	36.75	37.65	37.09
Japan	22.95	23.24	22.07	22.98	23.56	23.05	20.44	19.02	18.64	16.56	16.09	16.35	17.39
Korea	3.46	3.98	3.19	2.87	3.26	3.58	3.98	4.49	5.26	4.53	4.38	4.48	4.62
ASEAN	10.68	11.39	10.94	9.71	8.96	8.09	7.32	7.39	7.61	7.65	7.94	7.93	7.88
ASEAN+3	56.74	59.89	59.21	59.92	60.75	60.20	61.32	61.95	62.71	63.68	65.16	66.41	66.99

Indonesia	1980	1981	1982	1983	1984	1985	1986	1987	1988	1989	1990	1991	1992
USA	13.00	13.53	14.34	15.50	18.44	16.75	13.82	11.01	12.85	13.46	11.45	13.10	14.01
EU	14.86	18.46	17.70	16.73	17.18	19.17	19.10	20.85	21.19	18.04	20.71	20.24	22.08
Euro Area	11.53	13.33	13.97	13.40	13.53	14.93	14.41	16.69	17.45	14.19	17.19	16.40	17.84
China	1.82	1.91	1.37	1.25	1.62	2.42	3.14	3.18	3.04	3.26	2.97	3.22	2.75
Hong Kong	1.28	0.51	0.51	0.40	0.62	0.51	0.88	0.81	0.99	1.09	1.24	0.89	0.84
China+HK	3.10	2.42	1.88	1.64	2.24	2.93	4.02	3.99	4.02	4.35	4.21	4.12	3.59
Japan	31.49	30.06	25.38	23.20	23.83	25.74	29.17	27.97	25.40	23.27	24.79	24.40	22.04
Korea	2.16	3.68	1.80	2.37	1.54	2.00	1.48	2.09	3.27	3.46	4.51	5.55	6.94
ASEAN	12.93	12.91	19.76	24.28	14.19	9.44	10.51	13.11	9.91	10.36	8.44	9.85	9.66
ASEAN+3	48.40	48.57	48.31	51.10	41.18	39.59	44.30	46.35	41.62	40.35	40.70	43.02	41.41
ASEAN+4	49.69	49.08	48.82	51.49	41.80	40.10	45.18	47.16	42.61	41.43	41.94	43.92	42.25

Japan	1980	1981	1982	1983	1984	1985	1986	1987	1988	1989	1990	1991	1992
USA	17.39	17.69	18.38	19.60	19.75	20.00	23.04	21.18	22.54	23.02	22.45	22.66	22.62
EU	6.58	6.87	6.64	7.57	8.07	7.99	12.18	12.96	14.14	14.69	16.27	14.75	14.66
Euro Area	4.51	4.29	4.67	5.22	5.19	5.64	8.12	9.64	10.52	11.24	12.81	11.34	11.24
China	3.08	3.70	4.06	4.02	4.37	5.01	4.49	4.96	5.26	5.29	5.12	6.02	7.29
Hong Kong	0.41	0.47	0.47	0.53	0.62	0.59	0.85	1.05	1.13	1.05	0.93	0.87	0.88
China+HK	3.48	4.17	4.53	4.55	4.98	5.60	5.33	6.00	6.39	6.34	6.05	6.89	8.17
Korea	2.15	2.38	2.49	2.69	3.09	3.17	4.18	5.42	6.31	6.17	4.99	5.23	4.98
ASEAN	17.51	16.72	16.80	15.67	16.19	15.66	13.25	13.23	12.19	12.44	12.74	13.73	13.93
ASEAN+3	22.73	22.79	23.34	22.39	23.65	23.84	21.92	23.60	23.76	23.89	22.85	24.98	26.19
ASEAN+4	23.14	23.26	23.81	22.92	24.26	24.43	22.76	24.64	24.88	24.95	23.78	25.85	27.07

Annex 4
(continued)

1993	1994	1995	1996	1997	1998	1999	2000	2001	2002	2003	2004	2005	2006	2007
7.41	7.15	7.72	7.89	7.77	7.46	7.08	6.80	6.69	5.68	5.50	5.34	5.15	4.79	4.88
10.36	10.44	10.84	11.23	11.11	10.70	9.24	8.85	9.77	8.90	8.55	8.05	7.59	7.28	7.13
7.86	7.88	8.32	8.36	8.07	7.88	6.75	6.39	7.41	6.65	6.66	6.17	5.81	5.62	5.65
37.51	37.62	36.18	37.15	37.67	40.61	43.61	43.03	43.44	44.24	43.54	43.49	45.03	45.91	46.32
16.60	15.60	14.84	13.56	13.72	12.59	11.69	12.00	11.27	11.29	11.85	12.14	11.01	10.32	10.02
4.50	4.61	4.91	4.77	4.54	4.83	4.70	4.87	4.53	4.70	4.83	4.76	4.42	4.61	4.17
8.34	9.23	10.01	10.51	10.45	9.99	9.98	10.38	10.77	11.11	11.76	11.95	12.72	13.04	13.48
66.95	67.06	65.93	65.99	66.38	68.03	69.97	70.29	70.01	71.33	71.98	72.34	73.19	73.87	73.99

1993	1994	1995	1996	1997	1998	1999	2000	2001	2002	2003	2004	2005	2006	2007
11.49	11.21	11.71	11.79	13.06	12.88	11.84	10.12	10.37	8.45	8.30	6.95	6.73	3.66	4.05
23.66	21.07	20.63	21.73	20.35	21.71	16.03	12.58	13.74	12.63	11.16	11.53	10.15	7.46	7.14
18.55	16.99	16.77	16.80	15.05	16.03	12.90	10.00	10.02	9.30	8.81	8.82	7.84	5.74	5.70
3.30	4.28	3.68	3.72	3.64	3.31	5.18	6.03	5.95	7.76	9.09	8.82	10.13	11.24	12.14
0.87	0.75	0.68	0.61	0.78	0.96	0.95	1.02	0.83	0.77	0.68	0.57	0.50	1.70	1.74
4.18	5.03	4.36	4.34	4.42	4.28	6.12	7.05	6.78	8.53	9.77	9.39	10.63	12.94	13.87
22.06	24.18	22.69	19.82	19.79	15.69	12.14	16.10	15.15	14.09	12.99	13.07	11.97	8.76	8.67
7.42	6.77	6.03	5.62	5.57	5.59	5.54	6.21	7.14	5.26	4.69	4.18	4.97	5.29	5.52
9.39	9.51	14.88	11.94	12.98	16.48	19.93	19.35	17.64	21.63	23.75	24.71	29.53	41.03	40.43
42.17	44.73	47.28	41.11	41.98	41.07	42.78	47.71	45.87	48.74	50.52	50.77	56.60	66.31	66.76
43.04	45.48	47.96	41.72	42.76	42.04	43.73	48.73	46.71	49.51	51.20	51.34	57.10	68.01	68.50

1993	1994	1995	1996	1997	1998	1999	2000	2001	2002	2003	2004	2005	2006	2007
23.14	22.99	22.57	22.85	22.43	24.04	21.73	19.10	18.25	17.38	15.64	13.98	12.70	11.98	11.62
13.86	14.30	14.70	14.31	13.57	14.21	13.98	12.57	13.05	13.30	13.08	12.76	11.44	10.33	10.46
10.36	10.72	11.09	10.82	9.93	10.70	10.49	9.32	9.83	10.17	10.16	9.92	8.95	8.14	8.23
8.54	10.05	10.69	11.56	12.35	13.20	13.86	14.53	16.55	18.33	19.73	20.74	21.05	20.47	20.54
0.83	0.78	0.81	0.74	0.66	0.62	0.58	0.44	0.42	0.42	0.35	0.36	0.30	0.27	0.23
9.37	10.83	11.50	12.29	13.01	13.82	14.43	14.97	16.97	18.75	20.08	21.10	21.35	20.74	20.78
4.86	4.93	5.16	4.57	4.31	4.32	5.19	5.39	4.93	4.60	4.68	4.85	4.74	4.73	4.39
14.66	14.30	14.40	15.05	14.81	14.14	14.92	15.69	15.57	15.30	15.28	14.82	14.09	13.86	13.94
28.06	29.28	30.24	31.18	31.47	31.66	33.97	35.61	37.05	38.22	39.69	40.41	39.87	39.06	38.87
28.89	30.06	31.06	31.92	32.13	32.28	34.54	36.05	37.47	38.64	40.04	40.77	40.18	39.33	39.11

Annex 4
(continued)

Korea	1980	1981	1982	1983	1984	1985	1986	1987	1988	1989	1990	1991	1992
USA	22.17	23.13	24.57	23.96	22.45	21.10	20.63	21.35	24.52	25.65	22.78	23.10	22.08
EU	7.71	8.51	7.92	9.33	10.14	10.88	11.71	12.34	12.59	11.65	12.22	13.35	12.79
Euro Area	5.99	6.49	5.65	6.55	7.07	8.31	9.13	9.86	10.10	9.35	9.80	10.27	10.16
China	0.00	0.00	0.00	0.00	0.00	0.00	0.00	0.00	0.00	0.00	0.00	4.20	4.49
Hong Kong	0.45	0.77	1.01	0.84	1.53	1.44	1.26	0.97	1.10	0.93	0.83	0.95	0.96
China+HK	0.45	0.77	1.01	0.84	1.53	1.44	1.26	0.97	1.10	0.93	0.83	5.15	5.45
Japan	26.55	24.37	21.88	23.82	24.94	24.33	34.25	33.29	30.59	28.51	24.96	25.81	23.46
ASEAN	6.75	6.37	7.86	7.92	8.06	8.72	6.52	6.99	6.59	6.77	6.84	7.53	8.58
ASEAN+3	33.30	30.74	29.74	31.74	33.00	33.05	40.77	40.27	37.18	35.29	31.80	37.55	36.53
ASEAN+4	33.74	31.50	30.75	32.58	34.53	34.48	42.03	41.24	38.28	36.22	32.63	38.49	37.49

Lao	1980	1981	1982	1983	1984	1985	1986	1987	1988	1989	1990	1991	1992
USA		0.46	0.58	4.74	0.27	0.41	0.00	0.28	0.65	0.29	0.74	0.57	0.38
EU		20.16	18.34	17.96	10.27	9.64	13.69	12.42	13.07	7.79	8.96	9.50	4.64
Euro Area		16.50	12.66	17.00	6.11	5.48	6.46	4.98	4.11	4.94	5.12	7.73	2.88
China		1.22	0.00	0.00	0.00	0.00	0.00	0.83	3.23	3.78	10.72	7.95	11.86
Hong Kong		3.05	0.58	3.65	0.82	0.41	0.92	0.83	0.99	0.48	0.89	2.35	1.58
China+HK		4.27	0.58	3.65	0.82	0.41	0.92	1.65	4.22	4.26	11.60	10.30	13.43
Japan		13.73	14.31	18.90	13.86	24.24	23.98	21.36	21.35	20.82	14.54	15.21	11.93
Korea		0.00	0.00	0.00	0.00	0.00	0.00	0.00	0.00	0.00	0.00	0.00	0.00
ASEAN		61.05	65.73	50.11	64.37	60.71	55.10	54.44	56.73	56.94	60.91	57.30	60.24
ASEAN+3		76.00	80.04	69.01	78.22	84.94	79.08	76.63	81.32	81.53	86.16	80.46	84.02
ASEAN+4		79.05	80.62	72.66	79.04	85.35	79.99	77.45	82.30	82.02	87.04	82.81	85.60

Malaysia	1980	1981	1982	1983	1984	1985	1986	1987	1988	1989	1990	1991	1992
USA	15.07	14.57	17.57	16.06	16.31	15.28	18.77	18.69	17.65	16.83	16.95	15.31	15.85
EU	17.52	15.68	13.56	15.83	15.48	16.57	16.22	14.67	14.60	15.27	16.07	15.36	13.93
Euro Area	10.18	9.28	8.26	10.91	10.12	10.54	10.11	9.13	8.55	8.68	9.41	9.24	9.40
China	2.34	2.37	2.23	2.03	2.03	2.04	2.60	2.95	2.91	2.70	1.92	2.18	2.44
Hong Kong	1.37	1.27	1.33	1.47	1.97	1.70	2.07	2.21	2.30	2.05	1.91	2.04	2.27
China+HK	3.71	3.64	3.56	3.50	4.00	3.73	4.67	5.16	5.21	4.75	3.84	4.22	4.71
Japan	22.81	24.41	24.97	25.37	26.24	23.01	20.49	21.64	23.03	24.07	24.18	26.07	25.99
Korea	1.87	1.42	2.09	1.80	1.79	2.24	2.26	2.63	2.59	2.49	2.54	2.92	3.04
ASEAN	16.69	18.15	20.16	19.24	19.71	22.70	21.74	21.02	19.03	19.05	19.07	20.01	20.78
ASEAN+3	43.70	46.35	49.46	48.45	49.77	49.99	47.10	48.23	47.57	48.31	47.72	51.18	52.25
ASEAN+4	45.07	47.62	50.78	49.92	51.75	51.69	49.17	50.44	49.87	50.36	49.63	53.22	54.52

Annex 4
(continued)

1993	1994	1995	1996	1997	1998	1999	2000	2001	2002	2003	2004	2005	2006	2007
20.72	21.10	22.51	22.19	20.74	21.87	20.83	18.25	15.90	15.19	13.94	12.88	11.79	11.04	10.45
13.00	14.47	13.74	14.39	13.34	11.99	10.79	10.10	10.86	11.55	11.13	10.85	10.50	9.71	10.23
10.49	11.63	10.86	11.26	9.96	9.09	8.13	7.70	8.38	9.04	8.80	8.36	8.47	7.93	8.34
4.54	5.34	5.48	5.69	6.90	6.95	7.40	7.98	9.43	11.44	12.25	13.18	14.80	15.65	16.62
1.08	0.64	0.62	0.76	0.59	0.58	0.74	0.79	0.87	1.11	1.53	1.46	0.78	0.69	2.04
5.61	5.98	6.10	6.45	7.48	7.53	8.14	8.76	10.30	12.55	13.78	14.64	15.58	16.34	18.67
23.11	24.81	24.13	20.94	19.25	18.04	20.16	19.83	18.88	19.63	20.31	20.56	18.53	16.76	16.34
8.44	7.67	7.50	8.04	8.63	9.80	10.23	11.32	11.28	11.02	10.32	9.97	9.98	9.64	10.15
36.08	37.81	37.11	34.67	34.77	34.78	37.80	39.13	39.58	42.08	42.88	43.71	43.30	42.05	43.11
37.16	38.46	37.73	35.43	35.36	35.36	38.53	39.92	40.45	43.19	44.41	45.17	44.09	42.74	45.15

1993	1994	1995	1996	1997	1998	1999	2000	2001	2002	2003	2004	2005	2006	2007
1.02	0.25	0.25	0.23	0.14	0.60	0.15	0.69	0.55	0.64	0.61	0.63	0.85	0.45	0.71
1.64	1.13	1.15	1.06	0.65	5.04	4.60	6.51	4.37	5.34	5.84	8.06	4.08	2.39	4.05
1.53	1.05	1.05	0.97	0.64	4.18	3.16	5.32	3.58	3.55	3.51	7.14	3.32	2.11	3.16
4.19	3.58	3.65	3.36	1.20	3.04	3.01	5.49	8.32	8.26	13.36	10.31	9.12	11.32	8.54
1.00	1.24	1.27	1.17	2.34	1.35	1.36	1.14	1.41	0.85	1.01	0.76	0.65	0.94	0.71
5.19	4.82	4.93	4.54	3.54	4.39	4.37	6.63	9.73	9.11	14.37	11.06	9.77	12.26	9.26
12.99	8.12	8.29	7.61	2.54	3.26	3.08	3.43	1.80	2.72	1.86	1.46	1.68	1.38	2.02
0.53	0.39	0.39	0.36	0.80	0.82	1.47	0.71	0.96	0.69	1.07	0.94	1.21	1.37	1.35
47.86	54.97	56.08	51.58	88.88	80.35	83.39	77.71	77.25	75.92	72.30	72.16	76.86	77.72	78.34
65.57	67.06	68.41	62.92	93.43	87.47	90.95	87.34	88.32	87.59	88.59	84.86	88.87	91.79	90.25
66.57	68.30	69.68	64.10	95.76	88.82	92.31	88.48	89.73	88.44	89.60	85.62	89.52	92.74	90.96

1993	1994	1995	1996	1997	1998	1999	2000	2001	2002	2003	2004	2005	2006	2007
16.93	16.62	16.30	15.46	16.75	19.62	17.42	16.63	16.14	16.47	15.53	14.63	13.02	12.59	10.84
12.86	14.94	15.40	14.65	14.44	12.08	11.89	11.03	13.14	11.62	12.06	12.13	11.76	11.45	11.87
8.73	10.63	11.44	10.85	10.66	8.99	8.70	7.85	9.64	8.67	9.43	9.37	9.33	9.25	9.66
2.40	2.29	2.20	2.39	2.82	3.17	3.27	3.94	5.19	7.74	8.82	9.91	11.60	12.18	12.86
2.02	2.00	2.16	2.32	2.43	2.60	2.51	2.75	2.58	2.92	2.73	2.74	2.51	2.65	2.91
4.42	4.28	4.36	4.71	5.26	5.77	5.78	6.69	7.77	10.66	11.55	12.65	14.11	14.82	15.77
27.47	26.71	27.28	24.52	21.97	19.66	20.81	21.08	19.37	17.82	17.26	16.08	14.64	13.29	12.98
3.05	3.19	4.09	5.19	5.15	5.76	5.21	4.46	4.03	5.32	5.51	5.01	5.02	5.42	4.93
20.14	19.01	17.40	19.76	20.44	22.68	23.44	24.02	22.79	22.98	24.39	24.17	24.87	24.55	24.46
53.06	51.19	50.98	51.86	50.38	51.27	52.73	53.49	51.38	53.87	55.98	55.18	56.13	55.43	55.24
55.08	53.19	53.14	54.18	52.81	53.87	55.24	56.25	53.96	56.79	58.71	57.92	58.64	58.08	58.14

Annex 4
(continued)

Myanmar	1980	1981	1982	1983	1984	1985	1986	1987	1988	1989	1990	1991	1992
USA	5.01	6.01	6.01	6.01	6.01	6.01	6.01	6.01	6.01	6.01	2.89	2.45	0.43
EU	21.44	25.35	25.35	25.35	25.35	25.35	25.35	25.35	25.35	25.35	15.98	10.24	8.97
Euro Area	11.07	13.38	13.38	13.38	13.38	13.38	13.38	13.38	13.38	13.38	11.24	6.37	5.65
China	3.73	3.16	3.16	3.16	3.16	3.16	3.16	3.16	3.16	3.16	20.62	29.48	27.25
Hong Kong	0.53	0.62	0.62	0.62	0.62	0.62	0.62	0.62	0.62	0.62	1.29	1.37	1.58
China+HK	4.26	3.78	3.78	3.78	3.78	3.78	3.78	3.78	3.78	3.78	21.91	30.85	28.83
Japan	43.66	39.02	39.02	39.02	39.02	39.02	39.02	39.02	39.02	39.02	16.59	8.50	10.15
Korea	1.28	0.07	0.07	0.07	0.07	0.07	0.07	0.07	0.07	0.07	3.49	2.97	3.28
ASEAN	8.28	9.03	9.03	9.03	9.03	9.03	9.03	9.03	9.03	9.03	26.04	35.68	38.53
ASEAN+3	56.95	51.28	51.28	51.28	51.28	51.28	51.28	51.28	51.28	51.28	66.74	76.63	79.20
ASEAN+4	57.48	51.90	51.90	51.90	51.90	51.90	51.90	51.90	51.90	51.90	68.04	78.00	80.79

Philippines	1980	1981	1982	1983	1984	1985	1986	1987	1988	1989	1990	1991	1992
USA	23.52	22.77	22.52	23.29	27.36	25.11	24.82	22.19	21.04	19.09	19.54	20.16	18.02
EU	11.79	11.67	12.18	12.90	12.00	9.40	11.70	12.83	13.08	12.29	12.14	11.22	12.78
Euro Area	8.28	8.64	9.00	9.31	9.03	6.78	8.96	9.81	10.26	9.75	9.21	8.50	9.77
China	2.67	2.48	2.70	1.01	3.64	5.43	2.31	3.12	3.08	2.17	1.40	1.88	1.26
Hong Kong	2.45	2.64	2.66	3.37	3.87	3.91	4.96	4.45	4.49	4.48	4.44	4.75	4.95
China+HK	5.11	5.12	5.35	4.38	7.51	9.34	7.27	7.57	7.56	6.65	5.83	6.62	6.21
Japan	19.91	18.98	20.11	17.07	13.59	14.01	17.01	16.56	17.35	19.46	18.44	19.44	21.19
Korea	1.75	1.39	1.94	2.05	2.48	4.00	3.23	2.90	4.01	3.98	3.84	4.93	4.78
ASEAN	6.74	8.03	7.46	9.34	12.45	14.52	10.07	9.53	9.85	10.23	10.57	10.07	9.53
ASEAN+3	31.07	30.87	32.21	29.48	32.16	37.96	32.62	32.11	34.29	35.84	34.25	36.32	36.76
ASEAN+4	33.51	33.51	34.87	32.84	36.03	41.87	37.58	36.56	38.77	40.32	38.69	41.06	41.71

Singapore	1980	1981	1982	1983	1984	1985	1986	1987	1988	1989	1990	1991	1992
USA	14.11	12.63	12.89	15.13	14.58	15.20	14.97	14.67	15.56	17.15	16.08	15.85	16.46
EU	12.52	10.99	11.35	11.56	11.26	12.33	12.64	13.44	13.23	13.84	14.03	13.22	13.83
Euro Area	7.80	6.88	7.61	7.68	7.78	8.45	8.35	8.97	9.16	10.01	10.01	9.42	10.02
China	2.62	2.80	3.12	2.94	4.70	8.64	5.61	4.33	3.86	3.42	3.44	3.36	3.12
Hong Kong	2.06	1.88	2.09	2.13	2.10	1.88	2.36	2.64	2.76	2.86	3.08	3.01	3.05
China+HK	4.67	4.68	5.22	5.07	6.79	10.52	7.96	6.96	6.61	6.28	6.52	6.37	6.17
Japan	17.95	18.81	17.90	18.02	18.35	17.10	19.90	20.46	21.95	21.35	20.12	21.30	21.06
Korea	1.14	1.13	1.23	1.52	1.28	1.61	2.32	2.69	2.88	2.99	2.91	2.85	2.95
ASEAN	17.34	15.95	16.73	17.82	18.97	18.51	17.73	18.05	18.32	16.41	17.12	19.29	19.56
ASEAN+3	39.04	38.70	38.99	40.30	43.30	45.87	45.56	45.52	47.01	44.18	43.58	46.80	46.70
ASEAN+4	41.10	40.58	41.08	42.43	45.39	47.74	47.91	48.16	49.77	47.04	46.67	49.81	49.75

Annex 4
(continued)

1993	1994	1995	1996	1997	1998	1999	2000	2001	2002	2003	2004	2005	2006	2007
1.07	0.79	0.76	1.31	0.77	1.49	0.53	0.62	0.48	0.39	0.23	0.37	0.16	0.22	0.18
9.48	9.03	8.42	8.47	7.38	5.93	5.62	3.96	3.33	3.31	2.12	3.13	3.19	2.95	4.75
6.56	6.71	5.91	6.27	5.83	4.76	4.64	3.25	2.42	2.69	1.66	2.89	2.53	2.68	4.56
27.90	26.40	29.02	21.41	21.90	24.85	17.69	17.97	20.55	26.85	30.96	29.82	28.82	35.06	35.70
3.49	3.17	2.96	3.77	2.71	2.17	2.80	3.22	2.63	2.36	1.50	1.41	1.10	1.17	1.05
31.40	29.57	31.98	25.17	24.62	27.02	20.49	21.19	23.18	29.21	32.46	31.23	29.92	36.23	36.75
8.59	4.85	7.40	10.43	8.11	8.71	8.05	7.09	7.71	4.27	4.25	3.36	2.83	3.01	3.76
3.61	4.03	4.06	5.37	5.26	6.94	8.15	10.47	9.59	5.31	6.27	5.16	3.70	3.08	2.81
41.10	46.33	43.63	42.00	47.43	42.93	49.23	45.31	43.62	42.68	44.08	47.41	50.80	46.77	44.64
81.20	81.61	84.12	79.21	82.70	83.44	83.12	80.84	81.46	79.13	85.56	85.75	86.14	87.93	86.91
84.70	84.78	87.08	82.98	85.41	85.60	85.91	84.07	84.10	81.48	87.06	87.16	87.25	89.10	87.96

1993	1994	1995	1996	1997	1998	1999	2000	2001	2002	2003	2004	2005	2006	2007
20.02	18.46	18.47	19.59	19.48	22.22	20.70	18.59	19.40	20.57	19.75	18.79	19.20	16.31	11.97
11.67	11.40	10.87	9.43	13.10	9.13	9.14	9.16	9.27	7.91	8.19	8.33	7.88	8.65	8.40
8.40	8.81	8.20	7.28	10.18	7.43	7.51	7.58	7.29	6.15	6.48	6.77	6.51	7.30	7.07
1.03	1.42	2.33	2.05	2.48	4.06	3.38	2.28	2.95	3.53	4.79	6.04	6.27	7.13	11.04
4.98	5.08	4.86	4.21	4.18	4.40	3.99	3.60	4.04	4.47	4.27	3.95	4.07	4.01	4.37
6.02	6.50	7.19	6.26	6.67	8.46	7.37	5.88	6.99	8.00	9.06	9.99	10.34	11.13	15.41
22.79	24.16	22.27	21.70	20.32	20.42	19.95	18.88	20.07	20.42	20.37	17.43	17.02	13.59	14.71
5.11	5.19	5.05	5.16	5.86	7.41	8.86	7.99	6.30	7.77	6.40	6.22	4.84	6.25	5.63
10.88	11.71	10.58	9.59	13.37	15.00	14.51	15.55	15.50	16.17	17.06	18.98	18.72	19.81	20.84
39.82	42.48	40.23	38.50	42.05	46.89	46.69	44.69	44.81	47.90	48.63	48.67	46.85	46.78	52.23
44.81	47.56	45.09	42.71	46.23	51.29	50.68	48.30	48.85	52.37	52.90	52.62	50.92	50.78	56.60

1993	1994	1995	1996	1997	1998	1999	2000	2001	2002	2003	2004	2005	2006	2007
16.34	15.23	15.05	16.41	16.88	18.49	17.13	15.06	16.51	14.26	13.21	12.01	11.73	12.71	12.48
12.67	13.39	13.78	14.82	14.39	14.45	13.40	11.96	12.27	12.47	12.43	12.85	11.66	11.41	12.38
9.27	9.75	10.14	11.15	10.46	10.52	9.77	9.10	9.31	9.62	9.60	10.03	8.81	8.74	9.62
2.82	2.81	3.25	3.38	4.27	4.77	5.13	5.29	6.20	7.61	8.12	9.39	10.25	11.41	12.11
3.15	3.37	3.30	3.20	2.95	2.80	2.87	2.61	2.40	2.44	2.27	2.11	2.10	1.72	1.46
5.96	6.18	6.55	6.58	7.22	7.57	8.00	7.90	8.60	10.05	10.39	11.50	12.36	13.13	13.57
21.86	21.93	21.15	18.15	17.56	16.74	16.66	17.22	13.87	12.51	11.29	11.06	9.61	8.35	8.18
3.22	3.81	4.34	3.70	3.12	2.99	3.76	3.58	3.29	3.69	3.64	4.02	4.30	4.39	4.87
21.98	22.63	22.27	22.24	22.43	23.34	23.75	24.72	25.00	26.16	29.03	27.35	26.04	26.11	24.99
49.87	51.18	51.01	47.47	47.38	47.84	49.29	50.81	48.37	49.98	52.09	51.81	50.20	50.25	50.15
53.02	54.55	54.31	50.67	50.32	50.64	52.16	53.42	50.77	52.42	54.35	53.93	52.31	51.97	51.61

Annex 4
(continued)

Thailand	1980	1981	1982	1983	1984	1985	1986	1987	1988	1989	1990	1991	1992
USA	14.45	13.02	13.40	12.63	13.53	11.35	14.28	12.45	13.56	11.20	10.78	10.51	11.74
EU	16.12	15.09	13.25	14.96	14.39	16.51	17.04	17.43	17.31	15.92	16.72	16.96	16.25
Euro Area	11.05	10.48	9.22	10.68	9.93	12.09	11.55	12.30	12.57	11.62	12.24	12.92	12.30
China	4.52	3.22	2.74	2.58	3.05	2.40	2.86	3.87	3.35	2.93	3.31	3.03	3.00
Hong Kong	0.95	0.90	1.05	1.14	1.24	1.16	1.52	1.45	1.24	1.33	1.24	2.04	1.21
China+HK	5.47	4.12	3.79	3.72	4.29	3.56	4.38	5.32	4.59	4.26	4.56	5.07	4.21
Japan	21.18	24.24	23.47	27.38	26.91	26.43	26.36	25.94	27.06	30.49	30.36	29.08	29.26
Korea	2.14	1.40	1.83	2.37	2.80	2.01	2.37	2.39	2.77	2.92	3.13	4.20	4.39
ASEAN	12.13	11.84	13.41	13.47	16.11	18.62	14.51	15.94	12.60	12.76	13.08	12.80	13.30
ASEAN+3	39.98	40.70	41.45	45.80	48.86	49.46	46.11	48.15	45.78	49.10	49.88	49.11	49.95
ASEAN+4	40.92	41.59	42.50	46.94	50.10	50.63	47.63	49.60	47.02	50.43	51.12	51.15	51.16

Vietnam	1980	1981	1982	1983	1984	1985	1986	1987	1988	1989	1990	1991	1992
USA		2.00	8.12	5.58	4.63	0.05	0.03	0.01	0.08	0.00	0.02	0.04	0.07
EU		51.18	34.93	28.34	27.83	7.55	6.72	6.33	7.57	4.54	12.28	13.25	8.92
Euro Area		31.37	17.61	15.55	12.54	2.42	1.93	2.14	3.87	2.05	8.88	11.20	7.83
China		0.00	0.00	0.00	0.00	0.00	0.00	0.00	0.00	0.00	0.16	0.74	1.05
Hong Kong		5.29	15.03	14.94	15.43	1.55	1.79	1.41	1.13	3.38	6.93	7.85	4.72
China+HK		5.29	15.03	14.94	15.43	1.55	1.79	1.41	1.13	3.38	7.09	8.59	5.77
Japan		21.21	23.33	32.19	24.88	7.71	5.65	4.21	5.03	3.48	5.95	6.35	7.91
Korea		0.02	0.00	0.00	0.00	0.15	0.29	0.28	0.16	0.51	1.87	6.13	6.98
ASEAN		15.02	10.07	13.19	17.53	1.56	2.53	2.20	2.09	1.73	18.99	32.67	31.49
ASEAN+3		36.26	33.40	45.38	42.41	9.42	8.46	6.68	7.28	5.72	26.97	45.89	47.43
ASEAN+4		41.55	48.43	60.32	57.84	10.98	10.25	8.09	8.41	9.11	33.89	53.73	52.15

Source: DTS.

Annex 4
(continued)

1993	1994	1995	1996	1997	1998	1999	2000	2001	2002	2003	2004	2005	2006	2007
11.65	11.71	11.04	12.33	13.66	13.85	12.80	11.77	11.60	9.58	9.48	7.70	7.38	7.49	6.83
18.59	16.96	16.42	15.83	15.21	12.66	11.98	10.48	12.62	11.30	10.32	9.99	9.13	8.71	8.52
13.16	11.66	11.57	11.06	10.75	9.83	9.55	7.92	9.81	9.01	8.23	7.77	7.27	6.82	6.76
1.96	2.52	2.72	2.61	3.56	4.17	4.95	5.45	5.98	7.61	8.00	8.67	9.44	10.57	11.59
1.16	1.25	0.97	1.14	1.29	1.75	1.40	1.43	1.33	1.41	1.42	1.41	1.27	1.20	1.03
3.12	3.77	3.69	3.75	4.85	5.92	6.35	6.88	7.31	9.02	9.42	10.08	10.71	11.76	12.62
30.23	29.84	28.05	27.29	25.47	23.28	24.34	24.73	22.37	23.03	24.09	23.71	22.03	19.93	20.29
4.22	3.59	3.21	3.58	3.55	3.42	3.52	3.50	3.42	3.90	3.85	3.80	3.29	3.98	3.78
12.46	13.31	12.00	12.70	12.61	14.68	15.85	16.66	16.19	16.84	16.64	16.84	18.29	18.32	17.90
48.86	49.27	45.98	46.18	45.18	45.56	48.66	50.35	47.96	51.38	52.59	53.01	53.05	52.80	53.56
50.02	50.52	46.95	47.32	46.47	47.31	50.06	51.77	49.29	52.79	54.00	54.42	54.33	54.00	54.59

1993	1994	1995	1996	1997	1998	1999	2000	2001	2002	2003	2004	2005	2006	2007
0.10	0.76	1.56	2.18	2.12	2.89	2.75	2.33	2.54	2.32	4.53	3.55	2.35	2.62	3.37
12.60	10.80	9.23	10.61	11.67	11.40	9.74	8.78	9.70	9.57	10.27	8.42	7.04	7.16	8.69
10.98	8.15	7.20	8.61	9.63	9.10	7.68	7.04	7.48	7.80	8.26	6.80	5.72	5.78	7.33
2.18	2.48	3.94	2.92	3.41	4.55	5.73	8.96	9.90	10.93	12.43	14.37	16.05	17.82	20.01
3.71	5.47	5.01	6.73	5.04	4.93	4.30	3.82	3.32	4.08	3.92	3.36	3.36	3.60	4.09
5.89	7.94	8.96	9.64	8.45	9.48	10.03	12.79	13.22	15.01	16.35	17.73	19.41	21.42	24.10
11.53	10.05	10.96	11.17	12.71	13.10	13.78	14.72	13.46	12.69	11.81	11.11	11.08	9.88	10.07
12.27	12.37	15.00	15.79	13.17	12.56	12.65	11.21	11.63	11.55	10.40	10.51	9.78	8.50	7.84
33.60	29.00	28.45	26.51	27.33	29.94	28.03	28.45	25.73	24.15	23.56	24.30	25.37	27.92	25.42
59.58	53.90	58.34	56.38	56.62	60.16	60.19	63.34	60.73	59.32	58.19	60.29	62.28	64.12	63.33
63.29	59.37	63.36	63.11	61.66	65.09	64.49	67.17	64.04	63.39	62.11	63.65	65.64	67.72	67.42

Annex 5
Annual GDP growth (percent), 1980–2007

	Brunei	Cambodia	China	Hong Kong	Indonesia	Japan	Korea	Lao	Malaysia	Myanmar	Philippines	Singapore	Thailand	Vietnam
1980	-7.00		7.91	10.21	9.88	3.18	-1.49	10.00	7.44	7.93	5.15	9.71	4.60	-3.50
1981	-19.83		4.74	9.24	7.60	2.93	6.16	15.33	6.94	6.36	3.42	9.73	5.91	5.80
1982	3.96		9.10	2.79	2.25	2.76	7.33	4.72	5.94	5.61	3.62	7.13	5.35	8.15
1983	0.50		10.90	5.80	4.19	1.61	10.78	3.00	6.25	4.43	1.88	8.52	5.58	7.09
1984	0.60		15.20	1.00	6.98	3.12	8.10	6.44	7.76	4.93	-7.32	8.34	5.76	8.40
1985	-1.49		13.50	0.72	2.46	5.08	6.80	9.12	-0.88	2.85	-7.31	-1.44	4.64	5.62
1986	-11.48		8.80	11.04	5.88	2.96	10.62	4.83	1.15	-1.06	3.42	2.12	5.53	3.36
1987	0.31	21.53	11.60	13.41	4.93	3.80	11.10	-0.96	5.39	-4.01	4.31	9.83	9.52	2.55
1988	-0.36	9.62	11.30	8.45	5.78	6.77	10.64	-2.10	9.94	-11.35	6.75	11.47	13.29	5.10
1989	2.21	3.33	4.10	2.22	7.46	5.29	6.74	9.89	9.06	3.69	6.21	10.01	12.19	7.80
1990	1.09	1.12	3.80	3.90	7.24	5.20	9.16	6.69	9.01	2.82	3.04	9.22	11.62	5.05
1991	3.15	7.59	9.20	5.69	6.95	3.35	9.39	4.00	9.55	-0.65	-0.58	6.56	8.11	5.81
1992	4.76	7.07	14.20	6.09	6.46	0.97	5.88	7.00	8.89	9.66	0.34	6.34	8.08	8.70
1993	0.30	4.04	14.00	6.04	6.82	0.25	6.13	5.87	9.90	5.92	2.12	11.73	8.25	8.08
1994	3.15	7.95	13.10	6.01	7.54	1.11	8.54	8.16	9.21	6.81	4.39	11.57	8.99	8.83
1995	4.48	6.52	10.90	2.29	8.22	1.96	9.17	7.05	9.83	7.20	4.68	8.16	9.24	9.54
1996	2.88	5.35	10.00	4.19	7.82	2.75	7.00	6.89	10.00	6.44	5.85	7.79	5.90	9.34
1997	-1.48	5.65	9.30	5.06	4.70	1.57	4.65	6.91	7.32	5.74	5.19	8.34	-1.37	8.15
1998	-0.56	4.96	7.80	-6.03	-13.13	-2.05	-6.85	4.00	-7.36	5.77	-0.58	-1.38	-10.51	5.76
1999	3.05	12.15	7.60	2.56	0.79	-0.14	9.49	7.28	6.14	10.95	3.40	7.20	4.45	4.77
2000	2.85	8.77	8.40	7.95	5.35	2.86	8.49	5.81	8.68	13.75	5.97	10.06	4.75	6.79
2001	2.75	8.10	8.30	0.50	3.64	0.18	3.84	5.74	0.52	11.34	1.76	-2.44	2.17	6.90
2002	3.87	6.60	9.10	1.84	4.50	0.26	6.97	5.92	5.39	12.03	4.45	4.18	5.32	7.08
2003	2.90	8.51	10.00	3.01	4.78	1.41	3.10	6.11	5.79	13.84	4.93	3.50	7.14	7.34
2004	0.50	10.30	10.10	8.47	5.03	2.74	4.73	6.37	6.78	13.57	6.38	8.99	6.34	7.79
2005	0.39	13.30	10.40	7.08	5.69	1.93	4.20	7.13	5.33	13.60	4.95	7.30	4.53	8.44
2006	4.40	10.77	11.60	7.02	5.51	2.42	5.13	8.11	5.78	12.70	5.40	8.17	5.11	8.23
2007	0.60	10.20	11.90	6.37	6.32	2.08	4.97	7.92	6.35	5.46	7.19	7.72	4.75	8.48
Mean	0.23	8.26	9.89	5.10	5.06	2.37	6.46	6.33	6.29	6.30	3.18	7.09	5.90	6.62
SD	5.23	4.24	2.85	3.93	4.07	1.87	3.82	3.22	3.87	5.81	3.60	3.84	4.41	2.65

Source: WEO.
Note: Data for Brunei (1980–1984) from WDI.

Annex 6
Inflation (annual percent), 1980–2007

	Brunei	Cambodia	China	Hong Kong	Indonesia	Japan	Korea	Lao	Malaysia	Myanmar	Philippines	Singapore	Thailand	Vietnam
1980			5.99	4.44	18.02	7.81	28.70	188.82	6.72	−0.10	18.20	8.54	19.70	25.16
1981	9.14		2.38	9.48	12.24	4.91	21.35	33.70	9.70	1.40	13.08	8.18	12.70	69.60
1982	6.36		1.93	10.95	9.48	2.74	7.19	70.38	5.83	5.23	8.98	3.93	5.30	95.40
1983	1.17		1.50	9.96	11.79	1.89	3.42	62.51	3.70	5.91	5.25	1.04	3.70	49.49
1984	3.10		2.83	8.57	10.45	2.25	2.27	27.18	3.90	5.24	46.24	2.61	0.90	64.90
1985	2.31		9.30	3.55	4.73	2.05	2.46	114.70	2.59	6.26	23.22	0.48	2.40	91.60
1986	1.78		6.50	3.58	5.83	0.62	2.75	35.00	0.35	14.74	−0.33	−1.37	1.80	453.54
1987	1.28	−31.25	7.30	5.72	9.27	0.12	3.05	6.11	0.74	17.63	3.04	0.48	2.49	360.36
1988	1.19	23.00	18.80	7.84	8.04	0.65	7.15	14.80	0.29	23.98	12.23	1.52	3.80	374.35
1989	1.31	63.80	18.00	10.19	6.42	2.24	5.70	59.70	2.56	23.82	11.37	2.29	5.37	95.77
1990	2.13	141.80	3.10	10.25	7.84	3.07	8.57	−26.32	3.04	21.91	13.20	3.45	5.89	36.03
1991	1.58	191.00	3.40	11.26	9.37	3.40	9.33	13.44	4.36	29.13	18.45	3.42	5.70	81.82
1992	1.26	75.00	6.40	9.54	7.51	1.64	6.21	9.85	4.77	22.29	8.93	2.27	4.15	37.71
1993	4.29	114.32	14.70	8.82	9.69	1.31	4.80	5.65	3.56	33.57	7.59	2.29	3.30	8.38
1994	2.45	10.57	24.10	8.80	8.52	0.60	6.27	7.67	3.70	22.44	9.01	3.10	5.08	9.48
1995	5.97	9.95	17.10	9.04	9.43	−0.10	4.48	19.08	3.20	28.92	8.50	1.73	5.77	16.93
1996	1.97	7.15	8.30	6.33	7.00	0.10	4.93	19.15	3.48	20.02	9.05	1.38	5.87	5.59
1997	1.71	7.96	2.80	5.80	6.19	1.89	4.44	19.54	2.66	33.90	5.88	2.02	5.58	3.10
1998	−0.42	14.78	−0.80	2.83	58.02	0.58	7.51	90.14	5.29	49.14	9.70	−0.27	8.08	7.89
1999	−0.01	4.03	−1.40	−3.95	20.75	−0.29	0.81	128.41	2.73	10.90	6.39	0.02	0.31	4.12
2000	1.17	−0.79	0.40	−3.74	3.77	−0.78	2.26	23.25	1.55	−1.72	3.97	1.35	1.55	−1.58
2001	0.60	0.22	0.73	−1.61	11.50	−0.69	4.07	9.27	1.43	34.50	6.83	1.01	1.66	−0.40
2002	−2.29	3.30	−0.77	−3.04	11.80	−0.89	2.76	9.18	1.79	58.10	2.94	−0.39	0.64	3.99
2003	0.30	1.15	1.17	−2.58	6.77	−0.30	3.52	15.48	1.07	24.94	3.48	0.49	1.80	3.20
2004	0.90	3.87	3.90	−0.38	6.06	0.00	3.59	10.46	1.42	3.77	5.98	1.67	2.77	7.72
2005	1.09	5.78	1.82	0.91	10.46	−0.30	2.75	7.17	3.05	10.70	7.65	0.47	4.54	8.25
2006	0.20	4.71	1.47	2.02	13.10	0.30	2.24	6.80	3.61	25.70	6.23	0.97	4.64	7.50
2007	0.30	5.85	4.77	2.03	6.17	0.00	2.54	4.52	2.03	33.90	2.80	2.10	2.23	8.30
Mean	1.88	31.25	5.92	4.88	11.08	1.24	5.90	35.20	3.18	20.22	9.92	1.96	4.56	68.86
SD	2.30	55.24	6.70	4.94	9.92	1.92	5.89	46.29	2.04	14.73	8.82	2.20	3.93	120.49

Source: WEO.
Note: Data for Brunei (1981–1982) from WDI.

Annex 7
Current account balance (percent of GDP), 1980–2007

	Brunei	Cambodia	China	Hong Kong	Indonesia	Japan	Korea	Lao	Malaysia	Myanmar	Philippines	Singapore	Thailand	Vietnam
1980			0.09	-5.01	3.04	-1.02	-8.30	-4.48	-1.14	-10.73	-7.66	-13.44	-6.39	-2.03
1981			0.78	-2.52	-0.56	0.41	-6.44	-9.86	-9.76	-12.73	-3.72	-10.64	-7.38	-5.33
1982			1.99	-0.55	-4.94	0.63	-3.35	-9.04	-13.20	-15.74	-5.35	-8.35	-2.74	-3.35
1983			1.37	0.57	-6.76	1.76	-1.80	-6.97	-11.46	-9.27	-5.33	-3.35	-7.18	-2.47
1984			0.63	6.87	-2.27	2.78	-1.39	-3.92	-4.84	-7.66	-0.52	-1.88	-5.05	-2.03
1985	82.17		-3.75	7.35	-2.08	3.77	-0.82	-3.22	-1.93	-8.87	1.70	0.33	-3.95	-6.29
1986	87.78	15.68	-2.43	6.48	-4.64	4.29	4.23	-5.00	-0.43	-3.98	4.04	2.08	0.57	-4.37
1987	88.88	17.67	0.09	7.69	-2.73	3.48	7.18	-9.02	8.19	-3.17	0.60	-0.53	-0.73	-3.30
1988	92.59	-41.87	-0.94	6.45	-2.15	2.70	7.73	-13.39	5.13	-2.59	0.84	7.62	-2.68	-3.31
1989	78.77	-25.75	-0.96	9.16	-1.53	2.15	2.32	-15.83	0.66	-0.69	-3.41	9.84	-3.46	-9.28
1990	71.90	-3.86	3.07	6.20	-2.55	1.45	-0.76	-8.93	-2.09	-21.95	-6.09	8.48	-8.33	-4.00
1991	69.30	-1.22	3.24	4.32	-3.13	1.98	-2.73	-2.43	-8.49	-15.85	-2.08	11.31	-7.50	-1.75
1992	44.67	-1.01	1.31	3.01	-2.03	2.98	-1.24	-3.49	-3.68	-12.43	-1.87	11.90	-5.50	-0.08
1993	31.98	-1.64	-1.94	4.76	-1.32	3.04	0.23	-3.21	-4.54	-11.09	-5.52	7.24	-5.03	-10.58
1994	39.00	-3.44	1.37	-0.83	-1.54	2.74	-0.95	-6.90	-7.44	-8.54	-4.45	16.13	-5.41	-11.50
1995	33.70	-4.99	0.22	-6.28	-3.04	2.11	-1.68	-6.93	-9.59	-3.71	-2.60	17.07	-7.88	-1.23
1996	29.36	-7.23	0.85	-2.52	-2.91	1.42	-4.14	-12.51	-4.36	-10.57	-4.58	14.97	-7.89	-8.19
1997	26.92	1.10	3.88	-4.38	-1.59	2.26	-1.57	-11.47	-5.84	-10.60	-5.17	15.52	-2.06	-5.42
1998	20.37	-5.78	3.09	1.50	3.79	3.08	11.59	-5.89	13.01	-11.70	2.27	22.21	12.78	-3.64
1999	35.32	-5.04	1.45	6.28	3.72	2.61	5.50	-6.54	15.69	-5.90	-3.77	17.38	10.17	4.06
2000	49.96	-2.83	1.71	4.14	4.83	2.56	2.39	-9.07	9.05	-0.80	-2.93	11.56	7.60	3.55
2001	48.38	-1.06	1.31	5.87	4.30	2.14	1.67	-12.76	7.85	-2.43	-2.45	12.53	4.43	2.10
2002	41.23	-2.43	2.44	7.58	4.00	2.87	0.99	-11.56	7.96	0.18	-0.36	12.60	3.69	-1.72
2003	47.72	-3.57	2.80	10.39	3.45	3.22	1.96	-12.08	11.98	-0.96	0.36	23.18	3.35	-4.88
2004	48.62	-2.17	3.55	9.48	0.61	3.73	4.14	-16.88	12.09	2.40	1.87	16.70	1.72	-3.49
2005	52.80	-4.23	7.19	11.35	0.10	3.63	1.89	-17.39	14.49	3.70	2.01	18.60	-4.33	-0.94
2006	56.30	-1.10	9.40	12.07	2.97	3.89	0.61	-10.82	16.05	9.50	4.55	21.80	1.05	-0.27
2007	48.80	-3.60	11.34	13.53	2.54	4.82	0.61	-17.30	15.63	6.80	4.41	24.27	6.43	-9.86
Mean	53.33	-4.02	1.90	4.39	-0.44	2.55	0.64	-9.18	1.75	-6.05	-1.62	9.47	-1.49	-3.56
SD	21.47	11.66	3.23	5.38	3.21	1.24	4.23	4.51	9.37	7.23	3.44	10.38	5.85	3.90

Source: WEO.

Annex 8

Government balance (percent of GDP), 1980–2007

	Cambodia	China	Hong Kong	Indonesia	Japan	Korea	Lao	Malaysia	Philippines	Singapore	Thailand	Vietnam
1980		-2.80	3.90	-2.42	-4.50	-2.50		-6.95	-1.39	0.70	-3.87	
1981		-0.52	2.90	-2.02	-4.00	-2.00		-15.65	-4.32	2.60	-2.81	
1982		-0.53	-0.40	-1.91	-3.90	-1.40		-16.65	-4.54	3.20	-4.89	
1983		-0.72	-1.20	-2.40	-4.10	-1.00		-9.84	-2.02	2.40	-2.48	
1984		-0.62	0.90	1.36	-2.50	-1.10		-6.00	-1.90	5.40	-3.36	
1985		0.25	1.00	-0.96	-1.40	-1.10		-5.69	-1.95	8.20	-3.69	
1986		-0.82	1.80	-3.27	-1.10	-0.10		-10.48	-5.03	2.80	-3.01	
1987		-0.53	3.20	-0.81	-0.20	0.40		-7.59	-2.45	-0.40	-0.68	
1988		-0.91	3.50	-2.94	0.60	1.50		-3.56	-2.91	5.60	2.31	
1989		-0.97	2.10	-1.87	1.50	0.20		-3.24	-2.11	10.00	3.52	
1990		-3.96	0.70	0.38	2.10	-0.60		-2.89	-3.45	11.60	4.90	
1991		-3.51	3.30	0.39	1.80	-1.80		-1.95	-2.11	10.30	4.01	
1992		-2.72	2.70	-0.39	0.80	-0.70		-0.82	-1.18	11.20	2.54	-1.82
1993		-2.04	2.10	0.61	-2.40	0.30		0.21	-1.48	14.30	1.76	-4.30
1994		-2.01	1.00	0.94	-3.80	0.10		2.26	1.07	13.90	2.79	-1.42
1995		-1.55	-0.30	2.22	-4.70	0.30		0.84	0.58	12.20	3.22	-0.53
1996		-1.27	2.10	1.16	-5.10	0.20		0.72	0.29	9.30	0.94	-0.18
1997		-1.24	6.40	-0.67	-4.10	-1.40		2.35	0.06	9.20	15.20	-1.72
1998		-1.59	-1.80	-2.95	-5.60	-3.90		-1.77	-1.88	3.60	15.50	-0.13
1999	-3.90	-2.46	0.80	-1.15	-7.50	-2.50	-2.50	-3.15	-3.75	4.60	15.40	-1.58
2000	-5.00	-3.10	-0.60	0.23	-7.70	1.10	-2.50	-5.74	-4.06	7.90	15.20	-2.81
2001	0.00	-4.45	-4.90	-2.40	-6.40	0.60	-4.50	-5.51	-4.05	4.80	15.10	-2.94
2002	-3.60	-2.87	-4.80	-1.27	-8.20	2.30		-5.60	-5.32	4.00	16.10	-8.17
2003	-4.60	-2.40	-3.30	-1.65	-8.10	2.70		-5.31	-4.63	5.70	16.90	-3.69
2004	-2.20	-1.42	-0.30	-1.16	-6.60	2.30		-4.34	-3.85	6.00		-3.19
2005	-0.10	-1.12	0.30	-0.95	-5.80	1.90			-2.71	6.00		-4.20
2006			3.97		-3.77	1.85				7.62		
2007			7.65		-3.20	3.75				9.00		
Mean	-2.77	-1.76	1.17	-0.92	-3.50	-0.02	-3.17	-4.65	-2.50	6.85	4.61	-2.62
SD	2.06	1.19	2.89	1.48	3.07	1.79	1.15	4.85	1.76	3.89	7.74	2.12

Source: WEO.

Annex 9
Estimated basket weights of East Asian currencies, 1999–2008

Brunei dollar	US dollar	Euro	Yen	Adjusted R-squared
1999	0.8264***	0.0825***	0.0753***	0.84
	(0.0410)	(0.0297)	(0.0223)	
2000	0.9252***	0.0327*	0.0161	0.91
	(0.0325)	(0.0185)	(0.0230)	
2001	0.8051***	0.0169	0.1214***	0.86
	(0.0374)	(0.0226)	(0.0277)	
2002	0.6692***	0.1190***	0.1474***	0.83
	(0.0348)	(0.0263)	(0.0293)	
2003	0.7180***	0.0963***	0.1480***	0.88
	(0.0371)	(0.0237)	(0.0334)	
2004	0.6002***	0.1739***	0.1579***	0.87
	(0.0329)	(0.0210)	(0.0263)	
2005	0.5984***	0.1963***	0.1250***	0.82
	(0.0364)	(0.0271)	(0.0339)	
2006	0.6154***	0.2044***	0.1547***	0.80
	(0.0369)	(0.0302)	(0.0314)	
2007	0.7179***	0.1903***	−0.1094***	0.74
	(0.0439)	(0.0344)	(0.0263)	
2008	0.5702***	0.2675***	0.0515	0.88
	(0.0394)	(0.0321)	(0.0332)	
1999–2008	0.7264***	0.1168***	0.0913***	0.85
	(0.0117)	(0.0082)	(0.0087)	

Cambodian riel	US dollar	Euro	Yen	Adjusted R-squared
1999				
2000				
2001				
2002				
2003	0.9315***	0.0440	−0.0204	0.91
	(0.0658)	(0.0412)	(0.0552)	
2004	1.0125***	−0.0077	0.0187	0.87
	(0.0394)	(0.0251)	(0.0315)	
2005	0.9415***	0.0475	0.0398	0.62
	(0.0722)	(0.0539)	(0.0673)	
2006	0.9979***	0.1232**	0.0965*	0.73
	(0.0600)	(0.0497)	(0.0507)	
2007	0.9652***	0.0393	0.0109	0.81
	(0.0417)	(0.0327)	(0.0249)	
2008	1.01240***	−0.0351	0.0828	0.61
	(0.1026)	(0.0835)	(0.0864)	
1999–2008	0.9836***	0.0239	0.0383*	0.72
	(0.0269)	(0.0202)	(0.0218)	

Chinese yuan	US dollar	Euro	Yen	Adjusted *R*-squared
1999	1.0023***	−0.0061	−0.0027	0.99
	(0.0080)	(0.0058)	(0.0043)	
2000	0.9949***	−0.0009	0.0101***	1.00
	(0.0047)	(0.0027)	(0.0033)	
2001	1.0002***	−0.0004	−0.0002	1.00
	(0.0006)	(0.0003)	(0.0004)	
2002	1.0184***	−0.0050	−0.0076	0.99
	(0.0078)	(0.0060)	(0.0066)	
2003	1.0221***	−0.0084	0.0010	0.95
	(0.0247)	(0.0158)	(0.0222)	
2004	1.0029***	−0.0002	−0.0006	1.00
	(0.0024)	(0.0016)	(0.0020)	
2005	0.9849***	−0.0051	0.0064	1.00
	(0.0065)	(0.0048)	(0.0060)	
2006	0.9542***	0.0014	0.0146	0.98
	(0.0132)	(0.0107)	(0.0111)	
2007	0.9284***	0.0016	0.0129	0.94
	(0.0205)	(0.0160)	(0.0122)	
2008	0.9269***	−0.0021	0.0145	0.98
	(0.0192)	(0.0157)	(0.0161)	
1999–2008	0.9860***	−0.0025	0.0085***	0.98
	(0.0039)	(0.0027)	(0.0029)	

Indonesian rupiah	US dollar	Euro	Yen	Adjusted *R*-squared
1999	0.7724***	0.0594	0.2124	0.13
	(0.2512)	(0.1797)	(0.1322)	
2000	1.0652***	−0.0711	−0.0040	0.38
	(0.1370)	(0.0781)	(0.0968)	
2001	1.1020***	−0.0686	0.1431	0.26
	(0.1960)	(0.1183)	(0.1448)	
2002	0.7151***	0.0688	0.1187	0.39
	(0.0948)	(0.0720)	(0.0799)	
2003	0.8961***	−0.0015	0.1376**	0.73
	(0.0653)	(0.0417)	(0.0588)	
2004	0.5893***	0.0974**	0.1920***	0.63
	(0.0617)	(0.0388)	(0.0488)	
2005	0.7439***	0.0992*	0.1503**	0.62
	(0.0676)	(0.0507)	(0.0623)	
2006	0.7244***	0.0175	0.2157***	0.45
	(0.0808)	(0.0644)	(0.0660)	
2007	0.9243***	0.0748	−0.2308***	0.51
	(0.0804)	(0.0630)	(0.0481)	
2008	1.0168***	0.0203	−0.1521***	0.90
	(0.0414)	(0.0337)	(0.0348)	
1999–2008	0.8669***	0.0228	0.1035***	0.35
	(0.0402)	(0.0281)	(0.0298)	

Annex 9
(continued)

HK dollar	US dollar	Euro	Yen	Adjusted R-squared
1999	0.9980***	0.0015	0.0014	1.00
	(0.0015)	(0.0011)	(0.0008)	
2000	0.9983***	0.0000	0.0017*	1.00
	(0.0014)	(0.0008)	(0.0010)	
2001	1.0000***	0.0001	−0.0001	1.00
	(0.0006)	(0.0003)	(0.0004)	
2002	1.0001***	−0.0001	0.0000	1.00
	(0.0004)	(0.0003)	(0.0003)	
2003	0.9707***	−0.0015	0.0254***	0.99
	(0.0086)	(0.0055)	(0.0077)	
2004	0.9784***	0.0094***	0.0073**	1.00
	(0.0043)	(0.0028)	(0.0035)	
2005	0.9901***	0.0045*	−0.0057*	1.00
	(0.0036)	(0.0027)	(0.0034)	
2006	0.9854***	0.0017	0.0069**	1.00
	(0.0036)	(0.0029)	(0.0030)	
2007	0.9847***	0.0044	0.0021	0.99
	(0.0089)	(0.0070)	(0.0053)	
2008	0.9731***	0.0091*	0.0068	1.00
	(0.0063)	(0.0051)	(0.0053)	
1999–2008	0.9885***	0.0024**	0.0048***	1.00
	(0.0014)	(0.0010)	(0.0010)	

Japanese yen	US dollar	Euro	Adjusted R-squared
1999	0.8378***	0.0406	0.35
	(0.1026)	(0.0834)	
2000	0.9038***	0.0053	0.54
	(0.0652)	(0.0495)	
2001	0.8277***	−0.0393	0.48
	(0.0667)	(0.0508)	
2002	0.4384***	0.0618	0.27
	(0.0686)	(0.0558)	
2003	0.6831***	−0.0285	0.52
	(0.0545)	(0.0441)	
2004	0.7097***	−0.0740	0.41
	(0.0639)	(0.0494)	
2005	0.5886***	−0.0616	0.37
	(0.0560)	(0.0498)	
2006	0.4391***	−0.1137*	0.15
	(0.0682)	(0.0597)	
2007	0.5209***	−0.1705**	0.10
	(0.0989)	(0.0809)	
2008	0.4193***	−0.1240	0.15
	(0.0878)	(0.0758)	
1999–2008	0.6607***	−0.0350*	0.35
	(0.0231)	(0.0187)	

Korean won	US dollar	Euro	Yen	Adjusted R-squared
1999	0.8432***	0.0093	0.1540***	0.74
	(0.0584)	(0.0423)	(0.0317)	
2000	1.0063***	−0.0668	0.1085*	0.67
	(0.0814)	(0.0463)	(0.0578)	
2001	0.8337***	−0.0492	0.3288***	0.75
	(0.0655)	(0.0387)	(0.0484)	
2002	0.5597***	0.1235***	0.1935***	0.58
	(0.0616)	(0.0472)	(0.0525)	
2003	0.7258***	0.0226	0.2629***	0.72
	(0.0644)	(0.0409)	(0.0582)	
2004	0.6804***	0.0285	0.2535***	0.85
	(0.0392)	(0.0241)	(0.0313)	
2005	0.5499***	0.1325***	0.1690***	0.67
	(0.0508)	(0.0370)	(0.0466)	
2006	0.6125***	−0.0501	0.2344***	0.54
	(0.0543)	(0.0445)	(0.0459)	
2007	0.9400***	0.0424	−0.1932***	0.67
	(0.0561)	(0.0440)	(0.0335)	
2008	1.1280***	0.0046	−0.1658*	0.60
	(0.1122)	(0.0914)	(0.0946)	
1999–2008	0.8135***	0.0170	0.1514***	0.66
	(0.0207)	(0.0145)	(0.0154)	

Lao kip	US dollar	Euro	Yen	Adjusted R-squared
1999				
2000				
2001				
2002				
2003	1.0161***	0.0100	−0.0449	0.98
	(0.0349)	(0.0211)	(0.0298)	
2004	1.0276***	0.0110	−0.0222	0.96
	(0.0195)	(0.0125)	(0.0156)	
2005	0.9355***	0.0750	0.0787	0.69
	(0.0646)	(0.0482)	(0.0599)	
2006	0.8943***	0.1126**	0.0767	0.64
	(0.0653)	(0.0534)	(0.0554)	
2007	0.9673***	0.0270	0.0372*	0.86
	(0.0348)	(0.0273)	(0.0208)	
2008	0.9334***	0.0529	0.0031	0.87
	(0.0484)	(0.0394)	(0.0407)	
1999–2008	0.9575***	0.0463***	0.0285*	0.81
	(0.0207)	(0.0155)	(0.0168)	

Malaysian ringgit	US dollar	Euro	Yen	Adjusted R-squared
1999	1.0044***	−0.0037	−0.0020	1.00
	(0.0041)	(0.0030)	(0.0022)	
2000	1.0000***	0.0000	0.0000	1.00
	(0.0000)	(0.0000)	(0.0000)	
2001	1.0000***	0.0000	0.0000	1.00
	(0.0000)	(0.0000)	(0.0000)	
2002	1.0000***	0.0000	0.0000	1.00
	(0.0000)	(0.0000)	(0.0000)	
2003	1.0000***	0.0000	0.0000	1.00
	(0.0000)	(0.0000)	(0.0000)	
2004	1.0000***	0.0000	0.0000	1.00
	(0.0000)	(0.0000)	(0.0000)	
2005	0.9826***	0.0183	0.0037	0.97
	(0.0151)	(0.0113)	(0.0140)	
2006	0.9886***	−0.1141***	0.0855**	0.74
	(0.0486)	(0.0398)	(0.0413)	
2007	1.0163***	−0.0319	0.0560***	0.91
	(0.0284)	(0.0223)	(0.0170)	
2008	0.9681***	−0.0186	−0.0029	0.88
	(0.0453)	(0.0369)	(0.0382)	
1999–2008	0.9888***	−0.0084*	0.0139***	0.96
	(0.0063)	(0.0044)	(0.0047)	

Myanmar kyat	US dollar	Euro	Yen	Adjusted R-squared
1999				
2000				
2001				
2002				
2003	1.0149***	0.0111	−0.0392	0.98
	(0.0345)	(0.0209)	(0.0295)	
2004	1.0270***	0.0136	−0.0166	0.97
	(0.0165)	(0.0105)	(0.0132)	
2005	0.9800***	0.0497**	0.0148	0.93
	(0.0261)	(0.0195)	(0.0243)	
2006	0.9720***	0.1476***	0.0457	0.88
	(0.0357)	(0.0292)	(0.0304)	
2007	0.9724***	0.0300	0.0333*	0.88
	(0.0321)	(0.0251)	(0.0192)	
2008	0.9875***	0.0348	0.0126	0.94
	(0.0332)	(0.0270)	(0.0280)	
2003–2008	0.9918***	0.0438***	0.0111	0.93
	(0.0119)	(0.0089)	(0.0097)	

Annex 9
(continued)

Philippine peso	US dollar	Euro	Yen	Adjusted *R*-squared
1999	0.8869*** (0.0619)	−0.0065 (0.0449)	0.1348*** (0.0336)	0.72
2000	0.9936*** (0.0584)	0.0123 (0.0332)	0.0145 (0.0413)	0.78
2001	0.8730*** (0.0740)	0.0920* (0.0548)	0.0710 (0.0446)	0.66
2002	0.7881*** (0.0399)	0.1089*** (0.0330)	0.0721** (0.0307)	0.82
2003	0.9553*** (0.0586)	−0.0076 (0.0374)	0.1165** (0.0528)	0.78
2004	0.8606*** (0.0220)	0.0495*** (0.0176)	0.0928*** (0.0141)	0.95
2005	0.7944*** (0.0371)	0.0726*** (0.0280)	0.1478*** (0.0346)	0.85
2006	0.8177*** (0.0480)	0.0176 (0.0396)	0.1371*** (0.0409)	0.72
2007	0.9320*** (0.0986)	−0.0024 (0.0773)	−0.1792*** (0.0589)	0.37
2008	1.1126*** (0.0970)	−0.0738 (0.0794)	−0.0665 (0.0811)	0.65
1999–2008	0.9016*** (0.0186)	0.0365*** (0.0131)	0.0675*** (0.0138)	0.72

Singapore dollar	US dollar	Euro	Yen	Adjusted *R*-squared
1999	0.7742*** (0.0455)	0.0947*** (0.0330)	0.0961*** (0.0247)	0.80
2000	0.9376*** (0.0333)	0.0540*** (0.0190)	0.0024 (0.0237)	0.91
2001	0.8222*** (0.0391)	0.0333 (0.0236)	0.0749*** (0.0289)	0.85
2002	0.6933*** (0.0363)	0.1601*** (0.0275)	0.1231*** (0.0306)	0.84
2003	0.7301*** (0.0350)	0.1518*** (0.0223)	0.0971*** (0.0315)	0.89
2004	0.6130*** (0.0320)	0.2416*** (0.0205)	0.1115*** (0.0256)	0.89
2005	0.6221*** (0.0356)	0.2573*** (0.0265)	0.0742** (0.0331)	0.84
2006	0.6303*** (0.0326)	0.3018*** (0.0267)	0.0921*** (0.0277)	0.86
2007	0.7229*** (0.0391)	0.2226*** (0.0301)	−0.0182 (0.0230)	0.82
2008	0.5900*** (0.0422)	0.2976*** (0.0343)	0.0598* (0.0355)	0.88
1999–2008	0.7316*** (0.0117)	0.1566*** (0.0082)	0.0742*** (0.0087)	0.85

Annex 9
(continued)

Thai bath	US dollar	Euro	Yen	Adjusted R-squared
1999	0.8624*** (0.0884)	0.0921 (0.0641)	0.1199** (0.0480)	0.57
2000	0.8972*** (0.0724)	0.0340 (0.0412)	0.0771 (0.0514)	0.69
2001	0.8195*** (0.0416)	−0.0046 (0.0251)	0.1130*** (0.0307)	0.83
2002	0.6120*** (0.0636)	0.1907*** (0.0482)	0.1250** (0.0536)	0.60
2003	0.7799*** (0.0441)	0.0340 (0.0281)	0.1404*** (0.0397)	0.83
2004	0.7220*** (0.0318)	0.0955*** (0.0199)	0.1299*** (0.0256)	0.89
2005	0.6653*** (0.0345)	0.1177*** (0.0257)	0.1521*** (0.0321)	0.84
2006	0.6992*** (0.0635)	0.1505*** (0.0519)	0.1326** (0.0539)	0.58
2007	0.8739*** (0.1699)	−0.0618 (0.1340)	0.0591 (0.1053)	0.15
2008	1.0045*** (0.1565)	−0.0018 (0.1274)	−0.0162 (0.1319)	0.39
1999–2008	0.7908*** (0.0240)	0.0683*** (0.0169)	0.1115*** (0.0180)	0.58

Vietnamese dong	US dollar	Euro	Yen	Adjusted R-squared
1999				
2000				
2001				
2002				
2003	0.9859*** (0.0546)	0.0298 (0.0349)	−0.0555 (0.0461)	0.94
2004	1.0240*** (0.0165)	0.0130 (0.0105)	−0.0119 (0.0132)	0.97
2005	1.0002*** (0.0130)	0.0153 (0.0097)	0.0128 (0.0122)	0.98
2006	0.9846*** (0.0284)	0.0587** (0.0232)	0.0107 (0.0241)	0.91

Annex 9
(continued)

Vietnamese dong	US dollar	Euro	Yen	Adjusted R-squared
2007	0.9448***	0.0584***	0.0397**	0.92
	(0.0261)	(0.0205)	(0.0156)	
2008[2]	1.0536***	0.0114	−0.0385	0.77
	(0.0740)	(0.0603)	(0.0624)	
2003–2008	1.0068***	0.0258**	−0.0021	0.90
	(0.0142)	(0.0106)	(0.0115)	

Source: Own calculations with daily exchange rate data from Datastream (Reuters and Tenfore).
Note: The currency weights were estimated using the methodology introduced by Frankel and Wei (1994) as presented in Section 3.2.2 with daily exchange rates. Time series for Cambodia, Lao, Myanmar, and Vietnam start from 10/7/2003. Estimates for 2008 were made with data ranging from 1/1/2008–4/8/2008.

Annex 10
A chronology of events in the EMS, 1979–1999

Year	Date	Event
1979	Mar 13	EMS starts operation (±2.25% band for all participants except the Italian lira with a ±6% band)
	Sep 24	German mark (+2%), Danish krone (–2.9%)
	Nov 30	Danish krone (–4.76%)
1981	Mar 23	Italian lira (–6%)
	Oct 05	German mark (+5.5%), Dutch guilder (+5.5%), French franc (–3%), Italian lira (–3%)
1982	Feb 22	Belgian franc (–8.5%), Danish krone (–3%)
	Jun 14	German mark (+4.25%), Dutch guilder (4.25%), French franc (–5.75%), Italian lira (–2.75%)
1983	Mar 21	German mark (+5.5%), Dutch guilder (+3.5%), Belgian franc (+1.5%), French franc (–2.5%), Italian lira (–2.5%), Irish punt (–3.5%)
1985	Jul 22	Belgian franc (+2%), Danish krone (+2%), German mark (+2%), French franc (+2%), Irish punt (+2%), Dutch guilder (+2%), Italian lira (–6%)
1986	Apr 07	German mark (+3%), Dutch guilder (+3%), Belgian franc (+1%), Danish krone (+1%), French franc (–3%)
	Aug 04	Irish punt (–8%)
1987	Jan 12	German mark (+3%), Dutch guilder (+3%), Belgian franc (+2%)
1989	Jun 19	Spanish peseta enters with ±6% band
1990	Jan 08	Italian lira (–3.7%) and adopts ±2.25% band
	Oct 08	British pound enters with ±6% band
1992	Apr 06	Portuguese escudo enters with ±6% band
	Sep 14	Belgian franc (+3.5%), German mark (+3.5%), Dutch guilder (+3.5%), Danish krone (+3.5%), Portuguese escudo (+3.5%), French franc (+3.5%), Irish punt (+3.5%), British pound (+3.5%), Italian lira (–3.5%)
	Sep 17	British pound and Italian lira suspend membership of ERM, Spanish peseta (–5%)
	Nov 23	Portuguese escudo (–6%), Spanish peseta (–
1993	Feb 01	Irish punt (–10%)
	May 14	Spanish peseta (–8%), Portuguese escudo (–6.5%)
	Aug 02	Widening of margins of fluctuations to ±15% for all ERM currencies; Germany and Netherlands agree to bilaterally maintain their currencies in the ±2.25% band
1995	Jan 09	Austrian schilling enters with ±15% band
	Mar 06	Spanish peseta (–7%), Portuguese escudo (–3.5%)
1996	Oct 14	Finish markka enters with ±15% band
	Nov 25	Italian lira rejoins with ±15% band
1998	Mar 16	Irish punt (+3%)
	May 02	Selection of qualifying members for EMU
1999	Jan 01	EMU comes into effect

Source: Pilbeam (1998: 446).
Note: –indicates a devaluation, + indicates a revaluation.

Annex 11
Total reserves (except gold) of East Asian countries and the euro area (in million USD), January 1980–August 2008

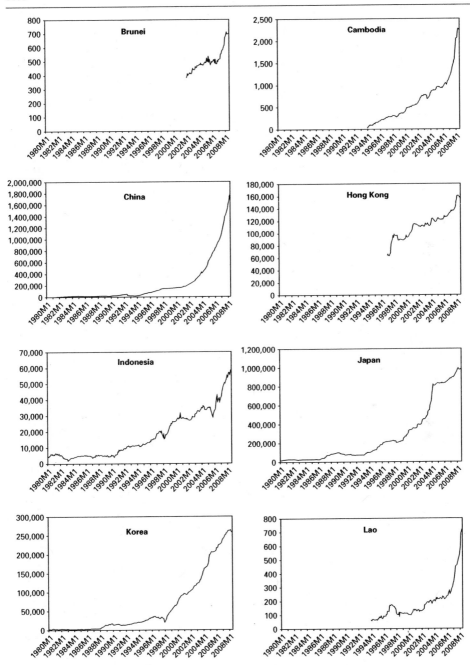

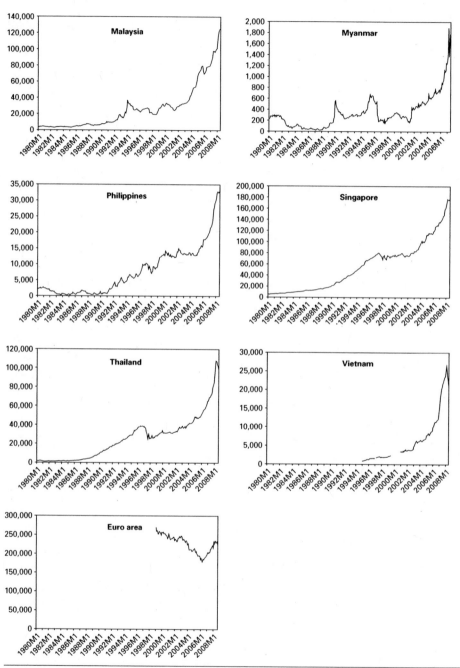

Source: IFS.
Note: Different scaling on left axis.

Annex 12
Construction of NEER weights

	Trade with …	Percent of total imports	Percent of total exports	Percent of total trade	NEER weights (% of total trade blown up to 100)
Brunei	United States	6.64	5.21	5.55	5.79
	Australia	1.08	12.22	9.55	9.96
	Japan	5.87	30.96	24.95	26.02
	United Kingdom	8.78	1.35	3.13	3.26
	China	4.82	2.31	2.91	3.03
	Indonesia	2.84	23.68	18.69	19.49
	Korea	1.17	16.98	13.19	13.76
	Malaysia	19.13	1.18	5.48	5.71
	Singapore	33.11	1.73	9.25	9.64
	Thailand	4.33	1.39	2.09	2.18
	Euro Area	4.41	0.07	1.11	1.16
Cambodia	United States	2.78	60.64	26.82	30.24
	Canada	0.11	4.82	2.07	2.33
	Japan	2.24	3.24	2.65	2.99
	United Kingdom	0.12	4.79	2.06	2.32
	China	16.73	1.17	10.27	11.58
	Hong Kong	12.28	0.44	7.36	8.30
	Korea	3.31	0.10	1.97	2.23
	Singapore	8.79	1.97	5.96	6.72
	Thailand	27.19	1.15	16.37	18.46
	Vietnam	6.11	2.39	4.56	5.15
	Euro Area	3.76	15.36	8.58	9.68
China	United States	7.36	19.52	14.14	26.02
	Japan	13.73	8.42	10.77	19.82
	China	2.84	14.83	9.52	17.53
	Korea	10.84	4.58	7.35	13.53
	Euro Area	9.51	14.97	12.55	23.10
HK	United States	4.88	13.73	9.15	11.60
	Japan	10.02	4.45	7.33	9.29
	China	46.32	48.67	47.46	60.14
	Korea	4.17	1.97	3.10	3.93
	Singapore	6.79	1.88	4.41	5.60
	Euro Area	5.65	9.37	7.45	9.44

Annex 12
(continued)

	Trade with …	Percent of total imports	Percent of total exports	Percent of total trade	NEER weights (% of total trade blown up to 100)
Indonesia	United States	4.05	10.71	7.57	9.41
	Australia	3.20	3.11	3.16	3.92
	Japan	8.67	18.50	13.87	17.24
	China	12.14	8.62	10.28	12.78
	India	1.46	3.38	2.48	3.08
	Korea	5.52	6.84	6.22	7.73
	Malaysia	4.95	4.39	4.65	5.78
	Singapore	28.18	10.33	18.74	23.29
	Thailand	4.56	2.84	3.65	4.53
	Saudi Arabia	3.33	0.57	1.87	2.33
	Euro Area	5.70	9.98	7.96	9.90
Japan	United States	11.62	20.38	16.30	23.10
	Australia	4.99	1.99	3.39	4.80
	China	20.54	15.30	17.74	25.13
	Hong Kong	0.23	5.45	3.02	4.28
	Indonesia	4.22	1.27	2.64	3.75
	Korea	4.39	7.60	6.10	8.65
	Singapore	1.13	3.06	2.16	3.06
	Thailand	2.94	3.59	3.29	4.65
	Saudi Arabia	5.72	0.94	3.17	4.49
	United Arab Emirates	5.23	1.13	3.04	4.31
	Euro Area	8.23	11.04	9.73	13.79
Korea	United States	10.45	12.42	11.43	16.89
	Australia	3.42	1.34	2.38	3.52
	Japan	16.34	6.88	11.63	17.19
	China	16.62	25.84	21.20	31.34
	Hong Kong	2.04	3.86	2.95	4.36
	Singapore	3.19	3.23	3.21	4.74
	Saudi Arabia	6.23	0.95	3.61	5.33
	United Arab Emirates	3.90	0.93	2.43	3.59
	Euro Area	8.34	9.31	8.82	13.04
Lao	China	8.54	6.24	7.69	9.86
	Thailand	69.91	35.75	57.31	73.50
	Vietnam	5.66	11.26	7.73	9.91
	Euro Area	3.16	8.80	5.24	6.72

Annex 12
(continued)

	Trade with …	Percent of total imports	Percent of total exports	Percent of total trade	NEER weights (% of total trade blown up to 100)
Malaysia	United States	10.84	15.62	13.45	16.79
	Australia	2.02	3.37	2.76	3.44
	Japan	12.98	9.13	10.88	13.59
	China	12.86	8.77	10.63	13.28
	Hong Kong	2.91	4.62	3.84	4.80
	India	1.40	3.34	2.46	3.07
	Indonesia	4.24	2.93	3.53	4.41
	Korea	4.93	3.80	4.32	5.39
	Singapore	11.48	14.63	13.19	16.48
	Thailand	5.35	4.95	5.13	6.41
	Euro Area	9.66	10.07	9.88	12.34
Myanmar	Japan	3.76	5.65	4.67	5.50
	China	35.70	6.84	21.85	25.72
	India	3.62	14.47	8.83	10.39
	Malaysia	4.49	2.66	3.61	4.25
	Singapore	16.59	1.17	9.19	10.82
	Thailand	20.44	44.20	31.85	37.50
	Euro Area	4.56	5.35	4.94	5.81
Philippines	United States	11.97	13.29	12.61	15.28
	Japan	14.71	11.77	13.28	16.09
	China	11.04	29.27	19.91	24.11
	Hong Kong	4.37	8.31	6.28	7.61
	Korea	5.63	2.60	4.16	5.04
	Malaysia	3.96	3.86	3.91	4.73
	Singapore	9.51	7.87	8.71	10.55
	Thailand	4.50	2.93	3.74	4.52
	Saudi Arabia	5.07	0.10	2.65	3.21
	Euro Area	7.07	7.57	7.31	8.85
Singapore	United States	12.48	8.91	10.58	13.51
	Australia	1.20	3.74	2.55	3.26
	Japan	8.18	4.81	6.39	8.16
	China	12.11	9.67	10.81	13.80
	Hong Kong	1.46	10.47	6.26	7.99
	India	2.23	3.34	2.82	3.60
	Indonesia	5.57	9.85	7.84	10.02
	Korea	4.87	3.55	4.16	5.32
	Malaysia	13.07	12.91	12.99	16.58
	Thailand	3.23	4.14	3.71	4.74
	Saudi Arabia	3.35	0.28	1.72	2.19
	Euro Area	9.62	7.50	8.49	10.84

Annex 12
(continued)

	Trade with ...	Percent of total imports	Percent of total exports	Percent of total trade	NEER weights (% of total trade blown up to 100)
Thailand	United States	6.83	12.63	9.84	13.39
	Australia	2.72	3.76	3.26	4.43
	Japan	20.29	11.89	15.93	21.68
	China	11.59	9.73	10.62	14.46
	Hong Kong	1.03	5.70	3.45	4.70
	Indonesia	2.85	3.13	2.99	4.07
	Korea	3.78	1.95	2.83	3.85
	Malaysia	6.16	5.11	5.61	7.64
	Singapore	4.49	6.25	5.40	7.36
	Saudi Arabia	3.27	0.90	2.04	2.77
	United Arab Emirates	4.88	1.45	3.10	4.22
	Euro Area	6.76	9.89	8.38	11.41
Vietnam	United States	3.37	22.49	11.52	14.62
	Australia	1.88	7.46	4.26	5.40
	Japan	10.07	11.99	10.89	13.81
	United Kingdom	0.42	3.40	1.69	2.15
	China	20.01	6.19	14.11	17.90
	Hong Kong	4.09	1.47	2.97	3.77
	Korea	7.84	2.04	5.37	6.80
	Malaysia	4.13	3.62	3.91	4.96
	Singapore	11.55	4.21	8.42	10.68
	Thailand	6.74	2.21	4.81	6.09
	Euro Area	7.33	15.68	10.89	13.82

Source: Calculation with data from DTS.
Note: Trade data are for 2007.

Index